Sixth Edition

Business Communication

with Writing Improvement Exercises

ANNOTATED INSTRUCTOR'S EDITION

Phyllis Davis Hemphill, M.S.
Rio Hondo College, Emeritus

Donald W. McCormick, Ph.D.
University of Redlands

Robert D. Hemphill, B.S.
Webstop.com, Inc., President

Prentice
Hall

Upper Saddle River, New Jersey 07458

Library of Congress Cataloging-in-Publication Data
Hemphill, Phyllis D.
   Business communication with writing improvement exercises /
Phyllis Davis Hemphill and Donald W. McCormick. — 6th ed.
     p. cm.
   Includes index.
   ISBN 0-13-089708-6
   1. Commercial correspondence.   2. Business communication.
3. Business writing.   I. McCormick, Donald W.   II. Title.

HF5721.H46   2000
651.7′4—dc21   00-041655
                                                  CIP

Acquisitions Editor: Elizabeth Sugg
Production Editor: Fred Dahl
Editorial Assistant: Delia Uherec
Director of Production and Manufacturing: Bruce Johnson
Managing Editor: Mary Carnis
Editorial/Production Supervisor: Inkwell Publishing Services
Design Director: Marianne Frasco
Manufacturing Buyer: Edward O'Dougherty

HF
5721
.H46
2001

Prentice-Hall International (UK) Limited, *London*
Prentice-Hall of Australia Pty. Limited, *Sydney*
Prentice-Hall Canada Inc., *Toronto*
Prentice-Hall Hispanoamericana, S.A., *Mexico*
Prentice-Hall of India Private Limited, *New Delhi*
Prentice-Hall of Japan, Inc., *Tokyo*
Prentice-Hall Singapore Pte. Ltd.
Editora Prentice-Hall do Brasil, Ltda., *Rio de Janeiro*

10 9 8 7 6 5 4 3 2 1

ISBN: 0-13-089708-6

Contents

PART I. INTRODUCTION

PART II. THE THREE BASIC QUALITIES OF EFFECTIVE BUSINESS COMMUNICATION: ATTRACTIVE APPEARANCE, GOOD WILL TONE, CLEAR, COMPLETE, CONCISE TONE

3   Qualities of an Effective Business Communication: Good Will Tone, 39

4   Qualities of an Effective Business Communication: Clear and Complete Message, 57

PART III. APPLYING THE THREE BASIC QUALITIES OF EFFECTIVE BUSINESS COMMUNICATIONS

5   The Routine Information, "Yes" or Good News Communication: News Releases, 83

6 *The Negative Communication: The "No" Message, 115*

7 *Sales Letters and Persuasive Claims and Requests, 143*

8 Credit and Collections, 175

9 Courtesy Messages You Don't Have to Send, But Should, 207

10 Oral Communications, 225

PART IV. BUSINESS COMMUNICATION IN THE WIRED WORLD

11 The Internet and Other Communication Technologies, 247

12 Healthy Computing: Preventing Eyestrain, Carpal (Wrist) Tunnel Syndrome, Back Pain, 269

PART V. EMPLOYMENT

13 Employment Guides: Finding a Job, Holding a Job, Earning Promotions, Changing Jobs, 289

Preface

Instructors from New York City to Singapore have used previous editions of this book in college classrooms, continuing education, corporate training, and vocational education programs since 1976. We detail some of the reasons that this book has been so successful for so long.

To the Student

According to a survey conducted by *The Wall Street Journal*, 80 percent of United States businesses cited written communication as their employees' biggest skill problem. We have written this book so that

- ☐ You will learn to communicate in a way that increases your credibility in business situations and in other business courses.
- ☐ You will learn to avoid embarrassing mistakes in your letters, emails, presentations and other communications.
- ☐ You will be able to create resumes, cover letters and other business communications that will help you get and keep a good job.

We have incorporated features that we know you care about. These include:

- ☐ A **real world emphasis** on **practical skills** that you will use in your jobs.
- ☐ **Up to date** coverage of the communication techniques you need in today's workplace.
- ☐ An **entertaining writing style** that uses humor and anecdotes.
- ☐ Our assignments match the experience level of **early college students**.
- ☐ **Job interview questions** are featured. We have included questions most commonly asked during job interviews.
- ☐ A **convenient and low cost** format is featured. *Business Communication 6th edition* combines a textbook with a workbook, so you don't need to buy two separate books.

To the Instructor

This new edition has many features that help make your teaching more effective and convenient.

☐ **Convenient annotated instructor's edition.** You don't have to fumble back and forth between the text and the instructor's manual while teaching.

☐ **Concise coverage of basic business communication.** We have made this book concise so you can cover all the basics of business communication in one quarter or semester.

☐ **Grading Guidelines.** We provide guidelines for grading.

☐ **Convenient textbook/workbook format.** For short answer assignments, this format allows students to simply write their answers in the workbook, rip out the page and hand it in. It also means that you and the students do not need to deal with two separate books—a workbook and a textbook.

☐ Up-to-the-minute coverage on the latest information technologies, including email, fax, voice mail, and the World Wide Web.

The Clear Organization of this Book

Originally this book was written to create a textbook with a coherent, progressive organization that makes it easy for students to grasp and apply the basics of business communication to many forms of communication—a textbook that avoided the "grab bag" form of organization that seemed to say to the reader "it's all in there.., if you can only find it."

The first chapter introduces a basic theory of communication and shows students the benefits of studying business communication. It introduces students to some of the ongoing themes that run throughout the book—including ethics in business communication and communication technologies.

The next three chapters present the basics of business communications: attractive appearance, a tone of good will, and clear and complete message.

The rest of the book applies these principles to different types of messages—routine and positive messages; negative, sales and persuasive messages; miscellaneous messages, communication on the internet, employment messages; and finally presentations, reports, and term papers.

The accompanying sidebar, "ORGANIZATION: BUSINESS COMMUNICATION with Writing Improvement Exercises" sets out Parts I to VI of the text in a progressive, logical order, showing how basic qualities of effective writing are first studied and then applied to all types of clear, complete concise messages. In the concluding Appendix, spelling and punctuation rules and exercises are included.

We must say: We believe we have written the right book for today's changing basic Business Communication classes and that *studying this book will help students get better jobs.*

ORGANIZATION: BUSINESS COMMUNICATION
with Writing Improvement Exercises

PART I: INTRODUCTION
Chapter 1: You and Business Communication

PART II: THREE BASIC QUALITIES OF EFFECTIVE BUSINESS COMMUNICATIONS
Chapter 2: Attractive Appearance

Chapter 3: Good Will Tone

Chapter 4: Clear, Complete Concise Message

PART III: APPLYING THE THREE BASIC QUALITIES OF EFFECTIVE BUSINESS COMMUNICATIONS

Chapter 5	Chapter 6	Chapter 7	Chapter 8	Chapter 9	Chapter 10
Routine Information, "Yes," Good News	Negative, "No"	Sales; Persuasive Requests	Credit; Collections	Courtesy Messages	Oral Communications

PART IV: BUSINESS COMMUNICATION IN THE WIRED WORLD

Chapter 11	Chapter 12
Computers; the Internet; Telecommunications	Healthy Computing

PART V. EMPLOYMENT

Chapter 13	Chapter 14
Finding, Holding Changing Jobs	Resumés; Other Employment Communications

PART VI: BUSINESS REPORTS AND TERM PAPERS; BUSINESS CONTRACT PROPOSALS

Chapter 15	Chapter 16
Planning Business Report or Term Paper	Writing Business Report or Term Paper; Contract Proposal

APPENDIX

A. Major Spelling Rules; Spelling Lists	B. Major Punctuation Rules with Examples

"The more things change, the more they remain the same" goes the old expression. Since this book was first published over twenty years ago, the forms of business communication have changed dramatically. But the basics of organization and writing have remained the same. So by learning the basics and how they apply to many different forms, students get a solid foundation upon which to face the ever-changing forms of business communication that will emerge.

Features Which Help Students to Learn

This edition has many features that will help students learn business communication. They include:

- [ ] **Designed for learning.** The chapters include many checklists and writing improvement exercises, and end with a review exercise.

- [ ] **More Examples.** This edition has an even stronger visual presentation, with more diagrams and with more examples of letters, forms, emails, and web pages.

- [ ] **Easy to read.** A clear writing style that uses clear vocabulary and sentences makes the ideas understandable to students from diverse cultural and educational backgrounds. We work to write at the high school reading level, which is the same level as most business publications such as *Business Week* and the *Wall Street Journal*. We work hard to write a clear and understandable book, without oversimplifying ideas or talking down to the student.

- [ ] **Checklists** that students can use as guides to writing messages (such as email, sales letters. etc.) and to check their work for this class.

- [ ] **Writing improvement exercises** which give students the chance to immediately apply what they have learned.

- [ ] **Boldfaced Key Terms.** We write key terms in boldface type when they are first introduced in the book. This makes it easier for the student to find key terms and identify the most important ideas.

Up to Date Coverage

The book contains up to date coverage of issues such as ethics and technology.

- [ ] **Ethics.** This book does not tuck moral issues in business communication away in one chapter or limit it to a few boxed features lightly spread throughout the text. These issues are so important that we integrate them throughout the textbook.

- [ ] **Technology.** Chapter 11 contains computers, the internet and other communication technologies. Also, technological issues are covered throughout the main body of the text. This includes information technologies such as email, voicemail, desktop publishing, cell phones, and more.

Acknowledgments

We are grateful to all those who have helped us with previous editions of this text, especially Hal Balmer, without whom there probably would have been no editions.

Currently, we thank Elizabeth Sugg, our Acquisitions Editor, and Fred Dahl, our Production Editor, for this and the fifth edition. Knowing we always had their direction available made this book, *Business Communication with Writing Improvement Exercises*, Sixth Edition, possible.

We are grateful to the nameless people of the entire Simon Schuster / Prentice Hall marketing staff. We praise those friends of the classroom, known or unknown to us, the Prentice Hall publishers representatives who help keep classes up to date by putting this and other current texts into the hands of instructors and students.

Introduction to Annotated Instructor's Edition

Transparency Projections

To add variety to the course and emphasize any point being made, overhead transparencies are helpful. Showing figures such as those in Chapter 1 can make the points clearer. Also, having the enlargements of letters makes it easy to show the specific matter being discussed.

As writing assignments are made, students find it helpful if the class goes over the end of the chapter checkpoints so they will know what their assignments should contain and how they will be graded.

I. Plan of Book

The plan of this book is to set up an organized manner of teaching Business Communication by explaining basic principles and then applying these principles to preparing any communication.

The plan of the book is shown in the Preface on page xiii. (It could be used as an overhead projection.)

Instruction is aimed at planning communications that might be prepared in early years of employment. Then, in later years, writing can be based on these same principles. Numerous examples are included, together with—we hope—lively illustrations.

Each chapter that has writing assignments closes with a checklist that can guide students in preparing these types of messages, and can also guide the instructor in grading them.

Chapters 2 through 14 have Writing Improvement Exercises, which give students hands-on practice in specific ways of improving any writing. Review and Discussion topics at the end of each chapter can be used as a basis for lecture/discussions, or can be given as assignments for grading.

II. Class Schedules and Assignments

The text is planned for one semester or for one or two quarters of study. As a chapter is assigned for reading, students should be instructed to complete the Review and Discussion questions at the end of that chapter. This procedure usually insures that the students read the chapter material assigned. It also enhances classroom discussions.

Standard Weekly Schedule

For a semester course, allow approximately one week to cover each chapter, including the Writing Improvement Exercise. An instructor would be justified in spending more or less time on a particular chapter, according to his or her own desire and background. In a two-quarter course, more time will be available for oral communications and report writing, making it possible to stretch late sections of the text beyond the basic one week for each chapter. Chapters 15 and 16 make a good introductory study of report writing even when this subject is taught as another course. A skeleton report writing assignment is included for abbreviated coverage of this assignment.

Because of employers' strong requests for us to improve student spelling, it is suggested that spelling tests be given weekly for at least ten weeks. This procedure not only improves student spelling; it also emphasizes the importance of spelling accuracy. Appendix A contains six basic spelling rules and current word lists. One list of 25 words can be assigned each week. Appendix B contains basic punctuation rules.

Weekly Variety Schedules

To give variety to daily classwork, you might cover the basic chapter material in the first two hours of a weekly class (for instance, on Monday and Wednesday of a Monday-Wednesday-Friday schedule). This leaves the third hour to cover Chapter 15, "Planning a Business Report or a Term Paper," and Chapter 16, "Writing a Business Report or a Term Paper," and "Writing a Business Contract Proposal." Study of these two chapters can then be spread throughout the term by assigning short sections at a time. Spelling tests can also be given on this later day, Friday, usually helping to increase attendance.

III. *Classroom Sessions*

First Classroom Session

You might use the first paragraphs of "Section I. Plan of the Book" to introduce the course to your students. Also, for a brief view of the entire course, you can scan the Table of Contents. Then, turn to the end of one of the letter-writing chapters and show the checklist for writing a specific type of communication to show how much help these lists can be.

At the first session, a syllabus with the explanation of the planned course should be handed out, mentioning that there may be some variation from the schedule. **(See Syllabus on next page.)**

Explain your grading system, showing that emphasis will be placed on student writing assignments.

In a communication classroom, students should become acquainted with each other. During the first or second session, ask students to stand and briefly introduce themselves by saying something about one or two of their special interests, such as career plans, hobbies, family, jobs, special experiences, and so forth. You may also choose to introduce yourself briefly.

Or, students could count off in groups of two or three and be given a ten-minute period (with you out of the room) to get acquainted. Then have them stand and introduce each other. Of course, you may prefer some other method of having them get acquainted. As much as possible, the atmosphere should be friendly and relaxed; it usually takes courage to register for a writing class.

During the first or second session, you might assign the writing of a letter in class, having students explain why they are taking this class; state that these letters will not be counted toward their final grades. This writing sample can help acquaint you with your students and can show types of writing improvement actually needed. The letters can also be used to *screen students* on the advisability of taking the course at this time

Assign the reading of Chapter 1 and the completion of Review and Discussion questions at the end of the chapter.

Succeeding Classroom Sessions

Students' interest is usually best stimulated if they do not know exactly what procedure will be followed each session. In other words, we should try for variety.

Individual sessions can vary. The instructor may choose to present a lecture made by listing major text headings with any needed subheadings. Another method of covering a chapter is to get students involved with a discussion of end-of-chapter questions. Of course, any important information not covered can be added by the instructor. For lecture or discussion, transparency projections can be shown of writing examples or illustrations from the text, from student assignments, or from other sources.

Through their own mail and through soliciting mail from others, instructors should gradually accumulate different types of communications—good and bad—to show the class. The original can be displayed if the room and the class are small. Most students have limited access to such correspondence; therefore, few assignments for bringing letters and memos to class have been made in the text. However, some students may have good sources.

Assignments

Writing assignments should be given with a three- or four-day advance preparation time. *When the assignment is made,* be sure to call attention to the checklist at the end of the chapter for that particular type of communication, emphasizing that assignments will be graded by these lists. When these letters or memorandums are returned, it is interesting and instructive to show some of the best and worst examples—protecting privacy. Common errors can be listed on the board to emphasize that these errors should be avoided in future assignments.

For grading individuals, it is helpful to have students prepare letters in the classroom for one or two open-book (but not open-mouth) assignments.

Syllabus: Business Communication (Business _____)
Spring, 20XX

Instructor Name: _____

Office: _____

Office Hours: _____

Course Description	Basic Business Communication principles applied to preparing letters, memorandums, oral presentations and reports, with exercises for improving any writing.
Required Text	BUSINESS COMMUNICATION *with Writing Improvement Exercises*, 6th Edition, Hemphill / McCormick / Hemphill; Prentice Hall, Inc.
Recommended Supplemental Text	A copy of the current edition of one of the following dictionaries, all recommended by the National Council of Teachers of English:

WEBSTER'S NEW WORLD DICTIONARY OF THE ENGLISH LANGUAGE, Simon & Schuster;
THE AMERICAN HERITAGE DICTIONARY OF THE ENGLISH LANGUAGE, Houghton Mifflin;
WEBSTER'S NEW COLLEGIATE DICTIONARY, Merriam Webster

Assignments	Read ahead of classroom discussion. Plan is to cover one chapter each week, including Writing Improvement Exercise and end-of-chapter Review and Discussion. Complete assigned writing.
Tests	Multiple choice test, Chapters 1-5. Multiple choice test, Chapters 6-10. Final Exam, Chapters 11-16.
Grades	Writing assignments, tests, spelling tests, classroom participation, attendance.
Calendar	(SUGGESTIONS) Fill in date classes begin and dates of holidays, last day to withdraw without penalty, last change of program day, and final exam date.

# # #

Entire sessions can be devoted to individual preparation of the letters.

Another method for adding variety is to cover different types of writing by "committees" of no more than five students. The graded letters can be shown on a projector enlargement. A change of pace is to show the letters ungraded, having the class grade them according to the checklist for that particular message, showing that this is your own grading system. You can probably expect brisk discussions.

Working together in class on the Writing Improvement Exercises provides a good, helpful change from standard lecture format. These exercises can be assigned for one day, collected and quickly recorded by a checkoff grade, then returned at the next session. During this later session, students can "volunteer" their solutions. Usually, the greater the variety, the better, within reason.

Additional Helps

Every classroom should have a good current desk-size or unabridged dictionary for ready reference when questions arise.

Also, audiovisual aids break up the routine and should be used if they are up to date and of sufficient value to supplement the course content. Your college audiovisual department can direct you to sources. Excellent slides, films, and videotapes are available free or at nominal charges. Showing a few current and past student letters on a projector is usually interesting and effective.

IV. Testing and Grading

An instructor's method of grading should be that instructor's own choice. However, in a writing course, most of the student grade should be derived from writing, not from multiple-choice tests. Letter and memorandum writing assignments, both inside and outside class, can serve as effective examinations.

Because the first five chapters contain basic background material, having a test at the end of Chapter 5 can be helpful. This plan should give the student a good grasp of important principles of preparing attractive communications that will carry clear and complete messages while retaining the readers' good will. Students are then prepared for writing assignments of other chapters as they are covered.

Grading Writing Assignments

Giving or receiving grades for a person's writing can be an unnerving process. However, the end-of-chapter checklists are helpful guidelines for students and instructors.

Writing is a creative process, and heavy criticism can be devastating to the student's psyche. Any text on business communications emphasizes "positive attitude," and we should remember this fact in grading student papers. Beside tackling poor writing points on student assignments, do give praise. In looking over a paper of a discouraged student, you can usually find some point or points for approval.

Proofreaders' Symbols. Before making writing assignments, be sure to cover "Proofreaders' Symbols" at the end of Chapter 12. These symbols are abbreviations for what otherwise would be repetitive wordy comments of writers and editors, saving time in editing and grading. They are exceedingly educational and useful to students, instructors, and anyone else working with the written word.

Proofreaders' symbols are universal, so proofreaders and typesetters know and use these plus a few more as the need arises. Longer lists can be found in dictionaries and encyclopedias. With desktop publishing flourishing, they can gradually be adopted in all offices and become great time-savers.

Helps in Grading. To make grading simpler, you might use a numerical equivalency system, marking letter grades on student tests and papers from numerical grades in your records. This makes averaging of grades easier and easier to explain.

A numerical system also makes it easier to explain letter grades clearly to students. Because low numbers are simpler to work with, you might like this system.

A+ = 0	B+ = 3	C+ = 6	D+ = 9	F = 12
A = 1	B = 4	C = 7	D = 10	
A– = 2	B– = 5	C– = 8	D– = 11	

Systems for Grading Writing Assignments

Letter and Memorandum Writing Assignments. These assignments should be the basis of grading for the course.

Tests. Each test should be weighted the equivalent of a letter-writing assignment.

Reports. A report should have double the value of a letter-writing assignment, reflecting more detailed and lengthy work. If a shorter report project (page 385) is assigned, the value of this assignment should be the same as that of a letter or test.

Proposals. If a business or industry bidding proposal is assigned, the grading system can be determined by the instructor according to time and emphasis given to this study.

Spelling Tests. A cumulative grade for all spelling tests should equal the value of a single letter-writing grade. It is suggested that the lowest spelling test grade be dropped from the averaging. This system permits *one* absence from these tests without penalty.

Writing Improvement Exercise Worksheets and Review and Discussion Worksheets. Any records of Writing Improvement or Review and Discussion worksheets might be used as the balancing factor when a term grade is between two levels.

Typical grades	*Total points or percentages*
Multiple Choice Test, Chapters 1-5	10
Multiple Choice Test, Chapters 6-10	10
Letters, Memorandums, Oral, Chapters 6-14	40
Report, Chapters 15, 16	20
Spelling tests	10
Final Exam, Chapters 11-16	10

Do you get tired of trying to play God to determine students' grades?

Instructors should have their own choices as to how to grade, but here is a method that should relieve you of worry about making grade choices. It is systematic and fair. Try it for this or for any other course. (The originator of the following system is not known.)

Optional Grading System

First. Work on the standard premise that 60 percent of the top grade is the lowest possible passing grade:

100 possible	50 possible	85 possible
$\times .6$	$\times .6$	$\times .6$
60 = lowest	30 = lowest	51 = lowest
passing	passing	passing
grade	grade	grade

Second. Count the number of steps from lowest passing grade to top score:

100	50	85
-60	-30	-51
40 steps	20 steps	34 steps

Third. Divide the number of steps by four to get *As, Bs, Cs, Ds:*

$40 \div 4 = 10$ $20 \div 4 = 5$ $34 \div 4 = 8 + 2$ extra steps to be placed somewhere.

Fourth. Make up steps within each grade: Example: 85 possible points.

1. $85 \times .6 = 51$ (lowest passing grade)
2. $85 - 51 = 34$ (number of steps for passing grade)
3. $34 \div 4 = 8 + 2$ extra steps

4. Pluses and minuses within grades:

	77		68		59		
85 A+	76 B+		67 C+		58 D+		
84	75		66		57		
83	74		65		56		
82 A	73 B		64 C		55 D		
81	72		63		54		
80	71		62		53		
79 A−	70 B−		61 C−		52 D−		
78	69		60		51		

When the first tests are returned, explain your grading system, showing that for the final grade, emphasis will be placed on student writing assignments.

V. Tests

Tests with answers are at the end of this text.

VI. Companion Website

This text has a Companion Website with the following:

1. Short chapter by chapter summaries.
2. Ten multiple choice questions for each chapter to let students know how well they understand the topics. They can submit their answers to the Website and get instant results. If programmed to do so, scores can be sent to the instructor.
3. Weblinks that connect the student to related interesting, revealing and sometimes amusing Websites: www.prenhall.com/business_studies.

Phyllis Davis Hemphill
Donald William McCormick
and
Robert D. Hemphill

1 You and Business Communication

The Communication Theory

Why Study Business Communication?

Basically, there are two reasons for learning to prepare good business communications: (1) to benefit you, the student, and (2) to benefit business and industry.

Benefit to Student

In a *Harvard Business Review* article that has become a classic, Peter Drucker, highly respected business management consultant and educator, asks what is taught in college to help a person in future employment and then gives this answer:

> ... they teach one thing that is perhaps the most valuable for the future employee to know. But very few students bother to learn it.
>
> This one basic skill is the ability to organize and express ideas in writing and in speaking.... The letter, the report or memorandum, the ten-minute "presentation" to a committee are basic tools of the employee.

Two thousand business executives from all levels of management supported this statement when asked which factors lead to promotion of employees. These people listed ability to communicate as the most important factor, above such other qualities as ambition, drive, education, experience, self-confidence, and good appearance.

Information from many other sources also supports this attitude. For example, a survey of former university business students asked if they had observed people having problems in written communication in their work. The response: 77 percent, "yes"; 14 percent, "no."

Of those answering yes, the following are some of the troubles that were reported:

> Given that the individual knows his business, the difference between a shot at the top job and being buried someplace lower is the ability to communicate that knowledge.

I feel that not enough emphasis is being placed on written communication in our colleges. Although most individuals are able to compose a letter of sorts, they are totally lost, particularly in ability to organize anything of substantial length.

I would never wish to sell drive, ambition, and technical expertise short. But, in order to succeed, the ability to communicate properly is more important.

The largest portion [of CPA—Certified Public Accountant—work] is for record purposes only and is not reviewed or edited for construction, grammar, etc., but only for content.... A prerequisite for advancement to higher levels is ability to write properly. Poor writing catches up with one eventually.

My business communication course was one of the most useful of my undergraduate courses.[1]

Benefit to Business

Many industry leaders believe so strongly in the importance of business communication training that their firms offer their own courses or pay employees' tuition for private college classes in the subject. Among such firms are the American Institute of Banking, the American Savings and Loan Institute, Bell & Howell, New York Life Insurance Company, Sears, and General Electric. When such emphasis is given, a student who has already studied college level courses in business communication will have a potential employment advantage over those who have not, and eventually should have a better chance of promotion.

Whenever representatives of business and industry meet with college educators to determine what courses are most needed by students entering the job market, these business leaders overwhelmingly put "need for communication skills" at or near the top of their lists of priorities.

Studies show that those at management or executive level spend at least 25 percent of their time on the job writing and about the same amount of time speaking. It must be acknowledged that the volume of writing must be kept in check so that email and paper work do not bury business. Yet at the same time, we must understand why it is often necessary to write letters, memos, reports, and other business messages.

A century ago, communication in business was simple because much work was done by hand, and customers were usually personal acquaintances of the craftsman or business person who was selling a product or performing a service. Also, people performed most of their own work and often prepared in their own homes many materials that are commonly bought today. When society and business became more complex, face to face contact between customers and suppliers became more difficult and time consuming. Writing business letters, reports, and memorandums was a natural development. And communicating by telephone eventually became routine in business. Computers have added to this complexity and made the study of business communication even more important.

---

[1]Homer Cox, "The Voices of Experience: The Business Communication Alumnus Reports," *The Journal of Business Communication,* Summer 1976, pp. 35ff.

The Internet Age

Business communication in the last decade has changed dramatically because of the invention and proliferation of new technology. The impact on both our personal lives and business dealings is immense. Technology affects how we live, work and play, and has made marked differences in how we communicate personally and professionally.

Fueled by the rapid growth of computer systems throughout the world, new forms of communication have appeared. Beyond the early uses of computer technology for word processing, spreadsheets (computer programs that organize data into horizontal and vertical columns), graphic presentations and page layouts, as well as other forms have emerged. The World Wide Web and internet have burst upon our lives faster than any other technological phenomenon. Our vast, interconnected communications network has resulted in an "Internet Age," in which the majority of people have increasing access to a rapidly growing number of electronic communications.

Bits over Atoms

Nicholas Negroponte, Director of the Massachusetts Institute of Technology multimedia labs, has adroitly described the quickening replacement of atoms with bits.[2] For example, creating a letter on paper results in the use of atoms to form the physical communication medium—a sheet of paper, an envelope, and a stamp. In contrast, an email message is created with computer "bits," which are electronic, digital representations of information. The email bits can be transmitted to another computer anywhere in the world and displayed on the screen without the use of any atoms (paper or the like) to store the essence of the message.

Why is this so? Availability and economics. The rapid expansion of lower-cost computing and the dramatic emergence of the internet as a means of connecting millions of computers has enabled email to become practical. With over 100 million computers connecting to the internet today, its availability is nearly universal. In economic terms, the cost of sending email is much less than the cost of paper manufacturing, mailing, and handling of postal mail. For many emerging communications uses, it's clear that bits will win over atoms, especially in an increasingly Internet-wired age.

Communication Technology Challenges

As in most areas of computer use, many business people find it increasingly difficult to keep up with the rapid changes wrought by new communication technologies. Using a computer to type memos, letters, and reports is a valuable skill expected of every college graduate. As many early users will attest, it is certainly a challenge to learn new methods of creating communications materials. Word processing allows great improvements in formatting, corrections, and composing for many, so the pain of learning is well worth it.

---

[2]Nicholas Negroponte, *being digital* (New York: Alfred A. Knopf, Inc., 1995).

Today, the most popular word processing program has hundreds of commands, format options, and font style settings, and it requires an astounding number of megabytes of disk storage to install. Professional computer software trainers indicate that their own expert level knowledge in the top word processing software is less than 25 percent of the total features and capabilities. Most competent users understand less than 10 percent even after years of use and training. Yet many of the often unused software tools, such as spelling and grammar checkers, can help improve the quality and accuracy of the message being communicated.

In the early days of personal computing, program software titles were sparse. Today, thousands of products in various releases are available. Incompatibility between programs makes interchange difficult. Even with the advent of improved user interfaces, our challenge is even greater than before.

And just when you thought it was safe to jump in, the internet has burst in and changed our lives in dramatic new ways. The impact of the **World Wide Web**—a whole new means of accessing global information, anytime, from almost anywhere—has fueled a business revolution.

Computer Literacy Is Not Enough

Today's youths are well versed in computer use. While older generations struggle to keep up, grade school children have no fear of figuring out what they must do to use their computers. But computer literacy is not enough. Effective, quality communications require skills and experience in technology and in composing business communications.

Business Communication Classes = Prestige Courses

In a business communication journal, Joel Bowman of Western Michigan University stated that, as employers continue to demand that employees write better, business communication classes have become prestige courses on the job market. Completion of college business communication classes is a plus on any employment resumé. If you write clearly in an organized manner, your work will stand out because of the obvious general lack of such talent. To people upstairs, organized writing means organized thinking. With today's information boom, there is always room at the top for people who can write.[3]

Because of the new easy operation and efficiency of desktop computers, increasing numbers of people at management and other executive levels are composing, writing, and creating sophisticated communications at their own desktop computers. They make diagrams, charts and electronic spreadsheets—much more than writing simple memos.

Communication Channels

To learn to communicate effectively, it is helpful to understand something about the various communication methods or **channels,** and also the ideas behind the communication theory. The following channels will be studied: nonverbal, oral, written, combining oral and written, and later will cover newer communication methods.

[3]Joel Bowman, "And Not a Shot Was Fired ...," *Bulletin of the Association for Business Communication,* December 1987, p. 33.

Nonverbal Communication

Nonverbal communication—that is, communication without words—is frequently more effective than any spoken or written message. (The word *verb* originally meant *word*; therefore, *nonverbal* means *without words*.) Nonverbal forms of sending messages include such things as red and green traffic lights, road pictographs directing traffic around the world, police and fire sirens, the telephone ring, the beeper's beep and the computer's alert ping. Although no words are used, each provides a clear message.

Another extremely effective means of nonverbal communication is the use of **body language,** which was originally given the scientific name **kinesics.** Body language is used in many forms, such as nodding or shaking the head, raising eyebrows, pointing thumbs up or down, pointing a finger, raising a fist, winking, smiling, frowning, glaring, kissing, clapping, or shaking hands. In fact, body language can often transmit a stronger message than verbal language. For example, if a man is asked if he likes another man, he might say, "Of course I like him." But if he should at the same time use a "thumbs down" gesture, or make a motion with his forefinger as if to slit his own throat, this would totally contradict the spoken verbal message.

Sign language such as that used for communicating with the deaf is considered a means of verbal communication because, although signs are used, communication is taking place by means of words.

Oral Communication

The chief advantage of **oral** (spoken) **communication** is that it furnishes an opportunity for a speedy and complete exchange of ideas—in other words, immediate **feedback**. This gives an opportunity to clarify any matters that may be questionable.

The first and highest level communication channel is speaking in person, face to face. This channel rates high because, besides immediately exchanging words, we can see all signs of body language. Also, when we hear another person speak, we can get additional information from noticing vocal cues of tone, loudness, pronunciation, emphasis, grammar usage, and so forth.

Telephoning and **computer voice mail**, the second level communication channel, are not always as completely effective as face to face because of the absence of body language. But they do furnish vocal cues and an opportunity for immediate feedback. Use of the telephone for business communication continues to grow because of the telephone's convenience and its real or imagined economy.

Written Communication

Written or printed communication such as **email** and **postal letters**, memos and reports, are generally considered the third level communication channel. Some of these communications are prepared on paper (hard copy), and others are stored on computer disks or displayed on computer terminals. Although these visual communications lack some advantages of personal oral messages, written ones are frequently preferred.

A business communication is often too important not to be put in writing. Correspondence within a company, contacts between customers and clients, monthly statements, credit and collection matters, and appointment confirmations are just a few examples where records might be needed.

As business grows, it becomes apparent that the chief advantages of having a copy of a communication properly filed are these:

1. **Having a written record.** A major advantage of written communications is that the writer and receiver may each have a copy for immediate and future reference. Letters, memorandums, and reports, written properly, can save hours that could be wasted in looking for facts and figures. *Attempting to recall all details of a face to face interview, a telephone call, or voice mail message often produces incomplete or inaccurate information.*

2. **Working when convenient to writer and receiver.** Another major advantage of written communication is convenience. One writer may be able to handle the bulk of preparing correspondence and reports at a regular time each day. Another might snatch a few minutes periodically throughout the day, thereby leaving time free for other pressing matters. Similarly, the person who receives the printed postal mail or email message can read it more leisurely at a convenient time.

3. **Preventing "Telephone Tag."** Written communication on paper or a computer screen also prevents the problem called **telephone tag.** In this frustrating game, you call Mr. Jones but reach only his answering machine or a secretary. When Mr. Jones returns your call, he gets your answering machine or secretary because you are likewise busy. You get the message and try to contact him, and so on. This back-and-forth game can go on for a long time before you actually reach the person you want. Most business to business phone calls do not reach the intended person immediately, and at least a short game of phone tag results.

The chief thrust of this text will be to teach the various types of written communications for these two reasons:

☐ A high percentage of traditional and electronic communication is done by the written word.

☐ The need for training in business writing is obvious.

Combining Oral and Written Communication

As noted earlier, some advantages of person to person meetings and telephone calls can be offset by the loss or confusion of actual details. Participants might remember (or forget) different parts of the spoken messages. As we will see later, surveys of all business communications show that a high percentage are unclear and completely misleading.

Therefore, a joining of oral and written message channels, combining the advantages of both, can be extremely effective to help clarify the information exchanged. Notes written before, during and/or after interviews, speeches, conferences, telephone calls, and so on can refresh memories of participants. At times, such notes have even held up as evidence in court. Important notes must be filed carefully.

However, taking and retaining too many unnecessary notes can create a glut of paper garbage in office files. (See Chapter 11, "Oral Communications.")

The Communication Theory in Action

Today, scientific researchers are studying the **communication theory** to help us improve our methods of communicating effectively. This research helps us formulate and send messages that are complete and clear—in other words, received with the same meaning that was intended by the sender. Studies show there are innumerable causes of misunderstandings, beginning with the formation of the message in the mind of the sender. Going through various stages where meaning might become unclear, it is recognized that the understanding and effect of a message can even be changed drastically by the mood of the person receiving it.

Input, Channel, Message, Output, Feedback

Figure 1.1 shows the communication theory in action. It shows the ideas of the *sender* being transmitted to the *receiver*, with the receiver's resulting **feedback** or reaction to the message.

The **communication theory** centers on a study of sending and receiving messages. The main steps of the process are as follows:

1. **Input:** information or ideas sender plans to give receiver
2. **Channel:** the selected type of message carrier: email, postal mail, telephone call, fax, interview, conference, etc.
3. **Message:** the actual message that is sent: memo, letter, form, report, etc.
4. **Output:** information the receiver gets
5. **Feedback:** receiver's response or nonresponse to the message
6. **Brain drain:** the possibility of misunderstanding at any step

FIGURE 1.1
Communication theory in action, showing ideas
being transmitted from sender to receiver.

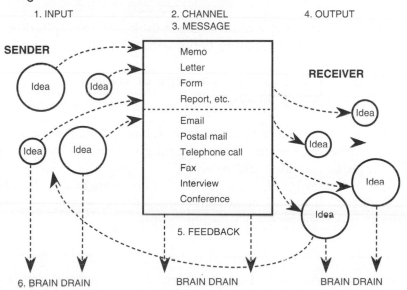

Obviously, innumerable barriers can block immediate understanding of a message. It pays to write clearly so a message can be understood on the first reading.

"Closing the Loop" of Communication

In communication research, the proper feedback of information from receiver to sender is called **closing the loop** of communications.

Following is a simplified example of the communication theory in action, showing **input, message, output,** and **feedback,** closing the loop of communication.

Input	*Message*	*Output*
I want a copy of the current catalogue of MNO corporation. $\rightarrow$	Would you please send me a copy of your current catalogue. $\rightarrow$	They want a copy of our current catalogue.

Feedback: Copy of current catalogue mailed to sender of message.

"Brain Drain"

Not all messages are as simple as the foregoing request for a copy of a company catalogue, and **brain drain,** a breakdown in the communication cycle, frequently occurs. This breakdown means the communication loop has not been closed properly. Such breakdowns result in all those unclear messages and can be due to one or more of the following:

Improper formulation of the message in the mind of the sender

Improper statement of the information in the message

Improper reception of the information by the receiver

The common occurrence of brain drain indicates an emphatic need for study in the field of planning and preparing better communications.

Communication Barriers that Damage or Destroy the Receiver's Understanding

Even when a message is planned and prepared well, it may not be received and understood properly. Poor understanding might be caused by **barriers** that can exist between the parties sending and receiving.

To help us communicate clearly, we must be aware that such potential problems increase the need for writing clearly and concisely. For examples, here are a few barriers that can block the receiver's understanding:

☐   Emotional status—pressures of receiver's job and personal life

☐ Differences in age, cultural background, gender, economic status or education between sender and receiver

☐ Time pressures on the receiver

Figure 1.2 pictures the process of trying to send a message of various ideas through a maze of potential mental and emotional blocks or barriers. Count the number of ideas being sent and the number of ideas being received.

Uses of Business Communication—External and Internal

Business communications perform many functions both inside and outside an organization. Inside a business, the chief **functions of communications** are these:

To inform management about operations to enable the business to continue successfully

To inform workers of job requirements—those that remain the same and those that change

To improve morale by keeping employees informed of overall business operations and personnel matters

FIGURE 1.2
Examples of barriers between individuals that might
cause the receiver to misunderstand a message.

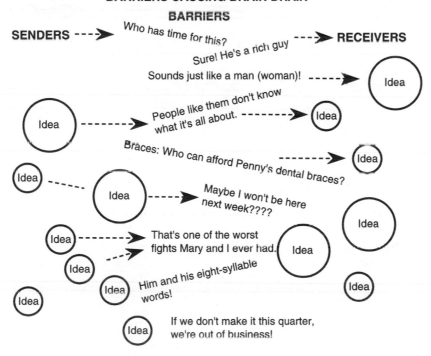

The major uses of communications outside an organization are as follows:

To receive goods and services

To sell goods and services

To make necessary reports to owners/stockholders

To make necessary reports to the government

To create and maintain good will for the business

How you express yourself not only affects your readers' confidence in you, it also affects your ability to influence your readers.

Figure 1.3 is a humorous example of a typical communications brain drain that can occur when a new product is developed [original source unknown].

FIGURE 1.3
A communications brain drain.

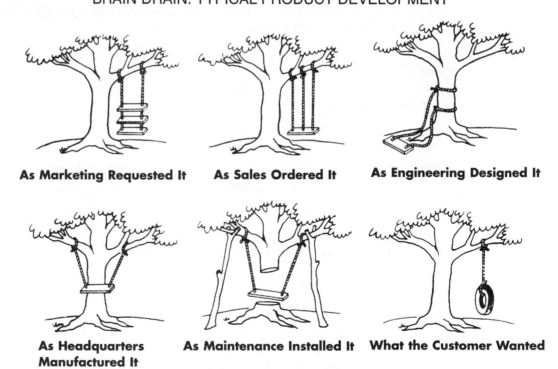

BRAIN DRAIN: TYPICAL PRODUCT DEVELOPMENT

As Marketing Requested It   **As Sales Ordered It**   **As Engineering Designed It**

As Headquarters Manufactured It   **As Maintenance Installed It**   **What the Customer Wanted**

Chapter 1   You and Business Communication:
The Communication Theory

REVIEW AND DISCUSSION

Please make answers brief. Draw a line through any incorrect response.

1. Peter Drucker, highly respected business management consultant and educator, said that the one thing most valuable for a future employee to know is <u>the ability to</u> <u>organize and express ideas in writing and speaking.</u>

2. How do some industry leaders show their support for employees to get training in business communication? <u>Some offer their own courses or pay tuition for college</u> <u>classes in the subject.</u>

3. In business communication today, atoms are increasingly being replaced by electronic bits. (True/~~False~~)

4. Today most competent users of word processing software say they use a (~~high~~ / low) percentage of their word processing features and capabilities.

5. On the job market, what kind of courses have business communication classes become? <u>Prestige courses.</u>

6. Give two examples of nonverbal communication that are not given in the text.
   a. <u>(Student input.)</u>
   b. _____

7. What is the chief advantage of oral communication? <u>Feedback: immediate</u> <u>exchange of ideas.</u>

8. What are the advantages of written records? <u>Having a printed record for both</u> <u>immediate and future use.</u>

9. The communication theory centers on what? <u>Sending and receiving messages.</u>

10. Name a barrier to clear communication that is not given in the text. _____
    (Student input.)

VOCABULARY

Give definitions of the following terms.

11. "bits" of an email message <u>Electronic pieces of information.</u>

12. closing the loop of communication <u>Receiver's response to message.</u>

2 Qualities of an Effective Business Communication

Attractive Appearance

> *The neater the document, the more competent the sender seems to be. Other factors being equal, readers pay closer attention to—take more seriously—the document with the better appearance.*
>
> Joel P. Bowman and Debbie E. Renshaw[1]

Are you insulting your readers?

When a shoddy, unattractive letter is received, the reader may not bother to pinpoint any reason for an initial negative reaction to the entire letter. But there may be an immediate mental response like this: "Well, if their way of doing business is like their letters, let's find someone else for our business!"

The appearance of an internet website is a crucial factor in the quality of good business communications. The best business websites are attractive, well designed, easy to use, and have valuable information content. What's amazing is the predominance of unattractive web pages today. Just because it's easy for anyone to create a web home page, you don't really want your web image to look like it was designed by a nonprofessional any more than you would have your company logo designed by an amateur.

Most of this book covers the *content* of business communications—how to write them. But this one early chapter covers the appearance of written communications because of the recognized importance of this element. Of course, not all information relating to appearance can be covered completely in one chapter. For greater detail, see an up-to-date secretarial manual.

Much responsibility for the appearance of a good letter should rest in the hands of people at management or executive level. Company letterhead, quality of paper, style of type, and other such matters should be studied thoroughly. The total appearance is important enough for the attention of top-level officials, who should understand the reasons for careful decisions on these matters.

Website appearance is a more complex issue, since there are many more factors to consider, and many more opportunities to succeed or fail in having a quality "look and feel." In Chapter 11, we'll review some of the qualities of a good website.

---

[1]Joel P. Bowman and Debbie A. Renshaw, "Desktop Publishing: Things Gutenberg Never Taught You," *The Journal of Business Communication*, Winter, 1989, p. 60.

Stationery

Stationery Size

Most business stationery is the standard 8½ by 11 inches. This size paper fits in standard office file drawers. Legal offices and courts have changed from the traditional 8½ by 14 inch legal size paper to the 8½ by 11 inch size.

In some states courts will not accept the old "legal size" paper unless needed for some special archival purposes.

Sometimes a special size of paper is used for executive prestige correspondence or for other special mailings. For the sake of appearance, this paper, usually 7½ by 10½ or 6 by 9 inches, may have a high rag fiber content. However, a disadvantage of the smaller sheets is that they tend to become lost in file drawers built to accommodate standard stationery.

Stationery Quality

The most common business **stationery quality** is 16 to 20 pound weight. Lighter weight paper usually is not opaque, showing the printing of the sheet underneath. Heavier paper resists wear; therefore, 20 pound bond, even though usually more expensive, might be preferred to 16 pound. Also, heavier paper gives the reader the impression of quality.

Paper that has 25 percent **rag content** might be used for more important communications. (Rag content refers to the percentage of cotton fiber contained in the paper—the more rag fiber, the better the quality.) Some better quality papers may have 50 to 100 percent rag content. To check the cotton fiber amount, hold the paper up to the light and you will see a watermark showing the percentage of cotton used. Rag paper is selected because it looks and feels attractive, is durable, and resists yellowing.

Stationery Color

While most business letters are written on standard white paper with black ink, use of color is a growing tendency. The greatest advantage of using softly tinted stationery is that it reduces glare.

Black ink on white paper gives off a great amount of glare and is therefore hard on eyes. Paper in soft tones of cream, green, yellow, blue, and gray are appearing. Accountants have long used accounting papers in soft greens or yellows.

Given the number of hours all office people spend reading various communications, we must give more attention to adopting any practice, such as use of color, that spares eyestrain. Good quality copying machines print on light tints as clearly as white. (See Chapter 12, "Healthy Computing: Avoiding Eyestrain, Carpal (Wrist) Tunnel Syndrome, Back Pain.")

Many organizations with environmental concerns use recycled paper in soft earth tones, such as light tan or green. In this way, even a company's stationery conveys its concern for the environment.

Care must be taken when using colored paper. Be sure to select tones that reproduce as clearly as white on copying machines. Red can show up as black or gray.

Blue often shows up as white. A light blue letterhead will not reproduce on many copy machines.

Multiple Page Letters

The second and any following pages of a letter should be of the same quality as the letterhead paper. Otherwise, it may appear that you are putting on a false front by having only the first page of top quality. Pages after the first should be numbered, and many businesses also have the date and the name of the addressee on these subsequent headings. This information should begin on the seventh line (leaving a one-inch top margin), and should be followed by a triple space (two blank lines) before the body of the letter is continued. To save space, this information can be shown horizontally on one line:

Dr. S. I. Chang   2   September 1, 20XX

Methods of Preparing Communications

Computers can be used solely for their word processing capabilities.

Typing errors can be completely removed before printouts, with no evidence of the error's having been made. A poorly made correction of a typing error can stand out so badly that it offends any reader. Typewriters on today's market are simple computers, and have technically advanced methods of removing errors totally and replacing them with corrected copy. There may always be a place for typewriters in offices so printed forms can be completed. But, as one newspaper columnist observed, "computers do word work infinitely better than typewriters."

Letter Placement

Standard Length Line Placement

The most popular form for **letter placement** today is the standard length line with uneven or "ragged" right margins. With computer word processing, letters can be reformatted, even after typing. Any letter placement pattern can be stored on the hard disk or computer network for future use.

For the **standard length line placement,** side margins for all letters are set for approximately $1\frac{1}{4}$ inch width. The space between date and address can be varied according to the length of the letter, leaving more space for a short letter, less space for a longer one. Space variation can also be made between the closing parts of the letter, such as the complimentary closing, signature lines, and typist's initials.

Simplified Placement; Memorandum Form

A different pattern is **simplified placement.** For efficiency and brevity, this form follows standard placement but leaves out the salutation and the complimentary closing. Many people like this style. Perhaps the lack of general acceptance, however, is a reaction against omitting the traditional personal touches of salutation and closing.

A natural development is that instead of using the simplified form, some firms use the memorandum form for routine communications not only inside an organization but also for outside mailings. Evidently this form is accepted because of its efficiency and also because of people's familiarity with it for in-house communicating. Also, it has no obvious omission of personal touches. The memorandum form usually has the following headings:

To: Date:
From: Subject:

Upper Placement

Another letter placement form, **upper placement,** is not yet accepted by many letter-writing purists. This form has the standard length line with the letter written in the upper portion of the page, leaving room for the return message to be typed at the bottom. The upper placement form originally came into use in letters and memorandums between individuals in or branches of the same business.

With routine messages, this placement form can also be used outside a business. If the entire message with reply is needed for the files, a print can be made on a copy machine. Frequently, no copy of this type of message is made, and the answered original is simply returned to the sender, requiring no unnecessary typing and filing. Or, a fax copy of the original with answers can be sent. *Frequently having one sheet substitute for two* is a big bonus for filing, when you consider how much space can be saved in the stacks of communications sent and received.

Picture Frame Placement

The **picture frame** pattern of placing a letter on a page has become less popular. In the picture frame form, the letter has side margins nearly equal and top and bottom margins nearly equal, framing the letter as if it were a picture, which takes time and therefore costs money. This placement is sometimes used for executive level correspondence, where more time and attention can be given to special appearance.

The following chart is a good rule of thumb for placing letters under the picture frame plan:

Words in Body of Letter	Side Margins
up to 100	2 inches
101–300	$1^1/_2$ inches
over 300	$1^1/_4$ inches

The inside address of the letter should begin from four to thirteen lines below the date line, with six to eight lines the most common space. Shorter letters will have wider top and bottom margins as well as wider side margins; longer ones will have narrower margins.

Choice of Letter Styles

Often, a particular letter style is selected for all correspondence of a firm. Such information is circulated by interoffice memorandum or through a company correspondence manual that contains materials relating to proper form for preparing company communications.

In studying business correspondence, we soon learn that every year, one or more new ideas will be adopted that previously would have been considered unthinkable. With office costs spiraling upward, most of today's changes have resulted from an interest in economy. One factor that changes from time to time is letter style. Currently, the two most popular letter styles in American business correspondence are block and modified block.

Block and Modified Block Letters

In the **block letter style,** shown in Figure 2.1, all lines, including those of new paragraphs, start at the left margin. This saves the time of setting the various indentions and reduces the chance of error in doing so.

Computers can also make the right margin blocked by justifying the right margin—that is, setting the machine to make all lines space out to finish at the right margin. However, some people object to the streams of space that sometimes flow down through papers because of adding extra spaces to many lines. Detailed research by a United States government agency shows that such letters are more difficult to read than letters with the traditional, uneven ragged margins.[2]

Figure 2.2 shows the first two paragraphs of the letter in Figure 2.1 written with justified right margins. Choice of right margin form is a matter of personal taste, but most people choose not to justify the right margin.

Still the most popular business letter style is the **modified block.** Most parts of this letter (Figure 2.3) begin at the left margin; the paragraphs may or may not be indented five, seven, or ten spaces. The date might be centered at the top, started at the center of the page, or placed so that it ends at the right margin. Then the complimentary closing and signature lines would start vertically in line with the starting position of the date line. Figure 2.3 also shows the proper notation for enclosures. If you have more than one enclosure, the number could be shown as "Enc. (3)" or "Enclosures (3)."

---

[2]*Guidelines for Document Designers,* American Institutes for Research, 1055 Thomas Jefferson Street, N.W., Washington, D.C. Not dated.

FIGURE 2.1

Example of block style letter with no punctuation after salutation and complimentary closing. Letter also shows picture frame placement.

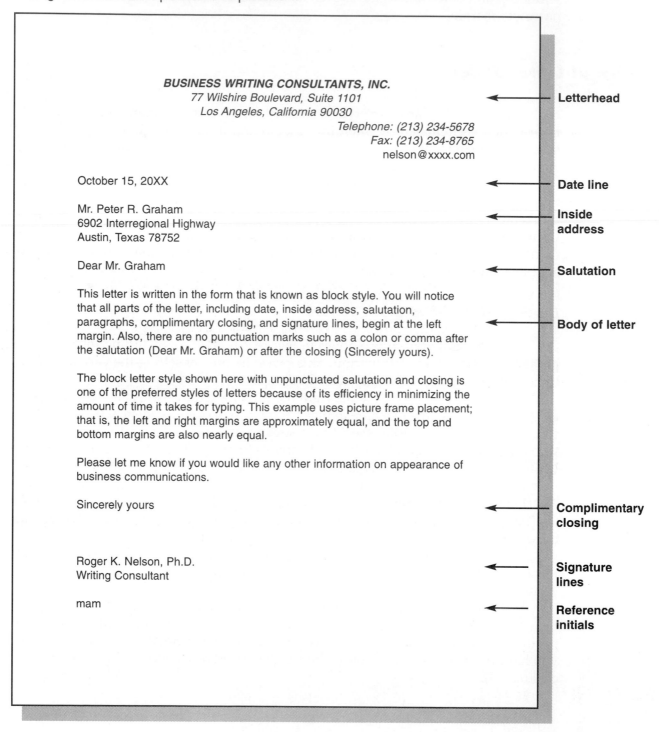

BUSINESS WRITING CONSULTANTS, INC.
77 Wilshire Boulevard, Suite 1101
Los Angeles, California 90030
Telephone: (213) 234-5678
Fax: (213) 234-8765
nelson@xxxx.com ← **Letterhead**

October 15, 20XX ← **Date line**

Mr. Peter R. Graham
6902 Interregional Highway
Austin, Texas 78752 ← **Inside address**

Dear Mr. Graham ← **Salutation**

This letter is written in the form that is known as block style. You will notice that all parts of the letter, including date, inside address, salutation, paragraphs, complimentary closing, and signature lines, begin at the left margin. Also, there are no punctuation marks such as a colon or comma after the salutation (Dear Mr. Graham) or after the closing (Sincerely yours). ← **Body of letter**

The block letter style shown here with unpunctuated salutation and closing is one of the preferred styles of letters because of its efficiency in minimizing the amount of time it takes for typing. This example uses picture frame placement; that is, the left and right margins are approximately equal, and the top and bottom margins are also nearly equal.

Please let me know if you would like any other information on appearance of business communications.

Sincerely yours ← **Complimentary closing**

Roger K. Nelson, Ph.D.
Writing Consultant ← **Signature lines**

mam ← **Reference initials**

FIGURE 2.2
First two paragraphs of block letter in Figure 2.1 written with right margin justified.

October 15, 20XX

Mr. Peter R. Graham
6902 Interregional Highway
Austin, Texas 78752

Dear Mr. Graham

This letter is written in the form known as block style. You will notice that all parts of the letter, including date, inside address, salutation, paragraphs, complimentary closing and signature lines, begin at the left margin. Also, there are no punctuation marks such as a colon or comma after the salutation (Dear Mr. Graham) or after the closing (Sincerely yours).

The block letter style shown here with salutation and closing not punctuated, and all parts starting at the left margin is one of the preferred styles of letters because of its efficiency in minimizing the amount of time it takes for typing.

Personal Business Letter

Important: Be sure to put your personal return address on a personal business letter. In an office, envelopes usually become detached from the letters.

Figure 2.4 is a good example of a form for a personal business letter. This form is used for handling your own business or personal affairs when you do not have a letterhead with address information. Your return address must be shown either above the dateline or below the signature with or without your telephone and other address numbers. If you do not include this information, people will not know where to contact you. Figure 2.4 is prepared in modified block style with indented paragraphs. (It is completely improper and illegal to appropriate your employer's stationery for your own use.)

Parts of a Business Letter

Major and minor parts of a business letter are shown in Figures 2.1, 2.3, and 2.4. At least one blank line should be left between all parts. To help make a short letter

FIGURE 2.3
Example of modified block style letter with no punctuation after salutation and complimentary closing.

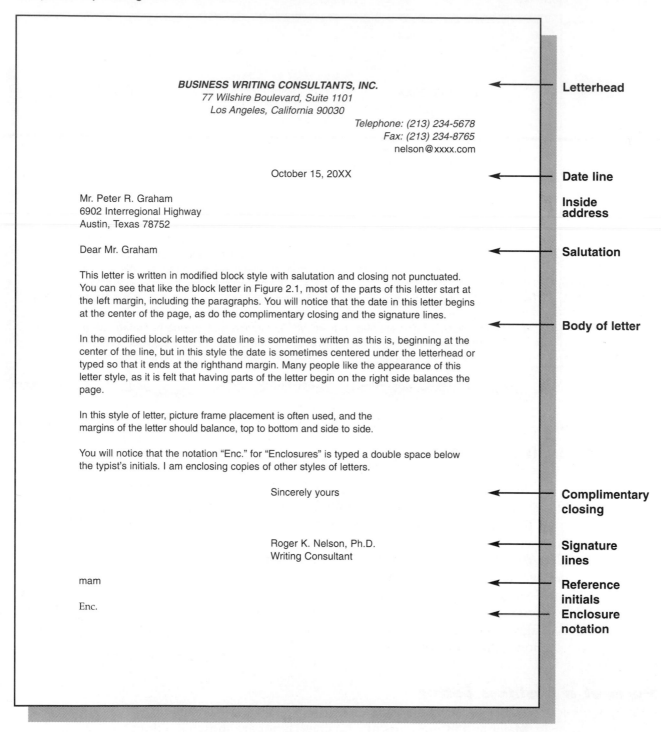

BUSINESS WRITING CONSULTANTS, INC.
77 Wilshire Boulevard, Suite 1101
Los Angeles, California 90030
Telephone: (213) 234-5678
Fax: (213) 234-8765
nelson@xxxx.com
→ **Letterhead**

October 15, 20XX
→ **Date line**

Mr. Peter R. Graham
6902 Interregional Highway
Austin, Texas 78752
→ **Inside address**

Dear Mr. Graham
→ **Salutation**

This letter is written in modified block style with salutation and closing not punctuated. You can see that like the block letter in Figure 2.1, most of the parts of this letter start at the left margin, including the paragraphs. You will notice that the date in this letter begins at the center of the page, as do the complimentary closing and the signature lines.

In the modified block letter the date line is sometimes written as this is, beginning at the center of the line, but in this style the date is sometimes centered under the letterhead or typed so that it ends at the righthand margin. Many people like the appearance of this letter style, as it is felt that having parts of the letter begin on the right side balances the page.
→ **Body of letter**

In this style of letter, picture frame placement is often used, and the margins of the letter should balance, top to bottom and side to side.

You will notice that the notation "Enc." for "Enclosures" is typed a double space below the typist's initials. I am enclosing copies of other styles of letters.

Sincerely yours
→ **Complimentary closing**

Roger K. Nelson, Ph.D.
Writing Consultant
→ **Signature lines**

mam
→ **Reference initials**

Enc.
→ **Enclosure notation**

FIGURE 2.4

Personal business letter in modified block style, not punctuated after salutation and complimentary closing. Letter shows placement of return address when none is shown on a letterhead.

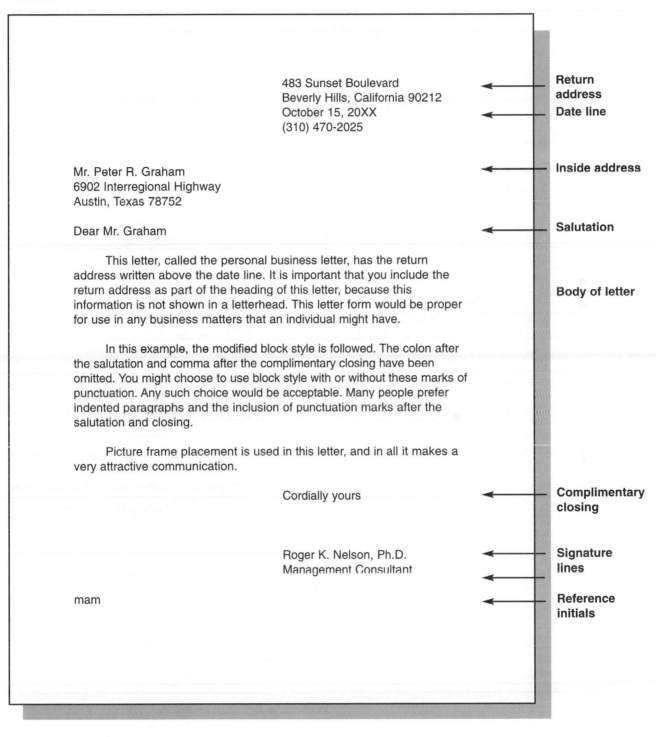

Return address

Date line

Inside address

Salutation

Body of letter

Complimentary closing

Signature lines

Reference initials

483 Sunset Boulevard
Beverly Hills, California 90212
October 15, 20XX
(310) 470-2025

Mr. Peter R. Graham
6902 Interregional Highway
Austin, Texas 78752

Dear Mr. Graham

     This letter, called the personal business letter, has the return address written above the date line. It is important that you include the return address as part of the heading of this letter, because this information is not shown in a letterhead. This letter form would be proper for use in any business matters that an individual might have.

     In this example, the modified block style is followed. The colon after the salutation and comma after the complimentary closing have been omitted. You might choose to use block style with or without these marks of punctuation. Any such choice would be acceptable. Many people prefer indented paragraphs and the inclusion of punctuation marks after the salutation and closing.

     Picture frame placement is used in this letter, and in all it makes a very attractive communication.

            Cordially yours

            Roger K. Nelson, Ph.D.
            Management Consultant

mam

fill a page, extra blank lines can be left between the date line and the first line of the address, and an extra blank line can be left between paragraphs. The complimentary close (when used) and signature can also be used as **elevator lines,** that is, extra blank lines can be left between these parts to further balance a page.

The standard order of letter parts is set out here. In this list, minor parts, those parts that might or might not be used, are set out in italics.

1. Letterhead
2. Date (at left margin or centered under letterhead)
3. *Special mailing instructions (in all capital letters) (or as last part)*
4. *File number*
5. *Personal or Confidential*
6. *Attention line* [3]
7. Mailing address
8. *Salutation*
9. *Reference (RE) or subject line (when used)*
10. Body of letter
11. *Complimentary close*
12. Signature
13. *Reference initials*
14. *Enclosures*
15. *Copies*
16. *Postscripts*

The following information about some specific letter parts may be helpful.

Letterhead

A letterhead should show business name, complete address including ZIP code, telephone number including area code, and email address. You may choose to include additional information such as names of officers, products or services, organization slogan, and so forth.

Many firms today join the growing tendency to place much of this letterhead information at the bottom of the page, where we might call it a **letterfoot,** thus clearing clutter from the top of the page. But the firm name is almost always at the top. Assistance in designing a letterhead can be obtained from stationery supply firms, printers, letter writing consultants, and advertising agencies. Many stationery catalogues with letterhead examples are available, and from these a style can be selected.

In-house computer-generated letterheads can be updated and changed at little or no cost. With a computer and good printer, you can prepare your own "classy" or conservative headings as you like them. And you won't have to hire a designer to help you. Then your own designs can be used on envelopes, memos, forms, routing slips, telephone message forms, and so forth. Or you can hire that professional designer.

---

[3]At the request of the United States Postal Service, the attention line should come before the rest of the address for speedy mail sorting and delivery in the post office and at the place of the receiver. (*Postal Addressing Standards,* Publication 28, United States Postal Service, January, 1992, page 6).

Letter writing today

Date Line

Unless there is a specific reason for doing otherwise, the **date line** typed on the letter should be the date the letter was dictated or composed, not the date it was typed. The receiver of the letter may need to know at what point in communications it was composed.

In block style letters, all lines, including the date line, begin at the left margin. In modified block style letters, the design of the letterhead often determines the placement of the date. In these letters, the date can be centered, it can be started at the center of the line directly aligned with the signature lines, or it can be typed so that it ends at the right margin of the page.

A space of at least three lines should be left between the date and the inside address. As stated, this space can be varied to balance placement, according to the length of the letter, leaving more blank lines for a short letter, fewer blank lines for a longer one.

Special Mailing Instructions

To catch the attention of mail room personnel or any others mailing letters, **special mailing instructions** such as *Express Mail, registered mail, certified mail,* etc., should be typed in all capital letters below the date with a blank line before and after these instructions. Mailing instructions are sometimes shown at the bottom of the letter, but they are less noticeable there, especially if the letter is more than one page.

These instructions also show the receiver that the letter had special mailing attention.

Inside Mailing Address

To simplify addressing letters and envelopes, the address parts of both should have the same information and should be in the same order. The United States Postal Service recently requested that, for speedier and more efficient mail handling, the attention line with the name of the person to receive the letter should be placed above the name of the firm or building to which the mail piece is directed. The Postal Service also requests that the address *on the envelope* be written in all capital letters. (See page 29, "Addressing Envelopes.") The following example of the format *for letters* shows standard capital and lower case letters.

```
Attention: Mr. Charles G. Rosselli
K and K Neighborhood Markets
Post Office Box 1000
City, State 00000

Dear Mr. Rosselli
```

Figure 2.5 is an alphabetical list of states with their standard abbreviations and two-letter abbreviations. A decision must be made as to the form for addressing mail. Objections arise about using the two-letter state identification because some codes can be taken to identify more than one state. Is AK Alaska or Arkansas? Is MI Michigan or Minnesota or Mississippi? Is CO Colorado or Connecticut? Also, a one-letter typing mistake (everyone makes these) can identify the wrong state.

Some firms require that all their mail show the standard state abbreviation or the full state name. However, for speedy, accurate distribution of mail, ZIP codes (numbers) must always be used because optical character reading (OCR) machines, which have become more widespread, read these numbers.

In the address line, the first name or initials should be used before the surname of the person to whom the letter is addressed, and the appropriate **courtesy title**, such as Mr., Miss, Ms., Mrs., or Dr., can precede the name. Although traditionalists do not like the trend, some courtesy titles are disappearing, as all men are addressed *Mr.* and all women *Ms.*

Because of a need for economy in addressing volume mail, *occupant* and *resident* mailings often do not conform with strict patterns for addressing letters, following only minimal postal recommendations.

The inside mailing address on the letter and the outside address on the envelope should contain the same information not only to simplify mailings, but also because the internal copy of the letter will be used for future reference in addressing letters.

All lines of the address must be checked carefully for absolute accuracy, particularly numbers, the spelling of names, and any words written in a foreign language.

FIGURE 2.5
Alphabetical list of state names with standard abbreviations and two-letter abbreviations.

Two-Letter Abbreviations and Standard Abbreviations of State Names

State	Postal Abbrev.	Standard Abbrev.	State	Postal Abbrev.	Standard Abbrev.
Alabama	AL	Ala.	Missouri	MO	Mo.
Alaska	AK	...	Montana	MT	Mont.
Arizona	AZ	Ariz.	Nebraska	NE	Nebr.
Arkansas	AR	Ark.	Nevada	NV	Nev.
California	CA	Calif.	New Hampshire	NH	N.H.
Colorado	CO	Colo.	New Jersey	NJ	N.J.
Connecticut	CT	Conn.	New Mexico	NM	N. Mex.
Delaware	DE	Del.	New York	NY	N.Y.
District of			North Carolina	NC	N.C.
Columbia	DC	D.C.	North Dakota	ND	N. Dak.
Florida	FL	Fla.	Ohio	OH	...
Georgia	GA	Ga.	Oklahoma	OK	Okla.
Guam	GU	...	Oregon	OR	Oreg.
Hawaii	HI	...	Pennsylvania	PA	Pa.
Idaho	ID	...	Puerto Rico	PR	P.R.
Illinois	IL	Ill.	Rhode Island	RI	R.I.
Indiana	IN	Ind.	South Carolina	SC	S.C.
Iowa	IA	...	South Dakota	SD	S. Dak.
Kansas	KS	Kans.	Tennessee	TN	Tenn.
Kentucky	KY	Ky.	Texas	TX	Tex.
Louisiana	LA	La.	Utah	UT	...
Maine	ME	...	Vermont	VT	Vt.
Maryland	MD	Md.	Virgin Islands	VI	V.I.
Massachu-			Virginia	VA	Va.
setts	MA	Mass.	Washington	WA	Wash.
Michigan	MI	Mich.	West Virginia	WV	W. Va.
Minnesota	MN	Minn.	Wisconsin	WI	Wis.
Mississippi	MS	Miss.	Wyoming	WY	Wyo.

ZIP Code and State Identification

For classroom exercise letters that will not be mailed, nonsense ZIP code[4] numbers of 00000 or 12345 can be used. This prevents looking up each ZIP code unnecessarily or using incorrect ZIP codes.

For heavy mailings, investigate the use of the nine digit (**ZIP + 4**) code. Your post office will furnish printed copies of a bulletin giving current rate information.

---

[4]The first digit of the ZIP code identifies a general geographic area consisting of three or more states; the second digit designates a state within that geographic area. The third digit pinpoints a large city or postal area, and the last two digits indicate a specific delivery zone, such as part of a heavily populated city or an entire smaller town.

Salutation

Titles in Salutation. The invention of the typewriter first brought women into the business office. In 1884, the Remington Type-Writer became the first mass produced machine of its kind. Seven years later, the New York City YWCA trained eight young women as experts on these typewriters. (At this time, people were trained to use two fingers of each hand for all typing. The choice of which keys were struck with which fingers was a matter of personal choice.)

The entry of these eight women—themselves called "typewriters"— seemed revolutionary in the business world. There were dire predictions of the dreadful social consequences of having men and women mingling in offices. Also, there was great fear that the delicate physiques of these gentlewomen could not take the rigors of such work.

But times, scenes and attitudes change. Today, we are instructed to use *Ladies and Gentlemen.* After all, the letter may be answered by a woman. Use appropriate titles: *Dear Supervisors, Dear Board Members, Dear Department Heads,* and so forth.

When addressing a person whose name is not known to us, instead of *Dear Sir,* we can use the title of the unknown person, such as *Dear Credit Manager, Dear Customer, Dear Subscriber,* and so forth.

When a person's name is known, we can use the acceptable title with the surname or use the full name. In salutations, capitalize all titles, names, and nouns.

Dear Ms. Bracken   My dear Mr. Brown   Dear Joseph Brewerton

Punctuation and Format of Salutation. As stated previously, a noticeable trend is to have open punctuation in letters, that is, no punctuation after the salutation and complimentary closing. If punctuation is used after the salutation, it should be a colon in a business letter or a comma in a friendly letter. The comma can be used in a business letter when the sender and receiver are well acquainted.

To conform with accepted letter styles, if the letter has a colon or a comma after the salutation, it should also have a comma after the complimentary closing at the end of the letter, to make these two parts match. Figures 2.1, 2.2, and 2.3 show letters without punctuation after the salutation and complimentary closing. Figure 2.4 shows punctuation after these two letter parts. As just noted, either form is acceptable, but the trend is away from the unnecessary use of these marks.

Dear Mr. Bracken	*or*	Dear Mr. Bracken:
Dear Dr. Wright	*or*	Dear Dr. Wright:
Dear Carol	*or*	Dear Carol,

There should be at least a double space—in other words, one blank line—between the last line of the address and the salutation. There should also be at least one blank line between the salutation and the body of the letter. The salutation should name the person or persons shown on the first line of the address. If a person's name is used in the address, be sure to use the name in the salutation, since it gives the letter a more personalized touch.

Subject Line or Reference

Subject lines are required in all emails as references for senders and receivers and that is how they are traced through the airwaves. In a postal memo or letter, if there is a **subject line** or **reference,** it is typed a double space above or below the salutation. This line may start at the left margin, or it may be centered if the letter is a modification of the block style:

Mr. Charles Rosselli
President and
   General Manager
Sunshine Markets
Post Office Box 100
Cleveland, OH 44106

Dear Mr. Rosselli

Re: Your Invoice #12310

There should also be a blank line between the reference line and the body of the letter.

Body of the Letter

The **body of the letter** is the main section and contains the message. Most of this text deals with the writing of the body of a letter, memorandum, or report.

Almost all business letters today, even short ones, are typed single spaced with one blank line between paragraphs if paragraphs are not indented. *If the letter is double spaced, leave an extra blank line between paragraphs.* In the modified block style, paragraphs indentions of five, seven, or ten spaces are commonly used.

Complimentary Closing

There should be at least one blank line between the body of the letter and the **complimentary closing.** In the block letter style, the closing begins at the left margin; in the modified block letter, it will usually line up vertically with the date line. Common complimentary closes of business letters today are *Sincerely, Sincerely yours, Very truly yours, Yours very truly, Cordially, Cordially yours.* Notice that only the first letter of the closing is capitalized.

As mentioned earlier, there should be a comma after the complimentary closing if there is a colon or comma after the salutation at the beginning of the letter.

Signature Lines

Leave at least three blank lines between the complimentary closing and the typed **signature** of the sender, making room for the signature, which should always be written in ink. Three lines is generally enough space, but sometimes more space is needed for a particular signature. The position of the sender, such as *President, General Manager*, or *Supervisor*, if included, is typed immediately below the name. If a person's name and title are shown on the letterhead, the title is usually not typed below the signature, since this is unnecessary repetition.

In signing a letter, a person should normally not give himself or herself a title. An exception to this rule is for the person who has a given name suitable for either a man or woman, such as *Cary, Shawn, Carol, Leslie, Terry*, and so forth. In these cases, when desired, it is acceptable to show a title. Also, women frequently indicate which title—*Miss, Ms.,* or *Mrs.*—they prefer. When a title is shown, it should be typed with the name below the signature rather than having the sender of the letter sign the title with the signature:

Cordially,

Leslie Taylor

Mr. Leslie Taylor

Cordially,

Nancy H. Angelo

Ms. Nancy H. Angelo

On legal papers such as business correspondence, checks, and other legal documents, a married woman should not sign her name with her husband's given name, such as *Mrs. Charles F. Stevens*, but should always sign her own given name, such as *Jane M. Stevens*, because this is her legal name. She should do this because there may have been or there may be in the future another person using her husband's name—for instance, another *Mrs. Charles F. Stevens*. To indicate that she wishes return mail addressed to her by social name (her husband's name) she would have that name typed below her signature or written in parentheses below her signature:

Jane M. Stevens   *Jane M. Stevens*

Mrs. Charles F. Stevens   *(Mrs. Charles F. Stevens)*

Reference Initials

When desired, **reference initials** identifying the person who typed the letter are placed at the left margin a double space below the signature lines. These initials often show on internal office copies only.

Enclosure Notation

If an enclosure is being sent with the letter, an **enclosure notation** is placed at the bottom of the letter at the left margin, a double space below the typist's reference initials, to remind the person mailing the letter that one or more enclosures are to be sent. The enclosure notation also reminds the receiver to look for enclosures. If more than one enclosure is being sent, the number can be shown in parentheses after the word *Enclosures* or the abbreviation *Enc.*

Enclosure   *or*   Enc.
Enclosures (3)   *or*   Enc. (3)

Copy Distribution

Copy distribution should be shown at the left margin, a double space below all other information. One "c" stands for "copy" or "copies"; "cc" stands for the old "carbon copy" or "carbon copies." Today few carbon copies are made.

c: James Finley

If you are sending copies to two or more people, list their names alphabetically, unless an executive is listed first.

Copies are often distributed without showing this information on the original outgoing communication. If this is done, the abbreviation *bc* for *blind copy* and the alphabetic list of recipients are typed on internal copies only.

Postscripts

If there is a **postscript**, it should start a double space beneath all other information except special mailing instructions and can be preceded by the initials *PS* or *PPS* (postscript, post postscript). However, the current trend is to omit these initials. The postscript may be signed or initialed.

A postscript is not necessarily an afterthought. The value of occasionally using one intentionally should not be overlooked. A busy person reading mail will often read the postscript while noticing very little else, knowing that here may be found the most interesting tidbit of the letter. Many business people write postscripts for emphasis rather than for afterthoughts, and they are frequently used for personal messages in business letters.

Addressing Envelopes

Identification of Sender

In addressing a business envelope, *first type the sender's name above the firm's name in the upper left-hand corner.* Better still, have a supply of envelopes ready with the name of the individual sender printed or typed above the return address. Figure 2.6 shows the name of the dictator or writer above the return address for possible quick reference.

Placing the name of the specific person who sent the letter above the return address on the envelope is important because a great deal of mail is returned to the sender. Much time is wasted by mail room or other personnel trying to route returned letters to the right people. Records show that one-fifth of the American populace move each year. Also, people die, are transferred, or are simply replaced.

FIGURE 2.6

The United States Postal Service makes the following requests:

□ The name of the individual within the organization sending the letter should appear on the envelope above the return address of that organization.

□ Special notations to receiver, such as "Confidential," should be placed beneath the return address.

□ Sender's special mailing instructions, such as "registered mail," should appear beneath the stamp area.

□ The entire envelope outside address should appear in all capital letters in the lower half of the envelope, leaving at least a $1/2$-inch margin clear at the left side, right side, top and bottom.

□ If there is an attention line, it should be above the name of the receiver organization.

□ Except for the hyphen within ZIP + 4 code, all punctuation may be omitted.

□ When using a foreign address, always place the country name by itself on last line.

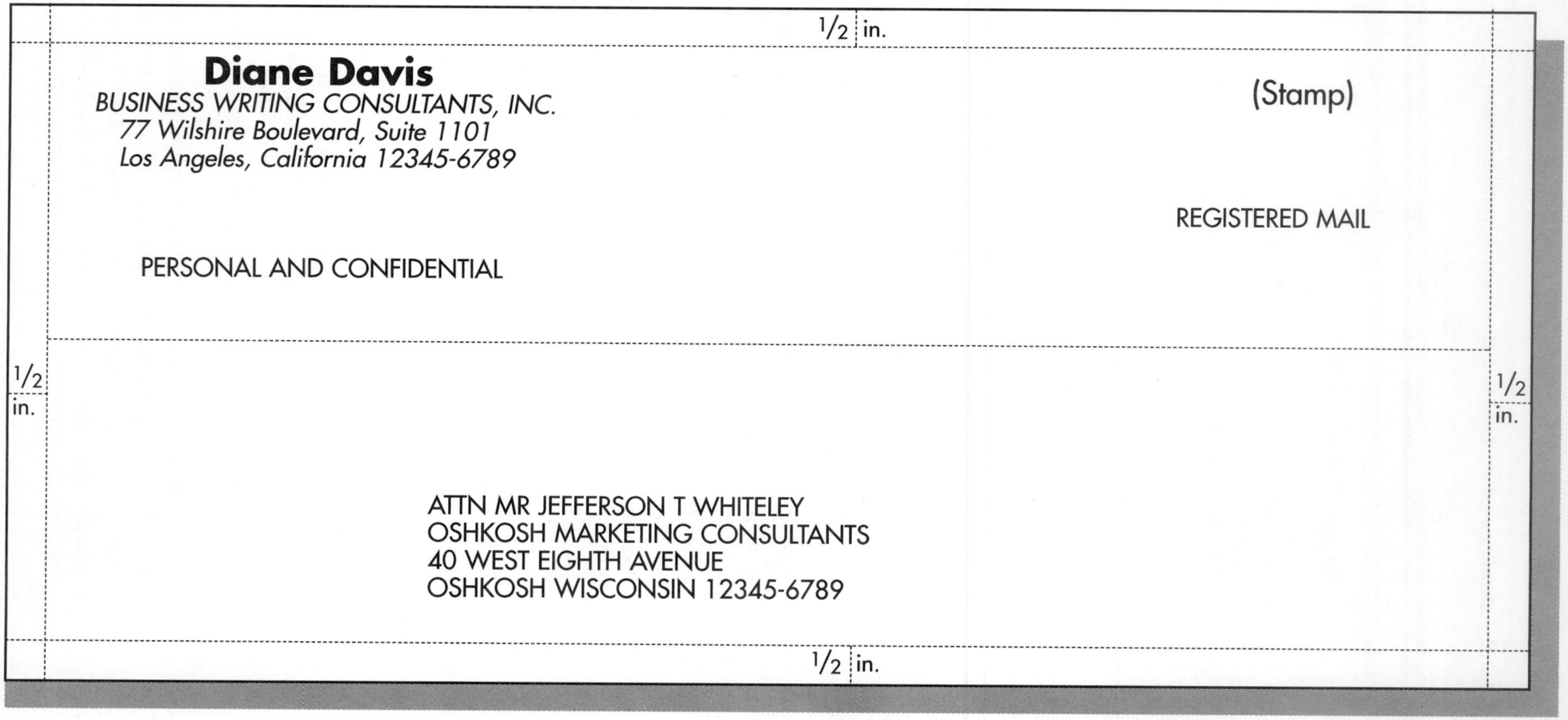

30

$1/2$ in.

Diane Davis
BUSINESS WRITING CONSULTANTS, INC.
77 Wilshire Boulevard, Suite 1101
Los Angeles, California 12345-6789

PERSONAL AND CONFIDENTIAL

(Stamp)

REGISTERED MAIL

ATTN MR JEFFERSON T WHITELEY
OSHKOSH MARKETING CONSULTANTS
40 WEST EIGHTH AVENUE
OSHKOSH WISCONSIN 12345-6789

$1/2$ in.

$1/2$ in.

$1/2$ in.

The Envelope Outside Address

The outside address on the envelope should contain the same address information as the inside letter address. This inside address, of course, should be written with capital and lower case letters like the rest of the letter.

For speedier sorting and delivery of the mail, *the United States Postal Service recommends that the envelope address be written in all capital letters.* Further, the *Postal Service requests that we not use dark-colored envelopes,* or if we do use dark envelopes, we should type the delivery addresses on white or light colored labels attached to the envelopes which are read more easily by human or machine. Figure 2.6 shows placement of envelope address parts according to the request of the Postal Service. These parts are as follows:

1. Name of the individual within the office who is sending the letter
2. Special notations to receiver, such as "Confidential"
3. Sender's special mailing instructions, such as "Registered"
4. Correct placement and form for address
5. Correct placement of attention line, if any
6. Lack of punctuation in address except hyphen in ZIP + 4

If a **window envelope** is used with a return address typed on an insert, the insert should be of a size that prevents it from moving beyond the window.

If you use **pull-out flaps,** put them on the right or postage side of the envelopes so that they do not blow open while passing left to right on the optical character reader (OCR) automated postal scanning machines.

For additional details on designing and addressing mail, contact your local post office marketing office and obtain a current copy of Publication 25 or its successor, *A Guide to Successful Mail Preparation.* The Postal Service points out that any postal regulation regarding the addressing of envelopes should be considered a *"voluntary guideline . . . UNLESS* it pertains to qualifications for a postage discount."

Folding Letters

If a letter is prepared carefully, it should not be stuffed haphazardly into an envelope. Rather, it should be folded to fit neatly inside the size envelope that will carry it. Entire letters have had to be rewritten because of careless folding.

Estimating Letter Costs

Today, letter writing labor has been reduced greatly, especially in computer word processing with revision and correction capabilities. Thus, the costs of creating a letter have shifted toward the expense of computer equipment, software, connecting networks among computer systems, and training. In this manner, a portion of the costs would have to be based on the estimated proportion of use for an individual letter.

In the future, you will have worlds of traditional and electronic communication choices in both your career and personal lives. Decisions. Decisions. Along the new and changing information superhighway, try to miss the chuckholes! Remember:

"New" doesn't mean it's good.

"Good" doesn't mean *you* need it.

"Expensive" doesn't mean it's worth the price.

If someone else has it, you don't necessarily have to have it.

Chapter 2   Qualities of an Effective Business Communication: Attractive Appearance

WRITING IMPROVEMENT EXERCISE: WASTED WORDS

Keep your writing tight and sharp. Don't waste words.

We beg to advise you and wish to state
That yours has arrived of recent date.
We have it before us; its contents noted.
Herewith enclosed are the prices we quoted.
Attached you will find, as per your request,
The forms you wanted, and we would suggest,
Regarding the matter and due to the fact
That up to this moment your order we've lacked,
We hope that you will not delay it unduly.
We beg to remain, yours very truly.

Why do phrases like these in this old rhyme appear in today's business letters? Undoubtedly, someone with little writing or dictating experience, confronted with preparing his or her first business correspondence, looked into the files to see how someone else composed a letter. And there was a letter dictated by someone else who similarly had had no business writing experience and also had checked into old correspondence files ... *ad infinitum.*

Make your writing concise—don't waste words!

Knowing that a reader's time is valuable, eliminate all unnecessary words in business writing. Concise writing benefits the writer as well as the reader, because the brief, clear message will probably be read more quickly and acted upon more promptly.

The following list contains stereotyped, outdated, or simply wordy expressions that can be shortened or altogether eliminated to make writing more concise and therefore clearer. Almost all writing can be improved by similar paring down.

Wasted Words

Wordy	Concise
1. a large number of	1. many, several
2. absolutely complete	2. complete
3. period of one week (day, month)	3. one week (day, month)
4. are of the opinion that	4. believe
5. at a distance of 50 feet	5. at 50 feet
6. at a later date	6. later
7. at all times	7. always
8. at an early date	8. soon; at once; immediately
9. attached please find	9. attached is; here is
10. at the present time	10. now
11. beg to remain	11. (omit)
12. circular in shape	12. circular; round

Wasted Words *(continued)*

Wordy	*Concise*
13. consensus of opinion	13. consensus *or* opinion (*consensus* cannot be anything but *opinion*)
14. costly from a money standpoint	14. costly; expensive
15. costs the sum of	15. costs
16. despite the fact that	16. although
17. due to the fact that	17. since; because
18. during the year 2006	18. during 2006
19. during the course of	19. during
20. enclosed herewith is	20. enclosed is
21. first of all	21. first
22. for the purpose of	22. to; for
23. for the reason that	23. since; because
24. in a satisfactory manner	24. satisfactorily
25. in addition	25. also; further
26. in order to; in order that	26. so; to
27. in regard to	27. regarding; about
28. in the amount of	28. for
29. in the event that	29. if
30. in the meantime	30. meantime
31. in the near future	31. soon
32. in the normal course of events	32. normally
33. in this day and age	33. now; today
34. in view of the fact that	34. since; because
35. information which we have in our files	35. our information
36. inquired as to	36. asked
37. is at this time	37. is
38. kindly be advised that	38. (omit)
39. long period of time	39. long time
40. made the announcement that	40. announced
41. my personal opinion	41. my opinion (it can't be anything but *personal*)
42. not in a position	42. cannot
43. please do not hesitate to write	43. please write
44. pursuant to our agreement	44. as we agreed
45. reached the conclusion	45. concluded
46. seldom ever	46. seldom
47. sign your name	47. sign
48. sometime in the early part of next month	48. early next month
49. the thing is … the thing is	49. (omit)
50. this is to inform you	50. (omit)
51. trusting you will …; trusting this is …	51. (omit)
52. under separate cover	52. separately
53. until such time as	53. when; until
54. we are in the process of	54. we are
55. we ask your kind permission	55. may we
56. we wish to acknowledge	56. we acknowledge
57. we would like to ask	57. please; would you
58. will you be kind enough	58. please
59. you know … you know … you know	59. (omit)
60. your letter under date of …	60. your letter of

Chapter 2   Qualities of an Effective Business Communication: Attractive Appearance

WRITING IMPROVEMENT "HANDS ON" ASSIGNMENT: WASTED WORDS

Rewrite the following sentences, deleting unnecessary words. (Acceptable answers may vary.)

1. You know, one of our major problems is a low inventory. → <u>One of our major</u> <u>problems is low inventory.</u>

2. As per your suggestion, attached hereto are the samples you requested. → _____ <u>Here are the samples you requested.</u>

3. Due to the fact that the supply shortage is past, we will ship your order in the very near future. → <u>Because the supply shortage is past, we will ship your order soon.</u>

4. The computer was installed during the time that our workload was heaviest, for the reason it was the only time that delivery could be made. → <u>The computer was</u> <u>installed while our workload was heaviest because that was the only time delivery</u> <u>could be made.</u>

5. In reply to your letter I wish to state that we are also sending the wall braces. → <u>We are also sending wall braces.</u>

6. Could you supply us with details of check #10017 before such time as the auditors arrive? → <u>Please send us details of check #10017 before the auditors arrive.</u>

7. Our bank is not in a position to furnish that information to the press. → _____ <u>No comment. or We cannot give out that information.</u>

8. This is information we have in our files. → <u>This is our information.</u>

9. Mr. Frost said that in the event you were absent again, you should complete this form. → <u>Mr. Frost said that if you are absent again, you should fill out this form.</u>

10. Could we make up the vacation schedule sometime during the month of April? → <u>Could we make up the vacation schedule sometime during April?</u>

11. It is our consensus of opinion that completion of the project will take a period of about one year. → <u>We believe that project completion will take about one year.</u>

12. The thing is, our opponents had the ball more of the playing time than we did. → <u>Our opponents had the ball most of the playing time.</u>

13. In the meantime, please be advised that we are in the process of clarifying the supervisor's opinion. → <u>Meantime, we are clarifying the supervisor's opinion.</u>

14. Kindly be advised that we seldom ever ask for additional details. → <u>We seldom ask for additional details.</u>

15. Would you be kind enough to fill in the enclosed form and return it immediately. → <u>Please fill in the enclosed form and return it immediately.</u>

16. You should take into consideration rising interest rates. → <u>You should consider rising interest rates.</u>

17. Permit me to take this opportunity to thank you for your help in preparing the new work schedule. → <u>Thank you for helping us prepare the new work schedule.</u>

18. The welding process ended, being of an unsatisfactory nature. → <u>The welding process ended because it was unsatisfactory.</u>

19. A check for the amount of $1000 was deposited in your account on the date of January 1. → <u>A check for $1000 was deposited in your account on January 1.</u>

20. Please be so kind as to furnish us the name of your bank. → <u>Please give us the name of your bank.</u>

Chapter 2 Qualities of an Effective Business Communication: Attractive Appearance

REVIEW AND DISCUSSION

Please make answers brief. Draw a line through any incorrect answer.

1. Why is the appearance of a business communication important?
   It is often the first impression others receive of your business. First impressions last.

2. True or False: The appearance of business communications should be the responsibility solely of the secretarial and word processing staffs. Explain.   People at top levels should help make these important decisions.

3. Name three major factors that must be decided concerning stationery.
   Quality, color, size.

4. What are the advantages of using paper with rag fiber content?   It looks and feels better, lasts longer, and resists yellowing. Gives a good impression.

5. Standard business stationery measures 8½ by 11 inches.

6. Give three advantages of using tinted stationery.
   a.   Stands out.
   b.   Color coding; tells where copies go; identifies company, etc.
   c.   Reduction of glare; accountants and data processing people have long used soft greens, yellows, etc.

7. How are margins usually set for standard length line letter placement?
   About 1¼ inches each side.

8. Describe picture frame letter placement.   Both side margins set about 1¼-inch width; top and bottom margins vary according to letter length.

9. In a block style letter, all lines begin   at left margin.

10. The most popular business letter placement is standard length line with side margins about 1¼ inch. Horizontal space between other parts can change according to letter length.

11. In a personal business letter, what information should be included at the top or bottom of the letter that is not needed on a business letter that has a printed letterhead?
    Complete return postal and email addresses plus phone, fax, other.

12. Should offices always use the two letter state abbreviations? Why or why not?
    Some offices do not because they can be confused.

13. What would be a good salutation for a letter addressed to Director of Human Resources, Federal Savings and Loan Association? <u>Director, Human Resources,</u> <u>Federal Savings and Loan Association</u>

14. If a letter is addressed to Mr. John J. Sims, Personnel Director, Second Security Bank, the salutation should read: <u>Dear Mr. Sims *or* Dear John J. Sims</u>

15. A woman whose maiden name was Ann Marie Carter and whose husband's name is Peter B. Steele should sign her name (~~Mrs. Peter B. Steele~~, Ann C. Steele*).

16. How can postscripts be used in letters? <u>For afterthoughts; for personal comments.</u>

17. The outside envelope address should be copied from <u>the inside letter address.</u>

18. What information should be placed above the firm's return address on an outgoing envelope? <u>The name of the specific individual sending the letter.</u>

19. With the exception of matters relating to postal rates, the United States Postal Service points out that any postal regulation regarding addressing envelopes should be considered a (~~rule or law that should be followed~~; voluntary guideline for speedier sorting of your mail).

20. Make this sentence shorter and clearer: I beg to inform you that it is the consensus of opinion of the committee that much of the eyestrain could be eliminated by studying the causes. <u>The committee has decided that much eyestrain could be prevented</u> <u>by studying causes.</u>

*Her legal name. In the past or future there may be another "Mrs. Peter B. Steele," her "social" name at times.

3 Qualities of an Effective Business Communication

Good Will Tone

> It's not what *you say*, it's the way *that you say it.*
>
> Old Saying

The **tone** of a message profoundly influences the effect that message will have upon the person to whom you are writing or speaking. The message should in no way offend its audience. Rather, it should have a good will tone that creates a favorable impression.

Remember: *Your written document is you and whomever you represent.*

An Oriental expression, **"between the leaves,"** is a somewhat poetic way of expressing our **"between the lines"**—the unwritten or unspoken message that comes across in communications. Broadly, this might be considered the tone of the communication.

The sender of a message—written or spoken—might think that snide remarks slipped "between the lines" will scarcely be noticed. But actually, such comments usually jump out and are exaggerated in the mind of the receiver, possibly damaging the total effect. Some readers will read no further.

Most businesses do not have to place a price tag on the value of their **good will**, but a business stays in business because it creates and maintains good will. To do this, its people try to hold current customers, bring back old customers, and bring in new ones.

Business good will is the value of the business in excess of its tangible assets. For instance, if you were offered $500,000 for your small business and the tangible assets of that business amounted to only $450,000, you would be getting paid $50,000 for your business' good will. This value would come from your reputation, location, new approach(es) to old problems, distinctive name and logo and/or your relations with customers, and so on.

Also, any business has an investment in the training and experience of its employees. It is advantageous to consciously apply the theories of good will in communications circulated within a company—its mail, memos, reports, and various announcements to employees.

Good will tone, then, is the overall unspoken courteous message coming across in a communication that promotes friendly relations with customers, suppliers, officials, employees, subordinates, peers, and others. A good will tone shows warmth, strength, sincerity. A negative tone can be overly formal, insincere, condescending, prejudiced, weak and/or disrespectful.

Identify Reader and Write at Reader's Level

Before starting to write, identify the person or persons to whom you are writing so you can set the right tone. One of the best ways to create a good will tone is to pretend you are sitting across the desk from the other person. Create a mental image of the reader; try to imagine what you would say directly and how you would say it. Try to imagine what the reaction would be if you were speaking in person. Then let your message have a tone of writing to one person, not to a crowd.

For instance, you might consider the following aspects of the reader or readers:

Background on the subject

Education

Relationship to you or your organization

Depth of the information desired

Personality traits

Pompous writing by an ego-inflated person usually repels the reader. But the writer should beware of the other end of the scale—becoming too humble.

The business writer should avoid writing either up to a reader or down, attempting instead to reach the reader at a neutral level. In order to find the neutral level of writing that should be used, try to employ **empathy.** That is, as the American Indians say, you should try to "walk in the moccasins" of the other person, saying, "How would I feel if I were the person receiving this message?"

Frequently, business or technical writing must be adapted to the understanding of a lay person. If necessary, replace long words and difficult terms with shorter, more common usages. If a difficult term must be used, it should be explained in understandable language.

However, a worker who receives a condescending memo might become resentful, thinking, "What do they think I am—stupid?" And the work might suffer.

Business writing that is obviously written down to such groups as youths and housewives is apt to miss its target or offend its audience. Today's general market is better educated, accustomed to more serious thinking, and more sophisticated than was the market of past generations. Consumer protection movements are undoubtedly part of a people's rebellion against being underrated.

Of course, if you are writing to a highly educated, professional person, you might write at a higher level than that for the very young or for a person of limited education. But keep in mind that even a pompous person rarely cares to receive pompous communications.

For many reasons, the best level of most business communications is a straightforward, eyeball to eyeball exchange of ideas. See Figure 3.1, a graphic of attitudes that would be appropriate for various levels of writing.

Watch the Tone of Speedy Email

With the rapid spread of new forms of electronic communication, messages are created at the click of a mouse. Email can be sent to anyone across the hall or around the world quickly and easily. These rapid-fire communications are often created and sent with less care than traditional postal letters and memos.

FIGURE 3.1
Summary of recommended attitudes for various levels of
writing.

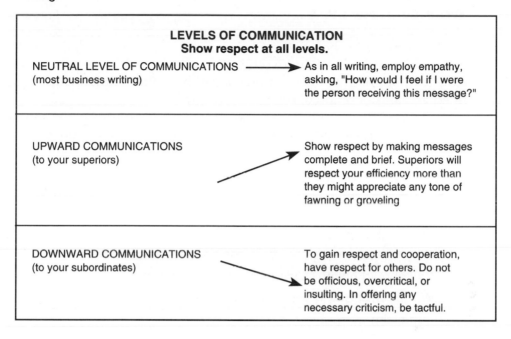

LEVELS OF COMMUNICATION
Show respect at all levels.

NEUTRAL LEVEL OF COMMUNICATIONS ——→ As in all writing, employ empathy,
(most business writing)   asking, "How would I feel if I were
                                                                     the person receiving this message?"

UPWARD COMMUNICATIONS   Show respect by making messages
(to your superiors)   complete and brief. Superiors will
                                                        respect your efficiency more than
                                                        they might appreciate any tone of
                                                        fawning or groveling

DOWNWARD COMMUNICATIONS   To gain respect and cooperation,
(to your subordinates)   have respect for others. Do not
                                                        be officious, overcritical, or
                                                        insulting. In offering any
                                                        necessary criticism, be tactful.

Email messages can have the same positive or negative tone results, but much quicker.
It's more important than ever to use care with both the message and the tone of email.

How to Create a Good Will Tone

Use Good Grammar

Using poor grammar in career and social situations gives others a bad impression. Nonstandard English marks a person as uneducated or careless. On the other hand, use of standard English makes a good impression, giving people confidence in you. Also, good grammar helps make what you say clearer, so people need not unscramble a message that might be clouded through the use of poor English.

Write Naturally

Allen R. Russon, author, lecturer, and business communications professor, says that before you can effectively write business communications, you must be in the proper frame of mind. Dr. Russon gives the following advice on how this can be achieved by writing naturally:

Let your reader understand that you are the sort of person who would be liked and trusted.

Talk   don't write. Let your reader hear the voice of a considerate person.

Relax. Reflect good manners, not dignity and formality. Avoid stilted expressions.

Don't be afraid to use I *and* me. Don't overuse these pronouns, but constantly avoiding them may be awkward.

Write Courteously

Five centuries before the Christian era, Confucius stated the **Golden Rule** in this manner: "Do not do unto others that which you do not wish done to yourself." **Courtesy,** or good manners, is practicing the Golden Rule, which could also be defined as "consideration of others before self."

The need for courtesy and a courteous tone in business communications seems so obvious that there should be no need to mention it. But studies of actual business communications show that many letter writers need to give this matter more thought.

In seeking a courteous tone, writers must avoid making accusations, asking awkward questions, or casting aspersions on the character of the reader. Here are some negative examples that would surely arouse an undesired response in the reader:

> You neglected to …
>
> Why haven't you given us all the necessary details?
>
> You should have realized what you were doing.
>
> What's wrong with your outfit, anyway?
>
> You claim …

Each of these expressions could be restated more courteously or could be eliminated altogether. The Writing Improvement Exercise at the end of this chapter gives practice in changing discourteous statements to more courteous forms.

Be Ethical

You are practicing good **ethics** when you are conscientiously honest, combining honesty with a sincere desire to meet the needs of others.

To be ethical, try to maintain that attitude of sitting across from the reader face to face. It is difficult for a conscientiously honest person to look someone in the eye and be dishonest or insincere. Phoniness usually comes through between the lines of

---

William Bennett, "Honesty"

☐ To be honest is to be real, genuine, authentic, and bona fide.

☐ To be dishonest is to be partly feigned, forged, fake, or fictitious.

☐ Honesty expresses both self-respect and respect for others.

☐ Dishonesty fully respects neither oneself nor others.

☐ Honesty imbues lives with openness, reliability, and candor; it expresses a disposition to live in the light.

☐ Dishonesty seeks shade, cover, or concealment. It is a disposition to live partly in the dark.

William J. Bennett
The Book of Virtues[1]

---

[1]William J. Bennett, *The Book of Virtues* (New York, New York: Simon & Schuster, 1993), p. 599.

a communication more clearly than much of the specific written message. When you have judged that the message is suitable to the people involved and the purpose that prompts it, and that you are being honest, then you can proceed with a straightforward message.

In the extremes, if you are unethical you may find yourself in trouble with the law, along with the person or people who ordered you to be dishonest. Words to live by might be taken from this old rhyme:

> *I have to live with myself and so*
> *I want to be fit for myself to know....*

Shakespeare might have explained ethics best when, like fathers today, Polonius was giving advice to his son Laertes, who was Hamlet's close friend:

> *This above all: to thine own self be true,*
> *And it must follow, as the night the day,*
> *Thou canst not then be false to any man.*

Emphasize the Positive

This is a must in business correspondence, as it is in business. Psychologists tell us that the person who works with a **positive attitude** will probably get results that match this attitude.

A conscious, continuing effort must be made to achieve a good attitude, but once this is practiced, it can become routine. You should avoid reference to any potentially negative situation, trying instead to provide information about what can be done to remedy it.

To write with a positive attitude, choose a positive statement over the negative one, avoiding, if at all possible, any negative reference. The following positive and negative words are helpful to keep in mind:

Negative (People Don't Like)	*Positive* (People Like)
neglect	please
sorry	thank you
anxious	welcome
fear	happy
mistake	enjoy
you claim	like
damage	appreciate
late	pleasure
rotten	you're right
overdue	generous
unhappy	free
wrong	praise
died, death	agree
negligent	benefit
disagreement	commendable
unpleasant	courtesy
unwelcome	cheerful
difficult	satisfactory

Practice in changing negative statements to positive ones with the same basic message is given in the Writing Improvement Exercise at the end of Chapter 6 on negative communications.

Write from the "You Viewpoint"

Dwight David Eisenhower, commander of Allied forces in Europe in World War II and thirty-fourth President of the United States, said: "Without optimism in the command, victory is scarcely obtainable."

Business writers will profit from noticing how frequently the words, *you, your,* and *yours* are used in today's advertisements. Advertisers have learned that they benefit from talking directly to individuals, bringing them immediately into the picture. Here are some headlines from current ads. For our purposes, the *you* words here are set in bold type:

- [ ] A hanging basket—Holds **your** favorite fruit, flowers, potted plant, or what-have-**you.**
- [ ] Nothing can convey **your** feelings better than a colorful scarf—the proper adornment for **your** casual or dressy outfit.
- [ ] **Your** new Honda Accord will get **you** there.
- [ ] Gives **you** twice as much as the best-known pain reliever.
- [ ] Now—**yours** at truly great savings—any 4 compact disks for only $5.99.
- [ ] Dry Yogurt Nuggets—Carry a Packet in **Your** Purse or Pocket.

Adopt the "you viewpoint" by showing advantages to readers and their interests, instead of expressing matters in your interests. You get the reader's attention and hold it by focusing on matters that concern that person.

Practice in changing letters from the writer's viewpoint—"we viewpoint"—to the "you viewpoint" is given in the Writing Improvement Exercise at the end of Chapter 7 on sales letters.

Watch Your Word Connotations

Euphemisms are sometimes employed to avoid unpleasant **word connotations**. A euphemism is the substitution of an acceptable word or term for a blunt expression that may be objectionable.

Study the meanings of the following terms and consider the advantage of using the second form of each:

Original *(Possibly Negative)*	*Euphemism* *(Positive Connotation)*
complaint department	customer service department
down payment	initial investment
pilferage	shrinkage
janitor	custodian
cheap	economical, inexpensive
poor	disadvantaged
died	passed away

Original (Possibly Negative)	*Euphemism* (Positive Connotation)
bossed	managed; supervised
stupid, ignorant	unsophisticated
dean of student affairs	dean of students
waiter/waitress	server
funeral	services
you're lying	Is your memory playing tricks on you? Aren't you going past the truth?
room deodorant	air freshener
cubes of jello	jeweled dessert
getting older	having too many birthdays

Although appropriate use of euphemisms is advisable, overusing them can lead to obscure writing that repels people. These terms can also be confusing. Consider the young man who was an assistant city administrator and accustomed to the gobbledygook of many government offices. Having been asked to find the names of some garbage collectors, he attacked the Yellow Pages of the local telephone directory. First he looked under *refuse collectors*—negative; then *sanitary engineers*—negative; *trash collectors*—negative. Finally, he found the desired listings—under *garbage collectors.*

Here is an example of an exaggerated euphemism. The late U.S. Senator Everett Dirksen, known for his mellifluous tones and his mastery of language, was once asked to define a euphemism. "Well," he answered, "*you* might say that your father was hanged. *I* would say that he died at a large public gathering when the platform collapsed."

Be Careful with Humor and Sarcasm

When used acceptably, humor can be a very effective tool in any communicating process. But heavy humor, which becomes **sarcasm,** can be hazardous and should be used only under limited circumstances between people well acquainted with each other.

The story is told that George Bernard Shaw sent tickets for his latest play to an old friend, Winston Churchill, with the note:

Here are two tickets to the opening of my new play—one for you, and one for a friend—if any.

Churchill returned the tickets with this note:

Sorry, am unable to attend opening night. Please send me tickets for second performance—if any.

Use of the appropriate light touch in even routine correspondence is often recommended. Business people state that they will shuffle through a stack of mail or a string of email and give immediate attention to something written by a person who

---

Humor on the Job Can Help

According to John Sosik of State College, Pennsylvania, "It's long been argued that good senses of humor are key communications tools that will bring about group cohesion and commitment." Sosik is co-author of a recent study that suggests a little levity can actually make workers perform better.

Sosik said, "Humor brings people together and helps them cope with their demanding jobs." Titled "A Funny Thing Happened on the Way to the Bottom Line," Sosik's study examined the effect of humor on job performance.

---

has a reputation for adding a little humor to everyday business matters. They claim they welcome such a break in routine because it is so unusual.

At a business education conference, two people were overheard discussing which presentation they should choose of two that were scheduled at the same time. "Oh, let's go hear _____. She always makes me laugh."

Finding a way to use humor appropriately often challenges a writer's imagination. But this light touch has a reciprocal advantage—it also gives the writer a lift.

Email presents a special case, because of its potential to travel fast, far and wide. We should not use email humor that pushes the edge of the envelope in matters of good taste.

The following information is taken from the Apple Internet Connection Kit:

☐ Be extremely careful with humor. Email tends to be much less formal than traditional paper mail. Even so, care needs to be taken when sending email to people you don't know very well; subtle wit travels poorly in email.

☐ If you use wit that might be mistaken as attack or criticism, you can clarify your intent with a "smiley." A smiley is a set of text characters that form a face when you look at it with your head tilted to the left. People use smileys on the internet to signify their real emotional intention. Here are a few common ones:

:-)   A smile, signifying a humorous intent.

;-)   A wink

:-(A frown, signifying unhappiness

8-[An angry face

:-o   A surprised face

☐ Remember that it's generally impossible to take back a letter once you've sent it.

Hold Your Temper

"Cool down before you crack down!"

Occasionally, almost anyone feels prompted to write a letter really "telling off" somebody. Perhaps it is a supplier who frequently misreads an order or a purchasing agent who regularly fails to include all the information for filling an order. Or it may be someone with a frequently overdue account.

No matter what the justification may seem to be, there is rarely, if ever, a time when losing your **temper** is justified. These are the reasons:

- ☐ Time often quenches or diminishes anger.
- ☐ When we think more calmly about it, we realize that we really don't want to have anyone know us at our worst.
- ☐ Old matters can come back to haunt us, and someone whose opinion does not seem to matter at one time may be in a different position at some later date.
- ☐ If threats are made, which might be done when a person is angered, there might be cause for legal action.
- ☐ Passionately unloading your anger on another person is rarely the best way to get the response you want.
- ☐ Temper flareups can damage your health.

If you are angry and all the will power you possess cannot stifle the luxury of blowing off, go ahead and write the letter. Then destroy it immediately!

In business and in personal life, a flare of temper is an extravagance you cannot afford. The great hazard of temper explosions is that they can become a pattern, and the symptoms may get worse each time. The phrase, "Cool down before you crack down!" might be changed to: "Cool down before you *crack up!*"

Some people believe that loudly expressing anger toward others is good because it "gets it off your chest" and makes you feel calmer afterward. However, psychological research has shown that people who lose their temper and express it usually are angrier after a period of time than people who do not express their rage.

The basis of showing good will in writing business communications is to present ourselves and our business at our very best.

Close in a Good Will Tone with a Positive Statement

We are constantly cautioned to make our letters as brief as possible. But you can always add the extra words to close with a positive statement. You might refer to some pleasant business or personal matter. Also, saying "please" and "thank you" doesn't cost anything, but it can pay high dividends.

Make Answers Prompt

How do you feel when you do not receive an answer to a message within a reasonable time? There is that nagging conviction that you and your concerns are not important to the person who should reply. Similarly, it is advantageous to you and your business to keep matters as current as possible.

Recognizing this, many firms establish a rule that letters must be answered within a given short period, sometimes 24 or 48 hours. To outsiders, immediate attention to correspondence is sometimes seen as a picture of the competence of an entire business enterprise. We have been impressed, for example, by customer service representatives at the Tom Peters Group and Apple Computer who have faxed us needed information within minutes of our call.

Sometimes there may be an understandable reason for delaying an answer. If so, it frequently pays to send a brief note explaining the delay, such as:

Thank you for your inquiry regarding specifications of our new rotary widget engine.

Our engineering department is preparing a paper containing detailed information, accompanied by diagrams, and we will send you a copy as soon as it is available.

Or, when the person to whom a business letter is addressed is out of town for an extended period of time:

Mrs. Baker is on vacation, but I am sure she will be able to give you full details when she returns next week.

Know Company Policy

Frequently, questions come up concerning procedures to be followed to maintain an organization's good will, such as knowing which printed materials are available free of charge, or the type of adjustments to be made on returned merchandise, and so forth. Most firms have established policies relating to questionable situations, but borderline cases must sometimes be handled. For questions on **company policies**, you should be well acquainted with established **company policy** and should get proper authorization for any variance from it. Your job could depend on this knowledge.

Use Resale in Business Communications

Resale is anything that helps assure customers that they made the right decision when choosing to deal with you, and encourages them to continue to do so. One type of resale is to reassure a customer of the wisdom of having made a purchase: "I am sure you will get several seasons' wear from your new suede jacket." Or, "Your new Bennox air conditioning unit will bring you many summers of unbelievable comfort."

Resale can also be used at any time by including promotional materials on items other than the specific ones purchased. Or, you might add information about other materials or services available through your firm: "You would probably also like to drop in and look over our new selection of microfiber skirts and jackets."

Names—Use Them Correctly

You know that you are particular about the correct spelling and pronunciation of your **name.** If your name is misspelled, you may even wonder if a letter is actually intended for you. Everyone, foreign or otherwise, feels the same about the treatment of his or her name.

Also, if a name is misspelled, it might be delivered to the wrong person. Because we may not be familiar with the spelling and markings of **foreign names,** it may be easy for us to make errors. Therefore, we must be especially careful to check spelling, capitalization, and especially diacritic markings of each foreign name every time we use it.

For some time, businesses that operate internationally have learned to investigate foreign interpretations of coined names and slogans. Until it was changed, the Flemish translation of General Motors' "Body by Fisher" was "Corpse by Fisher." Then, there seemed to be no explanation for the fact that the Chevrolet Nova did not sell in Puerto Rico. Translated literally, *no va* in Spanish means "doesn't go," or, "It doesn't run." When the car was renamed "Caribe" for that market, it sold well.

Courtesy = Good Manners = Good Will

An article in *The Royal Bank Letter* in Canada summarizes a discussion of **courtesy,** which is the basis of good will, as follows:

> Courtesy is the lubricant that eases the friction arising from differences among human beings... Concern about people is what courtesy is all about ... if there is courtesy, manners will look after themselves.[2]

This chapter ends with an exercise on changing discourteous statements to courteous ones.

---

[2]"The State of Courtesy," *The Royal Bank Letter,* Royal Bank of Canada, March/April 1981.

Chapter 3   Qualities of an Effective Business Communication: Good Will Tone

WRITING IMPROVEMENT EXERCISE
DISCOURTEOUS → COURTEOUS

Your manners are always under examination, and by committees little suspected, awarding or denying you very high prizes when you least think of it.
                    Ralph Waldo Emerson,
                    19th-century American writer
                    and philosopher

A few generations ago most business was conducted on a face-to-face basis, frequently between friends and acquaintances. However, as business and industry have grown, it became necessary to conduct business by other means—letters, faxes, memos, the internet, reports, phone calls, and so on.

Now, as a result of email and various other types of electronic communications dominating the scene, we should be even more cautious of the tone that our communications carry because they might spread farther than we wish. Also, they might carry unintended meanings.

When methods of communication become less personal, it may be easier to overlook courtesies that would be routine if people were meeting in person. As we have discussed, the tone of a discourteous word or phrase, intended or not, is often exaggerated in the mind of the receiver. A hazardous result is that an inconsiderate statement—even a snide remark—might cause the receiver to overlook part or all of the main message.

To improve the tone of communications, you should avoid writing or saying anything that could be interpreted as the following.

☐ *Accusations, such as "You claim," "you neglected," "you must think," etc.*

☐ *Negative overtones or connotations*

☐ *Anger*

☐ *Ultimatums, like "Do this or else…"*

☐ *Unflattering or insulting implications*

Following are a few examples of discourteous statements that have been restated in more acceptable forms. Perhaps you have other suggestions for improving them.

☐ You'll have to wait. I have a call on the other line. →
   Please excuse me; I'll be right back. I have to answer another call.

☐ You neglected to tell us the time your plane arrives. →
   Could you tell us when your plane arrives?

☐ We expected you to read the instructions before assembling Model #1009. →
   Enclosed is a second copy of instructions for assembling Model #1009.

☐ Here is the repair kit for your waterbed. We hope it comes in handy. →
   Here is the repair kit for your waterbed—which you probably will not need.

51

☐   The employees therefore request that you give us a 10 percent hourly increase in wages or nothing. [They got nothing.]→
We therefore ask that you give us a 10 percent hourly increase in wages.

☐   We cannot grant you credit until you complete the enclosed forms. →
We should be able to grant you credit as soon as you complete the enclosed forms.

In today's world there is forever someone else eager to take over an account that is being lost because of someone's bad manners. Offensive communications can be costly. *There is always time for courtesy.*

Chapter 3   Qualities of an Effective Business Communication: Good Will Tone

WRITING IMPROVEMENT "HANDS ON" ASSIGNMENT
DISCOURTEOUS → COURTEOUS

Rewrite the following sentences in a more courteous tone. One or two sentences could be omitted altogether.

1. Your letter did not state clearly what your problem is. → <u>Would you please give</u> <u>us details concerning . . .</u>

2. We are surprised that you expect a refund when you did not fill in the necessary form. → <u>As soon as you fill in this form and return it, we will send your refund.</u>

3. Although you claim that the order was mailed three weeks ago, we have not yet received it. → <u>We have not yet received your order.</u>

4. Now that you are getting older, we would like to help you make plans for retirement. → <u>Let us help you make plans for a pleasant retirement.</u>

5. Why didn't you enclose your check with your order and get the 5 percent cash discount? → <u>When you enclose payment with your order, you will receive a</u> <u>5 percent cash discount.</u>

6. Bank employees must limit personal telephone calls to their regular breaks. → _____ <u>Please limit necessary personal calls to five minutes.</u>

7. Although you didn't attend the meeting, it doesn't matter. The rest of us had a good time. → <u>We missed you at the last meeting.</u> <u>I wish you had attended the last meeting.</u>

8. Why don't you study the directions folder that we furnished with the garbage disposal unit? → <u>We are enclosing a copy of the directions folder that is packed</u> <u>with each unit.</u>

9. Your assumption that defective merchandise was shipped to you is entirely wrong, and we are surprised that a man in your position would not realize that damage might have occurred in shipment. → <u>Damage must have occurred in shipment.</u>

10. In the case of a new business with as little capital behind it as yours, we can do business only by cash or c.o.d. orders. → <u>With new firms that do not have a line of</u> <u>credit, we can do business by cash, credit card or c.o.d.</u>

Chapter 3 Qualities of an Effective Business Communication: Good Will Tone

REVIEW AND DISCUSSION

Make answers to the following questions as brief as possible. Answers will vary, of course. Draw a line through any incorrect response.

1. Define *good will* as used in a business sense. <u>Bringing in new customers, bringing</u> <u>back old ones, and holding current customers. Value in excess of tangible assets.</u>

2. Name two advantages of using good grammar.

   a. <u>Helps make meaning clear in speaking and writing.</u>

   b. <u>Gives good impression on job. Gives good impression socially.</u>

3. How does a person practice good ethics? <u>Being conscientiously honest, combining</u> <u>honesty with a desire to meet needs of others.</u>

4. How can we put the "you viewpoint" into our letters? <u>Speak of advantages to</u> <u>reader, not writer. Use *you, your, yours*.</u>

5. Name a word or term that has a negative connotation to you that is not given in the book. <u>(Student input.)</u>

   _____

6. Name a word or term not in the book that has a positive connotation to you. <u>(Student input.)</u>

   _____

7. When can humor be used appropriately in business communications? _____ <u>When you feel it will not offend—usually between people who are well acquainted.</u>

   _____

   _____

8. Email is often casual; therefore, we do not have to be concerned about courtesy. (~~True~~/False)

9. A flareup of temper is frequently a good manner of treating a business or personal situation. (~~True~~/False)

10. What is "company policy"? <u>A firm's established policy for handling</u> <u>questionable situations.</u>

11. Is your name ever misspelled? _____ If so, how? <u>(Student input.)</u>

   _____

12. How is resale used in company communications? <u>Information that reinforces an</u> <u>individual's desire to do business with you.</u>

13. Give your personal definition of *courtesy*.   <u>Consideration of others above self.</u>
   <u>[Other definitions?]</u>
   _____

14. It does not matter if you offend your readers in your business communications as long as what you say is true. (~~True~~/False)

   Make the following sentences courteous. One or two sentences could be omitted altogether.

15. You should have kept the instructions booklet that came with the printer. → _____
   <u>We are sending you another instructions booklet.</u>
   _____

16. Sometimes you lie when you are trying to convince us. → <u>Are these the facts?</u>
   <u>[Other?]</u>
   _____

17. You failed to tell us the number of the paint color you chose. → <u>Please tell us the</u>
   <u>paint color you chose.</u>

18. What are you babes up to? → <u>I'm sorry, but we do not understand your request.</u>
   <u>Or omit?</u>
   _____

19. We will take care of your problem when your number comes up on our list. → _____
   <u>. . . is a very popular item. Your request will be handled in the order it was received.</u>
   _____

4 Qualities of an Effective Business Communication

Clear and Complete Message

> *Don't inflate an incident to make it more flamboyant than it actually was. If the reader catches you in just one bogus statement that you are trying to pass off as true, everything you write thereafter will be suspect. It is too great a risk, and not worth taking.*
>
> William Zinsser
> On Writing Well[1]

Why Is English Spoken Around the World?

While exploring, trading and establishing settlements during the eighteenth and nineteenth centuries, passengers and crews of English sailing vessels spread their flag and their language around the world. The common phrase, "The sun never sets on the British Empire," was certainly not an exaggeration.

English is the native or official language of one-fifth of the world's population, and is the major foreign language taught in most South American and European countries. Japanese students must study English beginning in the seventh grade.

---

[1]William Zinsser, *On Writing Well*, 6th ed. (New York: Harper Collins Publishers, 1998), p. 78.

A person who can speak English can travel all over the world and rarely find a place where it is necessary to speak another language. Internationally in business, education institutions, scientific research, aviation, and in many other fields, it is also the common accepted language.

Following the early trade and travel beginnings, worldwide radio and television English language broadcasts continue to make it the most universally known and studied language on earth. And it spreads farther.

Benefits of Mastering English—and Other Languages

You are aware that using good English benefits you both on and off the job. In our world where boundaries continue to shrink, we are also becoming aware that mastering a foreign language can help in the many firms that deal with other countries. We must take special care to avoid potential language difficulties.

Be careful which language is used in your communications. Use English unless you are certain that your use of another language is exceptionally good.

For clearer understanding, it is far wiser to write well in English than poorly in another language. Many foreign firms have their own English translators; many foreign people doing business in the United States will know English or have access to translators. English is the second language of millions of people around the world and is a mandatory foreign language requirement in many schools in other countries.

Because of growing international traffic in business, bilingual or multilingual ability is a great asset on the job market. Job seekers who speak English are not only encouraged to speak and write English well, but are also encouraged to master other languages. But you should write your letters in a foreign language only if you are absolutely certain of your competence. Otherwise, when necessary, use the talents of a person with full competence in that language.

Tips for Writing to Foreigners

For **correspondence with foreigners**, Patricia S. Beagle gives the following guidelines. Ms. Beagle has translated engineering and general business documents from French to English and English to French.

1. Do not use abbreviations. Write out words to avoid errors in translation.
2. Use simple words and simple sentences. No sentence should be too long.
3. Avoid slang and colloquialisms. They do not translate well.
4. Write out names of months in dates; 4-5-90 means April 5 in the United States and May 4 in France.
5. Courtesy is exceptionally important in some countries. Be particularly careful to be courteous.[2]

---

[2]With special permission.

> ### "Speak Up"
>
> In a college computer lab an English instructor overheard two of her students discussing their computer assignment in strongly accented English.
>
> When she complimented them for speaking English on campus, as she had suggested, one of them replied, "We have to. He speaks Arabic and I speak Farsi."

And Now Email

your last msg made me LOL. Lets do lnch today.

Email often uses a computer shorthand. "Msg" is clearly "message." "LOL" is "laugh out loud." These are the informal messages that zip through phone lines from one computer mailbox to another and are read on computer screens all over the world. A professor of English grammar and linguistics says, "Conventions of correctness are usually suspended. What we're seeing is the democratization of communication."

A conclusion is that in email nothing is being printed on paper; communications don't have a "real existence." Grammar is casual and misspellings might be considered typos. Further, unless a communication is written on paper, the rules of punctuation and capitalization often do seem suspended.

So here enters a new kind of communication in the speed-up casual spirit of what email is all about. Receivers of more formal **printed** communications, however, still expect good grammar usage.

As to the quality of our emails: Recently on his television program *Wall Street Week*, Louis Rukeyser commented, "We can thank the internet for bringing back the practice, if not the art, of letter writing."

The Non-Message

Including a non-message category in a business communication text may seem questionable. However, it is so important we are listing it first.

Businesses, industries and other organizations are struggling to reduce today's avalanches of unnecessary paperwork. An unwarranted amount of money goes for time spent preparing, composing and typing such correspondence. Further, storage costs for paper printouts also become unreasonable. Compared to costs for storing hard copies, computer data storage is minimal. But try to keep in memory only information that may be needed in the future and trash documents according to charts showing how long specific types of records must be kept.

Further, as the volume of messages we send continually increases, problems with mail, phone, electronic and other services naturally increase. *Offices should eliminate unnecessary correspondence.*

Establishing a category of non-messages emphasizes the fact that there are messages you don't have to write and shouldn't. There is of course another category of messages that might be considered—courtesy messages. These are covered in Chapter 9, "Courtesy Messages: Messages You Don't Have to Send, But Should."

"I'm looking at your paper right now."

Planning the Message

The first step in writing a message is to plan it ahead.

Your List

To write clearly, you must organize your thoughts logically. An old slogan states, "Disorganized, illogical writing reflects a disorganized, illogical mind." Undoubtedly, one problem of letter writing is that too much preparation is done from mental notes. Even those who are practiced in dictation or writing find that their written and spoken communications benefit from lists or notes.

If you are writing in reply to another letter, you must thoroughly read the letter you are answering. Highlight each statement that requires a comment, whether the comment is specifically requested or the request is merely implied. Then, in the margin of the letter, between the lines or on a note pad, you can list each highlighted item in any order and later renumber items in the order you want them to appear.

If you've received the message electronically, your word processing software will allow you to insert specially highlighted comments right into the document itself. You can then "cut" and "paste" any parts of the document into your reply.

If you are not writing in reply to another letter, simply make a brief list of all information to be included. Usually, all that is needed is a word or phrase to remind you of each topic. The next step is to identify by number the order in which each item could logically be covered. Notes or a list might include such notations as those given in the following example. Numbers are assigned to items in random order, followed by the list in logical order—very easy to follow. For composing the message, these numbers can be taken from random order, or a different list can be set up with items in order.

List in Random Order

5. How will it be shipped?
1. Which brand modem?
2. $$ estimate
4. Delivery when?
3. $$ for faster modem

List in Logical Order

1. Which brand modem?
2. $$ estimate
3. $$ for faster modem
4. Delivery when?
5. How will it be shipped?
6. Thanks [added]

The bank letter in Figure 4.1 shows written notes in the margin telling what is to be covered in the answer letter.

Arranging Ideas in Logical Order

In a recent university survey, graduates of business communication courses said that **"arrangement of ideas"** came first as the training most needed to improve the writing of their co-workers. Various types of writing training were given the following order of importance:

1. Arrangement of ideas
2. Practice in solving problems and explaining the solutions in writing
3. Sentence construction
4. Selection of ideas
5. Spelling
6. Grammar
7. Punctuation
    Other: Conciseness, practice in dictating, handwriting, reducing arguments to writing

Making Your Message Clear

Well Planned = Well Written

How often have you said, "I know what it is. I just don't know how to explain it"? Go back and think it over. If you can't explain something, you probably do not understand it well yourself.

FIGURE 4.1

Bank letter simulation showing underlining of items to be covered in reply and numbered notations in margin for assistance in responding.

THE THIRD NATIONAL BANK OF BANKTOWN
BANKTOWN, MINNESOTA 12345
(612) 654-3210
Fax (612) 000-0000
NABA @xxxxx.com

October 30, 20XX

The First National Bank of Weston
Weston, Minnesota 00000

Gentlemen:

We shall appreciate it if you could tell us of the financial responsibility, the credit standing, and the management characteristics of ⟵
    1. Will appreciate
    2. Financial
    3. Credit
    4. Mgmt.

    Phoenix Auto Supply
    301 Main Street
    Weston, Minnesota 00000

based on your dealings with this company.

This inquiry is made to enable us to get information to help us furnish banking services to this company, and should not be construed as being in any way unfavorable to this company.

Please consider this request as confidential, and you are assured that any information ⟵ **5. Confidentiality**
you may furnish to us will be treated in a similar manner.

We appreciate your cooperation and will of course be willing to be of similar service to ⟵ **6. Reciprocate**
you at any time.

Sincerely,

Juan Perez
Vice President

So it is in writing, and this is the "input" stage of planning a communication. When you have all the information necessary, you yourself must understand exactly what you want to say. Then ideas and words begin to fall into place easily and quickly. Each time you write from a list or notes, it becomes easier. Soon, well planned, clear and concise messages become almost automatic.

That is the best type of writing—when it sounds so simple that it seems to have written itself. Truly good writing is uncomplicated. What is clearly understood by the writer is more readily transmitted to the reader.

Business Writing Consultants' Complaints

In identifying problems in today's business correspondence, business writing consultants agree that vague or murky messages lead to many hazardous consequences of actions taken or not taken because of misunderstood messages. One costly consequence is that an unclear message can require still another message. Obviously, there are hazardous results of actions taken or not taken because of misunderstood messages.

The Reader

When we write a letter or report, we sometimes like to picture the person who receives it as saying, "Well! Here is that letter (or paper) from Smith. Don't disturb me with any phone calls, messages, or callers. I want to read this without interruptions." Actually, there may be many matters calling for the attention of the person to whom you are writing. As your letter is being read, there may be business or personal interruptions, as well as a waiting stack of correspondence that sometimes overflows onto a table.

When we think about the attention that our written material receives, we might keep in mind the picture of the man in Figure 4.2 who is going through his daily mail.

FIGURE 4.2
Going through the daily mail.

Writing the Message

Accuracy

Gather all your information; then, before you start to write or dictate from your list, check all that information for **accuracy.**

Occasionally, checking for accuracy can take more time than writing. When all facts are in, you may even find no need for the communication. If something you want to say is doubtful, do not report it, or report it as being doubtful and explain why you have some question. Otherwise, any matter you recount then or in different circumstances might be suspect to others and your ethics might be questioned. Making sure your information is honest and correct helps give validity to the rest of what you say and do. Suspicion can damage your reputation in many ways. Check the display quote at the beginning of this chapter.

One author who conducts grammar and writing seminars for editors regularly emphasizes the need for accuracy so much that he leaves his audiences by saying: *"Suspect everything. If your mother tells you she loves you, check it out!"*

Advantages of Being Concise

The clearest, most effective writing is concise. That is, it does not contain words or phrases that could be eliminated or stated in simpler language. You owe it to your readers and listeners to write and speak not only in a manner they will understand but in a manner they will understand as easily and quickly as possible. This does not mean all communications must be short; some require several pages. But many lengthy messages can be shortened to one page or less. We should remember how busy most readers are. When we make our letters, memos, and other communications concise, we are being considerate of the reader.

Business writing consultants firmly believe that 50 percent of business writing could be eliminated if material were written more carefully. A typical editing of one business report planned for wide distribution changed the original 50-page report to 20 pages. Everyone agreed the shortened report was much clearer. Undoubtedly, more of the people who received it would read it.

"Pascalize It!"

Blaise Pascal (1623–1662), genius French mathematician, physician, and philosopher. He invented the first calculator, and is still so respected that the current high-level computer language, PASCAL, still a favorite of many, was named after him.

At one time he apologized to a friend for a letter being too long, explaining, "I lack the time to make it short."

From this we coin the term, "Pascalize it," meaning "Rewrite to make it shorter, better, and clearer."

Rewriting for clarity takes time.

Elimination of Unnecessary Words—Wasted Words

Examples of editing that can be done to improve writing by eliminating words:

at ~~the hour of~~ one o'clock	during ~~the year of~~ 1995
~~in the~~ meantime	enclosed ~~herewith~~
if ~~it is at all~~ possible	~~at a~~ later ~~date~~
because ~~of the fact that~~	~~absolutely~~ complete
~~in order~~ to	after ~~the time of~~
on ~~the~~ average	in ~~the~~ future

Here are further examples of making writing more concise by simple rewording:

Long Version	Concise Version
at this point in time	now; at this time; at this point
under separate cover	separately
during the time	while
at all times	always
we are not in a position to	we cannot
under date of	on; by
in the normal course of events	normally

Of course, these lists could go on and on. A Writing Improvement Exercise about eliminating "wasted words" is at the end of Chapter 2.

Concise: "To Be or Not to Be"

You can improve your writing by checking carefully for words, phrases, sentences, and even paragraphs that can be omitted. The remaining message is cut to its essentials.

However, when you are working with complicated business, technical or professional material, you might make improvements by certain rewriting that makes the writing somewhat longer. In many places you should probably use a few short words to replace a difficult long one.

Also, *do not progress too speedily through difficult material*. To smooth the flow of the writing, back up and use some of the transition devices. These steps tie ideas together or smooth abrupt changes. For instance, repeat the core idea briefly by restating the idea to help the reader understand for sure what you are talking about. Then, try adding other transition words and phrases (*next, therefore, also, consequently, nevertheless, unless,* and so on). These words bridge the gaps, helping you grasp the reader by the hand so you both glide along more easily.

Remember to look for a place to break up any sentence much longer than 23 words. You might remember that number as a place to check whether your meaning will be clearer if you rewrite with shorter sentences. Breaking them down smoothly may mean you must repeat some words or add others. Then, when you read these shorter sentences you will see that your writing is clearer. With **shorter sentences**, more people will read it; more people will understand it. Feedback will be right.

However, do not convert your writing to a series of short, choppy sentences. This can be as bad as, or worse than, overlong sentences. Writers sometimes try to impress others by displaying their "mastery" of writing by using **overlong words and sentences**. Too much of their writing is often not readily understood even by people in their own fields. Such papers often just add to the never-read papers sitting on their desks. David Brinkley, well-known TV newscaster, says that people don't read these papers—they just step over them.

Strive to have your writing understood on the first reading so it is inviting at the first glance. So what about impressing your readers? If you write concisely and clearly, most readers will respect and envy you for your writing style. And, as said, more will read and understand you.

Caution: Not Too Brief

In striving to make messages brief, however, you can overdo it and become ambiguous. A good example of this is the story of the Hollywood reporter who wanted some personal details about a movie star. He wired the star's agent:

> HOW OLD PAUL NEWMAN?

The reply came back:

> PAUL NEWMAN FINE. HOW YOU?

Clear Words, Sentences, Paragraphs

Words

In general, short words are easier to understand than long ones. From one government administration to another, officials try to make government writing clearer—to eliminate **gobbledygook.** According to dictionaries, gobbledygook is talk or writing, especially of officialdom, that is pompous, involved, and full of jargon and long words. Each of the following items listed in the left column actually appeared in offices in print. Suggestions for improvement are given on the right.

Gobbledygook	*Improved*
As a general rule, and certainly not applicable in all situations, the briefing E-mail forwarded to the secretary had been loaded with an excessive amount of verbiage.	Most of the briefing E-mail forwarded to the secretary had been too wordy.
The airplane engine experienced high temperature distress.	The airplane engine overheated.
It is envisioned that this sort of writing will not require more than a page and a half to two pages at the most.	No more than two pages should be required.
Loose aggregate could be ingested into the engine.	Gravel could be drawn into the engine.

Gobbledygook	*Improved*
Due to metabolic inability to cope with a recent shift change, I did not respond to external stimuli, thereby remaining in a comatose condition.	I overslept.
motorized attendance modules	school buses
fuel exhaustion	empty gas tank
physically handicapped	physically challenged
interior intrusion detection systems	burglar alarms
acoustical attenuation for ball activity area	soundproofing of the gym

Jargonistic, longwinded writing frequently keeps people from reading technical and professional papers that they should read for the benefit of their clients.

Because business and professional writing by their nature must often use technical and specific terms, you should increase your vocabulary in order to use these terms when necessary. But you should discipline yourself to use long and technical words only when necessary, when they cannot be replaced by shorter ones.

Dictionary. Owning a good, reliable, current **dictionary** is extremely helpful to students in any field. Educated people constantly improve their vocabularies and knowledge by reading the dictionary and checking it for meaning, pronunciation and spelling of unfamiliar words.

The advice "Never use a long word when a short one will do," is valid. But an enlarged vocabulary enables a person to use clearer, more specific language in both speaking and writing. Any business, profession, or technical field has its own vocabulary, and learning new terms quickly is a job asset.

Further, a good desk-size or college dictionary is actually a condensed encyclopedia.

Most personal computer word processing software includes a spelling checker, which is quite valuable in identifying and correcting spelling mistakes and type. However, a spelling checker doesn't provide the meaning and usage of words—there's no substitute for a good dictionary.

Also, authorities claim that 50 percent of any college course is learning the vocabulary of that course. When you learn the new terms, you have the major grasp of the subject.

Thesaurus. A **thesaurus** is a reference book containing word synonyms and antonyms, and using a thesaurus will broaden your vocabulary.

A thesaurus also provides all writers and speakers with new words and phrases to substitute for overused ones. Probably the best and most popular books of this kind are *Roget's International Thesaurus* (Thomas Y. Crowell Company, New York) and *Webster's New World Thesaurus* (Simon & Schuster, New York). The electronic version of a thesaurus provides a fast way to determine word substitutes, and as they improve, they can be used when available.

Other Helps. Since you are studying business, a good business dictionary can prove very helpful. The author's recent review of current business dictionaries showed that these two are probably the most understandable and authoritative: *Webster's New World Dictionary of Business Terms* (Simon & Schuster, New York), and *Dictionary of Business and Management* (John Wiley & Sons, New York).

An exercise on using a thesaurus is at the end of Chapter 14.

To gain a better education you will benefit from word study with a standard dictionary, a thesaurus, a specialized business dictionary, textbooks, general news and business periodicals, and other worthwhile publications.

Sentences

There is no specific rule about the best length of either **sentences** or **paragraphs**. But there is no doubt that short sentences and paragraphs are usually clearer, and therefore better. People who make their living by teaching others how to write effective business communications state that 15- to 23-word sentences are easily understandable. Therefore, it is recommended that most sentences not be much longer than that.

Also, people understand sentences written in active form more readily than sentences written in passive form. This means simply:

Active   *More effective*—subject performs action.
              Subject $\rightarrow$ Verb

             The committee prepared the report.

Passive   *Less effective*—subject receives action.
              Subject $\leftarrow$ Verb

             The report was prepared by the committee.

It must be pointed out that both active and passive sentences are good grammar forms. However, a good writer uses the direct statement, the active sentence, more than the passive, thereby making the writing move along faster and more clearly.

Paragraphs

William Caxton became known as the Father of English printing when in the 1400s he brought the printing process from Germany to England. He translated and produced many select foreign and British works, besides composing and printing his own writing.

At this time printing was done in large solid blocks of type uninterrupted by **paragraphs.** But Caxton decided this style tired the eyes, making reading difficult. Therefore, he said, he began to mark resting places for the eyes with paragraph marks (¶). Later he used these marks as a signal to end one line and indent the first line of the next unit. See Figure 4.3 for an example of Caxton's printing made in 1481 before anyone used paragraph marks.

Appendix B contains condensed rules for the correct use of punctuation. Grammar texts and some dictionaries contain more thorough studies of these punctuation guides.

FIGURE 4.3

A page from William Caxton's 1481 copy of Godfrey of Boloyne, printed before Caxton originated paragraphs. The Boloyne manuscript was translated by Caxton from the French version of a Latin history.

Grammar, Spelling, Punctuation

Good English Grammar

For both white collar and blue collar jobs, better positions can depend on a person's ability to use **good English grammar.** When more than one person's job performance is expected to be satisfactory, the one selected for hiring or promotion will often be one who makes a good impression on others by using good English. Besides earning respect, that person will communicate more clearly and accurately on the job.

Spelling

You may think it unreasonable, but right or wrong, errors in spelling are usually looked upon as gross. Right or wrong, they usually identify the writer as being ignorant, uneducated, careless, lazy, or any combination of these.

Correct spelling also helps make our meaning clear and specific.

One young executive was asked if business communication courses place too much emphasis on spelling, grammar, and punctuation now that, especially with email, administrators and executives at all levels often prepare their own letters and memos on their personal computers. The young man's reply:

Too much emphasis? I'm not sure. I am not a great speller, I am above average, and when I read a *printed document*, I am miffed if it has an excessive number of misspellings. This must be in part because I've had to work hard to become an adequate writer, and spelling well goes along with it. If you can't spell well, there is no excuse these days in school or in business not to use a computer spell checker or dictionary. *None!* Even though you may not have a computer or dictionary on your desk at work, whoever does the email and letters probably does, and should have a spell checker as well!

If you are fortunate enough to have a personal or group secretary, a dwindling luxury these days, that person should have strong skills in **grammar, spelling, punctuation,** and **business communications,** as well as a computer spell checker.

The sad thing is that a brilliant idea can be disregarded because of sloppy writing. It's really hard to write well. **Spelling, grammar,** and **punctuation** skills are difficult, but certainly are the most teachable. Every educated person should have a decent set of these skills. You need to use them to write carefully and edit even more carefully.

Email is the fast new way to communicate ideas—easily and quickly. Some email software programs include spell checkers, but few people use them. It's so easy to dash off an email, click on the reply, and in seconds you've sent your message around the world. Because it's so easy, it's also twice as easy to send a poorly written business communication. Careful writing is as important in the wired age as it ever was!

Another young executive, knowing her own weakness in **spelling,** claims she owes part of her success to the fact that she regularly carries a small speller's dictionary in her purse or pocket. Do you need one?

For student study or for office use, the National Council of Teachers of English recommend desk-size or college editions of the following dictionaries:

Webster's New World Dictionary, of the American Language, Simon & Schuster

Webster's New Collegiate Dictionary, Merriam-Webster

The American Heritage Dictionary of the English Language, Houghton Mifflin Company

Whether the attitude is right or wrong, errors in spelling have come to identify the writer as being ignorant, uneducated, careless, lazy, or any combination of these. You may think this is unreasonable, but spelling errors on printed documents are considered gross.

Correct spelling helps to make our meaning clear and specific.

Punctuation

Why study punctuation? Some people may think that **punctuation** is scattered around a page only to make it look better. Others may even think that the main use for studying punctuation is to keep English teachers employed. Authorities agree that punctuation is used for only one purpose: to help make meaning clear. Punctuation makes the meaning of these couplets clear.

Woman without her man is a savage.
Woman! Without her, man is a savage.

Carter acted fairly honestly and conscientiously.
Carter acted fairly, honestly, and conscientiously.

The professors said the students are stupid.
The professors, said the students, are stupid.

After she finished eating the cat crawled into her basket.
After she finished eating, the cat crawled into her basket.

Authorities on grammar and punctuation recommend that questionable marks be omitted if the meaning is clear without them.

Summarizing and Listing

Summarizing and **listing** items can be genuine timesavers to the reader. In many instances, they can also save time and money for the writer who is giving a list of information, making a number of requests, or asking a number of questions. When the writer summarizes each statement and puts it in a list at the end of the letter or memorandum, the reader should understand the message more clearly. For instance, at the end of a letter that asks several questions, it is worthwhile to restate each question in a summary form, and number the questions in the order in which they appeared in the earlier part of the letter. Then the receiver can simply check each item to see if all the necessary information has been given. If more on any item is needed, additional details can be learned from the preceding sections of the letter.

Figure 4.4 is a good example of a letter that effectively summarizes information already given. To aid the reader, the fifth paragraph summarizes information given in detail in paragraphs 2, 3, and 4.

FIGURE 4.4

Letter in which paragraph 5 summarizes information contained in paragraphs 2, 3, and 4.

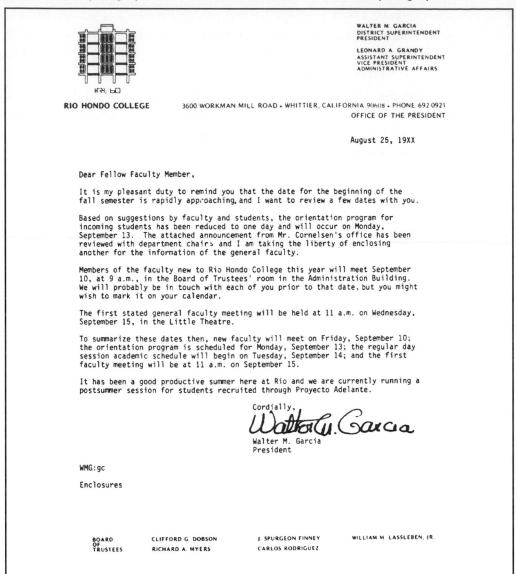

Checking the Final Document

Clear and Complete?

Checking Your List

Surely, checking a letter or other communication to make sure it is clear and complete is as important as any other part of its preparation. By referring to your earlier list, you can see if all planned points were covered and presented in the order you prefer.

Legality

Occasionally, the contents of a letter or other document come under **legal examination**. Courts generally hold that when a person signs a letter about company business on company stationery, that person is acting as an agent for the business.

Since the originator or dictator is a legal agent, the business is responsible for the letter contents. Of course, few letters will come under such scrutiny, but mistakes and inadvertent typos can be perilous.

Check all statements that could be interpreted as defamation of character, invasion of privacy, fraud, contracts or implied contracts. Also look for statements related to laws regarding employment, credit and collections. Later chapters covering specific types of communications will refer to their legal aspects. See Index under "Legal aspects of" regarding legal matters relating to some specific types of communications.

Careful Proofreading

Before sending your communication, **proofread** it for major and minor errors. Nobody is perfect, not even you or your secretary. Besides checking the general content of the document, check technical details such as money amounts and other figures, verifying them carefully for complete accuracy.

Remember this: In cautioning their authors to proofread carefully, the *Prentice Hall Author's Guide* points out that errors can slip through: "The eye has a way of seeing what it wants and expects to see and it is very easy to skip over misspellings and even omissions."

American English Language Traps

New colloquial expressions regularly come into our language. Some eventually become accepted as standard; some do not. Today we have American English language traps ready to confuse—and sometimes abuse—us all: slang, buzz words, and profanity.

Slang

We notice that even foreigners who have studied our language well will be puzzled at many of our colloquial or slang expressions. Native born speakers of American English might easily understand certain colloquial words and phrases that might pose problems to those who have learned the language in foreign classrooms.

After a discussion about writing to pompous people, one very studious foreign student approached the instructor. With thumb and forefinger of each hand holding the front of his white shirt out stiffly, he questioned, "What do you mean, 'stuffed shirt'?"

For example, think of the picture a foreigner might get in trying to give a literal translation to any of the following: *hang in there, shipshape, haywire, easy mark, cold feet, highbrow, brainchild.*

When translated literally, English can come out quite strangely: Various translations of the advertisement, "Come Alive with Pepsi," came out as, "Pepsi Brings Your Ancestors Back from the Grave," or "Come out of the Grave."

Then again, a newly appointed United States Ambassador to Japan had just arrived in Tokyo. Trying to be relaxed and friendly at his first press conference, he said, "Ladies and gentlemen, I'm the new boy on the block. Shoot!" His stunned interpreter hesitated and finally translated "new boy" as kozokko, meaning junior apprentice. "Shoot" was just ignored. For some time puzzled Japanese reporters were questioning U.S. embassy officials, trying to learn what the esteemed gentleman had said.

Buzz Words

A new type of colloquial term seems to be creeping into our language by leaps and bounds. These terms are classified as **buzz words**, which are defined as words or phrases used by members of some in-group, having imprecise meaning but sounding impressive to outsiders.

Buzz words seem to fit into business interchange. Such terms might not be clearly understood by people in other fields, of course, but actually they have a spontaneous origin and are often regional. Like other slang, buzz words should not be used in international correspondence because they do not translate literally.

Some of these terms will be accepted and will eventually spread from their places of origin, but it is predicted that, like slang, most will disappear from the language entirely. Also like slang, a few will have clear meanings and will be used by so many people that, after several decades, dictionaries will show them as being acceptable for standard usage. (English teachers abhor the day that *ain't* is accepted. That day has not come yet!) Therefore, questionable terms should not be used in standard business communications until and unless they become adopted into standard language. Also, colloquial words can often give writing a tone that is too casual for a business image.

Here are some business buzz words with their current regional definitions:

Buzz Words	Current Definitions
run it up the flagpole	to give something a tryout
fiscally impacted	financially ruined
reinventing the wheel	thinking you are doing something new when in fact it has been done before
back to square one	to go back where you started
GIGO	Garbage In, Garbage Out; originated with computer operations
ballpark figure	a roughly estimated general figure
paid my dues	to have done one's share
comes with the territory	anything that can be expected as part of an assignment, as part of a promotion, as part of any activity
old boy (girl) network	a system whereby men of a specific common background help each other; where women who are part of a network (system) help out other women
loose cannon	anything or anyone that cannot be controlled and might cause considerable damage (has nothing to do with ballistics)
neat freak	one who is exceptionally tidy
culture shock	a shock or disturbance caused by moving into an environment different from one's own
bottom line	basic element; in finance, net income or loss
MBO	management by objective
control freak	one who must be in charge, no matter what, right or wrong, must be in charge

Profanity

Profanity can leave a negative impression. People may be shocked. We caution against such usage in written business communications because people may be offended.

On top of that, some people are seriously religious. Rough language could turn them off. It is difficult to tell when others will become offended and see you as crude and uneducated. *Use of profanity often indicates to others you lack a wide vocabulary.*

Offense at this usage, of course, occurs in situations other than business. A judge once cautioned attorneys and clients against using expletives in the courtroom saying, "When a person has to resort to foul language it's because he isn't able to come up with more articulate and meaningful words."

Further, with increased international activity, we must be aware that objectionable language can deeply offend peoples of other cultures. In many places they are accustomed to using extremely courteous, formal terms in business dealings.

To the instructor: Apprehensive about teaching his first English class in a prison, a teacher decided to start with the basics. Looking around the class, he announced, "I suppose you all know what a sentence is."

Anonymous

"The Blind Men and the Elephant"

When figures show that a high percentage of our writing and speaking is not clearly understood, we must look for all methods to help us communicate more clearly. It is a sad fact that, given the same information, different people will sometimes report it differently. We must always be aware that such a situation can occur. The following classic parable represents this situation graphically:

It was six men of Indostan / To learning much inclined,
Who went to see the Elephant / (Though all of them were blind),
That each by observation / Might satisfy his mind.
The First approached the Elephant, / And happening to fall
Against his broad and sturdy side, / At once began to bawl:
"God bless me! but the Elephant / Is very like a wall!"
The Second, feeling of the tusk / Cried, "Ho! what have we here
So very round and smooth and sharp? / To me 'tis very clear
This wonder of an Elephant / Is very like a spear!"
The Third approached the animal / And happening to take
The squirming trunk within his hands / thus boldly up he spake:
"I see," quoth he, "the Elephant / Is very like a snake!"
The Fourth reached out an eager hand, / And felt about the knee:
"What most this wondrous beast is like / Is very plain," quoth he;
"Tis clear enough the Elephant / Is very like a tree!"
The Fifth, who chanced to touch the ear/ Said: "E'en the blindest man
Can tell what this resembles most; / Deny the fact who can,
This marvel of an Elephant / Is very like a fan!"
The Sixth no sooner had begun / About the beast to grope
Than, seizing on the swinging tail / That fell within his scope,
"I see," quoth he, "the Elephant / Is very like a rope!"
"And so these men of Indostan / Disputed loud and long,
Each in his own opinion / Exceeding stiff and strong.
Though each was partly in the right, / They all were in the wrong!

John Godfrey Saxe (1816–1887).

Chapter 4 Qualities of an Effective Business Communication: Clear and Complete Message

WRITING IMPROVEMENT EXERCISE
PRONOUNS IN SUBJECT OR OBJECT FORM

Pronouns in Compound Usage

Usually, the acceptable use of pronouns is not a problem. However, there are two chief places where personal pronouns might raise a question. The first and most common is when a pronoun is joined to a noun or another pronoun **(compounds)**.

Compounds are formed by joining parts of a sentence with words like *and, or, nor.* Here are examples of compounds:

John *and* I	John *and* me
she *or* you	her *or* you
they *or* he	them *or* him

When a pronoun is joined to a noun or another pronoun, it is usually very easy to select the preferred pronoun by mentally leaving out the other word or words of the compound momentarily and selecting the preferred form of the pronoun.

The two chief pronoun forms that might give trouble are subject and object:

Subject	Object
I	me
we	us
you	you
he	him
she	her
it	it
they	them

Subject Form of Pronoun

1. *Pronoun as compound subject (more than one subject).*
   (Her, She) and Curt read his poetry.
   She ... read his poetry.
   She and Curt read his poetry.

   (He, Him) and (I, me) can complete the project.
   He ... can complete the project.
   ... I can complete the project.
   He and I can complete the project.

With choosing the pronoun when it is part of a compound subject, a question can sometimes arise. When part of the compound is dropped, the subject can momentarily change from plural to singular. Then, you must mentally change the verb momentarily to the singular form to select the preferred pronoun. *(Selecting the correct pronoun really can become an easy habit.)*

Karen and (I, me) *are* taking the lead.
... I *am* taking the lead.
Karen and I *are* taking the lead.

Jeff and (he, him) *work* the late shift.
... he *works* the late shift.
Jeff and he *work* the late shift.

Object Form of Pronoun

2. *Pronoun as compound direct object. (Direct object receives action).*
The coach sent Lou and (he, him) to the showers.
The coach ... him to the showers.
The coach sent Lou and him to the showers.

We appointed (she, her) and her assistant to complete the work.
We appointed her ... .
We appointed her and her assistant to complete the work.

3. *Compound object of a preposition.*
They assigned the work to Dean and (she, her).
They assigned the work to ... her.
They assigned the work to Dean and her.

For (we, us) and our crew; it was a piece of cake.
For us ..., it was a piece of cake.
For us and our crew, it was a piece of cake.

Subject or Object Form of Pronoun: Pronouns with Appositives

Pronouns are sometimes joined with appositives. That is, they are sometimes joined with a noun or another pronoun that gives additional meaning to the noun or the first pronoun. Here too, there can be a question about choosing the better form. A simple solution is to temporarily drop the noun appositive, letting your "ear" select the preferred form.

(We, Us) workers make the finest West Texas rope.
We ... make the finest West Texas rope.

We *workers* make the finest West Texas rope.

Please send fax copies to (us, we) *architects*.
Please send fax copies to us ...
Please send fax copies to us *architects*.

Chapter 4   Qualities of an Effective Business Communication: Clear and Complete Message

WRITING IMPROVEMENT "HANDS ON" ASSIGNMENT
PRONOUNS IN SUBJECT OR OBJECT FORM

Select the correct form of the pronoun by drawing a line through the incorrect form.

Compound Subject

1. (He, Him) and Judy will attend the concert together.
2. Mr. Prince and (I, me) have worked together for some time.
3. (They, Them) and their staff will start their own agency.
4. Did you and (he, him) write your speeches?
5. Chris and (me, I) are preparing a new agenda.

Compound Direct Object

6. The president sent Hoskins and (I, me) to the meeting.
7. Yesterday the supervisor selected Ruben and (he, him) as shop foremen.
8. They introduced Jean and (she, her) during coffee break.
9. Janice invited (him, he) and (me, I) to the ceremony.
10. We met (he, him) and Matt at the entry door.
11. We want (she, her) and Andrew for the opening ceremonies.

Compound Object of Preposition

12. Between you and (I, me), I am in favor of Shawn.
13. Give this bouquet to (she, her) and Doris.
14. Let's hope the matter is settled in favor of (they, them) and their staff.
15. These designs were especially prepared for Ari and (she, her).
16. Between Don and (I, me), there is no sharp difference.

Pronouns with Appositives

17. (We, Us) secretaries are prepared to assist Nick.
18. The work should be assigned to (us, we), the ones who are responsible.
19. Please help (we, us) employees in our negotiations.
20. (She, Her), the person in charge, is expected to be on time.

Chapter 4   Qualities of an Effective Business Communication: Clear and Complete Message

REVIEW AND DISCUSSION

Make answers to the following as brief as possible. Where a choice is given, draw a line through any incorrect answer.

1. How did the English language begin to spread around the world? _Passengers and_ _crews of early British sailing vessels spread their language and flag around the world._

2. The demand for speakers of English to learn other languages is (growing/~~decreasing~~).

3. The text suggests that there are many planned letters, memos, etc., that need not be written. (True/~~False~~)

4. In the first stage of writing a message, your first warning is to check _all information_ _for accuracy._

5. Complete this old statement: "Disorganized, illogical writing reflects _"disorganized,_ _illogical thinking."_

6. When your receiver gets your letter, you can be sure it will get the attention you want. (~~True~~/False)

7. In general, __short__ words are easier to understand than __long__ ones.

8. *Gobbledygook* means __talk or writing that is pompous, involved and full of long__ ~~words. Often found in officialdom.~~

9. Authorities claim that __50__ percent of any college course is learning the vocabulary of that course.

10. The text says that cutting a message short, if it retains the planned meaning, can
    a. make it clearer.
    b. save space.
    c. make it more welcome to its audience.
    d. all of the preceding.

11. William Caxton, the father of English printing, first devised the paragraph mark (¶) in the 1400s as _a place to rest the eyes._
    _____.

12. Give two valid reasons for using good English grammar in business communications.
    a.   _To make meaning clear and specific._
    b.   _To gain respect._

13. Why study punctuation? _To help make writing clear on first reading._
    _____

14. Now that administrators and executives are preparing many of their own communications, using correct grammar, spelling, and punctuation can be ignored. (~~True~~/False)

In the following sentences, choose the correct pronoun by drawing a line through the incorrect one.

15. Yesterday (~~her~~, she) and Judy met us for lunch.

16. Write the report for Ms. Bronson and (~~I~~, me).

17. I telephoned (~~he~~, him) and Abdul.

18. Between (~~he~~, him) and Bozo, I would choose Bozo.

19. Between you and (~~I~~, me), Bozo was the right choice.

20. You annoyed Roger and (me, ~~I~~) with that movie.

5 Routine Information, "Yes" or Good News Communications

News Releases

> When you improve your ability to write clear, concise, persuasive, and natural English (which is the desirable language of business), you will also gain accuracy and naturalness in phrasing anything else you have to write or say.
>
> J. H. Menning and C. W. Wilkinson
> Writing Business Letters[1]

Most business communications can be prepared by following one of these three letter patterns:

1. Routine information, sometimes "yes" or good news
2. "No" or negative
3. Sales or persuasive request

We will now cover how to prepare the first, a routine information, "yes" or good news communication. This message simply sends information, says "yes" to a request, or announces good news. More than 80 percent of business communications fall into this category, which is fortunate, because they are by far the easiest of all letters to write.

Planning a Routine Information, "Yes" or Good News Communication

A routine information, "yes" or good news message basically requires just direct statement of facts.

First: A List

Before starting to write, make a list of everything you want to include. The list may be short or long, each item taking a word or a few words. This easy early step actually shortens the time it takes to prepare the message. You have in front of you the listed items you want to cover.

[1]J. H. Menning and C. W. Wilkinson, *Writing Business Letters*, rev. ed. (Homewood, IL: Richard D. Irwin, Inc., 1959), p. 1.

Moving List Items Around

Remember, your list is not cast in concrete. You can move entries at any time, adding, removing, combining, shifting positions until you find a workable draft. Chapter 4, page 61 shows a list going through changes in form.

Writing a Routine Information, "Yes" or Good News Communication

Of course, all elements of an effective business communication are necessary here: satisfactory appearance, good will tone, and a clear and complete message. Figure 5.1, a pattern for routine information communications, shows the message starting high with the main message, then gradually going down, giving all necessary information, usually in order of importance. It should close pleasantly, often ending with a brief upturn looking toward future contacts.

FIGURE 5.1
Pattern for the routine information communication.

First: Main Idea of the Message

The routine information message begins immediately with the main idea. This is what the reader wants to know and what you want the reader to know. Further, no purpose is served by delaying the main impact of the message.

Next: Middle Section—Necessary Details

Give all details necessary to support the main idea. The middle section may be short or long, depending upon the nature of the information being sent. To make sure that the message is clear and complete, check it for the following points:

Does it leave out any essential information? Go back to the list of items you made out naming what you want to include in the letter. Check your list with your message.

Does it include more information than necessary? Concise writing will be emphasized throughout this text. We might be inclined to include unnecessary extraneous information. Writing is improved by eliminating unnecessary words, phrases, paragraphs, and so forth, leaving the intended message short, clear, understandable to the receiver, and more inviting to read.

Closing: Pleasant Ending

The routine information message should close quickly and pleasantly. It usually has a slight upswing at the end, often looking toward the future. You might make a statement like one of these:

I hope this meets with your approval.

Let us know if we can be of further help.

I will appreciate receiving this information as soon as possible.

Multiple Copies and Form Letters

As we know, multiple copy communications—such as form letters—are not always welcomed by those who receive them. However, people are learning to accept them for many routine messages. We know that copy machines and other technology make it simple to run off tens, hundreds, thousands and more copies.

Routine they may be, but they can be very important to the sender and/or receiver. Because many people will be receiving them, they should be prepared even more carefully than single copies.

Someone must compose them; someone must see that information in them is clear, complete and up to date.

Outside Professionals or In-house Talent

For large multiple mailings, both outside professional and in-house printing processes can be used. Of course, making multiple copies should save money by not having someone compose individual letters for each piece of correspondence, which should make more time, talent and money available to produce necessary single copy communications.

Email

Email was used by more than 50 million individuals in 1999, and has rapidly become one of the primary means of business and personal communications. Internet email addresses are listed on most business cards and letterheads. Businesses that long ago implemented internal email have for some time used the internet to send and receive messages outside their own organizations—even outside their own countries. Recent studies indicate that 50 percent of U.S. households have at least one personal computer and the number of modems that connect to the Internet grows rapidly.

Email fills the gap between fast, interactive phone communications and the Postal Service mail. Email is much faster than the postal mail, and more flexible and interactive than using fax technology. It can be sent any time of day or night. Also, when wanted, part or all of it can be easily copied and "pasted" into other computer documents.

Email is an excellent way to send routine messages. We know we can write one message and it can go far and wide. We can also make a hard copy of email when desired. Chapter 12 describes how to use it most effectively in business communications.

Technology Highlight
Email Netiquette: Making Your Email Easy to Read

Email is often good for sending routine messages. Take, for example, distributing minutes to a meeting. You can easily send an email message to everyone who receives the minutes. However, whenever possible, email messages that you distribute should be done as part of your email message, not as an attachment.

"What is an attachment?" you ask. Well suppose you write up the minutes of an important meeting of the Veeblefetzer product development committee using the latest version of your word processing program. You can attach your word processing document to your email message and send it along to the committee members. The email message might read "I've attached the minutes for the Veeblefetzer product development meeting."

Now it goes to everyone in the committee, including the product development consultant, Teri. But since she doesn't use the same word processing program, she can read your email message but not the minutes that you sent in the attachment, since her program can't open the attachment.

Your message also goes to Jim, who works for the same company you do and uses the same word processing program you do. But Jim doesn't have the latest version of the program, so he also can't read the attachment.

Cheryl also receives your email, and although she has the same version of the same word processing program, she uses a different email program which handles attachments incorrectly, and turns the document into unreadable characters.

Finally, the email message goes to Ken, who has the same email program and same word processing program as you do, and can open the attachment you sent. However, because you sent it as an attachment, he has to take extra time and additional steps to open his word processing program and open the document to read the email message.

So the moral of this story is, when you send messages via email, if you want to be kind to your readers, make it part of the email message itself whenever possible.

Postcards

Postcards for brief, routine messages save time, paper and postage. The standard 3 by 5 inch postcard is completely acceptable when mailings are extremely common and open to public scrutiny.

Also, a card measuring up to $4^{1}/_{2}$ by 6 or 7 inches can be sent for the same amount of postage as the smaller postcard. The larger card has other advantages: It is more easily located in the mails, and more information can be included in the message.

Postal regulations forbid mailing cards or letters smaller than 3 by 5 inches.

The Postal Service requests that the name of the specific sender should appear in the return address directly above the name of the sending organization. This speeds delivery when mail is returned to sender—a frequent occurrence.

Figure 5.2 is a 4 by 6 inch postcard with return address.

FIGURE 5.2
Postal card measuring 4 by 6 inches, printed with complete return address.

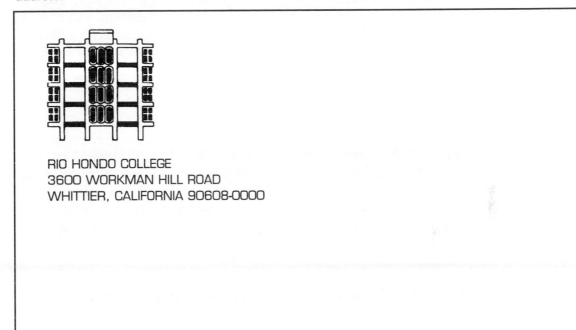

RIO HONDO COLLEGE
3600 WORKMAN HILL ROAD
WHITTIER, CALIFORNIA 90608-0000

Help! Help! Too Many Copies = Junk Mail!

We should become more deeply concerned about the volume of mail we send out, and we should try to cut down on this volume, hoping receivers don't put them in their **junk mail** categories.

We should regularly ask:

Is this message necessary?

Are all these copies necessary?

Who will/won't read it?

Environmentalists point out that we are depleting worldwide forests to feed our continually growing hunger for wood and paper products—even while some paper is actually being recycled. People who study the potential of the world's paper supply ask that we give more support for these efforts, regularly asking ourselves the preceding three questions.

The twentieth century American writer/humorist Ogden Nash once said, "Progress might have been all right once, but it has gone on too long."

Setting Up a Multiple Copy System

It may seem there often is no need for preparing template styles for multiple copies or forms. However, even the smallest operation will have frequently recurring situations for which the same or similar letters will suffice. Computers have ideal software for showing how to set them up initially in logical order so specific types of communications can be readily accessed.

To set up such a system, an extra hard copy of all office communications should be kept for a period of time—such as one month for a large office, two months for a smaller one. These copies should be classified by subject matter. In any office, even a large number of communications will fall into a small number of categories. In one study, 12,000 papers were classified under 23 subject headings.

Starting with the category that has the largest number, make up a postal or email message that includes all essential information. Continue this procedure for all frequently recurring types. To give outgoing mail some variety, more than one original can be prepared for the largest categories. However, strictly routine matters may be stated succinctly with no variation.

A Standard Printed Form or a Mail Merge Format?

Computer word processing software with mail-merge features makes it possible to create a template so that batches of letters can read like custom-written personal communications. The individualized words that are merged into the template will be spaced automatically—a great improvement over standardized form letters, which require fixed spacing.

To create a mail merge communication, first set up a main document template (memo, letter, form, etc.). In the proper locations, insert merge fields in the places you want to insert personalized information. (Merge fields are special entries that are specific to your computer's word processing software.) Create a second data document which contains the individual data records of the information to be merged into the main document template. An example of the data document would be names and addresses of a group of people who are to receive the form letter. You are now ready to create personalized mail automatically. Your computer software should give specific directions for creating and producing mail merge documents.

A mail merge example showing specific different information to be inserted into the main document template is shown in Figure 5.3.

FIGURE 5.3
Mail merge letter showing how a list document with personalized information for one receiver can be merged into a main document (form letter).

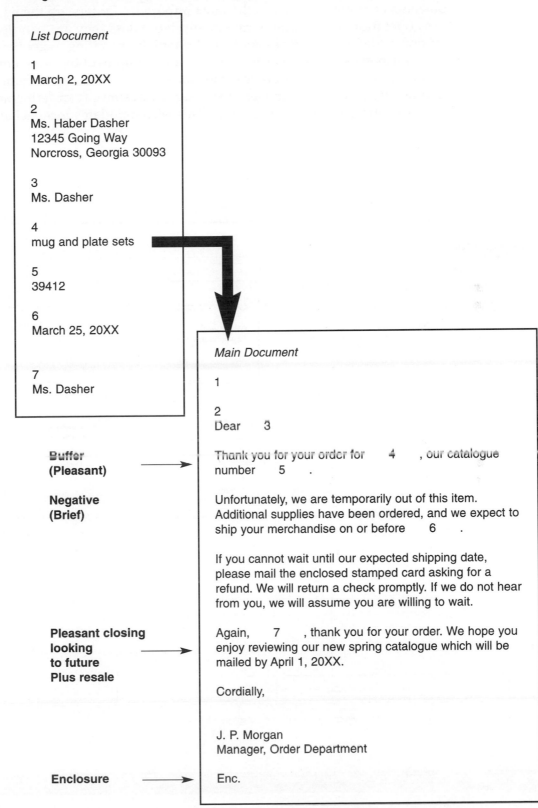

List Document

1
March 2, 20XX

2
Ms. Haber Dasher
12345 Going Way
Norcross, Georgia 30093

3
Ms. Dasher

4
mug and plate sets

5
39412

6
March 25, 20XX

7
Ms. Dasher

Main Document

1

2
Dear   3

**Buffer
(Pleasant)**

Thank you for your order for   4   , our catalogue
number   5   .

**Negative
(Brief)**

Unfortunately, we are temporarily out of this item.
Additional supplies have been ordered, and we expect to
ship your merchandise on or before   6   .

If you cannot wait until our expected shipping date,
please mail the enclosed stamped card asking for a
refund. We will return a check promptly. If we do not hear
from you, we will assume you are willing to wait.

**Pleasant closing
looking
to future
Plus resale**

Again,   7   , thank you for your order. We hope you
enjoy reviewing our new spring catalogue which will be
mailed by April 1, 20XX.

Cordially,

J. P. Morgan
Manager, Order Department

Enclosure

Enc.

Orders

Orders from customers and orders to suppliers are the most common types of business communication and the most important. Orders are the heart of any business operation, and business cannot survive unless they are handled properly. Attention to details eliminates additional phoning or writing to get needed facts.

Businesses regularly order supplies and equipment by using email, postal mail order blanks or purchase order forms. Increasingly, ordering is being done over the internet at no charge, with websites designed to simplify ordering and, when helpful, even showing pictures of items. This accommodates incapacitated individuals

FIGURE 5.4

Example of a standard retail customer order blank.

Company Name
Address
Phone Number
Fax Number

Place peel-off address label from back cover here. If address is incorrect, please provide correct information at right (including code from top of label).

Name

Address

City   State   ZIP

Account # _ _ _ - _ _ _ _ - _ _ _

Telephone Number(s)

☐ Check or money order enclosed

Charge: ☐ MasterCard   ☐ Visa   ☐ American Express

Account Number

To telephone please have catalogue and credit card handy.

Expiration date _____ Signature _____

Page	Description of Item	Item Number	Size	Initials/ Monogram	Qty	Item Price	Packing/ Shipping/ Insurance	Gift Wrap (add $2.00)	Item Total

* Please add packing, shipping, and insurance charges as shown in parentheses following item price.

Georgia residents add sales tax:

Total Order

and others who cannot do all their shopping in person. The working woman has become a major mail order buyer.

Because an order in any form is the first step in a legal contract to buy, proper completion of the order is vital to both the buyer and seller, and all information, especially numbers, should be checked carefully. Normally, the buyer has a number, the seller has a number, and the merchandise has a number. Merchandise can get totally lost if a single digit is lost in the morass.

Figure 5.4 is a typical printed postal mail order blank.

Ordering Online

Internet websites with online ordering capability are a recent phenomenon. E-commerce, or electronic commerce, allows anyone with internet access and a credit card to shop any time, day or night, at any store in cyberspace from the comfort of their home or office. In Figure 5.5, an example of an online order entry page, displays thumbnail images of the products available, similar to a printed catalog. By simply clicking on the "Add to Order" button next to the desired item, and then filling in the shipping address and credit card information, customers can shop for products they need without the time and expense of traveling to a "bricks and mortar" store.

FIGURE 5.5
Online order form.

Website privacy and financial security are two issues you should consider. Most quality websites will list a privacy policy on a web page that describes their promise to keep your information confidential, which is very important. Otherwise, your identification may be sold to others who can then use it to contact you with unwanted email promotions, currently known as "spam"—email jargon for "junk mail."

The best websites also use special means to protect your financial security. When you use a credit card over the internet, be sure the website uses secure pages to encrypt your card number and name. Information explaining the use of secure pages can be obtained from the maker of your internet web browser software.

Order Acknowledgments and Confirmation

If ordered merchandise is being sent within a reasonable time, there is often no need for an acknowledgment or confirmation. They are sent for two reasons: (1) to explain delayed shipments in order to assure the purchaser that the order was received, and (2) to promote good will toward the company filling the order. For online orders, an order acknowledgment or confirmation is sent to confirm to the user that the website received the order correctly, and to give the user an electronic "trail" of the transaction.

When merchandise is being shipped promptly, an email or fax order acknowledgment is quick and easy to use. Or a preprinted postcard or form letter to this effect can be sent to the purchaser in frequently occurring matters.

Figure 5.6 shows a typical email acknowledgment or confirmation.

FIGURE 5.6
Email order acknowledgment.

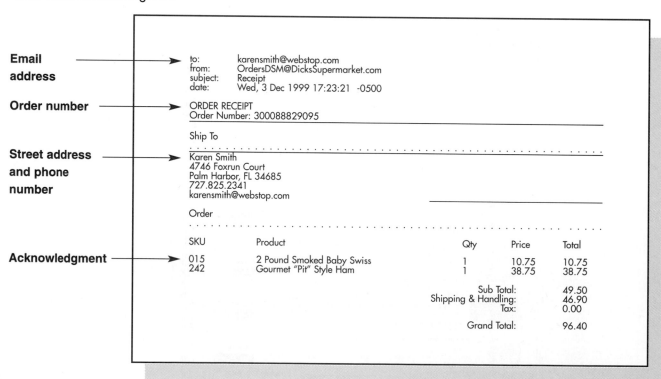

Order Delay

If there is delay, you might send a postal or email form letter or postcard with individual information placed in the blanks confirming the disposition of the order. Such an acknowledgment might read:

Thank you for your order for _____.

The order will be shipped by _____.

We hope you will remember us when making future orders.

Custom Order Acknowledgments

Sometimes, to acknowledge first orders, custom orders, or exceptionally large orders, a postal or email letter should be sent that is individually prepared or appears to have been individually prepared. Purchases that might be routine to the seller are often not routine to the buyer, who likes to know that the patronage is appreciated. This letter follows the routine information pattern.

1. The first sentence should state that the order has been received; it is common courtesy to thank the customer.

2. The next part of the message should state what is being done with the order.

3. Then, if appropriate, the closing can contain a "you attitude" reference to the use of the merchandise, and it can use resale material promoting the firm or its products. It can also close with a service attitude, offering help or information. At any rate, it should indicate pleasure in doing business with the customer. Give them your postal and email addresses and also enclose an order blank.

FIGURE 5.7
Custom acknowledgments.

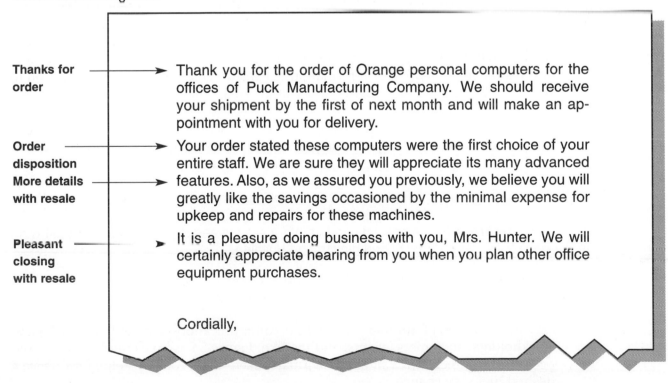

Thanks for order → Thank you for the order of Orange personal computers for the offices of Puck Manufacturing Company. We should receive your shipment by the first of next month and will make an appointment with you for delivery.

Order disposition → Your order stated these computers were the first choice of your entire staff. We are sure they will appreciate its many advanced **More details with resale** → features. Also, as we assured you previously, we believe you will greatly like the savings occasioned by the minimal expense for upkeep and repairs for these machines.

Pleasant closing with resale → It is a pleasure doing business with you, Mrs. Hunter. We will certainly appreciate hearing from you when you plan other office equipment purchases.

Cordially,

FIGURE 5.8
Custom acknowledgment.

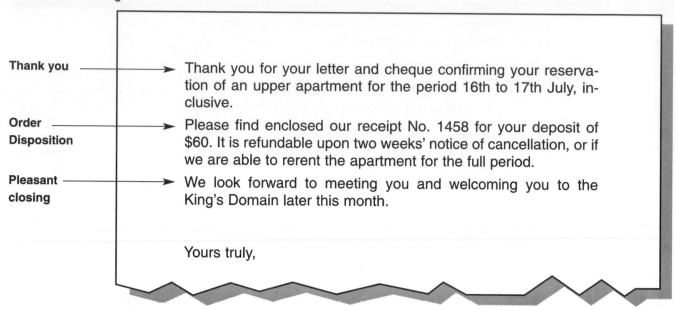

Thank you → Thank you for your letter and cheque confirming your reservation of an upper apartment for the period 16th to 17th July, inclusive.

Order Disposition → Please find enclosed our receipt No. 1458 for your deposit of $60. It is refundable upon two weeks' notice of cancellation, or if we are able to rerent the apartment for the full period.

Pleasant closing → We look forward to meeting you and welcoming you to the King's Domain later this month.

Yours truly,

This message can be very brief, according to the nature of the transaction. Figure 5.7 is a brief custom order acknowledgment where it was felt special attention should be given for a large order obtained when many suppliers were competing. Figure 5.8 acknowledges a room reservation for a hotel in Canada. (Note the British spelling, *cheque.*)

Sending Information, Making Announcements

Many routine communications simply send information or make announcements. Quite often, such information can be posted on a bulletin board where several people may read it. For information of considerable importance, in addition to being posted on bulletin boards, individual copies may be distributed to people concerned.

As far as possible, such messages should be stated in positive terms. That is, even when handling a negative subject, rather than saying what cannot or should not be done, if possible, say what can or should be done. As examples:

    Original: Employees should not use the administrative and customer parking lot.
    Improved: A special parking lot for employees is provided at the east wing of the administration building.

    Original: The newsstand is closed from 10 P.M. to 7 A.M.
    Improved: The newsstand is open from 7 A.M. to 10 P.M.

Many types of routine information communications are sent to employees, stockholders, customers, clients, and the like. Figure 5.9 is an example of a custom postal letter directed to a single individual citizen who probably helped influence a desired highway change.

FIGURE 5.9
Good news.

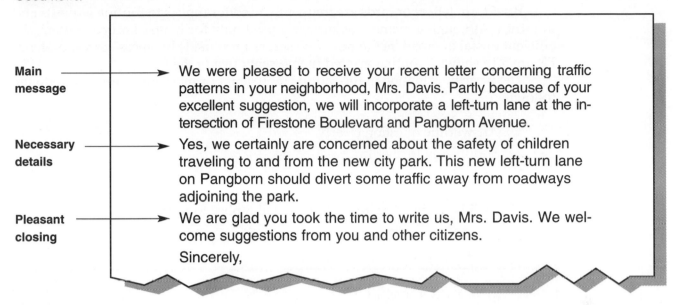

Main message → We were pleased to receive your recent letter concerning traffic patterns in your neighborhood, Mrs. Davis. Partly because of your excellent suggestion, we will incorporate a left-turn lane at the intersection of Firestone Boulevard and Pangborn Avenue.

Necessary details → Yes, we certainly are concerned about the safety of children traveling to and from the new city park. This new left-turn lane on Pangborn should divert some traffic away from roadways adjoining the park.

Pleasant closing → We are glad you took the time to write us, Mrs. Davis. We welcome suggestions from you and other citizens.

Sincerely,

FIGURE 5.10
Routine request.

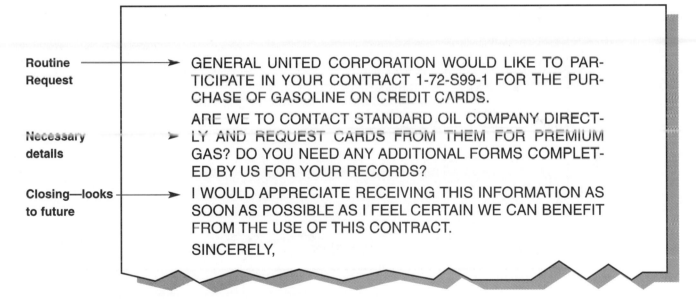

Routine Request → GENERAL UNITED CORPORATION WOULD LIKE TO PARTICIPATE IN YOUR CONTRACT 1-72-S99-1 FOR THE PURCHASE OF GASOLINE ON CREDIT CARDS.

Necessary details → ARE WE TO CONTACT STANDARD OIL COMPANY DIRECTLY AND REQUEST CARDS FROM THEM FOR PREMIUM GAS? DO YOU NEED ANY ADDITIONAL FORMS COMPLETED BY US FOR YOUR RECORDS?

Closing—looks to future → I WOULD APPRECIATE RECEIVING THIS INFORMATION AS SOON AS POSSIBLE AS I FEEL CERTAIN WE CAN BENEFIT FROM THE USE OF THIS CONTRACT.

SINCERELY,

Routine Inquiries and Requests

Businesses welcome inquiries requesting information about their products and services. When you write asking for information or material that you can expect to receive automatically, it is routine. See Figure 5.10. If you expect possible resistance to your request, that letter would be considered a type of selling letter, which will be covered in Chapter 7, "Sales Letters and Persuasive Claims and Requests."

Replies to Routine Inquiries and Requests

Brief form letters or cards are frequently used for replies to routine requests and inquiries. Although a memo was formerly used only for internal office matters, the efficient postal or email memo now also serves for outside business correspondence Figure 5.10 shows a routine printed memo sent outside the firms.

The basic information in the routine reply letter or memorandum would do the following:

1. Answer the question clearly.
2. Supply any further information necessary.
3. End with a good will closing.

Figure 5.11 shows examples of two email replies to routine requests:

FIGURE 5.11
Routine reply.

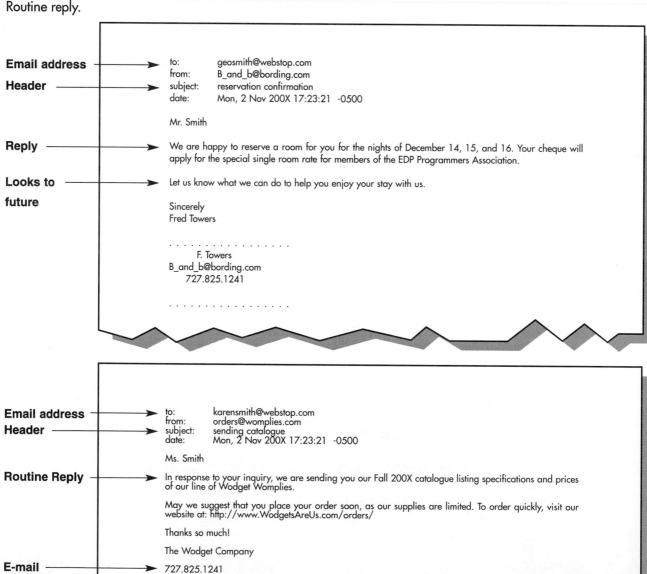

Email address → to: geosmith@webstop.com
from: B_and_b@bording.com
Header → subject: reservation confirmation
date: Mon, 2 Nov 200X 17:23:21 -0500

Mr. Smith

Reply → We are happy to reserve a room for you for the nights of December 14, 15, and 16. Your cheque will apply for the special single room rate for members of the EDP Programmers Association.

Looks to future → Let us know what we can do to help you enjoy your stay with us.

Sincerely
Fred Towers

. . . .
F. Towers
B_and_b@bording.com
727.825.1241

. . . .

Email address → to: karensmith@webstop.com
from: orders@womplies.com
Header → subject: sending catalogue
date: Mon, 2 Nov 200X 17:23:21 -0500

Ms. Smith

Routine Reply → In response to your inquiry, we are sending you our Fall 200X catalogue listing specifications and prices of our line of Wodget Womplies.

May we suggest that you place your order soon, as our supplies are limited. To order quickly, visit our website at: http://www.WodgetsAreUs.com/orders/

Thanks so much!

The Wodget Company

E-mail "signature" → 727.825.1241

Routine Claims

Occasionally, it is necessary to make a routine claim against a business for money, materials, or service that the company can be expected to agree with automatically. This is routine information letter, where the request is made early in the letter, with the necessary supporting facts following immediately. The letter can end with a statement of what is wanted. Figure 5.12 is an example of such a letter.

FIGURE 5.12
Claim letter.

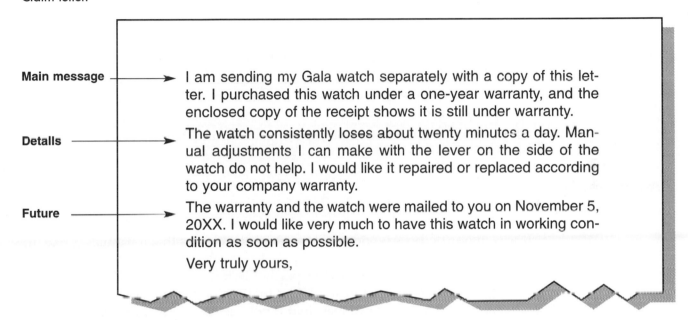

Main message — I am sending my Gala watch separately with a copy of this letter. I purchased this watch under a one-year warranty, and the enclosed copy of the receipt shows it is still under warranty.

Details — The watch consistently loses about twenty minutes a day. Manual adjustments I can make with the lever on the side of the watch do not help. I would like it repaired or replaced according to your company warranty.

Future — The warranty and the watch were mailed to you on November 5, 20XX. I would like very much to have this watch in working condition as soon as possible.

Very truly yours,

Routine Claim Adjustments

A routine claim adjustment letter is a good news letter, and states very simply that the claim or request has been satisfied. This letter should be brief. Resale material might be used here, because you have shown that your firm treats customers fairly.

The best way to write this letter is to avoid the use of negative words like *problem, trouble, damage,* and so forth. Instead, refer to the fact that the product is now in good condition and can be expected to operate properly.

Notice that the closing section makes no reference to the previous unsatisfactory condition of the watch. Neither does it suggest that more trouble might occur. In this manner, the letter ends on a positive tone rather than negative. Repeat: Eliminate or avoid negatives.

Quite often it is necessary to make a nonroutine response to an order or claim when there must be a long delay or when it is impossible to comply with the request. These responses would be negative communications, which are covered in Chapter 6, "The Negative Communication: The 'No' Message."

Checklist for Routine Information, "Yes" or Good News Communications

1. Identify your reader(s) and write at that level.
2. Is the appearance satisfactory?
3. Is it courteous?
4. Is the message clear and complete? Check your list or notes.
5. Is the main information given early?
6. Have you included all necessary details? Have you removed unnecessary information?
7. Does the letter end pleasantly?
8. Have you eliminated unnecessary words, sentences, or paragraphs.
9. For variety in sentence form, some sentences should start with descriptive words, phrases, or clauses. (See Writing Improvement Exercise starting on page 105.)
10. Check for correct grammar, spelling, and punctuation.

News Releases

News releases in a basic business communication text. If not here, where?

It was in one of those wonderful late afternoon classes that a woman spoke up, "Why doesn't your book tell us how to write news releases?"

Caught by surprise, the instructor paused before answering, "I have used or studied every business communication text that anyone else is using, and none of them covers news releases. I can't see that it belongs in a basic business communication text."

The interrupter continued, "Almost the first day of my job I was asked to write a news release."

From across the room a man's voice chimed in: "The same thing happened to me about the first week on my new job. That's why I'm here."

Coincidentally, their instructor had worked as a college campus correspondent, a "stringer," for the downtown newspaper for three years. The job was part-time during the school year and full-time during summers. This included a six month period as pro tem department editor for the sabbatical leave of her regular editor.

So that is how and why the topic "News Releases" was introduced into business communication textbooks.

Your News Story: Why You?

To their surprise, new employees frequently receive an assignment to write a news release. Why? Probably because no one else on staff has shown the talent or desire to write them. Most people do not write well and must study hard to do so. But, showing an aptitude for any writing can often be an upward career step.

In well established organizations that want to promote their product, services, or other interests and activities, news releases are usually prepared by the marketing or customer relations staffs. Or well paid outside advertising agencies handle these accounts.

In any case, people writing these publicity articles must work closely with their top management to make certain that information is accurate and is being handled in accordance with company policy at the time.

In Figure 5.14, a news release pattern is shown, together with an illustration of a long article being clipped shorter. When space is at a premium, which can be often, editors frequently clip the article from the bottom up. Further, looking to the future, with experience, if you are interested, you might have a chance at a career in writing.

Spreading the News

Any news release is distributed to print and/or broadcast media with hope of obtaining free publicity. Frequently, the same article is distributed to several different media. You should know that it is in stiff competition with other articles, and the better it conforms with regular news writing standards, the better its chances for publication. If it is written acceptably and is used, the news outlet benefits in getting a story already written by outsiders.

Small News Outlets

Also, you might have better success getting your news release accepted by small local or trade publications than by major newspapers, wire services, radio stations, or TV channels.

Don't discount **small news outlets.** Small outlets are hungrier for news, and even if your news releases don't get published in *The Los Angeles Times,* the article that was published in the *Beverly Hills Weekly* might land on the doorstep of an executive who reads it and becomes interested in doing business with you.

If you are going to write news releases on a regular basis, keep a list of newspapers, magazines, radio, and TV stations that might be interested in your firm's stories.

FIGURE 5.14
Outline for a press release, showing effect
cutting might have.

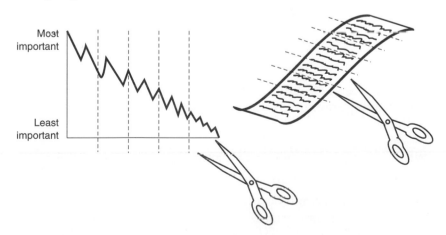

Typical Items for News Releases

Below are some typical topics for **news releases:**

New products or services	Special support of community interests
New plants or facilities	Number of new employees to be hired
Election of new officers	Contests
Appointments of top personnel	Environmental concerns and activities
Promotion of personnel	Prominent visitors
Mergers and acquisitions	Research breakthroughs
Grants to community, arts, or other organizations	New contracts
Community work done by employees	Employee activities

Getting Started

A Catchy Story

The editor who decides if your article will be published is looking for a lead to **catch the reader's eye.** Try to find an interesting twist—some novel angle—to start your story. Ask yourself, "What is the most interesting, exciting, or unusual aspect of this story?" But stay within reason. Don't get too far out. If you find and use an acceptable twist, your story will probably get earlier attention than 50 percent of competing stories.

Your Audience

Always, always consider your audience just as you do in writing letters or reports, and write to that audience. Newspaper readers and broadcast audiences are part of a general population, so do not use in-house or trade jargon not understandable to outsiders. Also, avoid overlong words. They won't impress the editor or your audience. You can consider using these terms for appropriate announcements to specific groups who will easily follow what you are talking about.

Who? What? When? Where? Why?

Editors recognize the work of professionals, and the more professional the wording and format of your release, the less rewriting needs to be done by the editorial staff. And the better are the chances for survival of your article under the editor's scissors.

A regular news staff member is trained to include in the lead of the story—the first one or two paragraphs—the answers to as many of these **"5 W's"** as are pertinent to the story:

Who?   Names make news: Name the people involved.

What?   Say what happened that is newsworthy.

When?   Say when it occurred. Remember: old news is usually not news. Timing is important.

Where?   Location is usually of great importance.

Why?   You often don't have information for this W. Yet, when it is part of a story, it can be the heart of the story.

With the "5 W's" in front of you, you can see that your job will be easier than you thought. These will be the notes or list you can follow to write the news release. *Make it catch the reader's attention!*

Writing a News Release

Like a good news story, a good news release will generally follow a modified routine information letter outline. The most important news must come early. Additional information should be included in decreasing order of importance, leaving the least important to last.

The modified outline that can be followed for a news release is shown in Figure 5.14, together with an illustration of a long article being clipped shorter. To fit available space, when brevity is needed, editors almost always clip the article from the bottom up.

Now follow these writing guidelines:

1. Make the story sound important—without false puffery.
2. Write in the third person, not in the first:
    This:
    Leo's Video store will give free Leo's T-shirts to *its* first 100 customers who show up at *its* store opening…
    Not this:
    We will give free Leo's Video T-shirts to the first 100 customers at *our* store opening…
3. Drop unnecessary words, phrases, sentences and paragraphs. Editors recognize puffery, knowing it also turns off readers.
4. Give your news release a final reading, making sure it is clear and complete. Also check grammar, spelling, and punctuation, making your article professional for the editor, the person with the fast scissors and the big wastebasket.

Most news releases are typed double spaced on plain white paper. At the top of the page in all capital letters, blocked against the left margin, type FOR IMMEDIATE RELEASE or NEWS. Above or below this heading, type the name, address, and telephone number of your company, together with the name of the person releasing the news. Also, the editor will appreciate your furnishing the approximate number of words in the article. Mark the end of the article by typing the journalistic symbol for the end (# # #) at the center of the line a double space below the copy. Figure 5.14 is a clipped form of a news release.

"... Your Morals First ...."

As a young man leaving for his first year at Harvard, President Theodore Roosevelt (1858–1919) was cautioned by his father: "Take care of your morals first, health next, and finally, your studies."

Submitting a News Release

Figure 5.15 shows a heading you might copy for the first page of a typical news release. Most are typed double spaced (for more room for easily reading and editing) on plain white or off-white paper or on gray newsprint.

In all capital letters, blocked against the left margin, type FOR IMMEDIATE RELEASE or NEWS. Above or below this heading, type the name of your organization, postal and email addresses, fax and telephone numbers of your company, together with your name as the person releasing the news. You can use the open white space at the right side of the heading to type your name and phone number with extension number and your email address.

Also, the editor will appreciate your furnishing the approximate number of words in the article. Mark the end of the article by typing the journalistic symbol for the end (# # #) at the center of the line below the copy. If there is more than one page, type MORE centered below the last line of copy on each page that has a following page.

FIGURE 5.15
Fragment of first page of news release.

FOR IMMEDIATE RELEASE

American Library Association
50 East Huron Street
Chicago, Illinois 60611
(312) 944–6780
annp@amlibasn.org

Contact Ms. Ann Parryman
Approximately 150 words

Checklist for Writing a News Release

1. Use that "catchy lead."
2. Choose the order of the 5 W's. You might mark them 1, 2, 3 and so forth.
3. Drop unnecessary words, phrases, sentences and paragraphs. Later, perhaps, you'll find that writing sometimes improves if you drop whole pages. Watch for unnecessary repetition—redundancies. Very important.
4. Stay with the truth. If you make one false statement, your news stories and your honor may be suspect at any time. Sometimes there goes the job!
5. Recheck grammar, spelling, punctuation, word usage. Use a thesaurus to find synonyms for avoiding awkward repetition of words; the thesaurus also enlarges your vocabulary.

> **To the instructor:** "Short words are best and the old words when short are best of all."
>
> *Winston Churchill*

Chapter 5   Routine Information, "Yes" or Good News Communications: News Releases

WRITING IMPROVEMENT "HANDS ON" EXERCISE
VARIETY IN SENTENCE FORMS

In each of the sentences that introduce this exercise, the first sentence follows the traditional pattern of the English language: Subject–Verb, followed by modifiers. Continual use of this pattern leads to extremely monotonous, unprofessional, singsong writing. The suggested improvement of each of these examples places modifying words, phrases, or clauses before the subject.

When a person's writing is not smooth, it often can be improved significantly by simply changing the order of some of the sentences. Frequently, amateurish writing becomes professional just through the use of such changes. You must be cautious, however. Moving an element to the beginning of a sentence tends to emphasize it. Do not emphasize negative information unnecessarily.

Applying this principle to their doctoral dissertations was the major re-write that helped some graduate students receive their doctorates which at first had been denied.

Here are some suggestions for varying the form of the traditional sentence.

1. Start these sentences with a descriptive word or phrase:
    a. These exercises can frequently be applied to my own writing. →
        Frequently, these exercises can be applied to my own writing.
    b. The jury brought in a verdict of guilty after deliberating five hours. →
        After deliberating five hours, the jury brought in a verdict of guilty.
    c. The tired and hungry board members ended their negotiations at 3 A.M. →
        Tired and hungry, the board members completed their negotiations at 3 A.M.
    d. Her opportunity to accept the job offer is gone. →
        Gone is her opportunity to accept the job offer.
    e. We found the lost files in the bottom drawer of Merlin's desk. →
        In the bottom drawer of Merlin's desk, we found the lost files.

2. Start the sentence with a dependent clause. (A *dependent* clause is a group of words with a subject–verb combination that cannot stand alone as a sentence. Within a sentence they act as adjectives, adverbs or nouns. An *independent* clause is a group of words with a subject–verb combination that can stand alone as a sentence.)
    a. They can participate in the discussion *if they desire to do so.* →
        If they desire to do so, they can participate in the discussion.
    b. We can paint them *if all else fails.* →
        If all else fails, we can paint them.
    c. We can be satisfied that we were honest, *even if the roof caves in.* →
        Even if the roof caves in, we can be satisfied that we were honest.
    d. He finished his work, not complaining even though he was tired →
        Not complaining even though he was tired, he finished his work.

Chapter 5 Routine Information, "Yes" or Good News Communications: News Releases

WRITING IMPROVEMENT "HANDS ON" EXERCISE
VARIETY IN SENTENCE FORMS

Rewrite the following sentences by placing something other than the subject at the beginning of the sentence. By all means, acceptable answers may vary.

1. Tellers must count the cash twice for each customer. → <u>For each customer the</u> <u>tellers must count the cash twice.</u>

2. Mr. Bernie left the meeting in a flurry of excitement. → <u>In a flurry of excitement,</u> <u>Mr. Bernie left the meeting.</u>

3. Replies to the mail order letter came in from all over the country. → <u>From all over</u> <u>the country came replies to the mail order letter.</u>

4. The exasperated bank manager called her staff together. → <u>Exasperated, the bank</u> <u>manager called her staff together.</u>

5. The record of the committee's work is somehow lost. → <u>Somehow, the record of</u> <u>the committee's work is lost.</u>

6. Many people will want to buy the stock when the market settles. → <u>When the</u> <u>market settles, many people will want to buy the stock.</u>

7. One member of the board of trustees was absent at the last meeting, while he took care of a family emergency. → <u>Due to a family emergency, one member of the board of</u> <u>trustees was absent at the last meeting.</u>

8. You may want to establish an education trust fund, since you have small children. → <u>Since you have small children, you may want to establish an education trust fund.</u>

9. Construction can start after the next meeting of the city council. → <u>After the next</u> <u>meeting of the city council, construction can start.</u>

10. We will open another branch if this one becomes a success. → <u>If this branch is</u> <u>successful, we will open another.</u>

Chapter 5 Routine Information, "Yes" or Good News Communications: News Releases

WRITING ASSIGNMENTS

1. Write a letter to Miss Carol Newman, Customer Service Representative, Sheraton-Tampa Motor Hotel, Cass and Morgan Streets, Tampa, FL 33602. Tell her that your firm no longer carries the cotton-linen banquet cloths and napkins she had ordered, but has substituted a new line of a linen-polyester banquet cloths, which have proved more satisfactory for appearance and long-wearing qualities. Although the regular price of the new line of linens is approximately 10 percent higher than the cotton-linen cloth, you have substituted these cloths for the Sheraton-Tampa at the price of the linens ordered. Sign your name to the letter, giving yourself the title of Manager, New Products Division.

2. Write a personal business letter with your fictitious home return address to Cable Car Clothiers, No. 150 Post Street, San Francisco, CA 94108. Order the following merchandise: a man's sleeveless sweater, catalogue #28C3, size 38, price $29.95, red; swim trunks, catalogue #27H3, size 32, blue-red combination, price $50.00; casual Knockaround Keds, catalogue #49AC, white, price $90.00. Enclose a personal check for the order, adding sales tax if you are a resident of California. Be sure to include your (fictitious) full name and address.

3. From Tiffany & Company, Fifth Avenue and 57th Street, New York, N.Y. 10022, order for yourself one bracelet of 18-karat gold, set with diamonds and emeralds, catalogue #A-65, price $3,950. Also, order earrings to match, catalogue #C-65, price $2,290. Ask that the merchandise be billed to your regular account and delivered to you by bonded messenger. Include your complete (fictitious) address.

4. Write a letter to yourself, thanking you for the order of bracelet and matching earrings in assignment 3. Sign the letter "Gott Roks, Director of Customer Relations."

5. Send an order to the University Shop, 3900 Jackson Road, Ann Arbor, MI 48103. Ask them to select for you a gift for your niece, Priscilla Winslow, a student at the University of Michigan, and ask to have it delivered to her at her college address, 2901 Wagoner Road, Apt. 201, Ann Arbor, MI 48103. You may make a suggestion, noting that you are not sure of her dress size so you cannot suggest specific wearing apparel. Ask them to charge it to your MasterCard Account #SZ31-00012-27AC. Specify a limit of $150.00.

6. You are employed by the Aspen Ski Hut and have received a letter from a new customer, Miss Terri Fick, saying that when she received her new short skis, the poles recommended were not included, although they were on the bill she received. Write a letter to Miss Fick saying that you are sending the ski poles and she will receive them by special delivery.

7. Write a letter that will be sent to all members of the Lakeside Junior Chamber of Commerce, of which you are program chairman. Announce that the next meeting will be held at the Lakeside Country Club at 12 noon, Monday, September 9, 20XX, in the Lakeview Room. The speaker will be Fred Snyder, Director of Community Relations of the local college. Lunch, including gratuities, will cost $15. Give details of the meeting and ask the members to inform you whether or not they will attend. Make up the name and address of one person to whom you are writing this letter.

8. You are the owner of a new business, Cyd's Cycle Shop, and are interested in participating in the local Thanksgiving Day parade either by preparing a float or by assisting a volunteer group in the preparation of its float. Write a letter to the head of the Thanksgiving Day Parade Committee, Ms. Lucia Stark, 4500 Nema Road, Tucson, AZ 85034.

Chapter 5 Routine Information, "Yes" or Good News Communications: News Releases

REVIEW AND DISCUSSION

Complete the following exercises. Be concise.

1. What is the most common type of business letter and the easiest to write? <u>The routine information, "yes" or good news letter.</u>

2. Name the three basic qualities of a good business communication.

   a. <u>Attractive appearance</u>
   b. <u>Good will tone</u>
   c. <u>Clear, complete, concise message</u>

3. Draw a diagram of a routine information pattern and identify the information that should be contained in the beginning, middle, and closing.

   [See page 84.]

4. What two questions can you ask to check if a letter or memorandum is clear and complete?

   a. <u>Does it include all necessary information?</u>
   b. <u>Does it include more information than necessary?</u>

5. How should the routine information communication end? <u>With a pleasant comment, possibly looking to the future.</u>

6. Why are form letters and postcards sometimes used for routine mailings? <u>To save time and money when message is routine.</u>

7. Name five types of communications that can be written following the routine information pattern.

   a. Orders

   b. Acknowledgments and confirmations

   c. Announcements

   d. Routine inquiries and requests

   e. Replies to routine inquiries and requests

8. Where should you look to get detailed information about composing mail-merge letters? In the software catalogue for your program.

9. Why is an order an important legal matter? It is the first step in a legal contract to buy.

10. What information should be in the last three sections of an order?

    a. Beginning: This is an order.

    b. Middle: Necessary details: description, amount, etc.

    c. Closing: What is being done with it.

11. Why is the number of people ordering online increasing? Ordering any time, easy payment by credit card, ordering any place, no need to travel.

12. List the information that should be included in a reply to a routine request or inquiry. Answer questions clearly. Supply necessary further information. Good will closing.

13. What information should be listed in a message sending material? Necessary details: what is being sent; how. Close on upbeat note.

14. What information should the first part of a routine claim give? State that claim has been satisfied.

15. Why is it especially appropriate to enclose resale materials or messages in a routine claim adjustment? You have shown that you treat customers fairly.

16. What are the 5 W's that should be considered for the lead section of most news releases? Who? What? When? Where? Why?

To give variety to these sentences, rewrite them so something other than the subject starts the sentence:

17. Applause broke out loudly when the new bank hours were announced. → <u>When the new bank hours were announced, the crowd applauded loudly.</u>

18. The managers were making the choice of computers without consulting the clerical staff. → <u>Without consulting the clerical staff, managers were making the choice of computers.</u>

19. Wage adjustments will be made for late night and early morning shifts. → <u>For late night and early morning shifts, wage adjustments will be made.</u>

20. Management frequently made adjustments on indoor and outdoor assignments. → <u>Frequently, management made adjustments on indoor and outdoor assignments.</u>

6 The Negative Communication

The "No" Message

> *I try to think of things very positive and nothing negative.*
> *Instead of saying, "Don't sit back," I say, "Always stay." Instead*
> *of saying, "Don't hang behind," I say, "Always attack." Instead*
> *of saying, "Don't be tense," I say, "Hang loose." Believe me, I*
> *think that is the difference.*
>
> *Jean Claude Killey*
>
> *Olympic Gold Medal Champion slalom*
> *skier, when asked how he managed to win*

Jean Claude Killey evidently believes a **positive mental attitude** pays off in his skiing. This optimistic viewpoint can also pay off in other experiences, especially in preparing postal and electronic letters, memos, reports and other communications.

Of the patterns for most common business communications—the routine information message, the negative message, and the sales letter or persuasive request—the negative communication presents the greatest good will challenge. This is because you are sending a disappointing or "bad news" message that might not be welcome. Your aim is to say the negative briefly in a manner that is acceptable, paying special attention to the hope that you retain the reader's good will.

Handling negatives acceptably requires considerable talent and attention. Studies show that many communications are unnecessarily offensive to their readers, who might take their business elsewhere. Intentionally, or unintentionally, negative wordings that do not help your purpose are sent too often. In fact, the wrong tone can completely cancel an otherwise clear, acceptable message. We must prepare our communications with an ear that is sensitive to the other person's feelings. If we approach negatives with a positive attitude, we will usually be more successful in making the unwelcome message sound acceptable.

Patterns for the "No" Message

Figure 6.1 shows a simple pattern that can be used for most negative messages, such as refusals, partial adjustment replies, and complaints. For a negative communication, this "no" pattern, contains three elements: (1) **buffer,** (2) **negative message,** and (3) **courteous closing.**

FIGURE 6.1
Pattern for a "no" or negative communication.

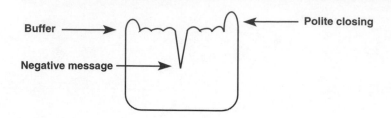

Another pattern to use for giving bad news would be to borrow from the entertainment industry and follow the format of a director giving actors suggestions after a rehearsal. This format also has buffer, negative message and pleasant closing. Called a **"praise sandwich,"** it consists of two slices of praise wrapped around a chunk of criticism. Figure 6.2 illustrates this negative "sandwich" concept.

First: The Buffer

An effective way to start a negative message is to open with a **buffer** as shown in Figure 6.1, or as a slice of bread covering a piece of meat, as shown in Figure 6.2. A buffer is used for the same purpose that a bumper was originally designed for on an automobile—to cushion a blow. If you give the "no" reply in the beginning, you will probably turn the reader away from the rest of the message where the reasons for the "no" are given. Instead, first make some pleasant statement with which the reader will agree. Next, lead in to the negative part of the message, generally giving the reason or some of the reasons for the coming negative. This plan is all part of the buffer leading to the main message.

The buffer should not sound so pleasant that the reader expects a "yes" or favorable reply. Sounding too positive would make the negative far more difficult to accept when it does come. You might have actually given false hope.

FIGURE 6.2
Pattern for a "praise sandwich."

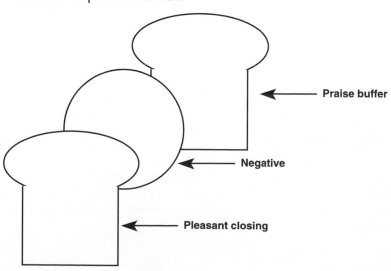

Middle Section: The "No" Message

After the buffer opening and possibly some explanation of the reasons behind the negative message, the "no" should be given very clearly and as briefly as possible. Good will is best served by saying it as pleasantly as possible and getting on with the closing.

Avoid Repeating Negatives

Whenever possible, avoid reciting here any of the negative aspects of your communication, such as repeating the details of a complaint. Repetition only serves to etch these details into the reader's mind.

Examples of How Not to Say It

We do not understand why you have had so much trouble with our watch for so long and why it does not keep good time for you. [This statement could be left out entirely.]

I am sorry that I cannot speak to your group, as I have a previous speaking engagement that night. I know it will be difficult for you to try to find another speaker at this late date, and I hope you won't have further problems with the rest of the program. [This paragraph could close with the first sentence.]

Do Not "Talk Down"

Regardless of how provoked you are, do not talk down to people. Don't "slap their wrists." They might retaliate behind your back, doing the opposite of what you have ordered—or worse. (See Chapter 3, "Qualities of an Effective Business Communication: Good Will Tone," and particularly the section on "Write Courteously.")

The Courteous Closing

After the tone of the letter drops down for the "no" message, the tone should come back up, closing on a positive note. When appropriate, the closing can contain additional reasons justifying negative message. If possible, try to show that a reason behind the refusal might be of potential advantage to the reader. This is done in the following credit refusal:

We are able to offer merchandise at these low prices only because of our credit policies. In the Miami district the costs of maintaining regular furniture delivery routes are tremendous. We have discovered that customers are able to arrange far more economical deliveries on their own, often carrying the purchases in their own vehicles.

Skillfully done, this closing section can often make a counterproposal and/or contain resale material, encouraging further business.

In the closing, care must be taken not to pretend to have done something you haven't done. Don't say:

We hope we can be of help to you again. [You weren't this time.]

We are sure this will meet with your approval. [It might not.]

Tone in Negative Communications

As contradictory as it seems, in negative messages we should avoid using negative words and phrases as much as possible. Letters set out in this chapter will demonstrate how this can often be accomplished. The German philosopher Friedrich (FREE drik) Nietzsche (NEE cheh) said, "We often dispute an opinion when what we really object to is the tone in which the opinion was uttered." Somebody else said, "It isn't what you say, it's the way that you say it!"

We want to give others a favorable picture of ourselves and our organization. Therefore, we should choose words for their connotations and their potential associations, as well as for their specific meanings. (See the discussion of words and their meanings in Chapter 3, "Qualities of an Effective Business Communication: Good Will Tone.") Avoid using words that have particularly unpleasant negative associations, and if necessary, go to a dictionary or a thesaurus for an acceptable euphemism.

"Flaming" Emails

In today's wired age, email messages are so easily sent that sometimes little thought is given before clicking on the "send" button. **Flaming** is the term used to describe very angry email replies—a habit that has little precedence with other forms of written communications. Although the pure shock value of such messages does certainly gain notice, it's not good form, and should be avoided.

Common Negative Phrases to Avoid

The following lists show how certain common phrases should not be used because of their unflattering connotations. Many words and phrases have negative, between-the-lines overtones. For example:

What You Say	*What They Hear*
Apparently you are not aware.	Stupid!
I question what you say.	Lying?
Our unassailable position…	We're always right.
We are not inclined to…	We don't care if we please you.
We cannot understand you.	You're not thinking clearly.
We differ from you.	So you must be wrong.
We question your…	Are you lying?
We repeated to you.	We told you this before!
When you question our decision,…	We're right.
You apparently overlooked…	Careless!

What You Say	*What They Hear*
You are wrong.	As usual.
You did not include…	Careless again!
You do not understand.	Dumbbell!
You failed to…	Can't you do it right?
You forgot to…	Ignoramus!
Your complaint…	Crybaby!
Your demand…	Don't be so bossy.
Your disregard…	Pay attention!
Your dissatisfaction…	Whine! Whine!
Your failure to…	You bombed again!

Humor in Negative Communications

Acceptable Humor

At a time when smoking was permitted on airplanes, a flight attendant's voice was heard on the intercom of a plane in flight: "Smoking in smoking sections only. *No smoking at any time in lavatories.* Violators of these regulations will be asked to step outside."

Use caution in employing humor in negative situations. Very often, the matter under discussion is too serious for the receiver to want to hear jokes about it. But under certain circumstances, humor can be used extremely effectively. This is usually more acceptable when the message is well intentioned and when you are certain it will be received in the manner that was intended. Also, it usually helps if the writer and receiver are acquainted.

Members of the Career Education Department of one college were continually plagued by having members of other departments block their driveway. Routine memos had produced fair results, but there were still trespassers, particularly the driver of a certain red Porsche. One morning, a member of the staff used a felt tip pen (with water-soluble ink) to draw a wide dotted line across the hood of the part of the car that protruded into the driveway, and attached the following note under the windshield wiper that finally produced the desired results:

> Attention: Mr. Mike Davis
> Plant Maintenance
> Rio Hondo College
> Please issue a work order for the necessary cutting of that portion of automobile projecting across the access road to Room T-106. See line of cut across hood of 1970 Porsche, red color.
> From: Larry Fickle
> Welding—Tech Dept.

The next day, Mr. Fickle found the following note in his mailbox:

Imagine my surprise when I went out to the parking lot and found my car so neatly trimmed off. Fortunately, the motor Is In the back and I was able to make it home. But imagine the sight it must have been to the other drivers to see a little gray-haired lady in half a car tooling down the freeway doing wheelies!

But I do know where to park what's left of my car from now on.

My best,

An effective whimsical approach was the request that an oceanfront hotel posted to put across a negative message to guests:

NO-NO'S: Barbecues, sleeping bags, surfboards in rooms (we have storage facilities).

Unacceptable Humor

Usually it does not take much talent or brains to show humor at the expense of other people. Rather, it takes more talent plus good sense to restrain yourself from ridiculing another person just for a cheap laugh. The nineteenth-century American educator Horace Mann, who is considered the father of American public education, said, "Avoid witticisms at the expense of others."

Among other matters, we should not resort to humor that focuses attention on a person's race, sex, disability, place of origin, sexual preference or religion, because it usually offends.

Being Candid

When things go wrong, there can be a tendency to "beat around the bush" or "pass the buck." However, when a person is ethical and therefore honest about a situation, even if it is not favorable, that person is respected for being **candid**. Openly and honestly admitting to a less than desirable fact can give people trust and confidence in you.

We should maintain our dignity, avoiding alibis and sour grapes. Others will recognize our honesty in a painful situation.

Some time ago, a successful New York advertising executive ventured into the treacherous waters of starting an advertising agency of his own. He met little success. After a while, he wrote a letter to each of his firm's clients, most of whom were old friends. The letter started: "You probably have noticed that lately I haven't been knocking on your door for material for our ... advertising agency." Then he went on to briefly explain his predicament.

He was candid, being open, honest, admirable.

Hiding Behind Company Policy

In a cartoon, the Moose was asked, "What's the reason?" "There's no reason," Moose replied, "it's just policy."

Unfortunately, this is what a person usually thinks when **company policy** is given as the only reason for the refusal of a request or for any other negative explanation. The automatic impression is apt to be, "That's a poor policy, and it ought to be changed."

Therefore, rather than hide behind the excuse of company policy, the negative reply should explain reasons for the answer in terms the reader can understand and presumably accept.

Forestalling Complaints

In the natural course of business, things occasionally go wrong. Delays in shipments to and from your business, production delays or foul-ups, even acts of God—fire, flood, earthquake, drought and so forth—can occur. The aircraft industry coined a word for an error that seems attributable to no identifiable cause: a *glitch*. To promote good will and prevent people from becoming annoyed or angered when a glitch occurs, try to forestall complaints before people go to pen, keyboard, typewriter or telephone, or before they press the key that activates voice mail.

Anticipating Developments

To forestall complaints, we should anticipate developments as much as we can. The number of service calls dropped dramatically when one major manufacturer began to include the following form with the delivery of any appliance. When advisable, additional information for a specific appliance is added.

Before You Call for Service:

As many as 25 percent of service calls are not due to improper appliance performance. Before you call for service, check the following:

- Is the unit unplugged?
- Has a fuse blown or is a circuit breaker tripped? (Check the outlet with another appliance or lamp.)
- Check the controls of the unit.

After living for years in apartments, one homeowner had just moved into a new house with all new electric appliances. She checked switches, appliances and so forth, and everything was fine.

But about a month after moving in she discovered that water stood about two inches deep in the bottom of the freezer. Her phone call soon brought a repairperson out immediately (times change). Looking at the machine, he opened the lid, reached behind and pulled up a loose electric cord. Plugged in, the freezer gave out its normal hum.

The repairperson seemed a little guilty. "Do you have any other electrical work I could check out?"

At her "No," he shook his head and commented, "We have a company rule that we must make the standard charge for any service call. Wow! Forty bucks to plug in a cord."

To give subscribers beforehand knowledge of the predicament in which one book club found itself, the following form was sent to all club members:

SPECIAL NOTICE

Dear Member:

The recent floods caused by Hurricane William devastated widespread areas of the eastern section of the country.

Our warehouse and shipping facilities and the serving post office are located in areas that were directly in the path of the storm, and unfortunately they suffered considerable damage. We are making every effort to restore our facilities, but if you should notice a delay in our service, we hope you'll be patient and will understand that we are doing our best to resume normal operations.

Thank you for your patience and cooperation.

Membership Secretary

The following memo was attached to pieces of wicker furniture being shipped to customers. The honest negative message is so well presented that readers would probably accept it totally. Also notice the uplift ending looking toward the future.

Congratulations!

Congratulations on your purchase! With proper care, you will probably enjoy your wicker furniture for many years. Please realize that no piece of wicker, no matter how carefully woven, will be like any other, and each will have its imperfections which are part of its charm. In no way was any part machine made, and its beauty lies in its handwoven artistry, using a natural fiber to create the piece you now own.

You will find that wicker is extremely durable, and with proper care will not break or wear out.

Writing in "Plain Talk"

People in business must learn that an amazing number of complaint letters are written because previous communications have not been written clearly, causing serious brain drain. To forestall complaints, we must be sure messages from our offices are written in "plain talk." Care must be taken in preparing individual letters, but greater care should be taken in preparing multiple copy communications, because of their repeated usage. Be sure that all terms can be easily understood by your readers, avoiding unnecessary technical terms and bureaucratic jargon.

Other firms are learning to follow the lead of insurance companies that are changing their policies to remove legalese and are rewording them in language the lay person can understand.

Let the Seller Beware

Today the old business concept of *caveat emptor, "let the buyer beware,"* is generally outmoded and is being replaced by an attitude of *caveat venditor, "let the seller beware."* This is due to the highly competitive nature of business and industry, and because of increasing consumer protection activities. Business people learn that following ethical practices retains customers.

To maintain the good will of customers, most businesses, including major retail chains, operate on the basis that "the customer is always right," or caveat venditor. The theory is that when a customer makes a complaint, in that customer's mind the complaint is justified. Therefore, all but the most flagrantly false claims are satisfied.

In responding to customer requests, claims or complaints, these businesses find it an economic necessity to draw the line somewhere, so they try to make adjustment decisions that are fair to both the customers and the firm. This makes it necessary to write adjustment letters to customers.

Types of "No" Messages

Probably the best way to learn how to write good negative messages is to study some specific types. Some common "no" replies are covered here.

Refusals of Claims and Requests

Some business people dislike making **refusals** so much that they try to avoid making them altogether. However, sometimes it becomes necessary to turn people down on outrageous requests. A refusal that retains a customer's good will, and therefore the customer, can be prepared only when the writer has the correct mental attitude. Although the writer may feel that the situation justifies frankness or even rudeness, the hope of preserving a good business image should prevent such an approach. True, some requests are ridiculous. But a humorous, cutting or snide comment would probably lose that customer as well as the business of some of the customer's friends or relatives.

A refusal of a request, claim or complaint can follow the pattern of the "no" letter, with a buffer, a brief negative message, and a pleasant closing. The closing can do any of the following:

- ☐ Suggest an alternative.
- ☐ Send an acceptable substitute for what was requested.
- ☐ Resell, suggesting future business under other circumstances.
- ☐ Wish them well in their plan without repeating your inability to assist.
- ☐ Discuss something off the subject, but acceptable.
- ☐ If compliance would be illegal, explain.

Following are three refusals with the buffer, negative message and closing labeled.

Refusal 1

**Buffer
(reader can agree)** ⟶   Yes, Mr. Nichols, we at American Home Service surely wish to retain our reputation as being the best friends of the do-it-yourself homeowner. One of the greatest services to the public, we believe, is maintaining low prices throughout our store.

**Negative message
(brief)** ⟶   Therefore, we cannot make a refund to you on the partial panels of plywood. We do not have storage facilities for all sizes of paneling and, as a matter of fact, are often unable to sell off the scraps we have left from our regular store merchandise.

**Polite closing
suggestion** ⟶   May we suggest, Mr. Nichols, that you try to find a place to store this paneling for your own possible use in the future. We have had many customers return after a period of time seeking to match some previously purchased woods. Because available supplies differ over the years, this is not always easy to do.

Upbeat ending ⟶   We hope to see you in our store taking advantage of our Annual Spring Sale from May 8 to 15. Check local papers for this big event. Special sales notices will be posted on items all over the store.

        Cordially,

Refusal 2

**Buffer (reader
should agree)** ⟶   Your survey of business reports should be of great interest to all businesses in our area.

**Negative
message (brief)** ⟶   However, because Axelradd Furniture Company is a wholly family-owned business enterprise, we do not publish reports for distribution to the public.

Polite closing ⟶   May we wish you luck in completing your study. And we surely wish you success in completing your work toward your college degree.

        Sincerely,

Refusal 3

        I agree with you, Ms. Bronson, that we should all do our best to support
**Buffer (reader
would agree)** ⟶ a cause that is worthy of our time and money. Certainly, I feel that your project of supporting underdeveloped nations is worthwhile.

        When our firm was founded, all joint partners agreed that, rather than
**Negative
message** ⟶ spread our support thinly among many good causes, we would give what we could to two community projects: the annual Community Fund drive and the Backman Geriatrics Ward at the local county hospital. Our support of these two worthwhile causes takes all the time, money, and effort our small organization can afford.

Upbeat closing ⟶   I have noted with interest some of the successes already obtained by the efforts of your organization, and I do wish you well in your fund drive.

        Cordially,

Partial Adjustment Replies to Requests, Claims, or Complaints

Frequently, in reply to a request, claim, or complaint, you may avoid an outright refusal by offering to comply with part of what was requested. This is called a **partial adjustment.** Regular adjustment letters where the writer complies with the request are covered in Chapter 5, "The Routine Information, "Yes" or Good News Communications."

In writing the partial adjustment, emphasize what can be done and deemphasize what cannot be done. A full explanation of the reason for the partial refusal should be given without offending the reader. It is very important that this letter lets the receiver know that your company looks forward to continuing to do business in the future.

Nonroutine Order Acknowledgments

Quite often it is necessary to make a nonroutine order acknowledgment when there must be a long delay in shipment or when it is impossible to make shipment at all. These nonroutine messages are written for the following reasons:

- The order received was incomplete.
- The merchandise ordered is temporarily out of stock.
- The order must be delayed or refused for some other specific reason.

These nonroutine acknowledgments are most effective when handled like other negatives: (1) buffer, (2) negative message, (3) courteous closing.

Acknowledging Incomplete Orders

Too often, a customer sends an **incomplete order** that does not contain all the information necessary for shipping the merchandise desired. When this happens, it is necessary to contact the customer requesting the missing details. Only a poorly run business will return the order—it may never come back! A copy of the order might be returned, or a form letter can be sent marking where needed details were left out.

Be careful with the tone of this letter, because the potential customer has, in fact, made a mistake in failing to supply all necessary information. Regardless of the temptation, avoid an accusing tone, and don't criticize. Write this letter with the "you attitude" toward the customer. That is, it is to the customer's advantage that additional information is furnished: "So that you may receive the merchandise promptly, could you please send this information." No matter how tempted you are, avoid a "between the lines" tone that suggests, "Hey, stupid, you forgot to tell us everything we need to know!"

Here is one place where the passive form instead of the active form may be preferred in sentence structure:

Not this   You did not specify color for the argyle sweater,source #3215, size 12.
Improved   Could you please tell us the color desired for the argyle sweater, source #3215, size 12.

Not this   You forgot to tell us how payment for this merchandise is to be made.
Improved   Please indicate how payment will be made.

Back Ordering Merchandise

When an article is temporarily out of stock and cannot be shipped within a time that is reasonable, you should advise the customer. Say that you are putting it on **back order** and that it will be shipped at a specific delayed date unless the customer sends notification to the contrary. Furnish the customer a postage-paid return card or envelope.

In a letter telling of delayed shipment, it is wise to use resale material promoting merchandise such as that on the order and other items you have available. In this manner you reinforce the ideas that caused the customer to do business with you in the first place.

Because back order situations are common in business, these letters can be prepared on a computer mail-merge system. With a computer properly programmed, the specific information about the merchandise can be in a list document and merged with general information of a main document, making the resulting letter an attractive personalized letter rather than a common form letter with specific information typed separately.

Mail merges are explained earlier in this book or you can consult your computer manual for more detailed instructions.

Substitutions for Orders

For any of a number of reasons, it may be impossible to ship the specific item requested, and the seller may be able to offer a suitable substitute. In this situation, the acknowledgment letter should tell the reason for the substitution. It should also fully explain similarities and differences between the one ordered and the substitute. The closing section of this letter should ask for an immediate reply. Following is an acknowledgment letter suggesting a substitution:

> Thank you for your order for 5,000 number 5001 Leviton electrical switches for use in your Smalltown School construction.
>
> The Leviton merchandise is of excellent quality, but we cannot obtain it because of the trucking strike. There is no way we can predict when Leviton products will be available.
>
> From the experience of other customers, we have found that Ideal switches can be substituted without loss of quality and at the same price. May we ship you 5,000 number 5-Ivory Ideal switches by the first available delivery?
>
> Yours truly,

Sometimes a substitution can be sent automatically when it is known that the customer will accept it without question. However, the substitution should be explained fully:

> Today we are shipping your order #3908.
>
> We have taken the liberty of substituting stock item #180329 bond paper for your requested #18328. The stock number we are sending has replaced the former item. The new paper has proven superior to the former.
>
> We do appreciate your order and look forward to continued business with the office staff of Bellows Chevrolet.
>
> Cordially,

Combination of Routine Orders, Incomplete Orders, Back Orders, and Substitutions

Although most orders are shipped out automatically, the order acknowledgment letter must sometimes be a combination of two or more types of acknowledgments if all the merchandise is not being shipped immediately. When this happens the most effective letter will, in separate paragraphs, list and itemize each article, making all information pertaining to each article completely clear. The reader should have no question concerning any part of this order. Today this information is often sent on a well planned form.

Refusing Orders

There are times in almost any business when an order must be refused. Some reasons are these:

☐ You cannot approve customer's credit. (Declining credit is covered in Chapter 8, "Credit and Collections.")

☐ You do not carry the merchandise desired and do not have a suitable substitute.

☐ You do not sell direct; the customer must order through the proper distributor or retailer.

☐ The sale would be illegal.

This negative letter should end with a positive tone, such as wishing the receiver luck in purchasing under other conditions or locating merchandise elsewhere, or giving specific information about where and how to make the purchase with another firm. This latter information must definitely be given if you are a manufacturer or wholesaler and are recommending a distributor or retailer who sells your own merchandise.

Following is a letter declining an order, which follows the negative communication pattern. The italicized items could be fill-ins for mail merge or form letters:

We appreciate your interest in purchasing a *Cherry Hill bookcase, Model 117C.*

However, as manufacturers, we do not trade directly with retail customers. You will be able to get this *bookcase* in one of the retail stores that carry *Cherry Hill furniture.*

We are enclosing a brochure that lists the names and locations of such dealers in your area.

If any store is out of stock, we have ample supplies in our warehouse. You could have the store order the *bookcase* and it could be in your home in four to six weeks.

Sincerely,

Enc.

Your Own Complaint

In your career or in your own personal transactions, you may find yourself on the "opposite end of the stick," having to make your own letter of complaint. Always remember that if you write at the height of displeasure or anger, what you write might be put in someone else's crackpot file. There might be that negative picture of you circulating—no one knows how far. You may experience great joy and relief in blowing off, but sooner or later your complaint could boomerang. The receiver may find a way to retaliate, and rather than complying, might respond spitefully.

Complain—to Whom?

Should you complain to a high official, or should you go through regular channels? An executive whose occupation is specializing in handling complaints suggests you first contact the head of the customer service department. That department has an established network for handling complaints. The suggestion is made that you should go to the top only when dissatisfied with service from the regular complaint people. In fact, going to the top first might only delay matters.

Then, if regular channels fail, take time to find the name of the top official of the organization, such as the president of the company or the chairman of the board. For your complaint, do not write to an office, like "Dear President" or "Dear Chairman of the Board," but honor that person by writing directly, using the full name. Over the phone or in person, your nearby reference librarian will get you the name and title of the chief executive officer along with the current address.

Buffer → Negative Message → Courteous Closing

Start your letter with a neutral statement with which your reader can agree, such as, "In the rush of business, we all know things can sometimes get out of hand." Or, "I am sure that you want to maintain the good reputation that your company has always enjoyed with its customers."

Then explain the negative, giving all the facts necessary to make your point, saying clearly what action you would like taken. If you remain cool and logical, your letter should not stir up heightened emotions in your reader. This should create a better chance of getting the complaint settled satisfactorily.

Next, the closing should be given with an optimistic attitude toward future relationships with statements like these:

> We believe that in fairness we can expect …
> If you continue to give us the same type of reliable service that we have learned to expect from your firm, we believe you will agree to [state clearly].

The Chinese have a proverb: "In the midst of great joy, do not promise to give a man anything; in the midst of great anger, do not answer a man's letter."

Figure 6.3 shows a sample complaint letter that can be used as for your personal or career business correspondence throughout the years ahead. Because your taxes have already paid for it, this letter can be copied verbatim with your own fill-ins. Keep copies of your letter and originals of all related documents and information.

Be certain you supply all the information suggested within the parentheses such as your complete address (people forget to do this and then complain that they did not get an answer), a complete description of the service or product including serial or model number. Describe the problem clearly; name the specific action you want taken; include *copies* of all pertinent records. *Do not send original records.*

FIGURE 6.3
Complaint letter example.[1]

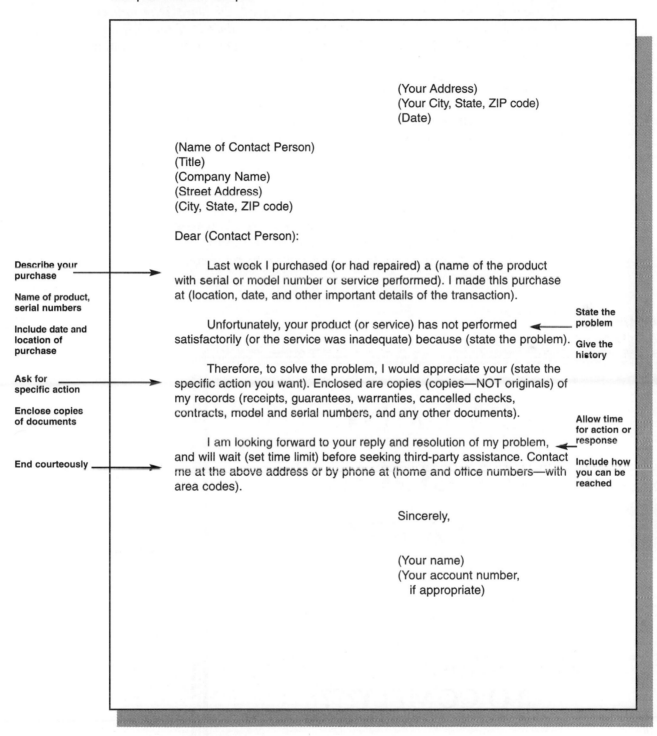

[1]Office of the Special Adviser to the President for Consumer Affairs, *Consumer's Resource Handbook* (The White House, Washington, DC, 1987), p. 3.

For a list of companies and their officers, check the company's Web page or the reference section of your college or public library for these sources: *Standard & Poor's Register of Corporations, Directors and Executives; Standard Directory of Advertisers; Thomas Register of American Manufacturers; Trade Names Directory.* Or a telephone call to the reference desk of your library will usually get you this information.

A Message with a "Bee Sting"

Never—repeat never—post a notice, write a postal or email memo, letter, report, or give any other message sending that tempting unwritten or unspoken snide remark or negative jab.

Figure 6.4 is an example of a message like this, which could be described as having a "bee sting." Such messages are borne of frustration that things or people are not working out the way they should. As mentioned in Chapter 3, be careful not to send unwritten negative messages "between the lines." You would be "talking down" to your reader(s), and, as stated earlier, instead of moving them to comply, the tone of your message might make them find a way to retaliate. As said, people do have some self respect.

FIGURE 6.4
A message with a "bee sting."

PLEASE
NO LOOSE
TRASH!

WHAT DOES IT TAKE TO
GET YOUR ATTENTION
TO COMPLY???

Answering—or Not Answering—the Crackpot

Almost every office—business, industry, government, profession—has what is sometimes called the "zero file," the file of letters from crackpots, whose correspondence usually can be easily identified. These are the unreasonable letters from irrational or angry people whose communications are hardly worthy of response. Some businesses do not even file these letters but discard them as soon as they are received. Other businesses or government offices, however, have a policy of answering all communications and, for this type of letter, will send off a perfunctory reply, discouraging continued correspondence, such as:

Thank you for your letter. We are taking the matter under advisement.

We have received your letter and are taking the proper action.

We believe that in fairness we can expect ...

If this sounds routine, it is meant to be. You do not wat to encourage further correspondence. Time is too valuable to be spent on unnecessary letter writing. A letter similar to this one would be appropriate in any instance in which your company simply desires to acknowledge receipt of a letter and end correspondence on the matter.

If a letter expresses contempt or attacks you or your company's reputation, never reply with a similar letter. Otherwise, you might leave yourself open to discipline on the job, or you might even be subject to court action for libel.

Some time ago, during a Panama Canal controversy, an aide to a United States senator did reply in an uncomplimentary manner to five or six letters that he felt were unnecessarily critical on the matter. For instance, to one resident of an eastern state, he wrote that her state was a "melting pot for neurotics, cranks, and other individuals with subnormal mentalities." Although mailed as personal letters at his own expense, his freedom of the mails cost him two months' pay.

Ask, don't command, and use positive terms such as "please," "we will appreciate," "we would like," and so forth.

The Negative Negative Message

Perhaps there is no need to give instructions on how to write the **negative** *negative* letter. You may never be justified in writing one. But at times, almost anyone might feel fully justified in "letting it all hang out," and might write a letter in which the good will tone is totally ignored. Such a letter should be sent only if the following two provisions hold:

1. Something constructive may come from it.
2. No illegal threats are made.

Chapter 3, "Qualities of an Effective Business Communication: Good Will Tone," cautions against writing postal or email letters in the heat of anger, pointing out that your anger might cool. Also, you might be embarrassed later because some people will remember you at your worst. Remember there is an old saying, "It is better to have the good will of a cur dog than its ill will." And again, you must think of the possibility that legal action might be taken against you if you say anything that might be interpreted as an illegal threat or defamation of character.

A strongly worded negative letter should be considered—we say considered—only when all other communication has failed. Then:

1. Cool off. Perhaps put writing off until tomorrow, or the next day, or next month.
2. If you must write, make the message clear and brief.
3. Explain steps you have taken that have been ignored.
4. Make the strongest *legal* threat that you can make to get compliance.
5. If you do not get satisfaction, follow through on step 4.

Or else FORGET IT!

The Bachelors and the Buffer

Two bachelors lived with their mother. One of the brothers had to leave town and gave the responsibility of caring for his cat to the other, Sam. A few nights later, the absent brother phoned and during the call asked how his cat was. "He died," said Sam.

"Wow!" was the response. "When you have news like that, Sam, you should lead into it gently."

"What do you mean?" his brother asked.

"Well, you might have said something like, 'Last night your cat was up on the roof ...' and then gone on to tell the news as less of a shock."

A couple of nights later, the traveling brother called home again. Upon hearing his voice, Sam said, "Well, last night Mother was up on the roof ... ."

Checklist for "No" Messages

1. Identify reader(s) and write at that level.
2. Is the appearance satisfactory?
3. Have you avoided offending the reader?
4. Is the message clear and complete? Check your list of items to be included.
5. Is there a buffer before the negative information?
6. Is the negative statement brief and clear?
7. Is the closing courteous, possibly looking toward the future?
8. Eliminate unnecessary words, phrases, clauses, sentences, paragraphs, and, for longer documents, pages.
9. Could any statement be interpreted as discourteous?
10. For variety in sentence form, see that some sentences start with descriptive words, phrases, or clauses.
11. Where possible, change negative words or statements to positive.

Chapter 6 The Negative Communication: The "No" Message

WRITING IMPROVEMENT EXERCISE
NEGATIVE → POSITIVE

Negative Why not visit our store?
Positive Come in and visit our store.

Negative You won't regret buying this Skill Saw.
Positive You'll be glad you bought this Skill Saw.

Negative We are sorry you are dissatisfied.
Positive We appreciate your frank comments.

In all business writing, we should assume PMA, positive mental attitude, especially when dealing with negative situations. There is the story that a pessimist says, "The glass is half empty," while the optimist says, "The glass is half full." Or you might say an optimist sees the roses; a pessimist feels the thorns.

This optimistic attitude should be conveyed in your business messages, whether they are prepared for people in your own office or for outsiders. Before a message is sent out, it should be checked for negative-sounding statements, and negatives should be dropped or rephrased positively.

It can be a challenge to make a potentially negative situation sound better. One woman, concerned about competing with younger job applicants, improved a potentially negative situation by stating, "My children are grown and I am free to re-enter the business world." Another woman, resuming her career after 25 years as a full-time homemaker, was asked, "What do you have to offer us?" Her convincing reply, "Maturity." A young girl applying for her first position successfully turned a potential negative to a positive. Instead of referring to her lack of experience, she wrote on her application, "I have no bad habits to unlearn."

Actually changing a few negative statements to positive ones can help make this feature of writing become almost automatic. It might even affect your personality favorably—"look on the bright side." Here are some tricks for changing negatives to positives. Of course, there are other acceptable changes than those given.

1. Change a negative statement to a positive statement:
    You will not be sorry if you purchase our Speedelectric shredder. →
    You may be the proud owner of a new Speedelectric shredder.

    Won't you please let us know? →
    Please let us know.

Why not mail a check? →
Please mail us a check.

The Senate failed to confirm three of the President's thirteen nominees.
→The Senate confirmed ten of the President's thirteen nominees.

2. To make a statement sound better, avoid saying what cannot be done and try saying what can be done. Emphasize the positive; deemphasize the negative.

We cannot give the discount rate on orders under $50. →
We can give the discount rate on orders over $50.

We cannot ship the order before the end of the month. →
We can ship your order by the first of next month.

Employee coffee breaks should not be longer than 15 minutes. →
Each employee may take a 15-minute coffee break twice a day.

3. Don't suggest a negative.

Do you mind if I use your phone? →
May I please use your phone?

I hope you are not too busy at this time to see me concerning a position with your firm. →
I will be available for an interview at your convenience.

Have you ever seen a worse report cover? →
Is this report cover OK?

Chapter 6   The Negative Communication:
The "No" Message

WRITING IMPROVEMENT "HANDS ON" ASSIGNMENT
NEGATIVE → POSITIVE

Change the following sentences to more positive statements. Of course, acceptable revisions may vary.

1. You did not specify whether you want 16- or 20-pound bond paper for your letter-head stationery. → Do you want 16- or 20-pound bond paper for your letterhead stationery?

2. I can type only 40 words a minute. → I can type 40 words per minute.

3. You will not regret buying our Office Hot Soup and Beverage Server. → You and your staff will enjoy using your own Hot Soup and Beverage Server.

4. Half the people present voted against your proposal. → Half the people present voted for your proposal.

5. We have a large backlog of orders and will fill yours as soon as your number comes up on our list. → Because ------- is a popular item, we have a large backup of orders, which will be shipped in the order we received them.

6. You will not qualify for our discount rate until your orders exceed $200 a month. → When your orders exceed $200 a month, you will qualify for our discount rate.

7. I cannot complete this work while this meeting is in session. → As soon as this meeting ends, I can complete this work.

8. We cannot print the report until all the revisions are received. → As soon as all revisions are received, we can print the report.

9. Why don't you bank trainees set up a workable break schedule? → Could you please set up a good break schedule?

10. Our warranty on computer parts covers only 90 days. → Our warranty on computer parts covers 90 days.

Chapter 6 The Negative Communication: The "No" Message

WRITING ASSIGNMENTS

1. You were chairman of the program for the Illinois City Managers' Association, which had its last meeting on March 13 and 14, 20XX, in the Krayton Hotel, 2108 Washington Boulevard, Detroit, MI 48231. Write to the manager of the hotel, Robert Hinshaw, telling him that you were dissatisfied with the meeting room accommodations because the public address system did not work satisfactorily and the room temperature could not be adjusted to the comfort of those in the meetings. You would like to know what assurance you can have that these matters will not recur at other meetings that you would like to hold at the Krayton. Start with something pleasant.

2. An irate customer has returned some carved mahogany bookends for refund, claiming that they were damaged when she received them. There is a deep scratch on the surface of one of the bookends. Since your store deals only in items of high value, you personally check every item carefully before having it wrapped for mailing. Compose an email stating that you cannot accept the returned merchandise and suggest that the customer have the bookends refinished professionally.

3. A recent fire has damaged your warehouse in Buena Park, California. Temporarily, shipments to the West Coast will have to be sent from the Phoenix, Arizona, warehouse. Compose a letter that can be sent to regular customers telling them why shipments might be delayed. Make up the name and address of an imaginary client and prepare a copy to him or her.

4. John Palladine, president of the El Camino College Business Club at El Camino College, 16007 South Crenshaw Boulevard, Los Angeles, CA 90506, has asked you to speak at the next meeting of the business club at the college at noon, October 30, 20XX. Write a letter refusing this request. Remember that you are interested in the group because you were president of the club when you were on campus.

5. A mail order customer has returned a pair of shoes and asked for a refund, saying the shoes are the wrong size. The shoes show evidence of use; the heels are worn and one toe is scuffed. *Refuse this request* and return the shoes, but try to retain the customer's good will.

6. It is the policy of your business to answer all letters, regardless of their tone and content. You have received a complaint from some possibly irrational person whose letter started, "What's wrong with you people, anyway?" and proceeded in a similar manner. Claiming that an order of a dozen "supposedly fresh roses" remained fresh only two days, the customer asks to have his $55 for the purchase returned. Write a refusal.

7. As Supervisor of the Mail Order Department, you have received another incomplete order from O. D. Trubble, Purchasing Agent of J. C. Nichols Company. This time he did not indicate the specific catalogue number of the computer paper he ordered. Write an email asking for this information, saying that with an immediate reply you can send the order out within 24 hours. You want to keep Mr. Trubble as a customer.

8. As manager of Panorama Towers, it is your duty to remind tenants that each must use only the parking space assigned to him or her, and that the front area is for 20-minute convenience parking only, as is marked on the curb. Write the form letter that will be placed at the door of all residents. Thank them for their cooperation while the parking lot was being constructed, and close with some pleasant comment about future operations or tenancy in the condominiums.

Chapter 6 The Negative Communication:
The "No" Message

REVIEW AND DISCUSSION

Make answers to these exercises as brief as possible. If given a choice, draw a line through any incorrect answer.

1. Why should we try to have a positive attitude when writing negative letters? _____
   We should try to make the negative as acceptable as possible.
   _____

2. Make an outline for a negative letter or make a drawing of a "praise sandwich," identifying what should be in the opening, middle, and closing.

3. How is the first part of the negative message, the buffer, used? To cushion a blow—
   the coming negative.
   _____

4. How should the negative letter close? On an upbeat note, if at all possible, saying
   something positive about the future.
   _____

5. "Ordinarily, a negative business message should be filled with negative words and
   phrases." Why or why not? No. Make it as pleasant as possible. Avoid negatives.
   _____

6. *Caveat emptor* means: Let the buyer beware./Let the seller beware.

7. Give two words or phrases not listed in the book that have negative connotations to
   you.
   a. [Student input.] _____
   b. _____

8. Can humor be used effectively in negative communications? Why? <u>Sometimes.</u>
   <u>Acceptable humor can relieve a tense situation.</u>

9. What is candor and what is the advantage of using it in your own negative situations?
   <u>Being honest under undesirable situations. Gains respect.</u>

10. Why is "company policy" a poor explanation of the reason behind a "no" message?
    <u>Public usually does not accept reasons behind policy and doesn't care.</u>

11. Describe how a merge letter is produced. <u>Having one form with general message</u>
    <u>into which different specifics can be merged from another form.</u>

12. What is "plain talk"? <u>Clear talk—short words, sentences, applied to speaking</u>
    <u>and writing.</u>

13. Give an example of circumstances where a letter might be written to forestall complaints? <u>When you know of a negative situation developing and can inform</u>
    <u>people who will be affected.</u>

14. For your own complaint letter, authorities suggest you first (try regular complaint channels/~~contact the head of the company~~).

Rewrite the following sentences in acceptable positive terms.

15. Why don't you pay attention when your supervisor is making work assignments?
    <u>Work assignments the supervisor is making are important. We should listen.</u>

16. From page 130 showing a "message with a bee sting," write here a brief courteous statement to replace the "bee sting." _____

    LET'S BE GOOD NEIGHBORS. To Keep Trash From Flying LET'S TIE IT IN BAGS.

_____

7 Sales Letters and Persuasive Claims and Requests

> *Some see private enterprise as a predatory target to be shot;*
> *others as a cow to be milked, but few are those who see it as a*
> *sturdy horse pulling the wagon.*
> Winston Churchill (1874–1965)
> British politician and writer,
> Prime minister 1940–1945 and 1951–1955

Writing sales letters is a talent that can be used in many ways. The sales letter pattern, widely used for selling goods and services can also be used for making persuasive requests and claims. This means that the sales letter formula can be used to persuade others to grant a request or claim you have made that was or might be disputed.

The employment application letter is a special type of sales letter wherein the product you are selling is yourself. These presentations are covered in Chapter 13 on employment communications. And on the job, your success could often depend on your being able to "sell" an idea.

Direct Mail Advertising

Writing sales letters is a form of **direct mail advertising.** Direct mail can be inexpensive compared to costs of most other types of advertising. Through sales letters, a firm, large or small, can reach select audiences chosen for the best expected return for the advertising dollar. Why is direct mail used so widely? *Because it sells.*

A more recent form of direct mail advertising is the use of unsolicited email, more commonly known as "spam," which is considered very undesirable by many internet users.

Writing Sales Letters as a Career

Being able to write effective sales letters can help in different types of careers. Direct mail advertising is usually the first kind of advertising done by any small business. Then later, perhaps when the firm is operating on a much larger financial scale, some forms of direct mail advertising will continue to be used. Because of this, there is a great need for people who are able to write sales letters for their own firms, or for another small or larger company.

Another way in which proficiency in writing sales letters might benefit a person is in a personally owned **mail order business.** Of course, considerable study must be made before launching such a career. Information concerning opportunities for employment in direct mail advertising, as well as information concerning the starting of one's own mail order business, can be obtained through writing the Direct Mail Advertising Association at 11 West 42nd Street, New York, NY 10036-8096, phone (800) 967-2637.

Because of their inherent advantages, properly planned sales letters can bring in a large return for the investment. A mailing is selective; that is, it can be prepared for one person or for a special segment of the market. Therefore, it can be very specific in its message.

By postal mail or email, sales letters have three general functions:

1. **Getting sales leads:** Following up requests for more information, such as brochures or samples, or asking for a call by a sales representative

2. **Bringing people into your place of business:** Introducing a new product or service; inviting people to special demonstrations, exhibits, or even parties

3. **Selling by mail** (mail order selling): Actually completing the entire process of advertising, selling, and ordering through the mail

The codfish lays ten thousand eggs,
The homely hen lays one.
The codfish never cackles
To tell you when she's done.
And so we scorn the codfish
While the humble hen we prize.
Which only goes to show you
That it pays to advertise.

Old rhyme

4. **Selling via the internet:** Using internet email and websites has become a powerful method of marketing. Whereas web pages cannot be delivered directly to consumers, email messages can be, and are often used to entice consumers to go to an online commerce website.

Selling in Today's Market

No one needs to be told that changes in today's business scene far outpace those in previous eras. Today, few factors in business remain constant, due to newly discovered needs, new methods for meeting old and new needs, and constant competition.

Currently, the internet has brought about a myriad of changes in numerous phases of our lives, and **advertising** by the internet fits into the picture. Internet advertising not only tries to catch up, but aims to lead in promoting goods and services.

Advertising

Advertising is essential to the free enterprise system, helping keep businesses competitive. As the worldwide market grows and changes, advertising helps raise the standard of living, making people aware of newly available products and services. They are also informed of improvements in older products and the obsolescence of others.

For instance, just think of the improvements made in a very short time in such common items as cellular phones and personal computers. Without advertising to inform people of the improved miniaturization, increased functions, and decreases in cost of these items, most people would not be aware of these features. When Maytag and others began advertising their wonderful electric wringer washing machines, our grandmothers and great-grandmothers threw away their washboards.

Although it is arguable that the Apple iMac computer was not necessarily better than most competing low-cost computers when it came out, the marketing concept, innovative design, and creative promotion strategy made it by far the fastest selling computer at the time. English teachers might shudder with their slogan, "Think different," but consumers responded to the tactics.

The market will always have a place for people who are sales professionals who sell products and services face to face or over the phone. But well written sales letters, widely used and effective, are becoming increasingly important.

"She's Your Wife"

David Ogilvy, New York advertising genius of the 1950s, said, "The consumer's not a moron. She's your wife. Try not to insult her intelligence."[1]

Successful Sales Letters: Product or Service, Prospect, Price

As with any other method of advertising, success with sales letters comes from identifying a **product** or **service** that appeals to a particular number of sales **prospects** at a suitable **price.** Many products are sold and promoted by postal and email letters, cards, and so forth. Also, many services—such as printing, telephone and power services, website and graphic design, product repair, and countless others—are also sold and promoted similarly.

When the correct marketing mix of product or service, prospect, and price exists, the expense of preparing and distributing sales materials is justified.

Product or Service

The first step in planning a sales letter is to study the product or service to be marketed. In order to do this, the person planning it should try as much as possible to become personally familiar with the item under consideration. If you are selling books, you should read them—or parts of them; if you are selling food, you should eat it; wearing apparel, wear it; laundry service, use it. If it is a product that you cannot test yourself, such as children's shoes or dog food, test it as much as possible on other suitable subjects.

[1]"People in the News," *U.S. News and World Report*, August 2, 1999, p. 10.

When you live with the item you are trying to sell, you may discover facets for promotion that even the manufacturer does not know. Further, you should discover that certain elements can be emphasized and others slighted. When possible, you should also study or use competing products and services. This way you can fully experience the advantages and disadvantages of yours compared to theirs.

The more thorough your knowledge of a product or service, the better equipped you are to write or talk about it. Another important matter to consider is timing. For example, normally you would not try to sell snow tires in summer.

The chief question to answer is, "Will the people buy it?" People will buy it if they are satisfied they will benefit from its use and if the price is right.

The Sales Prospect

The Target Market

Once it has been determined that a product or service is worthy of promotion, you should identify the **target market**, the prospects to whom the sales letter should be sent. Although the general public may believe that sales letter prospect lists are taken at random from the telephone book, in most instances this would be too expensive. Mailings of sales letters, particularly as postage rates increase, are generally sent to a special segment of the market. To minimize costs in large mailings, it is helpful to identify the expected "heavy users"—that is, the segment of the market that would be the main purchasers—and mail letters only to them.

Long ago, test mailings proved there is a considerably higher rate of return answers if letters are addressed to individuals by name. Therefore, consider obtaining a mailing prospect list so that specific names and addresses can be used.

When specific names and addresses are not used, and sales letters are sent "blind"—that is, to **"Occupant"** or **"Resident"**—an effort can be made to individualize the letter so that it appears to be addressed to a specific person. One device that is used for giving the appearance of being individually addressed is the simulated inside address. This impression is created by writing some introductory words or phrases in the position of the inside address of the letter and following it with an appropriate salutation. An example of this device is:

To you
If you are owned
By a cat
Dear Cat Lover:

Sales Mailing Lists

The best **mailing list** of prospects is often the easiest to obtain. It is the list of the firm's current and past customers. However, you may get other good lists of prospects chosen for occupation, area of residence, income, family size and age of family members, hobby and recreation interests, or other characteristics. Some of these lists are free, and others, such as lists of book club members, magazine subscribers or regular mail order buyers, must be purchased.

We should know there is a lively market for exchanging customer lists among firms selling competing products and services.

Following are some good sources for mailing lists:

Telephone company	Telephone companies sell frequently revised lists of names by city, street, and ZIP code.
Membership lists	Officers of churches, service clubs, or social, professional, or business organizations will often supply you with current lists of members.
Credit rating books	Standard & Poor's, Dun & Bradstreet, and other widely used reference sources are of value in building a worthwhile list of names by income.
Directories	Where available, the city directory is useful in selecting prospects by occupation, home ownership, and size of family. Trade and professional directories provide worthwhile prospects, including top executives of local companies.
Public records	Generally, public records may be examined without cost, and they are extremely accurate sources for names. They include tax lists, license and permit records, property valuations, and street lists, when available.
Local newspapers	These contain news of births, promotions, transfers, business and other activities that could add potential customers to your mailing list.
List brokers	If you want to get started right away on some special promotional activity, you can get lists from a broker—who is a specialist in compiling mailing lists of general and specific markets.[1]

Internet Advertising Companies

A number of internet-savvy organizations are developing vast lists of potential customers using web and email technology. Cooperative arrangements between companies allow use of a common pool of registered email addresses for different marketing ventures.

Finding a Target Market

A study should be conducted to determine the target market for a mailing list for any specific product or service. The following factors should determine the mailings for your sales promotion:

☐ Where do potential buyers live?

☐ What is their buying power?

☐ Under what conditions can they use your product or service?

☐ Do general conditions in the target area favor your promotion? For example, economic conditions; climate, season, or region for types of clothing, sports equipment; and acceptance of this type of product from other producers.

Computerized Sales Mailing Lists

Most of the preceding mailing lists are available electronically on CD-ROM, email, or via internet download. These lists give you the opportunity to send out large numbers of sales letters addressed to specific individuals.

For example, suppose you were selling a new training program in the Atlanta area and you wanted to send personalized sales letters to local training directors. To find your target market you might start by contacting a local professional association for trainers (such as the American Society for Training and Development) or a magazine that reaches training directors (such as *Training* magazine). Such organizations and publications will often rent you their mailing lists or the parts of it that are in the ZIP codes of the Atlanta area.

Use of selective **computerized lists** of names and addresses puts your mail directly in the hands of **heavy users**, people who most likely have an interest in your project. It also helps get your mail out of the possible **junk** category of "Occupant" or "Resident" mailings, which often aren't even opened.

Test Mailings of Sales Letters

Various formats of essentially the same sales letter are used for **test mailings** to learn which format brings in the best reader response. Detailed records are kept of the comparative responses to each format. This information is obtained by changing the return coupon or order form in some detail, such as having it addressed to a different department number or a different box number. Sometimes an identifying number or symbol is printed in small type in a corner of the mailing piece that is returned by the reader.

When it is determined which format brought the best reader response, then copies are made of this best-selling letter and sent to target markets, sometimes nationwide. If other formats of the letter receive an acceptable return from the sample of readers, these formats are often filed for future use in another mailing to an appropriate large customer list.

Usually, the parts of the letter that are tested most are the attention-getters—the envelope, possible enclosures, and the first part of the letter itself. The success of the entire letter depends on getting the receiver to read it and not cast it aside.

It is advisable to pretest results of different formats for even a small mailing.

The Price

Once a product or service has been identified and a prospect list for sending out a sales letter has been selected, the mailing should be prepared only after a **price** for the commodity is set within which the operation can expect to show a satisfactory margin of profit. The cost of the mailing itself is determined by simple mail order arithmetic. If a mailing costs $1,000 and it results in 200 orders, the cost per order is $5. This figure is justified only when the total profit per sale is a sufficient margin over the $5 cost per order.

Frequently, a firm makes a test mailing, or several test mailings, before committing itself to an expensive mailing campaign. "Expensive," of course, is a relative term. For a person beginning a small business, $300 for the preparation and mailing of a first sales letter may be a considerable expense. For a larger business, the term is equated with much larger figures.

The Purpose of the Sales Letter

Sales letters must be written with the knowledge that they are in stiff competition with the wastebasket. This type of mail is often identified by the unflattering term **junk mail**—once you have successfully done business by direct mail, you will hesitate to think of it as junk.

An independent research firm conducted a survey that revealed the following:

- ☐ Three out of four people open and read thoroughly, or at least glance at, advertising and sales letters.
- ☐ Three out of four open and read thoroughly, or glance at, catalogues.
- ☐ Three out of four use samples received.
- ☐ One out of two usually use coupons.

The Advertising Style Spiral

Figure 7.1 is a drawing of an original advertising style spiral. The *new style* in advertising at first is an **innovation;** if effective, it invites **imitation;** if very effective, it can become a standard style of advertising and moves into the area of **competition,** where most advertising styles remain the longest. Then, if overused, the once innovative style enters a stage of **saturation,** where it tends to repel the buying public. At this point, the market is ready for a different innovation, which marketing tries to discover or invent, and the advertising style spiral starts again. It can be read-

FIGURE 7.1
The advertising style spiral, showing a new style going through the stages of innovation, imitation, competition, and saturation, with another new style starting around the spiral as a different innovation.

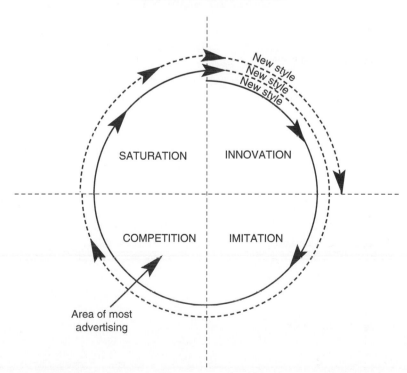

THE ADVERTISING SPIRAL

ily observed that different styles proceed around the advertising spiral at differing rates of speed.

The length of life of any advertising style can be unending, or it can stop at any stage of the spiral. An innovative style was used by the politician who sent voters in her district a mailing with her advertising slogan on an enclosed kitchen potholder. When her opponent copied this idea, the ad was in the imitation stage. However, partly because of the cost of large mailings, this style did not proceed into common usage, or the competition area of the cycle, and of course went no further.

At one time, the style of placing special designs and advertising gimmicks on sales letter envelopes was an innovation; but students of advertising did not recognize them as attention-getters. Now advertising on envelopes has progressed from innovation through imitation, and into competition. We might think envelope attention-getters entered a saturation stage, because they are becoming so common. However, test mailings will undoubtedly reveal whether enough readers respond to the message inside. Today we might predict that these designs will undoubtedly continue to be used as attention-getters—especially if something "FREE" is offered.

In writing sales letters, we should seek effective innovative sales letter styles, avoiding, if possible, styles that have been used a great deal, particularly those that might be considered to be in the saturation stage of the advertising spiral.

The Sales Letter Pattern

Figure 7.2 is a diagram of the traditional AIDA selling letter pattern. The star at top is for getting **A**ttention; the central circles are for the buildup of **I**nterest and **D**e-

FIGURE 7.2
Diagram of a sales letter, sometimes called
the AIDA selling letter pattern.

Sales Letter Pattern

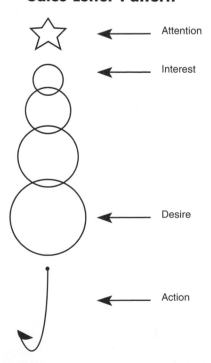

Attention

Interest

Desire

Action

sire; and the hook indicates the reader is to be hooked or "grabbed" and moved to Action.

The entire letter should be written in the "you attitude," emphasizing reasons the reader would be interested in the item you are selling and the item's benefits. The Writing Improvement Assignment at the end of this chapter is on changing the "we attitude" to the "you attitude."

The position of information in a selling letter generally determines whether that information is being used to attract **attention,** create **interest** and/or **desire,** or move the reader to **action.**

The first part of the letter must get the reader's attention, or the rest of the letter will probably not be read. (As noted, attention-getters frequently begin even on the envelope.) The middle section of the letter is long or short, depending on what is being promoted or sold, how it is being promoted, and for whom it is intended. The last part of the letter is probably what the reader will remember best. This section should, in as few words as possible, move the reader to specific action, giving all the details necessary for that action.

Since the advent of email, the difference between letters and memos has blurred.

Some time ago the "Simplified Style" for letters gained a large following. In this style the subject line is used but the salutation and complimentary closing are omitted. This same style arose anew in email. So now we have postal mail letters and memos and also email letters and memos. In most offices, email has become the preferred "message of the day."

Today "You've got mail!" usually means email. But it surely can mean postal mail delivered by the U.S. Postal Service.

But there will always be a place for letters, formal and informal. Daily, hourly or by the minute, decisions are made as to which to use.

"Occupant" or "Resident"—No!

It seems that the world probably could not revolve without a certain percentage of "Occupant" or "Resident" mailings.

However, their numbers are being reduced because computers simplify the process of inserting individual names and addresses economically. Using one of these systems helps personalize the mail and can help stop the reader from giving your letter a quick brush-off.

By all means, individually prepared letters should use the name of the receiver both in the address lines and in the "salute," the salutation. Also, you might use the name within the message, making it even more personalized.

Mistakes in Multiple Mailings

Check carefully for spelling and number errors when using the merge letter format or any other form letter in which different names and addresses are inserted into different copies of the same letter (as shown in Chapter 6). Otherwise, your efforts to please your readers by personalizing the mail can go awry and offend. Author Don Mc-Cormick, while a graduate student in organizational behavior, received a letter addressed to "Professor Cevmuick, Dept. of Original Behavior." An editor with Prentice Hall named "Rymer" often gets letters addressed "Rhymes." (Pretty appropriate!) A city manager named Tom Orr received a letter properly addressed to him, but the letter started: "Dear Mr. City."

While such mistakes may get a few laughs around the office, they probably won't generate a desire for the receiver to accommodate the lazy, careless or cheap sender.

Use These Annoying E-Mail Ploys If You Want to Destroy Customer Good Will

Like many overloaded recipients of junk E-mail, I've learned to automatically hit the delete button upon spotting "amazing opportunity" of six dollar signs in a row in the subject line of a message—sure signs of a "spam scam." The mailers have now retaliated with an amazing range of annoying ploys to trick me into reading their messages. I've gotten E-mails with subject lines that read, "Re: Your Marketing Question." "Here's the Information You Requested!" and "Returned Mail: Cannot Send Message." Of course, the latter message I immediately opened, thinking it was the note I had just sent out. It wasn't. It was a message touting another get-rich-quick report. The most irritating trick had to be the message with the subject line: "Are you still going tonight?"

The legitimate small businesses that are trying out E-mail marketing for the most part don't seem to realize how many computer users vehemently dislike unsolicited E-mails.[2]

First Section: The Attention-Getter

The first element, the **attention-getter,** must:

☐ tie into the product or service or idea that the letter is promoting, and
☐ bring the reader into the picture.

Usually, the big questions in the mind of the person reading the sales letter are, "What is the purpose of this message" and "What's in it for me?" If the attention-getters do not directly lead into the subject of the letter, the reader's attitude is apt to be "So what!" And the letter is tossed. If an otherwise good attention-getter is used, such as a funny story or an eye-catching illustration, but it has no relation to the selling matter, you've probably lost the reader's attention.

To catch attention and get the reader involved, traditional rules of business letter appearance are sometimes badly bent or even broken. A firm that employs a conservative, traditional letterhead for standard mailings might use a variety of striking designs, such as bright colors, oversized print, and vivid illustrations. Results are far different from the appearance recommended for standard business correspondence, but they frequently serve their purpose.

[2]Margaret Mannix, "Spamfest: Junk Mail Invasion at the Speed of Light," *U.S. News and World Report,* December 8, 1997, p. 48.

Attention-Getters on Envelopes

It has become a common practice to have attention-getters on the outside of the selling letter envelope in the form of printing, illustration, or splashes of color. This attack is most successful when it follows the precepts of tying into the matter being promoted and involving the reader. Listed here are some attention-getters used on envelopes as slogans, questions, or leading statements:

$100,000 CASH OR ONE OF 8,835 PRIZES!

PRIVILEGED INFORMATION!

Test ride this motorcycle today!

This may be your last chance!

Join your neighbors in an evening of fun and education.

Latest reports on next year's cars.

Enclosed: Flight Ticket, Round Trip. Two Persons.

Please RSVP. Pencil enclosed.

Attention-Getters on Websites

Website attention-getters such as animated graphics, audio sound bytes and "screaming" quickly became standard fare for getting the eyeballs of Internet web users. Web page banner ads, which had a very rapid rise in "click-through" rates (the number of people to click on the banner in order to find out more about the product of service), eventually fell in effectiveness. Market saturation? New techniques are being developed to keep users' interest, such as offering free recipes linked from online grocery ads. These and other ideas are attempts to make a website more "sticky" so that the user will stay and not click off to another website immediately.

Attention-Getters in Letters

Because the first paragraph will usually determine whether the rest of the letter will be read, this is the most important part of the letter. Here you must hold the reader's attention.

There are many emotional or rational appeals that can be used to gain attention. However, care should be taken to avoid gimmicks that have been used so much that they are in the saturation stage of the advertising spiral.

Here are some good examples of attention-getters:

Offer of a gift:

The card in the window of this letter will bring you the Handy Tool Set illustrated above. Please accept this with our compliments.

Flattery:

If the list on which I found your name is any indication, this is not the first—nor will it be the last—subscription letter you receive. Quite frankly, your education and income set you apart from the general population and make you a highly rated prospect for everything from magazines to mutual funds.

His or her better self:

As you know, the asthmatic children of Sahuaro School are boys and girls of every race, color, and religion, who came to the school because they couldn't gasp enough air into their frightened lungs to say even the first syllable of the most important word they know, "Mother."

Bargain:

Give me your permission and I will send you a His 'N' Her Car Coat ensemble in the popular *new* "crushed Buckskin" leather-look for the unbelievable price of only $69.95!

Special interests:

Do you love fishing, boating, water skiing, swimming? And have you found your favorite public beaches and waterways getting impossibly crowded and more hectic each year?

The overworked word "free" is still the most powerful word in the attention-getter lexicon. Of the three ways to say the same thing—"50 percent off," "half price," or "buy one, get one free," tests show that "buy one, get one free" draws a 40-percent higher response than the other two.

Another method of getting the reader's attention early in the letter, as mentioned previously, is to avoid "Occupant" or "Resident" in the address and use the reader's name not only in the inside address but also early in the body of the letter, and at appropriate points in the letter. It is said that to the average person, the sweetest sound in the world is the sound of his or her own name.

Frequently, **enclosures** are also used to gain attention. Or, because they often give information about the product or are actual examples of the product, such as a swatch of fabric or paint, enclosures might be considered part of the buildup of *interest* and *desire,* which is continued in the middle section of the letter. "Hands on" experience with something being sold is very compelling.

The Middle Section: Interest and Desire Buildup

The buildup of both the reader's **interest** in a product or service and the **desire** to own or use it follows the introductory section. This is also the section of a persuasive request where you try to build up the reader's interest by presenting appeals to convince the reader to agree to your request. You should include all the details you decide should be used, and follow a good plan. Superfluous details must be omitted, but all necessary information should be included.

Identifying Appeals That Attract Prospects

In general, people respond to two basic types of **appeals:** emotional and rational. For your letter to be successful, study the positive emotional and rational appeals that you can tie in with your product or service.

Emotional appeals involve our basic senses of feeling, seeing, tasting, smelling, and hearing. Some strong emotional drives appeal to our feelings of love and friendship, pride, fear, pleasure, safety, and appearance.

Rational appeals include such matters as making money, saving money, getting more for the dollar spent, maintaining a respectable position among family and friends, doing a good job, saving time and energy, protecting the environment, and getting greater use out of a product.

There are many other emotional and rational appeals. Study your product or service, or the project or favor you are requesting, and determine the best appeals for specific prospects.

- ☐ Promise money, a bonus, gift, or prize.
- ☐ Promise personal safety or property safety.
- ☐ Promise economy—a bargain.
- ☐ Flatter the reader—appeal to pride.
- ☐ Promise their children a better world.
- ☐ Appeal to a special interest: occupation, community service, hobbies, home improvement, etc.
- ☐ Appeal to a person's better self—charities, community service, civic responsibility, environment concerns.
- ☐ Appeal to the sense of humor—use an appropriate story or cartoon.

Different People React Differently to Same Appeals

We must recognize that all people do not view the same object in the same way. Figure 7.3 shows possible differing perspectives that family members might have toward the new family car. Whatever the merchandise, we must try an appropriate appeal for specific prospective buyers.

The Short or Long of It

Some believe that all selling letters should be short, since readers will not spend a great deal of time reading them. But a study of sales letters will show that long letters, as much as three or four pages, are frequently sent to get the interest of new subscribers to some of our major magazines, potential subscribers to book clubs, purchasers of technical and professional materials, investors in various plans, and so forth. We must acknowledge that a great deal of research must be done before preparing and sending these letters.

But if the material can be explained briefly, a short letter is preferred by almost all readers, and it is recommended that most selling letters should be short—no longer than one page.

Figure 7.3
The new family car.

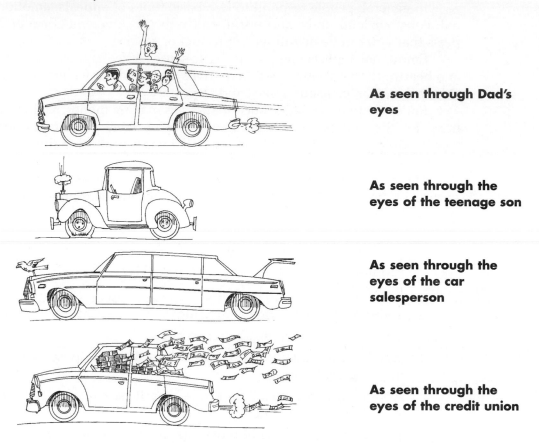

As seen through Dad's eyes

As seen through the eyes of the teenage son

As seen through the eyes of the car salesperson

As seen through the eyes of the credit union

Following is the middle section of a letter offering a complimentary tool set as an attention-getter with the hope of building interest and desire in purchasing insurance:

> With this practical gift you will also receive details about another fine tool—one that will help you *measure* and *build* your entire family's security. The John Bancock Family Plan makes it simple and sure with a plan tailor-made to fit *your* family's needs.
>
> The plan includes Father, Mother, and *all* children under age 18. You'll see how its flexibility adapts to any expansion in your immediate family circle, at *no* extra cost.
>
> Future children will be included when 15 days old—fully protected until the 25th birthday.
>
> This worthwhile protection *really* grows with your family, *every step of the way* ... provides guaranteed security for your loved ones—and builds for your own future at the same time!

Here are the selling parts of a letter planned to build interest in and desire for enrollment in a data-processing course:

In 10 workshop days you'll learn how to plan a logical systems study... how to review a system ... how to conduct a survey and make recommendations to management ... you'll gain an understanding of what management wants out of systems. You'll leave the workshop ready to perform with minimum help as a systems analyst.

Fast Start shaves months of trial and error into 10 intense days! It has won national acclaim as the fastest way to get a person productive in systems work.

After the introductory paragraph, a letter promoting resort property reads:

Can you remember the way it was 14,000,000 people ago? And do you know when that was?

Can you remember Lido Isle when the only building you could see from the sand dunes was the Lido Isle Recreation Building?

Consider today's waterfront lot prices: out of this world in many areas—but not at Canyon Lake.

What we have to offer now is the opening of the very best section of WATERFRONT lots at Canyon Lake—only about 150 in all. Excellent long-term financing available.

How would you like owning a choice waterfront lot here for summer swimming, fishing, boating, water skiing—maybe building later for retirement?

The Closing Section: The Action "Hook"

The closing section of the sales letter, the **action hook** shown in Figure 7.2, is diagrammed as a hook to indicate that it must "grab" the reader and move that person to action.

The hook should be specific, as illustrated by this story:

Once a businessman paid a writing consultant a high fee to edit a letter he had written to his Senator asking for help with a problem that he obviously considered important. The final paragraph of the letter read, "Could you please do something about this?"

The consultant left the bulk of the letter almost as it had been prepared, but said to the man, "You realize, of course, that the Senator has many different matters on his mind, and it will take time for him or his aide to study your letter—if they are able to give it much time at all. Why not say specifically what you would like the Senator to do?" After a short discussion, a clear closing paragraph was composed, explaining the action the writer wanted. Within a short time the Senator replied, saying he had contacted a certain government agency, which sent very helpful assistance.

The price of the item being promoted is often mentioned in the last paragraph. It is generally wise to make the price sound reasonable except for certain prestige items. You would not try to sell a Porsche by its "low price."

In other instances, one device is to bring the dollar amount down in a manner similar to this: Instead of saying "six dollars a month," say, "only twenty cents a day."

As far as possible, the closing hook of the letter should do five things. It should:

1. Tell the reader specifically what to do.
2. Say how to do it.
3. Make it easy, or make it sound easy—the word *just* is often used effectively.
4. Make the price sound right—perhaps use the word *only*.
5. Urge the reader to do it soon (before it is forgotten); sometimes a deadline is given.

The hook is the final part of the letter except for possible postscripts. This closing should be brief, preferably one sentence or a short paragraph that fulfills all five specifications.

To make ordering easy, you can attach or enclose self-addressed coupons or prepaid postcards or envelopes. Above all, as in the letter to the Senator, state the specific action desired.

Following are some letter endings that can serve as good examples of the sales hook. To show how frequently and effectively they are used, the words *you* and *your* have been printed here in italics.

☐ To be sure of receiving *your* Permanent Press Flannel Slacks while the supply lasts, just mail *your* free trial order form TODAY.

☐ We'll be looking for *your* card in the mail. Please mail it today. Postage has already been paid. Thank *you*.

☐ An order form is enclosed, along with a postage-paid return envelope. Do initial and return the order form today. We'll be looking for *you* to enjoy refreshments and pick up *your* free gift.

☐ But PLEASE be sure to bring this letter. Present it to the guard at our entry gate. It will identify *you*. Note directions and map on back of enclosure. We're looking forward to seeing *you!*

☐ To order, simply remove the Half-Price Savings Certificate near the back of this book and drop it in the mail. *Your* name and address are already on it, postage is paid, and *you* needn't send any money now—we'll bill *you* after *you've* received *your* first issue of *Apartment Ideas*.

Figure 7.4 is a good example of a short letter that would be considered very satisfactory for the product being sold, a gas climate control system. This letter could be sent to all gas customers of the firm. Note the perforations that permit a tear-off return card at the end of the letter, making replying easy.

Signatures

One of the proven principles of direct mail is that a letter that looks more personal receives a better response than one that is obviously totally mechanically or electronically printed. A letter asking you to purchase the latest version of Windows can be more persuasive if it appears "signed" by Bill Gates.

Postscript

Also, don't forget to add a postscript to your letter. After an attention-getter, the P.S. (or PS) is usually the number two spot that people read as being potentially interesting. It is a good place to light-heartedly restate some product salient benefits for the customer. Or an appropriate comment about some other business or personal matter could be welcome.

Forms for Letters

There is a wide choice of letter forms that can be used for the sales letter, from a postal card to a multipage production. Figure 7.5 shows the most common forms of mailings: (A) single mailing card; (B) one-fold mailer; (C) two-fold (3-section) mailing card or letter; (D) two-fold (4-section); (E) French fold; (F) four-page letter; (G) broadside.

FIGURE 7.4
Selling letter with perforated reply card
attached.

Dear Customer:

YEAR ROUND CLIMATE CONTROL is now available for your home.

Fresh, circulating air keeps your whole house warm in the winter and cool in the summer. (We know we don't have to tell you the advantages of being cool when it's hot. Remember last summer?)

Your CLIMATE CONTROL package will also include special low gas rates during the summer months for gas used for air conditioning. And as you know, gas air conditioning is more dependable and lasts longer because it has fewer moving parts.

Right now, and during the next few months, installers are not as busy and can provide
you with fast, dependable service. So think ahead and let us help you begin planning
your own YEAR ROUND CLIMATE CONTROL now. You'll be glad you planned for summer this winter.

For complete information, return the tear-off portion below with your gas bill.

Please tell me more about CLIMATE CONTROL for my home.
I understand this does not obligate me in any way.

Name _____
Address _____
_____
City _____ ZIP code _____
_____ A.M.
Telephone _____ Best time to call_____ P.M.

FIGURE 7.5
Card and letter forms that can be used for sales letters.
[Courtesy: Direct Mail Advertising Association, Inc.]

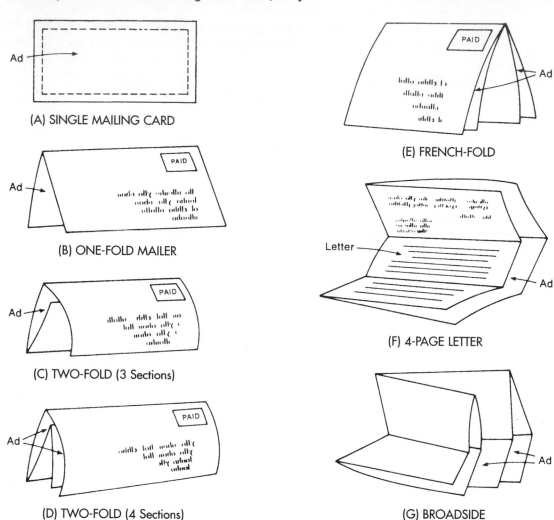

(A) SINGLE MAILING CARD

(B) ONE-FOLD MAILER

(C) TWO-FOLD (3 Sections)

(D) TWO-FOLD (4 Sections)

(E) FRENCH-FOLD

(F) 4-PAGE LETTER

(G) BROADSIDE

Persuasive Claims

Sometimes you may realize that the receiver of a claim you make may be reluctant to grant it automatically. These situations call for a **persuasive claim**. You know that you must make a strong case to get what you want. Therefore, you should try a selling letter to persuade the other person. (Routine or direct claims that are usually granted promptly are covered in Chapter 5.)

The first section of the letter should start with some statement you feel the reader will agree with. You might make reference to previous business transacted between the two of you that has been completely satisfactory. Or you might say something like, "I know that you want your customers to be satisfied with the performance of your ..." This sentence introduces the topic in a positive manner.

The second section of this letter should state clearly and *calmly* all the facts that are pertinent to your claim. This section should also be as brief as possible. Yet it may take time to explain all the details leading to the responsibility of the reader to grant the claim. Reread carefully to try to eliminate verbiage that might clutter your message. Enclose *copies* of any papers that support your claim. Again, do not send original papers.

This closing section should tie the first two sections together, saying specifically what you want done. Do not say something like, "I think you should do something about this." Rather, as stated earlier, by having made a logical explanation leading to the other person's responsibility, say exactly what you want done.

Following is a persuasive claim written after a routine claim for an insurance refund was ignored. The letter brought the $860 refund immediately.

FIGURE 7.6
Example persuasive claim letter for insurance refund.

Date: December 1, 20XX
Re: POLICY #678910 Mr. Joseph Jacobsen

My father, Joseph Jacobsen, has had a life insurance policy #23456 with Blank Insurance Company since 19XX and we have had a good business relationship with you. ← **Pleasant opening**

However, on September 3, 20XX we applied for a Skilled Nursing Care Facility policy for him and gave your agent, Jeremia Jack, a personal check for $860 for this coverage for one year. At the time, Mr. Jack advised us that because of my father's health history, he might not qualify for the particular policy and we were prepared for this refusal. ← **Complete details (brief)**

However, we received our cancelled check in late September but have received no policy. Mr. Jack has not answered my letter nor our phone messages left on his answering machine.

We are enclosing a copy of the front and back of our cancelled $860 check made out to your company and also a copy of the form signed when we applied with Mr. Jack for your policy. ← **Copies of proof**

We feel that Blank Insurance Company must send us the approved Nursing Care insurance policy or refund our $860 immediately. ← **Action**

Very truly yours,

Enc. 2

Persuasive Requests

In any career or in your personal life you may have occasion to make a special request to get someone to do you a favor or perform some other act that would take special motivation to get that person's agreement. A **persuasive request** that follows the form of a selling letter pattern should get the desired results.

For example, many companies have social organizations, and special urging is frequently needed to prod people to attend. Figure 7.7 shows two very persuasive requests.

FIGURE 7.7
Example persuasive letter.

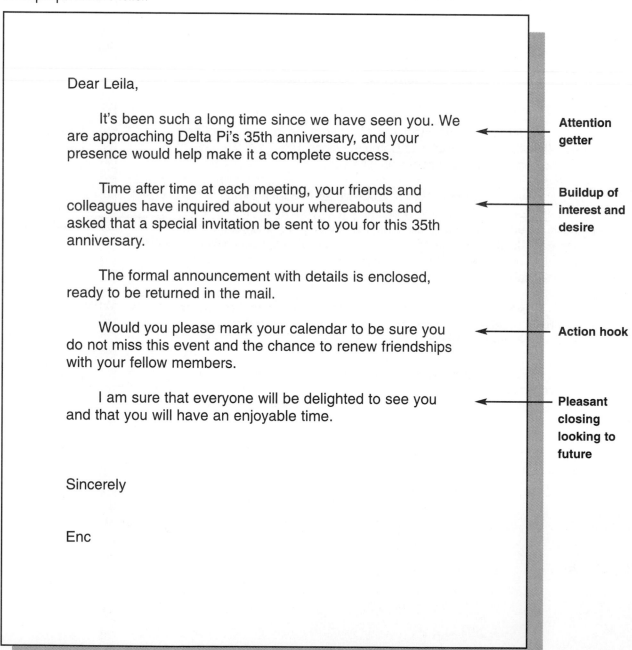

Dear Leila,

It's been such a long time since we have seen you. We are approaching Delta Pi's 35th anniversary, and your presence would help make it a complete success.   ← **Attention getter**

Time after time at each meeting, your friends and colleagues have inquired about your whereabouts and asked that a special invitation be sent to you for this 35th anniversary.   ← **Buildup of interest and desire**

The formal announcement with details is enclosed, ready to be returned in the mail.

Would you please mark your calendar to be sure you do not miss this event and the chance to renew friendships with your fellow members.   ← **Action hook**

I am sure that everyone will be delighted to see you and that you will have an enjoyable time.   ← **Pleasant closing looking to future**

Sincerely

Enc

(Courtesy Janet Matsuyama, Fullerton College).

FIGURE 7.7 (Continued)

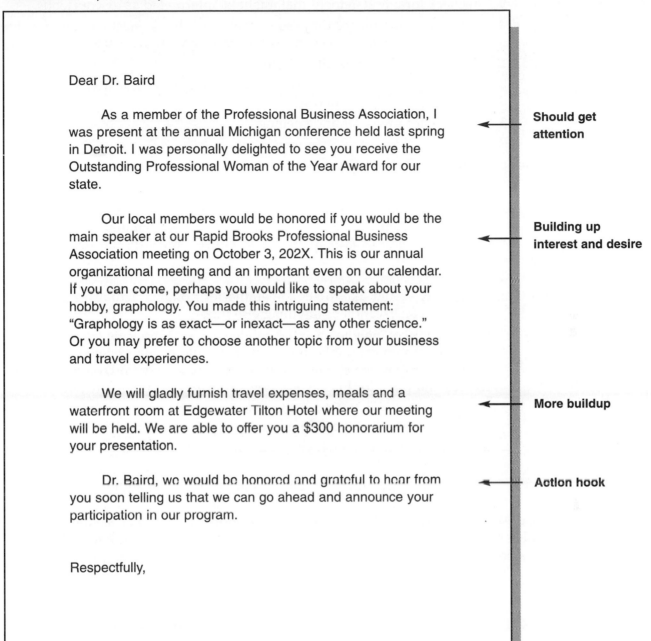

Dear Dr. Baird

As a member of the Professional Business Association, I was present at the annual Michigan conference held last spring in Detroit. I was personally delighted to see you receive the Outstanding Professional Woman of the Year Award for our state. ← **Should get attention**

Our local members would be honored if you would be the main speaker at our Rapid Brooks Professional Business Association meeting on October 3, 202X. This is our annual organizational meeting and an important even on our calendar. If you can come, perhaps you would like to speak about your hobby, graphology. You made this intriguing statement: "Graphology is as exact—or inexact—as any other science." Or you may prefer to choose another topic from your business and travel experiences. ← **Building up interest and desire**

We will gladly furnish travel expenses, meals and a waterfront room at Edgewater Tilton Hotel where our meeting will be held. We are able to offer you a $300 honorarium for your presentation. ← **More buildup**

Dr. Baird, we would be honored and grateful to hear from you soon telling us that we can go ahead and announce your participation in our program. ← **Action hook**

Respectfully,

Checklist for Sales Letters and Persuasive Claims and Requests

1. Identify reader(s) and write at that level.
2. Is the appearance satisfactory?
3. As you go over your letter, check your spelling, grammar, and punctuation.
4. Does the letter carry a good will tone for you and/or your firm?
5. Is the message clear and complete? Check your list of notes.
6. Does the letter follow the AIDA (Attention, Interest, Desire, Action) plan?
7. Have you used a fresh, effective selling or persuasive approach?

8.   Eliminate unnecessary words.

9.   Recheck for any statement that might be interpreted as discourteous.

10. For variety in sentence form, some sentences should start with descriptive words, phrases, or clauses instead of starting with the subject.

11. Restate negatives in positive terms.

12. Check for a "you attitude." Are statements made in the reader's interest instead of the writer's interest?

13. Recheck for grammar and spelling.

Your Own Look at Mail Order Buying

We can all expect to receive many sales letters in our lifetimes. While we are studying how to prepare such letters, it might be worthwhile to study them defensively for a moment from a consumer's standpoint for our own **mail order buying.**

Most sales offers made by mail are legitimate. However, we should remember the following:

- ☐ Everybody would like to get something for nothing; actually, you are not going to get a vacation or anything else free.

- ☐ Land frauds continue to snag the gullible. Federal and state laws have been passed to protect the public, but all offers should be investigated thoroughly *on the site.* If you are seriously interested, consult city and/or county legal records and plans for future developments before you sign any papers.

- ☐ If the quality of a product you see advertised seems miraculous, you needn't necessarily believe in miracles.

- ☐ In trying to make a killing, you might lose your shirt.

- ☐ Even questionable deals can sound good on paper—especially if you have the attitude, "My mind's made up; don't confuse me with the facts."

Don't be victimized. Movie star Clint Eastwood is quoted as saying, "You can fool some of the people some of the time, and usually that's enough to make a pretty good buck."

That must be the theme song of con artists, who do exist.

Chapter 7   Sales Letters and Persuasive Claims and Requests
"We Attitude" → "You" Attitude

WRITING IMPROVEMENT EXERCISE

The story is told of a highly successful sales consultant who moves around the country on assignment. Whenever he arrives in a new territory, he places a large cartoon on his bulletin board. The cartoon shows a tough-looking buyer demanding across his desk, "What's in it for me???"

When you begin to write a business letter, you might benefit from remembering the picture of the "tough-looking buyer." A letter satisfactorily answers his question when it has the "you attitude." This attitude reflects interests of the reader and is far more appealing than the letter with the "we attitude," which reflects the interests of the writer. The "you attitude" generally satisfies the tough customer and the not-so-tough customer or reader; both are primarily interested in their own potential benefits.

In business writing, of course, it is permissible to use the first-person forms—*I, we, my, our,* and so forth. But the purpose of this exercise is to emphasize the potential advantage of phrasing letters, particularly letters of a selling or persuasive nature, in terms of *you* and *yours.*

Following are examples of changing "we" sentences to "you" sentences:

☐ We believe our Baccutron is the best battery-operated watch on the market. →
You may enjoy the luxury and accuracy of your own Baccutron watch.

☐ We offer four different makes of cars at the Lakewood Auto Park—Ford, Toyota, General Motors, and Mercedes. →
For you to choose the car that best fits your needs, Lakewood Auto Park offers you four different makes of cars: Ford, Toyota, General Motors, and Mercedes-Benz.

☐ We have been in the dry-cleaning business here for 25 years. →
You can rely on a dry-cleaning firm that has been in business in your area for the past 25 years.

Chapter 7   Sales Letters and Persuasive Claims and Requests
"We Attitude" → "You" Attitude

WRITING IMPROVEMENT "HANDS ON" ASSIGNMENT

Rewrite the following sentences from the "we attitude" to the "you attitude." Suggestion: Try to think of an advantage to the reader, and use that idea. One student called these "minicommercials."

1. We have put all our floor models on sale to make room for our new spring consoles.→
   <u>Find your dream entertainment center in our Fall clearance sale.</u>

2. Our laboratory has worked three years to develop our newest Vitamin-Pack, which we feel will give people the pickup they need. → <u>Choose the pickup your body</u>
   <u>wants at Smith Brothers.</u>

3. We believe we have the best TV on the market. → <u>You can now own the best TV</u>
   <u>on the market.</u>

4. We also sell an edger that can be attached to any lawnmower. → <u>You can have a</u>
   <u>double-duty machine by attaching this edger to your mower.</u>

5. We are anxious to have you try our new Doggie Bisquit that we have just added to our line. → <u>Your pet likes treats too—get him our new Doggie Bisquits.</u>

6. We have been selling real estate in this area for 20 years. → <u>Get the benefit of doing</u>
   <u>business with a realtor who has sold homes in your area for more than 20 years.</u>

7. I have had three years' experience as a program analyst. → <u>Put my three years of</u>
   <u>experience as a program analyst to work for you.</u>

8. We have a seven-piece cutlery set that comes with a free knife sharpener. → <u>You'll</u>
   <u>like the free knife-sharpener that will come with your new seven-piece cutlery set.</u>

9. Our policy is for the customer to sign the sales slip for verification of the purchase. →
   <u>For your protection, you are asked to sign the sales slip for verification.</u>

   _____

10. After an initial probationary period, we try to have each new bank employee assigned
    to work in a branch bank of his or her choice. → <u>After an initial probationary</u>
    <u>period, we will try to have you assigned to a branch bank of your choice.</u>

    _____

Chapter 7 Sales Letters and Persuasive Claims and Requests
"We Attitude" → "You" Attitude

WRITING ASSIGNMENTS

1. After working part-time for a neighborhood florist, you have been able to purchase the business from the elderly couple who owned it. In your plan for expansion, you want to promote "flowers of the month" to try to sell to residents of the area. From the telephone company, you have obtained names and addresses of residents in your local ZIP code area. You plan to feature such bouquets or plants as azaleas in January, violets in February, roses in June, chrysanthemums in September, and poinsettias in December.
    a. Write a letter introducing and promoting the general plan of your "flowers of the month" campaign.
    b. Write a letter promoting a particular flower for a specific month.

2. You have a list of all the freshmen at your local community college. Write a letter promoting this year's model of a personal computer, using the name of Pete Zorria as one student. Make up special selling features that you feel will help sell the machine to this age group.

3. Write a sales letter for Neutrogenus soap. This is a rich, transparent, amber-colored bar soap that cleans thoroughly without being drying or irritating. It is a chemically balanced soap, beneficial to all complexions, and contains glycerin, an ingredient found in many hand and body lotions. Users write in that it is excellent for clearing teen-age complexion problems, and it also keeps the skin of older people smooth and nice. There is no better soap for babies, and men find it refreshing to use as a shaving lather. The soap sells for $1 a bar. You have a list of people living in the upper-middle-class and upper-class areas of Dallas, Texas. Prepare a letter to send to these people, using individual names and addresses.

4. You are one of the three students at Cruz College who are preparing the college's first poetry magazine, which will sell for $2. The poetry is the original previously unpublished work of Cruz students. If successful, the publication of the magazine will become an annual event. Your promotion funds are limited, so you have decided to prepare a sales letter on the magazine to be placed near campus mailboxes of students. You will also be able to place copies of the letter at other strategic places around the campus. Write this letter.

5. Choose a product or service, real or imaginary, that would be of interest to college students, and write a letter that could be sent to each student. Go ahead. Wing it.

6. You own and operate a pet store in the New Rockwood Shopping Center, and from the licensing bureau you have obtained the names and addresses of pet owners in the ZIP codes in your area. Write a letter that can be sent to all the names on this list to advise them of your newly opened store, the pets and pet products you carry. Also tell them of any special services you offer.

7. You have recently been hired by the Bay Company Department Store as college shop coordinator. Write a letter that will be sent to all homes in the community. Announce the opening of the new college shop with wearing apparel for college women. Mention the hours that the store is open and that ample parking is available.

8. You are secretary to the Community Relations Director of your college and have been asked to compose a letter inviting members of the community to an arts and crafts show and sale of students' work. The show will be October 30 and 31 from 10 A.M. to 10 P.M. Light refreshments may be purchased. The show is under the direction of Ms. Nancy Redburn, Community Relations Director. Decide what type of arts and crafts will be shown for selling. Make up the letter.

9. Write a form letter that will be sent to all customers of the AyZee Plumbing Company, along with a copy of the new 200X catalogue. Use resale information, urging them to come in.

Chapter 7   Sales Letters and Persuasive Claims and Requests
"We Attitude" → "You" Attitude

REVIEW AND DISCUSSION

If given a choice, draw a line through any incorrect response.

1. The book names two types of careers that require ability in writing sales letters. What are they?

   <u>Direct mail advertising (writing sales letters) and conducting a mail order business.</u>

2. Name three functions of sales letters.

   a. <u>Getting sales leads.</u>

   b. <u>Bringing people into a place of business.</u>

   c. <u>Selling by mail.</u>

3. Success of a sales letter depends on identifying *product or service, prospects,* and _____

   <u>price.</u>

4. How should you familiarize yourself with the product or service you are trying to sell? <u>Use it or have suitable others use it and report to you.</u>

5. Name four sources of names and addresses for use in mailing sales letters.

   a. <u>(Accept any four of these responses.) Telephone company. List brokers.</u>

   b. <u>Organization membership lists. Credit rating books.</u>

   c. <u>Directories. Public records.</u>

   d. <u>Newspapers. Other?</u>

6. What are the advantages of using computerized sales mailing lists? <u>If used to</u> <u>full advantage, can keep lists current and save time and money.</u>

7. Name in order the four stages of the advertising style spiral.

   <u>1. Innovation, 2. Imitation, 3. Competition, 4. Saturation</u>

8. Bring to class an ad you like from a printed source, and identify its stage of the advertising style spiral.   [Student participation.]

9. What is the purpose of test mailings of sales letters? <u>Saves money by showing</u> <u>which format brings in the best response and is worth advertising.</u>

10. Diagram the sales letter pattern given in the text or make your own rendition of a praise sandwich. Identify the main elements of the one you chose.
[See page 150.]

11. Name the two functions of the sales letter attention-getters.

a. <u>Get reader into picture.</u>

b. <u>Must tie into product, service or idea you are promoting.</u>

12. Bring to class one letter with an outstanding attention-getter on the envelope as an enclosure, or in the first paragraph of the letter. [Student participation.]

13. Name five appeals to the reader that are recommended as being effective in sales letters. Be brief.

a. <u>(Accept any five of these responses.) money, bonus, gift, prize, safety, economy,</u>

b. <u>pride, better future, community service, hobbies, home improvement, other?</u>

c. _____

d. _____

e. _____

14. Is the use of "Resident" or "Occupant" in the address of sales letters preferred to the use of a person's name? Explain. <u>No. Puts it into "junk mail" category.</u>

15. Name the five things the action element of the sales letter should do.

a. <u>Tell reader what to do.</u>

b. <u>Say how to do it.</u>

c. <u>Make it easy or make it sound easy.</u>

d. <u>Make the price sound right.</u>

e. <u>Urge reader to move fast.</u>

16. What devices are sometimes used in sales letters to make ordering sound easy?
<u>Coupons, prepaid postal cards or envelopes.</u>

17. You need not be suspicious that people may try to use the mails to defraud you. (~~True~~/False)

    Change these statements to the "you attitude."

18. Our price for bulk orders of one-pound Choco-lat bars is $4.50, and they can retail for $8.95. → <u>You make a great profit: Our $4.50 Choco-lat bar can retail at $8.95.</u>

    _____

19. My interest in mechanical operations has always made it easy for me to learn how new machines work. → <u>Put my mechanical gift to work for you!</u>

    _____

20. Because I enjoyed my part-time work in an office, I am applying for the office assistant position I saw in this morning's paper. → <u>My training for the office position you advertised should be brief. I have done well in my part-time office work.</u>

8 Credit and Collections

> *The two most beautiful words in the English language are:*
> *"Check enclosed."*
>
> Dorothy Parker
> (1893–1967)
> *American poet, short story writer,*
> *drama and book critic; known for her satirical wit*

Successful operation of a business depends largely on the harmonious interaction of three departments of that business: sales, credit, and collection.

Many problems of the credit and collection departments would not occur if sales forces were not aggressive. Similarly, the work of the collection department would be simplified if the credit department were extremely cautious in granting credit. But actually, most businesses would suffer, perhaps to extinction, if salespeople were not properly forceful. Further, a great percentage of total business would be lost if credit were not granted to certain marginal credit risks. Although credit privileges must be granted with care, figures show that the total credit losses for any given year amount to less than 0.5 percent of sales.

Is it necessary to use credit in business?

As a matter of fact, more than 85 percent of business operates on a credit basis, from the small individual shop owner to the large corporation. Credit is a way of life.

CREDIT COMMUNICATIONS

The Four Cs of Credit

Most studies state that credit should be granted by evaluating the applicant under the four Cs of credit: character, capital, capacity, and conditions.

1. **Character:** The person's basic ethics, such as honesty, dependability, and sense of moral values, indicated by a past credit record and/or satisfactory honest answers in a credit application.

2. **Capital:** The money behind the debtor. This may be cash, securities, real estate holdings, copyrights, etc. In case of necessity, these could be turned into cash. When a person is being judged for credit potential, capital holdings

175

should be rated for **liquidity**—that is, the ease with which they can be converted to cash.

3. **Capacity:** current or anticipated earnings as wages, salary, royalties, or cash returns on investment.

4. **Conditions:** any problem conditions that are not directly related to the credit applicant but could affect the applicant's credit condition, such as general or regional economic conditions, general employment conditions, or employment conditions in a given business, industry or profession.

Legal Aspects of Credit Communications

Communications that ask for or supply information on the credit record or credit potential of an applicant must fit into the legal category of a **privileged communication.** A privileged communication should be furnished only to somebody who has an interest to protect. This information should not be given for a random inquiry made out of curiosity or malice.

In making your report, check records to see that your information conforms with facts. In legal terminology, you should report what a **prudent person** would report. You can give personal evaluations and opinions to authorized inquiries, as long as they are given in good faith, without malice. You should protect the interests of both the applicant and the person making the inquiry.

Anyone handling credit applications or credit reports must be familiar with the provisions of the **Consumer Credit Protection Act of 1969** and its amendments. A free copy of this act can be obtained by writing the Board of Governors, Federal Reserve System, Washington, DC 20551.

Following are some major provisions of this legislation:

1. The credit applicant must be informed that a check is being made of his or her credit.

2. The person or agency making the report must be reasonably sure that information furnished will be used only for the stated reason for which it was requested.

3. Consumers may at any time or for any reason examine their credit records of debt as recorded by any credit reporting agency. If a recent negative report has been made on the applicant, this examination may be made free of charge. Otherwise, the reporting agency may charge a reasonable fee. The applicant has the right to have inaccurate or incomplete information reinvestigated. If information is inaccurate or cannot be verified, it must be removed from the file. If there is a dispute about the information, the applicant may have his or her own version added to the file, and this information must be included in subsequent reports on that person. Consumers can get the names of all who have received copies of the questionable reports.

4. Credit reporting agencies must not report adverse information that is more than seven years old, except for bankruptcies, which may be reported for fourteen years.

Amendments to the Consumer Credit Protection Act provide that:

☐ A retailer must resolve a customer's credit inquiry within 90 days after the inquiry is made.

☐ A retailer may not refuse credit on the basis of sex or marital status.

☐ A creditor must supply a written statement of reasons for denying or terminating credit if a rejected applicant requests such explanation.

Applying for Credit

Today, most credit applications are made by filling in a form furnished by the business. Occasionally, it is necessary to write a letter applying for credit.

The credit application would be a simple routine information letter. State clearly in the first sentence that it is a letter applying for credit; give your full name, address(es), telephone number, place of employment, and previous and/or current credit account references. Any other information that might be helpful should be supplied. If you are new in the area, give all pertinent information relative to your prior place of residence.

Different methods are used in getting credit information for retail customers and for trade or mercantile accounts.

Getting Retail Credit Information

The chief sources of information concerning the retail credit applicant's ability to pay are the following:

☐ The customer, the best source for information on the applicant: The credit applicant can furnish details about employment, residence, financial responsibilities, indebtedness, and so forth.

☐ Credit card agencies and/or the firms with which the applicant has done or is doing business.

☐ Employers, for verification of employment and earnings.

☐ Local retail credit associations.

Getting Retail Credit Information

The world's three largest credit bureaus are TRW, Inc., Trans Union Corporation and Equifax, Inc. **Retail credit bureaus** compile the following information: identification of the customer, including full name, address, and spouse's name; present employment information; personal history, including the customer's former address, former employer, spouse's employer, number of dependents, and so on; credit history, indicating in what manner the customer has paid bills in the past; and public record information covering lawsuits, judgments, and other litigation that may have some bearing on the person's ability to pay bills.

The information of the credit bureau is available only to those firms that prove to the bureau that they have a legitimate business need for the information.

Getting Trade Credit Information

Getting **trade credit** information about another business firm usually involves a more detailed study, using many sources.

The credit manager of a large eastern firm says that financial conditions of business change rapidly and trade credit statements, "like eggs, age fast." Every effort must be made to keep information current.

Sales representatives of your own firm can be your best sources of up-to-date information. They can report on such matters as condition of the premises, changes in product or service lines, and changes in personnel, ownership, location or management.

Valuable sources of information on the trade account also include those furnished by the account itself, such as references, financial data, and suppliers. National trade reporting services like Dun & Bradstreet, Moody's Investors Service, Inc., and Standard and Poor's Corporation can furnish reports. Further, information obtained from private or mutual trade agencies for a particular industry can be helpful.

Granting Credit

Although the letter **granting credit** is routine, it should certainly express a tone of welcome to the new credit customer. It will also undoubtedly carry with it a spirit of good will if it can be personalized as much as possible, such as having an original signature and calling the customer by name in the text. It should go without saying that new customers are important to a business, and new customers like to hear they are important to you.

Letters granting credit are good news, stating immediately that credit has been granted, giving details of credit terms, and closing with a lift that looks toward a pleasant business relationship. Promotional resale materials might be included such as any news that might be important to them.

A good example of a letter granting credit to a retail customer follows:

Robertson's welcomes you as a new credit card customer, Mrs. Rogers, and we hope you will use your credit privileges freely.

As a credit customer you will regularly receive announcements of private sales that are held for two days before sales events are announced to the public through newspaper ads. You will also receive special announcements of other credit customer benefits, such as fashion shows and Silver Club specials.

With this letter is an announcement of the Private Back-to-School Sale on August 15 and 16. We hope you enjoy having first selection of this merchandise.

Terms of Credit

Details of **credit terms** must be furnished on the credit application, in the letter granting credit, or in some other communication. Letters from wholesalers to dealers should indicate clearly the date from which the credit discount will be figured:

delivery date, invoice date, shipping date, receiving date, or e.o.m. (end of month). Also, you should state clearly when the net amount is due if a cash discount is not claimed.

Not this: Our credit terms are the standard 2/10, net 30.

This: Our credit terms are the standard 2/10, net 30, or 2 percent off if paid within ten days of invoice date; net amount due in 30 days of invoice date if cash discount is not claimed.

Interest charges may be given according to the monthly rate, but current law requires that the true annual interest rate also be stated clearly.

Refusing Credit

The letter refusing credit is, of course, more difficult to write than the letter granting credit. The refusal is a negative that must carry the "no" and still try to retain the good will of the credit applicant.

Credit officers should know the philosophy, "Success is not permanent. The same is also true of failure." However, do not make the opening buffer so pleasant that you give the reader a first impression that credit is being granted. Then, the refusal would be more difficult to take. Following is a letter that is probably too cheerful in handling a credit refusal:

Congratulations! Getting your college degree is a great accomplishment. This degree should enable you to get a good job.

When you get the job, we will be happy to reconsider your application for credit.

Credit refusals should be courteous, written with the knowledge that a poor credit risk today may be a good credit risk tomorrow, next month, or next year. Basically, the intent should be to try to get the business on a cash basis. A retail customer might be willing to put merchandise on layaway.

Here is a more acceptable credit refusal:

Buffer ⟶ Thank you for the order for your company name-imprinted stationery.

As yours is a new business, we can locate no information upon which to make a credit approval.

Details (Includes resale) ⟶ From our own experience, we know that new businesses generally find it necessary to watch even small expenditures. Could we have permission to send this order C.O.D., as we are sure that ours are the best prices on the market for first-quality stationery. Morton's stationery will give your business associations a good first impression.

Closing looking to future ⟶ We wish you success in your new enterprise, and would like to look forward to a long and pleasant business association.

May we send the order on cash or C.O.D. terms?

Exchanging Credit Information

Although most **exchanges of credit information** are done through credit rank-
ing bureaus or rating services, occasionally it is necessary to write letters asking or
giving details of an individual's or firm's credit status. These privileged communications must not contain libelous statements. Legally, postcards cannot be used because credit information, although routine, is confidential.

Information in these letters should relate to the following:

1. How long has the applicant had an account with you?
2. What is the usual size of the account?
3. What is the current status of the account?
4. Do you have any special comments about the applicant?

Because letters requesting credit information are usually quite routine, many
businesses use a form letter for these inquiries. A typical letter of this nature is shown
in Figure 8.1.

With a letter like that, the original letter (with the desired information filled in)
may be returned to the sender, saving much of the time of preparing the reply. It also
should eliminate the need for the person furnishing information to file the letter. If
desired, you can print your own copy.

FIGURE 8.1
Sample form request for credit information.

APPLICANT: _____

    Applicant wishes to establish a line of credit with us and has given
your name as a reference.

    Would you please give us the confidential information requested in the
form at the bottom of this page and return this letter in the enclosed
business reply envelope.

    We would appreciate your help and would be glad to furnish similar
service to you at any time.

                                               Very truly yours,

Period of time sold on credit _____ to _____
Credit limit, if any _____
Current amount due _____ Past due _____
                   (Discount)
Paying habits   (Prompt)
                   (Slow)
Comments _____
_____

Checklist for Credit Letters

1. Identify the reader(s) and write at that level.
2. Is the appearance satisfactory?
3. Is the message clear and complete?
4. Making credit inquiries and granting credit: Does the first paragraph contain the main message?
5. Refusing credit: Is there a pleasant buffer beginning and a pleasant closing? Is the refusal stated reasonably and briefly?
6. As you go over your first draft check for grammar, spelling; especially check for subject–verb agreement.
7. Eliminate unnecessary words, sentences, paragraphs.
8. Recheck for any statement that might be a violation of libel laws.
9. Where possible, change negative statements to positive ones.
10. Check for "you attitude." Are statements made in the reader's interest rather than in the writer's interest?

COLLECTION COMMUNICATIONS

Background for Making Collections

If orders are the heart of a business operation, then collections are surely its lifeblood. The importance of the duties and responsibilities of collection personnel cannot be overestimated.

We must write collection letters and they must be effective for these reasons:

1. We want the money that is rightfully ours to use for our own purposes.
2. We want to save the expense of further collection letters or collection procedures.
3. We want to regain the business of a customer who is probably doing business elsewhere because of money owed to us.

As a result of the detail work involved, those processing accounts sometimes "can't see the forest for the trees." Occasionally they should mentally step back to observe the collection process objectively. Such periodic reviews may be far more fruitful than continually making out the same type of collections on the same schedule as always. Well run organizations regularly check various collection approaches and various types of communications to determine whether or not they are bringing satisfactory results.

Personal contacts by telephone can be more productive than words on a written page, and in-person contacts can be most productive of all but usually are the "last resort." The personal telephone call can be used effectively at almost any stage

Bill paying day

of collection. Telephoning has the advantage of getting an immediate response. Of course, long-distance calls can be justified for any but small amounts. With competition among carriers today, you might get reasonable reduced rates for frequent use of long-distance lines.

The person with an innovative plan for collections will be ahead of competitors for the slow paying account and may be first in line of those debtors who are playing games in paying bills, settling a few at a time.

Classifying Your Accounts

Overdue accounts should be classified by type. Late payment from financially well rated businesses, government agencies, or municipalities can be simply a matter of paperwork and not a lack of funds. A good collection department officer can organize a personal campaign to devise a means of making these accounts pay on time.

To help reduce the need for collection notices, a brightly colored sticker telling of the rewards of cash discounts and on-time payments might be gummed or stapled to the statement.

With large organizations that have a consistent record of losing a cash discount because of late but sure payment, a letter might be written to a person in authority suggesting the hand-carrying of large account statements to get cash discount benefits. If no improvement results, at least an effort was made.

Making Collections by Telephone or in Person

In business, most collection communications are letters. Even with rising letter-writing costs, this procedure seems to be most economical and usually as effective as necessary. Competitive rates for heavy usage of long distance lines are usually available. However, earlier sections of this text have related that contacting people by telephone or in person might be more effective than writing letters. Evidently people can more easily ignore a letter than they can ignore a live human.

Certainly, a person in charge of collections should periodically try different collection procedures.

After sending one or two notices of overdue payments, you may find that telephoning or even calling in person is often well worth the time and effort. But it is necessary to do some homework before you make any kind of personal call:

1. *Check to see that your information is correct.* Was the material delivered? Checking all numbers, see that the billing was correct. Were all payments noted?
2. Check to see if the amount due justifies a planned collection procedure.
3. Check the past payment record.
4. Decide who is the right person to contact.
5. Figure out a possible different payment plan.
6. Plan your opening statement:
   a. Introduce yourself and identify your firm.
   b. Give the reason for your call.
   c. Wait a moment. Many calls are successfully completed during this pause.

Contacting High Officials

In the late stages of trying to collect on overdue accounts, the collection call or letter should be to the owner or manager of a small organization. In a larger organization, it should be to a person of high authority, such as comptroller or supervisor of accounts.

Guidelines for Writing Collection Letters

The plan behind writing collection letters is to collect the money and retain the good will of customers.

Important guidelines for writing good collection letters follow:

1. Understand that customers know they owe and expect to hear from you.
2. Be positive. Understand also that very few people are dishonest; most pay their bills. There are often good reasons why some people don't pay: carelessness, temporary financial difficulties, temporary personal problems, dissatisfaction with goods or services. But most come through. When their times are better, they will probably first pay those who treat them with respect.

3. Be specific. Do not refer to the "balance," but give the exact amount due. Always refer to the customer's purchase order number. Good idea: send a copy of the order, so all information is at hand.

4. Check that you have billed and shipped according to directions on the purchase order. This is a good plan for all orders. Major accounts operate under strictly defined procedures, and everything must match before an order can be processed for payment. A simple error in account number, order number, or dollar amount can delay or stop payment.

Collections: Multiple Mailings and Custom Mailings

Most collection letters are form letters, but on occasion, important accounts with long overdue balances are prepared as custom letters, mentioning matters that apply only to that account.

In-Office Preparation of Form Letters for Collections

Because of the large volume of collection letters that must be sent, most are prepared as in-office form letters. With the **mail merge system**, the individual date, name, amount due, date originally due, and so forth can be inserted automatically in the appropriate positions.

Commercially Prepared Software for Collection Letters

Also, various computer software firms prepare sets of collection letters that can be purchased from software suppliers. Some of these form letters may sound too "canned," but if chosen selectively, they can be very effective. As time passes, competition gives us better selections of commercially prepared software.

In unusual cases involving large dollar amounts, the cost of preparing individual custom letters might be justified. The tone of such a letter must be acceptable in the hopes of retaining a potentially valuable customer. However, the message must show clearly that the amount is long overdue. After all, that amount is rightfully yours and is earning them interest in their bank accounts or paying their other bills instead of being available to you for your purposes.

Using the Collection Letter Series

Collection letters should be written promptly, regularly, and with increasing forcefulness. Records prove that the older an account gets, the less chance there is of collecting it. United States Department of Commerce figures show that for the probability of collecting on it, $1 due becomes worth these amounts:

90¢ after two months

67¢ after six months

45¢ after a year

23¢ after two years

15¢ after three years

1/2¢ after five years

At early stages of collection, letters should be simple reminders. As the unpaid account becomes older, the later-stage letters should be firmer messages of serious steps that may be taken. Collection letters can be set up in a series, according to the tone or level of the communication.

The four stages of the collection letter series are (1) **reminder,** (2) **inquiry and appeal,** (3) **pressure,** and (4) **ultimatum.** If your first-stage reminder letters are ignored, you should proceed through these four stages of the series until a response is received.

More than one letter can be sent in each stage. However, a reasonable time should be allowed between letters, giving the customer a chance to pay. A follow-up letter every five days or so can be frustrating to both sides. Yet, waiting too long may cause the customer to pay another creditor who is more persistent.

Be sure to acknowledge that payment and your letter may have crossed in the mails. Debtors like to know that the people to whom they owe money are aware that this occurrence is common. Figure 8.2 is a copy of a form regularly sent out by one firm for this purpose. Incidentally, one self-designated authority states that the world's biggest lie is "Payment is in the mail." Your letter could move the debtor to make the statement true.

All collection letters can end with a statement like this: "If this notice and your payment have crossed in the mail, please ignore this letter."

Stage 1: Reminder

As soon as an account becomes delinquent, a **notification** or **reminder** letter should be sent. It is very important that this first collection letter appear routine, so that it will not offend the good customer who has merely overlooked payment or who has had a personal emergency. Although payment should have been made

FIGURE 8.2
Form that is included in collection letters to indicate that
payment and collection letter may have crossed in the mails.

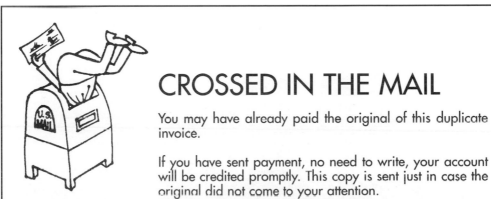

CROSSED IN THE MAIL

You may have already paid the original of this duplicate invoice.

If you have sent payment, no need to write, your account will be credited promptly. This copy is sent just in case the original did not come to your attention.

GEYER-McALLISTER PUBLICATIONS, INC., 51 Madison Avenue, New York, NY 10010

by the due date, you might lose the continued business of a faithful customer if you send what might be considered a premature dunning notice that demands payment.

Often, this notification simply takes the form of a second copy of the original statement with a stamped notation or a gummed label attached, saying something like, "Second Notice," "Have you overlooked?" or "Please." Figure 8.3 shows a collection of inexpensive gummed labels that can be used effectively in this manner. These labels can be purchased in most office supply stores.

In other instances, a printed form enclosed in an envelope with a reminding message is often sent:

Most likely the following charges have been overlooked:

May 15	$200.00
May 23	$301.75

Here are other examples of collection reminders.

Collection Reminder 1

HAVE YOU FORGOTTEN US?

We don't want to take it personally, because we do appreciate the business you have given us. Probably you have already sent us your check for $148.12 for the past two months' bills. If this is so, we do thank you.

But if you have not yet sent in your check, could you please mail it at once and then forget this little reminder.

Thank you.

FIGURE 8.3
Gummed labels that can be attached to second copy of customer statement at "reminder" stage of collection.

Collection Reminder 2

We'd like to fill your order …

BUT

… your account of $245.39, as shown on the attached statement, prevents us from doing so.

Won't you please mail your payment now, along with the enclosed form, so we can release your order.

If you have recently paid the $245.39, just note this information on the enclosed form and return it in the postpaid envelope we have provided.

Thank you!

Collection Reminder 3

Apparently through an oversight you have neglected to send us payment for the outstanding amount on your account. The amount, according to our records, is shown on the accompanying statement.

Won't you take care of this now, while the matter has your attention. Just return the enclosed statement with your check or money order, using the envelope provided.

Humor may be effective in early reminder stages of collection procedures, but use it cautiously. Most people do not feel that being reminded of overdue accounts is a humorous matter. Sometimes among members of social organizations or other membership groups, mild humor might be effective. Or some appropriate humorous touches might be used in other cases. Here are two oldies that could be used, together with two more modern messages.

How do you do?
Some pay when due.
Some pay when overdue.
Some never do.
How do you do?
Balance $_____.

Man is dust.
Dust settles.
Be a man.
Amount due: $_____.

Here are some reminders that attempt to humanize the computer.

Hi.
This is your friendly computer. Your loan is past due. If payment is not made, I will have to refer this to a human. Please include the late charge shown below with your payment.

HELLO! I AM THE COMPUTER. As yet, no one but me knows that you have not been making regular payments on this bill. However, if I have not processed a payment of $214.92 from you in 10 days, I will tell a Human who will resort to other means for collection.

Stage 2: Inquiry and Appeal

In this, the second stage of the collection letter series, the **inquiry** and/or **appeal** stage, attempts are made to try to draw out a response from the customer who has remained silent. This letter asks for the customer's side of the story before matters get out of hand. Here, you are trying to touch some human chord that will bring action from a customer who has so far ignored you—and possibly other creditors. These letters may take the form of inquiry about the reasons for nonpayment, appeals for response or payment, or a combination of both. Resale material can be used here, confirming the advantages of keeping accounts current so the customer may continue to do business with you.

More than one reminder might be sent. But it is recommended that only one or at the most two letters of inquiry or appeal be sent. This will make it possible to get on to stronger messages of the pressure and ultimatum stages if the customer fails to respond. After all, the original statement has been sent, as well as one or more reminders. At this stage, however, it is a good idea to suggest an excuse for slow payment to help the customer save face. You could still be saving the business of a potentially good account.

For customers with running accounts, at the **inquiry stage** you could send a printout of recent purchases and payments. They may have a valid question about the activity on the account, and you are trying to get part or all the money due or get some response that explains the reason for nonpayment.

Or the customer may in fact be dissatisfied with goods or services received and may be reluctant or too busy to communicate this information. Unusual circumstances may make prompt payment impossible. You are asking for an explanation. The following serve as good letters of inquiry.

Collection Inquiry 1

Inquiry ⟶ This is the third time we have reminded you of your overdue account of $200. Surely there must be a logical reason for your not answering our letters.

In view of your past good record with us, we would like to offer to rewrite your credit agreement, perhaps allowing you to make smaller payments over a longer period of time at the same interest rate.

Please come in and make both of us feel better by arranging to settle this account.

Collection Inquiry 2

We have mailed two monthly statements, and we have also written you on June 30 that your account was overdue $319.25. So far, we have received no response.

Inquiry ⟶ We like to assist our customers whenever possible, if we know what the problem is. To do so, we must have partial payment of the account or an explanation for the delay in payment. Meantime, you

Resale ⟶ are missing some really good buys in our Annual Fall Clearance Sale.

Your prompt reply as to the cause for withholding payment is expected.

There are many suggestions that can be used at the appeal stage of collection. Frequently, inquiries and appeals are combined. Here are some of the most common appeals:

- *Pride:* Self-respect, respect of others
- *Economic self-interest:* Good credit rating, advantages of continuing to do business with you
- *Sympathy:* "We both have our bills to pay."
- *Courtesy:* "Do as you would have others do."
- *Fair play:* "We have helped you; now you can help us."

Any one of these appeals could be phrased in many different manners. The following letter is an inquiry combined with a self-interest appeal:

Collection Inquiry and Appeal 3

Buffer ⟶ A few years ago we suffered through our city's first electrical brownout. Today we are "in the dark" again, but in a different manner.

Economic self-interest ⟶ Surely, it is in your best interest to maintain the good credit standing you have enjoyed with us and pay this bill today—$301.75—which is now almost two months past due.

Inquiry ⟶ If there is some reason why you haven't paid this bill, let us know what it is and perhaps we can help.

Goodwill Looking to future ⟶ We have always valued your business and we believe it is in the best interests of both of us if we continue to do so.

Here are two letters that use different appeals in their attempts to get some response:

Collection Appeal 4

Sympathy ⟶ Mr. Bucher, you have your bills to pay and we most certainly have ours.

Can't you help both of us by mailing a check for $280, the amount that has been due to us since March 31?

Collection Appeal 5

I'd like to take care of the problem you seem to be having with your past due homeowner's payment.

Inquiry ⟶ Let's look at some of the choices you have. If extra cash will help, I'll do my best to arrange it. If your budget isn't working, I'll help you develop a new one. If you're faced with a financial difficulty that extra cash won't solve, I'll try to suggest some practical solutions.

Sympathy ⟶ Over the years we have learned to sympathize with those who have temporary troubles meeting their expenses. I can't help unless I know what your problem is.

Please call or come in today so we can talk things over.

Sincerely,

P.S. Perhaps you don't feel a need to contact me. If so, I'll look for your payment of $_____ no later than January 26, 20XX.

Stage 3: Pressure

If you have heard nothing as a result of your earlier communications, you are dealing with a person with poor paying patterns. Your plan at this stage of the collection procedure is to try to break the ice with some form of **pressure** to try to get a response from the account. In the normal course of business, you would probably telephone the customer or make a call in person. Or you might have another representative of the firm call.

To force action here, letters with a stronger tone are sometimes sent. If contact has been made by telephone or in person and no response has resulted, a letter should follow.

The tone of the **pressure letter** is firmer than that of earlier communications, with a clear understanding that the customer is in the wrong by not having paid the amount due and by not even responding to your many communications.

At this stage, certified letters with a return receipt requested can be effective. You then know that the customer or someone authorized to act in that person's behalf has received your letter. The customer knows it and knows you know it. Although the expenditure for certified letters is minimal, it would not, of course, be recommended for attempting to collect small amounts. But for most accounts, it is well justified.

The pressure letter shows little friendly attitude but should in no way offend the customer. This may still eventually be a good customer again if you are patient through some difficulty. But the seriousness of the situation must be made clear. The tone of the following letter is firm, with reference to unspecified action, obviously serious, that might be taken:

Collection Pressure 1

The matter of your long overdue balance of $300 has become critical.

We have received no response to several letters we have written, although we have given you every opportunity to let us help you with your financial difficulties.

Frankly, you leave us no alternative but to inform you that unless we hear from you by April 30, we will have to consider other action.

Won't you give this matter urgent attention?

Another letter of the pressure stage of collection follows:

Collection Pressure 2

It has been brought to my attention that your current account is six months overdue. Previous efforts to contact you have gone unanswered. Your account shows a balance of $147.67 on one portable laser printer.

I will expect to hear from you by April 24, 20XX, or we will consider more drastic action.

The threat of impairing an individual or a business credit record is quite powerful. Most people want to maintain a good credit record to their own advantage, and most businesses cannot remain in operation without one. Therefore, the threat to report an account unfavorably frequently brings the desired results. The following letter has been effective.

Collection Pressure 3

As a businessperson, you know the value of a good credit rating. As a matter of fact, today it is all but impossible for a business to operate without the advantages of being able to purchase on credit.

Yet it seems that it will be our unpleasant duty to report your nonpayment of your account of $402.25, due since November 1.

Could we just have partial payment of this amount and a suggestion for scheduling payments that you will be able to meet?

Of course, form letters are used at any stage of the collection letter process. Here is a form letter for the pressure stage, as late stage letters are more difficult to write.

Collection Pressure Form Letter

We are worried because our efforts to reach you concerning the past due condition of your account have not resulted in the balance being reduced to a current condition.

Previous balance	Interest	Credits	Payments	New balance	Amount due
434.44	4.34	.00	.00	438.78	438.78

Your account has reached the point where we would ordinarily refer it to our Collection Department. However, we at Buffums value your patronage highly, and it is our desire to aid you in maintaining a prompt payment record.

Please contact me so that we can work out some arrangement that will be mutually satisfactory.

Stage 4: Ultimatum

After you have sent one or two gentle reminders, a letter of inquiry and/or appeal, and one or more messages showing firmer pressure, if there is no response, the messages take on a different tone. Letters of **ultimatum** are written at the final stage of the collection letter series.

In preparing these letters, it is helpful to try to get a mental picture of the person to whom you are writing: the poor credit risk. This person is accustomed to getting reminders and has a rather hard shell against most reasoning or appeals. If there is one appeal that is effective, it is fear—fear of something that the person does not wish to happen.

The letters written at this stage are among the few kinds that violate the rule of promoting good will. Your competitors are welcome to these customers. They are poor at paying obligations and are too much trouble to the collection department. Further, negatives are more effective here than positives—these customers have brushed off your more positive "nice guy" approaches.

The letter of ultimatum can take several forms. It can threaten to turn the account over to collection agencies—to have a caller come to the door— or to have attorneys take legal action. If legal action is to be taken, the debtor can be reminded that court costs of both the debtor and the creditor will be charged to the debtor. Some merchandise can be repossessed for money due and, in some states, wages can be garnished. Of course, credit privileges can be canceled. Since none of these avenues appeal to either the sender or the receiver of the letter of ultimatum, it is imperative that the message be as strong as legally possible to try to effect payment.

Legality is the key. Legally, the threat can be only for action that is within the limits of the law, such as a suit to collect a debt on a contract, or other actions as just set out. Libel laws prohibit name calling or threats of damaging a person's reputation. Other laws prohibit threats of violence.

Federal law sets out specific things you cannot do in debt collection:

□ You may not communicate by postcard (outsiders can read it).

□ You may not threaten violence.

□ You may not call repeatedly with intent to annoy.

□ You may not use obscene language to abuse.

□ You may not falsely say you are a lawyer.

□ You may not misrepresent the legal status of a debt.

□ You may not falsely suggest that the debtor has committed a crime.[1]

Guidelines for writing the letter of ultimatum in collection processes are shown here:

1. Give specific details of the debt: amount due, how long overdue, late payment charges, and interest charges.

2. State clearly that previous notices have been ignored or refused.

3. State clearly what action is desired.

4. State clearly what action you will take if no response is received.

5. Give a specific deadline, such as, "If we have not heard by _____ ." Give the person ample, but not too much, time—about a week or ten days.

Examples of effective collection letters of ultimatum follow.

Collection Ultimatum 1

As you have failed to answer our earlier requests for payment of $300.17, now six months overdue, we will be forced to put this matter in the hands of a collection agency.

If by January 31 we do not have in our hands the money due us, you can expect to be contacted by members of Brownson Collectors Group knocking at your door.

Collection Ultimatum 2

You are undoubtedly aware that federal law provides that anyone using the mails to defraud may be fined or imprisoned or both.

We do not like to report a customer to postal authorities, but we feel we have the right to collect what is legally due us. As you have ignored our many

---

[1]Iris I. Varner and Carson H. Varner, "Legal Issues in Business Communications," *The American Business Communication Association Bulletin,* September 1983, p. 14.

FIGURE 8.4
Ultimatum letter that brought desired results.

The Marina
601 Ocean Park Place
Long Beach, California 00800

September, 20XX

Edward Jaxson
Unit #1060

Dear Edward

I received your response explaining your refusal to pay the $5.75 increase in cable TV costs.

This is a problem that is encountered all the time by people living in condos. It is the need to conform and go along with the majority of owners that drives a lot of people away from condo living. I don't use the pool and sauna, but I still must help pay for their upkeep.

Through July of 20XX the breakdown of your maintenance fee was as follows:

Unit	Parking Space	Cable TV	Basic Maintenance Fee	Total Maintenance Fee
1060	6.00	16.00	175.00	219.00

Starting August 1 your maintenance fee is as follows:

1060	10.00	21.00	200.00	231.00

Let me know how you intend to proceed in this matter. I hope you will not force us to use legal action.

For the Board of Governors

A. D. Dunkin
Treasurer

c   Alfred Hunter—as you suggested
Law Offices
141 Beach Boulevard
Westminister, Calif. 92683

letters, we have no alternative, because your merchandise was ordered through the United States mails.

If we have not heard from you by August 23, you will be reported.

Collection Ultimatum 3

Because you have failed to pay the premium when due, your policy #121467892 is being canceled today, in line with our formal announcement mailed to you April 30, effective May 20.

Please remember that we wanted to keep you as a client—you are the one who is responsible for the cancellation.

Upon receipt of a check for the $97.20 due, we will suggest reinstatement of your policy to the underwriting department.

It might be risky to use humor at this stage. Dartnell Corporation gives us this story:

A few years ago, a furniture company attempted to collect some overdue bills with this threatening letter:

Dear Sir:

What would your friends and neighbors think if our truck pulled into your driveway some afternoon, and our men came into your house to pick up the items of furniture for which you have not paid us?

Shelby Furniture Company

Back came this prompt reply:

Gentlemen:

I have talked this over with my friends and neighbors and they all agree it would be a pretty lousy trick.

Henry Jones

Checklist for Collection Letters

1. Identify the reader(s) and write to that audience.
2. Is the appearance satisfactory?
3. Is the message clear and complete?
4. Does the message carry good will for you and/or your firm? *Exception:* In the late stages of collection, retaining good will is not a major concern. However, do not make libelous insulting statements or threats of violence.
5. As you go over your first draft, check for grammar, spelling, punctuation.
6. Eliminate unnecessary words, phrases, sentences.
7. Recheck for any statement that might be interpreted as discourteous.
8. Check for variety in sentence form: Some sentences should start with descriptive words, phrases, or clauses (subject performs action).

9. Where possible, change negative words to positive. *Exception:* late stages of collection letter series.

10. Check for the "you attitude." Are statements made in the reader's interest, rather than in the writer's interest?

To the instructor: Oral communication diversion: Have each student pronounce the following words.

nuclear	NOOK • lee • er
realtor	REE • uhl • tor
statistics	stuh • TISS • ticks

Print words and pronunciations on board.

Chapter 8   Credit and Collections

WRITING IMPROVEMENT "HANDS ON" EXERCISE
AVOIDING REDUNDANCIES—AWKWARD REPETITION
OF SAME OR SIMILAR WORDS

Original	The difference in results occurred because the new owners followed different routines.
Improved	The change occurred because the new owners followed different routines.
Original	This term would not be proper terminology.
Improved	This would not be proper terminology.
Original	They are located in convenient locations around the area.
Improved	They are located in convenient places around the area.

Each of these examples in its original form contains a needless awkward repetition of the same or similar words. One evidence of poor communication style in writing or speaking is such repetition, which is monotonous to the reader or listener. A way to catch this type of usage in written material is to read it aloud, since repetitions are usually picked up more readily by hearing them.

Some of these sentences can be improved by simply rephrasing them and omitting one of the repetitious words. In other instances, it is necessary to use another word of similar meaning. To find such synonyms and to improve your vocabulary, refer to a dictionary, thesaurus, or both.

Not all word duplications can be considered improper. When used intentionally for emphasis, repetition of the same or a similar word or phrase can be effective. For example:

Your report is excellent, really an excellent piece of work.

A cartoon character once said, "The critic claimed that new movies are either neurotic, erotic, or tommy-rotic."

I like to communicate in writing; then we both know what we both know.

Chapter 8   Credit and Collections

WRITING IMPROVEMENT "HANDS ON" ASSIGNMENT
AVOIDING REDUNDANCIES—AWKWARD REPETITION
OF SAME OR SIMILAR WORDS

In each of the following sentences, underline the words that are the same or that have awkward repetition of the same or similar sounds. Then rewrite the improved form in the space provided. If the repetition is not apparent, read the sentence aloud. Too many of these sentences were taken from public print or broadcast.

1. Greg <u>initiated</u> the <u>initial</u> action. → _____

   _____

2. One <u>important</u> lesson she learned was that getting along with people could be more <u>important</u> than being able to do the work. → _____

   _____

3. Management should <u>set up</u> a program whereby written instructions are <u>set up</u> for each machine operation. → _____

   _____

4. Andrew David's staff is <u>working</u> out <u>working</u> arrangements. → _____

   _____

5. Rising costs are mostly <u>due</u> to our own <u>doing</u>. → _____

   _____

6. What is the <u>use</u> of studying word <u>usage</u>? → _____

   _____

7. He <u>repeats</u> this <u>repetition</u> frequently. → _____

   _____

8. The marketing department has <u>laid out</u> the <u>layout</u> for next month's magazine ads. → _____

   _____

   _____

9. After all the information was obtained, the <u>contract</u> was <u>contracted</u> by the survey team. → _____

   _____

10. This <u>provision</u> <u>provides</u> insurance coverage for all dependents. → _____

   _____

11. This morning, the sectional weather roundup will not be <u>available</u> owing to <u>unavail-ability</u>. → _____

_____

12. Ask them to make a <u>record</u> of each <u>recording</u> sold between 6 and 9 P.M. → _____

_____

13. They want us <u>to</u> send <u>two</u> copies <u>to</u> them <u>too</u>. → _____

_____

14. <u>Reporters</u> <u>reported</u> detailed activities of each candidate. → _____

_____

15. At the wedding, her <u>presents</u> of cash made her <u>presence</u> most welcome. → _____

_____

Chapter 8   Credit and Collections

WRITING ASSIGNMENTS

1. You are employed as general office assistant for C. E. Lukes, D.D.S. Dr. Lukes has suggested that you try to collect his overdue accounts for an agreed percentage of the amount you can collect. The accounts range from 30 days to nine months past due. (You are to make up fictitious names and addresses.)

    a. Write a reminder to a client whose account is 30 days past due. The amount due is $60.

    b. Write a letter to a client whose account is 60 days past due, amount $172.

    c. Write a letter to a client whose account is nine months past due, amount $163.

2. As vehicle loan officer of First City Bank, you are in charge of collecting loan payments on all motor vehicles. Write a collection communication for each of the following overdue accounts. Make up individual names and addresses:

    a. A 20XX VW with a $123 balance one month past due.

    b. A 20XX Oldsmobile Cutlass with $1,330.78 balance. Payment has not been made for three months.

    c. A 19XX Wagoneer Motor Home with a balance of $4,272 on which payments have not been made for six months.

3. You are new to town and want to apply for credit at a local department store. Write to the store of your choice with a request to open an account. Give them information of satisfactory accounts you have had previously in Tucson, Arizona, at Goldwater's, Rosenzweig's, and Jacome's. Also mention that you have a current Texaco credit card under your name, account #75 141 0000.

Chapter 8 Credit and Collections

REVIEW AND DISCUSSION

Give concise responses to the following:

1. For successful operation of a business, three departments must work closely together. What are they?

    a. sales

    b. credit

    c. collection

2. What percentage of accounts are usually uncollectable? 0.5 percent.

3. 85 percent of business operates on credit.

4. Name the four C's of credit, and define each.

    a. Character: person's basic ethics, honesty, dependability.

    b. Capital: money behind debtor.

    c. Capacity: current or anticipated income.

    d. Conditions: economic situation not necessarily related to applicant.

5. Name four sources of retail credit information.

    a. Credit applicant himself or herself.

    b. Other businesses with which applicant trades.

    c. Retail credit association.

    d. Employer(s).

6. Name three sources of trade credit information.

    a. Salespeople and other contacts from your own firm.

    b. Trade reports.

    c. Suppliers, "word on the street."

7. Instead of explaining a credit term as "1/10, net 60," how should it be explained? __ Credit terms vary; should be explained in full.

8. What is a "merge letter"? A letter made up from a main letter holding common message with blanks to be filled in for each customer.

9. Name the four topics that should be covered in exchanging credit information.

    a. How long applicant had account with you.

    b. Usual size of account.

    c. Current status of account.

    d. Special comments that are legal.

10. Give three reasons why collection letters must be written and must be effective.

    a. You want money that is rightfully yours.

    b. You want to save expense of further collection procedures.

    c. You want to regain business of customer who is probably trading elsewhere.

11. What do well run organizations do to see that collection letters are continuing to be effective? They regularly review collection procedures, revising them if indicated.

12. In collections, personal oral contacts are usually (more/~~less~~) effective than written contacts.

13. Sometimes late payments from well rated businesses or government agencies are due not to a lack of money but to red tape—paperwork.

14. Give four guidelines for writing good collection letters. Be brief.

    a. Understand that he or she knows he or she owes and expects to hear.

    b. Few people are dishonest—almost all pay up.

    c. Be specific and up to date about details.

    d. Check that order was filled correctly.

15. The text says: "Collection letters should be written promptly, regularly, and with what kind of communication? Increasing forcefulness."

16. In business, most collection communications are by letter.

17. The older an account gets, the (~~more~~/less) chance there is of collecting on it.

18. Name the four stages of the collection letter series.

    a. Reminder.

    b. Inquiry and appeal.

    c. Pressure.

    d. Ultimatum.

19. Why should the first collection letter appear routine? Could have been overlooked. Could be a very good customer.

20. Name three types of inquiries or appeals that can be used in those stages of collections.

    a. Pride.

    b. Economic self-interest.

    c. Sympathy, courtesy, fair play.

Improve each of the following sentences by replacing words or phrases that have the same or similar sounds.

21. Your <u>reference</u> <u>refers</u> to faxes we sent earlier. → _____

_____

22. The road is still <u>closed</u> because the supervisor's office is <u>closed</u>. → _____

_____

23. Ed understands the operation of <u>fairs</u> and <u>carnivals</u> quite well. → _____

_____

24. The outdoor <u>scene</u> of the first act can be <u>seen</u> in the distance in the third act. → ____

_____

25. Among the <u>important</u> products they <u>import</u> are many electronic components. → ___

_____

9
Courtesy Messages You Don't Have to Send, but Should

> *Life is not so short but that there is always time for courtesy.*
> Ralph Waldo Emerson,
> *U.S. Essayist, philosopher and poet, 1803–1882*

It is difficult to set a dollar value on that intangible asset of a business, **good will.** But when a business is sold, the new owners will often pay money for the privilege of operating the business under the old name if that name has a favorable reputation. At such a time, an estimate of a reasonable value is placed on this asset, and the value of good will is included in the selling price as part of the cost of taking over the business. The new owners can then use the name to their own advantage.

In the crush of making money, business people should not concentrate so much on other important aspects of business that they overlook the value of creating and maintaining good will among present, past, and potential customers and among peers and employees. Although this text cautions against writing unnecessary letters, there are times when a personal message would be welcomed and should be written. Customers usually receive only two types of communications from a business: either those trying to sell goods and services or those trying to collect money. Other types of communications are rare and are therefore appreciated.

Various organizations have become so large and impersonal that sometimes we do not show the thoughtful personal consideration of people that we should. One top executive of a large corporation says he spends a high percentage of his time writing "letters you don't have to write, but *should.*"

Personal Communications Within an Organization

Besides pleasing employees, which is exceedingly important, showing good will to them helps a business prosper because employees, of course, have much to do with the successful operation of any business. Lines of communication can be kept open between employer and employee by the judicious writing of personal letters or notes that show an interest in the other's well-being. An occasional **message from an employer to an employee** noting a special event would undoubtedly be well received.

An occasional message from an **employee to an employer** may also indeed be welcome. Even in a large business this act gives a favorable impression to an employer who is aware that it is impossible to become well acquainted with all employees. An employee might compliment an employer on such an occasion as an honor received, a promotion, a speech, or some other notable personal event in his or her life or in the life of a member of the family. After all, the boss, too, is a human being! You should not be too effusive—just short and clear.

Remember—customers are your most priceless possession. Next best are the customers who bought from you in the past but have stopped.

Be aware that **special good will letters—courtesy letters—**are appropriate not only for many business situations but also for professional and personal contacts. These are messages you don't have to send, but should.

Types of Courtesy Communications

Thank You Letters and Other Letters of Appreciation

Thank you letters and other **letters of appreciation** are probably the most common type of special good will messages written in business. These can be sent to show appreciation for such things as doing business with the firm, completing payments on an installment account, paying open accounts on time, performing work beyond regular duties, doing favors, or doing anything else that is especially appreciated.

Here are some typical letters in this category;

Thank you 1

On behalf of the management and the entire staff of the Queen Mary Restaurants, we would like to thank you for affording us the pleasure of hosting your recent dinner.

It was a pleasure working with you, and whenever we can be of further assistance to you in any way, do not hesitate to contact us.

Thank you again, and we shall look forward to serving you again in the near future.

Thank you 2

Thank you for opening a new account with Bank of South America. It is a pleasure to serve you, and we look forward to a long and cordial relationship.

If at any time we can assist you in any of your other banking needs, please do not hesitate to call upon me.

Thank you 3

Dear Friends:

Today I am back at work feeling better than ever, and I can tell you it's a good feeling. Health is a big blessing. No one knows more than I how fortunate I am.

Having friends is another big blessing, and I want each of you to know how grateful I am for your prayers and good wishes. I received so many cards and get-well messages it would be impossible to acknowledge them all, so I am taking this means to thank you and tell you how much I appreciate your thinking of me.

There has never been any doubt in my mind that _____ is the greatest family in the world—always concerned and caring for its own. We have excellent benefits, but you have shown me that our concern for one another is the greatest benefit of all—and that's a benefit that money can't buy. I am truly grateful.

It's good to be back!

Sincerely,

[Personal note to individual recipient.]
P.S. Thanks for your nice letter. I appreciated hearing from you.

Thank you 4

Dear Mr. and Mrs. Hansen:

This is just a short note to let you know I very much appreciate the concern you expressed to me in Mrs. Hansen's letter of July 12. This has been a tragedy for the family, and we sincerely appreciate all the support we have received from family and friends.

Thank you for your thoughts.

Sincerely,

Congratulations

Letters, emails, memos, and cards of **congratulations** are some of the more common good will messages. They are sent for reasons like promotion, birthday, wedding, length of service, civic honor, published writing, research, an exceptionally fine piece of work, and so forth.

Here are typical congratulation letters:

Congratulations 1

Congratulations on moving into the new headquarters of your bank. The building is very attractive, and it should be a pleasure to do business with you there. It is really a fine addition to our community.

I will expect to call on you one of the first days the building is open for business.

Congratulations 2

Dear John,

Well, it really doesn't seem as if it was fifteen years ago that I interviewed you for your first position with Bankers Trust and Company. But it surely was, and I have enjoyed watching you grow with the organization, assuming different new duties and performing them well.

It will be my pleasure to be among those honoring you at the annual employee awards dinner-dance.

I just wanted to send you a note of congratulations and say how much I personally appreciate your work with us.

Congratulations 3

It has just been brought to my attention that last Friday evening you received the Silver Beaver Award in honor of your active participation as a leader in the Boy Scouts of America for the past fifteen years.

I am sure your work with the Scouts has not only been of much value to the boys, but also has been gratifying to you. I am also gratified to have such a person as a member of our staff.

I certainly congratulate you on receiving this distinction, and wish you continued success and enjoyment in your work in our community.

Congratulations 4

Congratulations on your daughter's graduation. You must be very proud of her. Congratulations to her—and also to her parents!

Letters, Cards, and Notes of Welcome

People always like to know that they are **welcome** as customers, as members of a group, as members of a community, or as new employees.

Here are some example letters of welcome:

Welcome 1

Tom Padia, the president of our local bank, just informed me that you have recently moved into our community. I wish to welcome you here. Big Springs has much to offer its residents, and the friendliness of our people is just one of its attributes.

I hope you enjoy living among us, and if I may be of service to you in establishing your business, please let me know.

Welcome 2

We are pleased to welcome you as a member of the Brandywine Museum of Art and to send you your official membership card.

Over the coming year, through the monthly calendar, you will be kept informed of special exhibitions and other events of particular interest to members.

On behalf of the Trustees, the staff, and the more than 2,000 members of the Museum, I extend warm thanks for your support and a firm hope that you will find your personal association with the Museum an enriching and stimulating one.

Concern

Letters of **personal concern** might be appropriately written on many different types of occasions, such as illness or injury, closing of a business, inactivity of an account, or damage of goods. The tone of this letter varies with the occasion and the relationship between the individuals involved. Six such letters are given here:

Concern 1

I just became aware of your recent operation through a communication from Ms. Angelo.

My initial thought was to contact your wife to inquire about your condition, but I realized such a contact from a person she hardly knows would scarcely be appreciated. I did call your secretary and was advised that your condition is improving splendidly and that you will probably be able to return to the office within the next two or three weeks. Needless to say, this assurance caused me much relief.

While I realize the unlikely need, if there is any way I may be of service to you personally, I would consider it an honor to accept.

It is my sincere hope that when you receive this letter you are feeling your old self again.

Concern 2

WE'VE MISSED YOU—

When we closed our books today, we found that your account has not been used for some time. Naturally, we are greatly concerned, because we value each of our patrons and miss them when they fail to visit us regularly.

Right now we are showing so many lovely new fashions at affordable prices that we are sure you will agree it's a good time for you to use your account again.

We trust that you will find it convenient to call on us soon. Just use your charge card. Your account is ready and waiting.

Concern 3

Well Lou!

We all knew you wanted to watch the World Series this week, but breaking your leg so you could do it was a bit much!

Seriously, I am sorry that you had an accident, and it certainly can't be fun. But we are pleased to hear that you are well on the mend.

We all miss you around here, and hope to see you back soon.

Best wishes,

Concern 4

Dear Dr. Albanese:

Tom and I are very grateful that Bob and Julie Ede recently referred you to us as our dentist. We surely appreciate the professional help you and your staff are giving to both of us.

Yesterday, Julie told me that the young Albanese woman who recently was the innocent victim of that shooting is your cousin.

Tom and I both express our regret that the incident occurred, and we want you to know of our concern for you and all your family.

Best personal wishes,

Concern 5

We were very sorry to learn of the flood that did so much damage to your warehouse. We hope that our man there, Martin Francis, arrived in time to be of some help to you.

Do be assured that any offer of assistance he makes to you is authorized by our entire organization.

We'll be happy to see you continue your operations as soon as possible.

Concern 6

The good will of old friends is of great value to us. And when we do not hear from our friends for a long time, it causes us concern. Because your last order was in July 20XX, we can't help wondering if our services to you may have faltered in some way unknown to us.

If it is simply that you haven't had the need of our services lately, you will be glad to know, I'm sure, that we have recently increased our capacity with additional equipment, incorporated a number of new features, and streamlined systems in our plant. Other customers are already finding these features most profitable.

Your good will and friendship are worth much to us, and we want to serve you well. May we look forward to the pleasure of hearing from you again soon?

Sincerely,

Condolence

At a time of bereavement, a person appreciates getting a card, but a personal letter of **condolence** from a friend or a business associate is appreciated even more. Because these letters are somewhat difficult to write, and also because they come at a time of deep emotional disturbance, they are probably more welcome than others.

There are certain guidelines that will help you compose such a letter. First, avoid long recitations of details that could sadden the reader. Avoid reference to anguish or suffering, and perhaps try to promote the thought that a person's good influence continues in the hearts and minds of those who knew him or her. You should not write of people's religious beliefs unless you are very close and fully understand their feelings. This is not the time to try to promote your own religious values.

A short message is very acceptable. The most important thing is that you took the time and effort to write. Here are letters you might follow as examples:

Condolence 1

I was deeply saddened by the sudden loss of my good friend, Eugene.

He was a strong and effective leader who had accomplished much, both in his business and community life. We will all certainly miss him.

I send my personal concern to you, Beth, and to your children.

Condolence 2

I just learned that you lost your mother last week and want to add my personal concern to those from your many other friends.

We all remember your mother as a friend of everyone—she left a good influence on those who knew her.

I will be sure to call on you the next time I am in town.

Seasonal Greetings

Many businesses send holiday cards and letters, mostly end-of-the-year or New Year greetings. Businesses should avoid religious references, concentrating instead on such phrases as "Season's Greetings," and "Happy Holidays." These can take any form, from a printed card to a personally written letter. This message should avoid maudlin sentimentality but should sound sincere.

Longhand Correspondence

There is still a place in business for **longhand correspondence,** although this form should rarely be used. But when someone does you a particular favor or supports a cause in which you have a personal interest, you might send off a brief longhand note. Or when you have a deep personal feeling about an event, the fact that you took the extra time and attention to prepare this communication will not go unnoticed.

Figure 9.1 is a copy of a longhand letter written by a Superior Court judge to a college instructor who had taken her class to visit the judge's courtroom. Writing the letter took some of her valued time, but it does make a good impression.

Communicating with Public Officials[1]

We can make this truly a government "of the people, by the people, and for the people" by communicating frequently with our elected officials. How? By letter, fax, telegram, phone, and personal visit.

Letters

Letters are probably the most effective means in most cases. A congressman recently stated that "letters are one of the best gauges of public opinion on issues that a busy member can have during a decision making period. While this is time-consuming to the citizen, it is valuable to the representative—and therefore, I encourage letters and welcome them."

---

[1]Courtesy of Lois M. Plowman, Professor Emeritus of Business Communication, Cerritos College.

FIGURE 9.1
Longhand letter from a Superior Court judge.

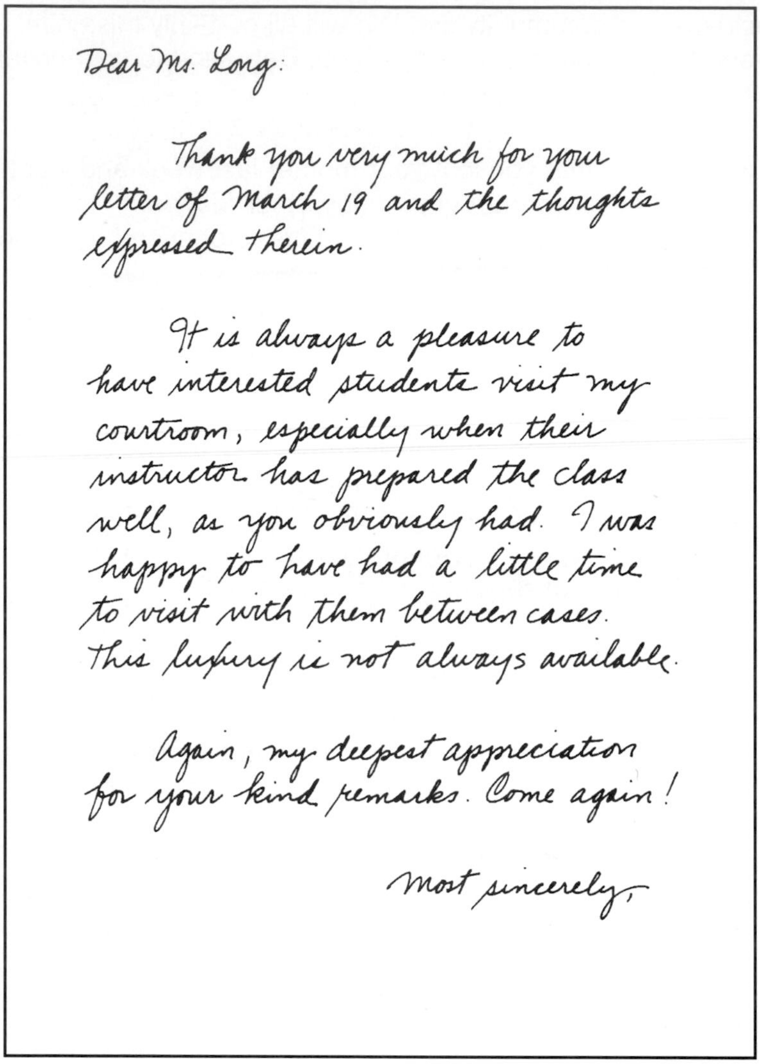

> Dear Mr. Long:
>
> Thank you very much for your letter of March 19 and the thoughts expressed therein.
>
> It is always a pleasure to have interested students visit my courtroom, especially when their instructor has prepared the class well, as you obviously had. I was happy to have had a little time to visit with them between cases. This luxury is not always available.
>
> Again, my deepest appreciation for your kind remarks. Come again!
>
> Most sincerely,

A Senator said, "citizens concerned about specific legislation should make their views known before the legislation is acted upon in Congress." This is important at *any* level of government.

Here are some guidelines for writing letters to our elected officials:

1. *Identify yourself.* State not only your name and address, but also which of your life roles you are representing. For example, you are requesting action as a businessman (give kind), parent, teacher, student, doctor, lawyer, officer of some organization, etc.
2. *Specify your concern.* If it is in regard to legislation, state the number and author if possible.
3. *Write briefly.* It is preferred that you limit your letter to one page. Give reasons for your position.

4. *Give facts.* Back your reasons for your position with facts, if you have them.

5. *Be courteous.* Show appreciation for the public servant's efforts. In no way be threatening.

6. *Cover one issue in one letter.* If you have concerns about unrelated items, write a separate letter for each issue. In other words, if you are writing a letter about legislation regarding oil rights, this same letter should not include your concern about sending troops to Angola. Instead, write two letters.

7. *The letter should be original with you.* There is strong aversion to form letters. One congressman has said that much more attention is given to a handwritten letter than to other kinds of letters. Congressmen know that it is fairly easy to get people to sign a form letter that they may not really understand or that may not truly reflect their views.

8. *There should be only one signature to a letter.*

9. *Use the correct name and spelling of the official being addressed.* You can get help on this from the following sources:
    a. Your local library (college or city). Ask the librarian over the telephone or visit the library.
    b. The local office of the official involved. Look in the telephone directory under the unit of government involved. For example, if you live in Jefferson County and it is a county matter, look under "Jefferson"; look under "United States" for a federal office; under the state's name for a state office.
    c. The city clerk in your city hall.
    d. The registrar of voters in your county or city.
    e. The League of Women Voters.

10. Where to write:
    a. *National affairs:*
        The President of the United States: The President, The White House, Washington, D.C. 20500. Or The Honorable _____ , President of the United States, The White House, Washington, D.C. 20500.
        U.S. Senators: United States Senate, Washington, D.C. 20510
        U.S. Representatives: United States House of Representatives, Washington, D.C. 20515.
    b. *State affairs:* State Capitol Building, name of your capital, state, ZIP code.
    c. *Local affairs:* Mayor _____ or Councilman or Councilwoman _____ c/o City Hall, name of your city, state, ZIP code.

Here is an example of a letter one might send to a member of the House of Representatives:

The Honorable Congressman _____
House of Representatives
Washington, D.C. 20515
My Dear Sir:

I ask that you oppose HR 2556, sponsored by Mr. Charles Wilson. This bill would close census records, which are now open, after they are 75 years old or older. This bill would not only keep them closed to the public but would also close them even to genealogists and historians.

I believe that the history of our country should be preserved so we can study events of the past to learn from them, thus avoiding mistakes of other times in the present and also benefiting from the solutions of problems of other times. This is the way we make progress.

It is important that every source of information be available so that a true picture of events can be made. How else can history be of value? Let us not close any sources! "And ye shall know the truth, and the truth shall make you free."

Yours respectfully, [Other appropriate closings are, "Sincerely yours," "Very truly yours," etc.]

Mrs. Lois M. Plowman

The federal government does want the average citizen to keep in touch, so much so that is has made available a free pamphlet, which comes out monthly, titled "How to Keep in Touch with the U.S. Government."

Telegrams

Western Union will send a Public Opinion Message to any elected state or federal official for a reasonable reduced rate. This message can be telephoned in and you will be charged on your phone bill.

Mailgrams

Also at a reasonable rate, Western Union will send a Mailgram electronically to a post office near any addressee. Printed on the distinctive blue and white Mailgram letterhead with envelope, the message will be delivered in the next regular mail, usually the next day, or sometimes the day it is sent.

Faxes

Fax copies of letters are common and receive attention because of their number.

> **To the instructor:** A woman who slipped and fell while shopping in a grocery store seemed to have hurt herself. Other shoppers offered to help—the store manager even offered to take her list and finish her shopping—but she refused. A nearby friend overheard the offer and, seeing her friend hobble off, asked, "Why didn't you let him?"
>
> "And let him see how I spelled 'spaghetti?'"

Chapter 9   Courtesy Messages You Don't Have to Send, but Should

WRITING IMPROVEMENT EXERCISE
AVOIDING REDUNDANCIES: AWKWARD REPETITION
OF WORDS OR IDEAS WITH SIMILAR MEANINGS

The weather is damp and wet.

I am tired and exhausted.

Each of the sentences above contains a repetition or a redundancy. In other words, each sentence needlessly contains a word that has essentially the same meaning as another word that has just been used. These sentences would be better if stated:

The weather is damp.

or

The weather is wet.

I am tired.

or

I am exhausted.

A professional writer or speaker avoids the use of redundancies, but owing to various pressures, speakers and writers occasionally make these grammatical lapses. Redundancies are also sometimes used as "filler" words, so that a person who has little to say can appear to be saying more.

Good business writing and speaking seek just the opposite. Here, words should be used economically—two words should not be used where one will do. Following are some examples of redundancies, all of which were taken from current writing and speaking:

1. But all these recommendations, however, will be put into effect. (*but* or *however*)

2. Basically, there are two fundamental reasons for following their progress. (*basics* are *fundamentals*.)

3. It was claimed that women charged with the exact same crime as men received longer sentences.

4. This matter is being used as a political football for various different reasons. (*various* or *different*)

5. They are laboring under a false deception. (What is a true deception?)

6. The Senator has a new and innovative approach to the problem. (Something *new* is *innovative*.)

7. Everything is agreeable and satisfactory. (*agreeable* or *satisfactory*)

8. Today's game will be broadcast at 3 P.M. this afternoon. (*P.M.* or *afternoon*)

9. I got a rebate back on my federal income tax. (*rebate* or *money back*)

10. We'll also broadcast from the locker room of the losing team, too. (*also* or *too*)

11. The alleged rumor is that the boss is dating his secretary. (*It is alleged* or *The rumor is*)

12. James reported the chance of a possible strike threat. (*the chance of* or *possible*)

13. The metal beams are about 30 feet long, approximately. (*about* or *approximately*)

Chapter 9   Courtesy Messages You Don't Have to Send, but Should

WRITING IMPROVEMENT "HANDS ON" ASSIGNMENT
AVOIDING REDUNDANCIES: AWKWARD REPETITION
OF WORDS OR IDEAS WITH SIMILAR MEANINGS

Make the following sentences shorter and clearer by drawing a line through any needless repetition.

1. I can take the bus and get to a <u>variety</u> of <u>different</u> places.
2. The company is <u>still</u> flourishing <u>today</u>.
3. We found this <u>ancient</u> <u>old</u> office memorandum.
4. This is the <u>same</u> <u>identical</u> piece of information that you got.
5. <u>Frequently</u>, profit anticipations of a business <u>often</u> do not materialize.
6. Friendly Inn policies are formulated by the governors and directors at an <u>annual</u> meeting held <u>each year</u>.
7. Don't be an <u>impediment</u> or <u>hindrance</u> to the campaign.
8. A <u>full</u> and <u>complete</u> report will be presented at that time.
9. <u>Possibly</u> they will <u>perhaps</u> be able to set the March meeting.
10. I believe these experiences have <u>prepared</u> and <u>qualified</u> me for a position as assistant manager.
11. I am <u>appreciative</u> and <u>grateful</u> that you attended our <u>recent</u> conference <u>last week</u>. It was <u>obvious</u> and <u>easy to see</u> that the session you led was very <u>successful</u>, as well as being <u>well received</u>.
12. You have said <u>too much</u>—it was <u>more than was needed</u>.
13. Our hero did not expect that his best friend would perform a <u>dishonest</u> act of <u>betrayal</u>.
14. Scott <u>openly</u> and <u>freely</u> discussed his pending legal action.
15. An <u>unknown</u> <u>stranger</u> contributed $50 to Edgerton's campaign fund.
16. We are <u>sure</u> that <u>without a doubt</u> we can remedy this situation.
17. They seem to be <u>sorry</u> and <u>concerned</u> about the results.
18. <u>Each</u> and <u>every</u> bit of evidence was presented.
19. Your firm and ours can <u>cooperate</u> <u>together</u> and agree.
20. All our representatives are <u>currently</u> speaking with customers <u>at this time</u>.

Chapter 9   Courtesy Messages You Don't Have to Send, but Should

WRITING ASSIGNMENTS

1. You own a print shop. Write a letter of concern to clients who have not done business with you in the past year. Let them know of the improvements in your shop, and tell them that you would like to do more work for them.

2. Mark Janowicz has just completed payments on his 19XX Accord, financed by your agency. Write Mr. Janowicz a brief letter complimenting him on the completion of his contract and the regular manner in which he made his payments, and thank him for the purchase.

3. The daughter of one of your employees, Mrs. Bonnie E. Brown, has just been chosen as commencement speaker at the Spring 20XX graduation exercises at the local college. Write a note of congratulations to Mrs. Brown.

4. Write a congratulations letter to Tom Padia for him and other members of the accounting division baseball team, which, although not placing as champions, fielded a team once a week for the entire summer season.

5. Write a letter thanking the members of the department where you work for the wedding gift they combined funds to purchase for you and your new bride or groom. Tell them to what use the gift is being put.

6. Write a letter that might go to a fellow employee who is in the hospital recovering from surgery.

7. John James, supervisor of your department, has recently lost his mother. Mr. James is out of the state attending her services and taking care of her legal and business matters. Write him a brief letter of condolence.

8. You are manager of the local Volvo agency and have decided to have a special letter printed to send to all recent customers. Make up this letter.

9. Write a letter to a public official expressing your concern about a matter in which that person might have some influence. If you actually plan to send the letter, make a note of this information and attach it to your letter so that the instructor will not place grading information on it. You should follow the pattern for a routine information letter, a negative letter, or a selling letter, according to your message. Your letter will be graded according to how well it follows the information contained earlier in this exercise.

10. Write a letter to a public official expressing your appreciation for some action taken by that official. Or, write a letter asking some official to support some cause or legislation.

Chapter 9 Courtesy Messages You Don't Have to Send, but Should

REVIEW AND DISCUSSION

1. What is "good will" in business?

   The value of a business over and above its tangible assets.
   _____

2. Is a dollar amount ever placed on the value of business good will? Explain.

   Yes, in the sale or inheritance of a business.

3. What are the two types of communications that customers usually receive from a business?

   Bills (statements) and sales letters.
   _____

4. Although mails and desks are frequently overcrowded with communications, why should we occasionally take time to write the "letters you don't have to write, but *should*"?

   Courtesy letters or other communications are usually noticed and appreciated.
   _____

5. Name some occasions that might prompt an employer to write a special courtesy letter to an employee.

   Special personal event: marriage, birth of child, birthday, bereavement, anniversary, and so forth. Letters of welcome.

6. Is it ever proper for an employee to write a courtesy letter to his employer? Explain.

   Yes. Bosses are human too. May help make you become human to your employer.
   _____
   _____

7. Name five occasions for which a thank you letter might be written.

   a. Appreciation for business.

   b. Completing payments on an installment account.

   c. Paying open accounts on time.

   d. Performing work well, beyond usual duties.

   e. Doing favors.

8. Name five occasions for which a letter of congratulations might be written.

     a.   [Choose proper events from Question 5 or others.]

     b. _____

     c. _____

     d. _____

     e. _____

9. Give guidelines to help someone write a letter of condolence.

     Avoid recitations that might sadden reader; avoid negatives such as reference to pain, anguish, loss; do not promote your own religion.

10. Is longhand correspondence ever acceptable in today's business? Explain.

     Yes. For special occasions, it can personalize a situation.

11. Do you believe public officials pay attention to messages they receive from their constituents?   (Student input.)

12. If you want to write to the same official about two different matters, how many letters should you write?   Two.

Oral Communications

> *I know you believe you understand what you think I said, but I'm not sure you realize that what you heard is not what I meant.*
>
> *Anonymous*

The ability to communicate orally is helpful in most careers, particularly careers in business. Business students are urged to take college courses that include training in various types of speaking, such as classes in speech, salesmanship, and business behavior. Summary discussions of major types of oral communications important in business and other career scenes will be presented here: telephoning, dictating, leading and participating in meetings and conferences, feeding the grapevine, winning the confrontation, making presentations, and listening.

Telephoning

Despite the intrigues of electronic communications, let's not overlook the power of the telephone.

Telephone techniques are extremely important in any business. A telephone call is frequently the first contact a customer has with a firm, and poor telephone manners—even by the telephone receptionist—can obviously lose the caller's good will and change a customer's mind about dealing with that firm. Each person along the line of the call must recognize that the company is being judged by its employees' telephone manners.

In a booklet entitled, "Every Time You Talk on the Telephone, You Really Are the Company," the General Telephone Company gives the following excellent advice:

- ☐ **Greet the caller pleasantly.** Be enthusiastic and yet sincere. Such treatment makes customers like you and be more apt to call again.
- ☐ **Use the caller's name.** There's no sweeter music to a person than the sound of his or her own name. And speak to the *person* at the other end of the line, not to the telephone.

225

☐ **Treat every call as an important call**. It is important to the person calling you. When the customer feels that you are giving **individual** rather that **routine** consideration, you'll create more confidence in you and your company.

☐ **Be tactful.** When it's necessary to refuse a request because of company policy, give a full and sympathetic explanation. Avoid expressions such as "you have to" or "you must." A reply such as, "If you come in Monday, we'll be happy to check that for you," is better than, "You'll have to come in Monday if you want that checked."

☐ **Apologize for errors or delays.** Maybe things won't always go right, but you can always be courteous. And if you're really sincere and natural, you won't sound artificially sorry.

☐ **Keep your promises.** If you make any promises to call back with more information, do everything you can to follow through. A broken promise may mean a lost customer.

☐ **Suggest an appropriate time for callback.** When you leave a message for someone to return a call and you expect to be out of your office for a while, it is courteous to suggest a time for calling back; for example, say, "Please tell him I'll be in after lunch."

☐ **Treat your co-workers like customers.** Handle inside calls with as much care as calls from the outside. Remember, you're building your personal telephone reputation too.

☐ **Take time to be helpful.** *Brighten up your day* by pleasant telephone contacts. It really doesn't take much more time to be helpful. It's better to spend minutes to keep a customer happy than months to regain good will.

☐ **Use basic phrases of courtesy.** Say, "Please," "Thank you," and "You're welcome." The use of such phrases is one way to put a smile in your voice. **THERE'S ALWAYS TIME FOR COURTESY….**

As pointed out in Chapter 1 on the theory of communications, face to face dialogue is in many ways more effective than other means of communicating. The other person is there—you can observe reactions, and there is immediate feedback from both sides. In the normal course of events, you will discontinue the conversation by mutual agreement. In telephoning, we must try to overcome some of the handicaps of not seeing each other in person.

The Name of the Game Is Names

Most telephone calls, of course, are made between people who know each other's identity. But too often, telephone calls giving or asking information are made without identifying the caller or the person answering the call. Business telephone calls, whether they are for personal business or otherwise, are most effective when both speakers know the **name** of the party on the other end of the line. Get the name of the other person even though you may only be seeking or giving routine information and it doesn't seem necessary to identify yourself or the person at the other end of the line. After all, a telephone call can become disconnected. Or you may need to get additional information later. It can be next to impossible to get reconnected with the right person in any way but by having the correct name. Also, calls can be transferred to many different departments, sometimes incorrectly. Having the name of the person to whom you were speaking makes reconnection easier and makes the call more personal.

FIGURE 10.1
Phonetic alphabet used by telephone operators.

A	Alice	J	James	S	Samuel
B	Bertha	K	Kate	T	Thomas
C	Charles	L	Lewis	U	Utah
D	David	M	Mary	V	Victor
E	Edward	N	Nellie	W	William
F	Frank	O	Oliver	X	X-ray
G	George	P	Peter	Y	Young
H	Henry	Q	Quaker	Z	Zebra
I	Ida	R	Robert		

Memorandum Forms for Telephone Calls

All offices should have **telephone call memorandum forms** similar to that in Figure 10.2, which contains blanks for typical information that should be written down for missed telephone calls: name of person calling, firm, name of person called, date of call, time of call, and message. Obviously, all the information is important, even the notation concerning the time of the message. The two parties involved may have contacted each other in person, and it might be important for the one getting the memorandum to know if the call came in before or after the other contact. Telephone memorandum forms can be purchased in bulk from a stationer or office supplies dealer, or they can be run off on the office copying or printing equipment.

Of course, telephone answering machines bypass some of these problems. But people do tire of hearing a string of mechanical voices.

Telephone Logs

Different offices maintain different types of telephone call records. Most keep date and time information on long distance and toll calls so that a central office can check the accuracy of telephone charges being made to the company. Many firms and individuals keep **telephone logs** of all calls made and received, information that can be helpful in future plans and in correspondence. Logs also corroborate other records of telephone charges and can be of legal assistance in checking telephone company charges.

Dictation

Because of the efficiency of computers, many supervisors, managers, and other officials today can compose and type much of their own work. Also, electronics make portable dictation easier than it was. If you are one of the decreasing fortunate few who dictate to a personal secretary, that person should be treated with respect.

FIGURE 10.2
Example of telephone memorandum form.

To _____

Date _____ Time _____

WHILE YOU WERE OUT

M _____

of _____

Phone _____

TELEPHONED		PLEASE CALL	
CALLED TO SEE YOU		WILL CALL AGAIN	
WANTS TO SEE YOU		RETURNED YOUR CALL	

Message _____

_____

_____

_____

_____

_____
Operator

In return, he/she will respect you and be one of your greatest assets on the job. In dictating to a machine, get adequate instructions and take the small amount of time needed to make yourself a pro in handling this equipment.

Gather together all material you will need for completing the session.

During Dictation

For dictation to a machine or to a person, keep in mind the transcribers' hours of work at the computer. Here are some of the transcribers' requests:

1. Dictate at a moderate speed; it is better to be slow, clear, and sure than to be too speedy.
2. Please do not eat and dictate at the same time.
3. Keep background noise down.
4. Please do not dictate from your car phone. *You would be a hazard to traffic.* Also, screeching brakes, honking horns, cars backfiring, and "background" music block out dictation.

5. Please do not dictate from your home if you are near a loud TV or radio, a baby crying, a running dishwasher, bathroom noises, or a family argument.

6. Explain any special paper or format needed.

7. If you make a mistake, erase and record over it. Don't tell the transcriber to "Change that to…."

8. Do not speed up when reading printed matter. If possible, furnish a copy to the transcriber, marking clearly what is to be typed.

9. When you pause for a long time, turn the unit off.

10. Unless you want dictation stored in the machine memory, have transcriber erase after use or someone else could retranscribe your old information.

Even the best secretary or typist appreciates having you spell out not only names and addresses but also any other terms or words that might be misunderstood. Use the phonetic alphabet of telephone operators, shown in Figure 10.1, for letters that may be misunderstood. If there is a question in your mind about anything you have said, do not hesitate to ask the secretary to read it back. Or learn the simple machine operation procedures that enable you to go back and listen to your dictation, erasing and redictating to make any desired improvements.

After Dictation

Nobody is perfect—not you, your secretary, nor a typist. Proofread everything you have dictated before you sign it. You and your firm are legally responsible for anything you sign. If any necessary corrections cannot be made neatly, a fresh copy should be made.

Keeping Your MIND on the Road

Law enforcement officers tell us that daydreaming is the cause of many traffic accidents, and you should **keep your MIND on the road.**

Surely when you dictate in a car, you often are not keeping your mind on the traffic situation. Further, don't follow unsound advice to save your office dictation for the trip to and from work in a car pool unless you are sure you are not disturbing the *other person driving*.

Computer Voice Recognition for Transcribing

Rapid advances in computer voice recognition now enable us to transcribe speech automatically into a word processing document. With the right combination of software, a microphone, and a fast personal computer, almost anyone can use voice recognition for dictating quickly and accurately. Originally developed for physically challenged people, voice recognition transcribes your words without requiring you to type a word or hire a secretary. Edits can be done on a keyboard, and the efficiencies this provides can benefit people who don't type and those who would simply prefer to compose orally.

Participation in Meetings and Conferences

Our discussion of participation in meetings and conferences can be set up under two headings: suggestions for the conference or meeting leader, and suggestions for other members.

The Leader

To accomplish the purposes of the meeting and hold the respect of members attending, the leader has several responsibilities in carrying out plans of the meeting. Some duties may be delegated, but they are ultimately the responsibility of the leader. "The buck stops here."

- ☐ The leader should set the time and place of the meeting and supply these details to those who are to attend in sufficient time for them to make plans to be there.

- ☐ The leader is responsible for preparing a meeting agenda—that is, a list of matters to be discussed and work to be done at the meeting. Copies of the agenda should be distributed to potential conference members either prior to the meeting or when they arrive, according to the topics being covered. This gives members time to study it enough to plan their own participation. It is very effective to give members a tentative agenda in advance, asking for suggestions that might be included in the final copy that will be used as a blueprint for the meeting.

- ☐ A conference or meeting should be called for a specific purpose or specific purposes, not because "it's about time we got together." If there is no purpose for calling a regularly scheduled conference, unless it is openly a social gathering, it should be canceled.

Maintaining Order

Maintaining order at the meeting is the responsibility of the leader. Parliamentary procedures are recommended for most meetings, since they not only give fair rulings on procedure but tend to smooth out disagreements among members.

In a small meeting, the leader is usually in charge of procedure. If unsure in this regard, the leader should assign this task in advance to another member who will study parliamentary procedure so that rulings can be respected and followed. In larger conferences, it is helpful to have a regular parliamentarian appointed who is (or will become) well grounded in procedural format. However, at all times the leader is in charge of the meeting and uses the parliamentarian only for reference.

Marguerite Grumme, parliamentarian, states:

The four basic principles of parliamentary law:
1. Courtesy and justice to all.
2. Consider one thing at a time.
3. The minority must be heard.
4. The majority must prevail.

Note: Parliamentary law is common sense used in a gracious manner.[1]

If parliamentary procedure is not followed strictly, the preceding four principles can serve as an excellent framework for **group discussions** and decisions.

Conducting the Meeting

As leader, you will gain confidence if you follow these guidelines:

☐ You are in charge of the discussion at all times, but you must show concern for others in attendance. Relinquish the floor properly to others. Avoid letting a few individuals monopolize discussions, and try to draw out comments from the more retiring persons who might make the best contributions.

☐ If you do not wish to take notes or minutes yourself, assign this duty to a responsible person. Notes should be taken; memory should not be trusted for details.

☐ Watch the time lapse, keeping your eye on the agenda.

☐ If a follow-up meeting is to be held with the same group, set an approximate or specific time and location for it after consulting with members present.

☐ When matters have been taken care of, conclude the meeting. Ample time should be scheduled for all meetings, but avoid the hazards of Parkinson's Law which states, "Work expands so as to fill the time available for its completion." If the full time set aside has not expired when business of the meeting is completed, give members welcome free time.

Handling Guest Speakers

Guest speakers usually do not appreciate sitting through proceedings in which they are not directly involved. Try to plan the agenda to avoid having these guests listen to the long (usually boring) reading of minutes, treasurer's report, business matters, and so forth. Such planning might help give the speaker a better attitude about addressing your group. Further, word gets around the speakers' circuit, and you may find it possible to attract some who would otherwise not be interested.

Participation of Members

Members of a conference or meeting are responsible for bringing any information in their possession that will aid the purposes for which the meeting was called. Each is also responsible for listening to others and asking pertinent questions if time is given for questions.

All members owe respect to others in attendance, even though they may not agree with what another is saying. Improper conduct at meetings reflects negatively on job performance and may even hurt possibilities for promotion.

When People Get Together

At formal and informal gatherings, when people get together, people talk. And they might be talking about you. In retaining and promoting personnel, the opinions

---

[1]Marguerite Grumme, *Basic Principles of Parliamentary Law and Protocol,* 3rd ed. (published privately at St. Louis, Missouri), page 3.

of peers and subordinates as well as the opinions of superiors are considered. A big question: Will this person get along well with people at all levels?

The Office Grapevine

Grapevines exist wherever people gather, and one of the ripest seems to be the **office grapevine,** office gossip. The term "grapevine" originated during the American Civil War (1861–1865) after the abundant grapes growing wild in the southeastern part of the country. At first it meant a false report circulated as a hoax. It was then called the "grape-vine telegraph." Today on the job, management accepts its existence. Sometimes the most judicious supervisors and managers learn to use the grapevine to their own advantage by circulating rumors, trying to test how workers would react if rumor became fact.

However, 75 percent of the stories circulated on the grapevine are accurate, according to a university study performed over several years. It concluded that wise managers learn to cultivate the office and factory grapevine, using it to their advantage because they cannot abolish it. The study states that the grapevine is as hard to kill as the mythical glass snake which, when struck, broke into a thousand pieces and grew a new snake from each piece.

Over the years, many officials have learned that the best antidote for the negative effects of false rumors is to keep people informed. Email is an excellent way to accomplish this. Having workers feel they are part of the organization can help them get more out of their work. In this way, they feel respected, do a better job, and are more productive.

Winning the Confrontation

When angry, count ten before you speak; if very angry, a hundred.

Thomas Jefferson
Third president of the United States (1801–1809),
drafted the Declaration of Independence.

In careers and personal lives, **confrontations** can occur. Patience and preparation can help you win them. For your own health and reputation, avoid **arguments.** But if you find yourself suddenly in a confrontation, follow these steps:

1. Take a deep breath. This will help you relax and gather your thoughts.
2. *Identify what you want to accomplish and concentrate on that objective.*
3. Speak clearly, concisely, using easily understood terms.
4. Maintain eye contact, showing that you honestly believe in what you are saying and cannot be intimidated.
5. Hold your temper—don't snap or yell at the other person.
6. If the opponent's position is weak, ask him/her to repeat that position. This might show how weak that position is, and you are gaining time to plan your strategy.

7. Pause. You can think of positive comments and counter the negatives.

8. Continue to concentrate on your objective.

Keep in mind that your performance will probably be described to others and remembered. Senator Barry Goldwater once said, "The important thing is to learn, become more gracious, and die as a gentleman."

Making a Presentation

Many speakers—and actors—say the thing they need most is *courage*.
But being prepared helps.

Speaking before a group, like many other communication processes, can best be improved with practice. As already mentioned, business students are encouraged to take courses in speech. It is also helpful to study **speeches** by others, noting their favorable and unfavorable aspects.

Planning the Speech

Having something worthwhile to say is the best possible asset for any public speaker.

Like a good letter or report, a good speech takes planning. Actually, a speech might be considered the oral presentation of a written report; it can certainly be prepared largely in the same manner. First, make a good list. Set up a central idea and then give introduction, details, and summary in an organized manner. (The topic of preparing reports is covered in Chapters 15 and 16.)

Notes can be helpful if you do not keep your eyes glued to them. Any notes or cards should be moved noiselessly and unobtrusively. Otherwise, listeners may feel the notes are more important than the audience or your message. Some speakers use a special large type font for their notes.

For Online Presentations: Computerized Slide Shows

For many business conferences, professional speakers have traditionally prepared color slides for their presentations. These slides are often prepared using presentation software such as Microsoft PowerPoint™ to create electronic slides. PowerPoint is flexible enough to let you create your slides one by one on your computer screen, or by entering your presentation material as an outline, and the program will create the slide file for you automatically. When completed, the PowerPoint file can be saved and given to a company that makes high-quality slides.

Many business users are now taking a further shortcut for their online presentations. After creating their PowerPoint presentation on a laptop computer, they simply hook up to a computer projector, and play their electronic presentation on the conference room screen just as if done via a slide projector. The advantages include savings on creating slides and more time to make last minute changes. Figure 10.3 is a copy of page for an online computer presentation.

FIGURE 10.3
Copy of page for an online computer presentation.

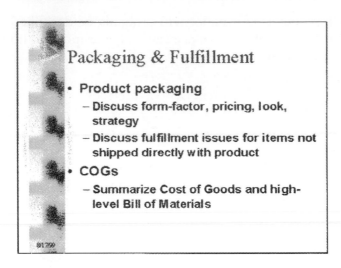

Putting your notes on 3 by 5 or 4 by 6 cards that have been arranged in numerical order is a good system. By jotting down just one phrase on a card, you will not glance at your notes and be confused as to which phrases you have already covered. Whether you use note cards or sheets of paper, you should never read your presentation word for word. Reading can bore your audience and make your presentation difficult to follow. Using brief note cards as reminders allows you to speak naturally and focus more of your attention on the audience.

Caution: Be sure to number your cards clearly in big print at the top in case they are dropped or otherwise get out of order. It happens.

Using a Microphone

If you are using a microphone, be sure that it is operating properly so that the entire audience is able to hear. It is always perfectly correct—actually, imperative if there is a doubt—to ask if everyone can hear you. If the answer is negative, show respect for the comfort and concern of your audience and get all the help you can in trying to rectify the problem.

You can build self-confidence before speaking over a microphone if you arrange a practice session. Even a few short minutes can be very helpful while you learn to adjust the microphone to your height and to determine the proper distance, usually a handspan, between your mouth and the microphone.

Some large auditoriums are equipped with electronic sound systems with microphones that can be attached to a lapel, collar or neckline of the speaker's apparel. Women should plan to wear an outfit with a small pocket convenient for holding the power pack that activates the mike. This is generally not a problem for men.

Bringing Life to a Speech

You can usually **bring life to a speech** by telling a story, joke or by giving an appropriate quotation. Also, almost any speaker will help the audience remember what is said by using visual aids. Listeners can follow your speech more easily if you give

them an outline. Further, slides, films, video tapes, flip charts, transparencies, or a blackboard are essential to some presentations and are helpful to most others. Improvements are constantly being made in visual aids. Each season, much equipment becomes simpler to operate, as well as more compact and lighter to carry.

Handouts are usually welcomed by audiences, whether they are copies of a list of major topics, information on the background of the speaker, additional sources of information on the topic, or appropriate gadgets.

Stand Up! Speak Up! Shut Up!

Stand Up! As a speaker, you should stand up comfortably, firm on your feet, showing confidence in your appearance. Of course, you should be dressed appropriately for the occasion. When in doubt about proper dress, inquire about suggestions from the program chairman or some other person in authority. In various organizations, at various times of day or night, and in various parts of a town, a country, or the world, different dress might be recommended for what essentially seems to be the same type of occasion.

Speak Up! Speak up so that people can hear you and get your message. This is done through many conscious efforts, such as speaking clearly, speaking loud enough for those assembled to hear, maintaining eye contact with your audience, and avoiding a monotone and any annoying mannerisms.

Speak Clearly. To get your message across and to be courteous to your audience, you should speak clearly by enunciating carefully and speaking slowly enough to be understood. If you mumble or mutter, or if you talk too fast, you may lose the attention of the audience.

Speak loud enough so everyone can hear you. It is usually possible to train yourself to project your voice so that even a relatively large audience can hear and understand you, with or without the use of amplifiers.

Speak directly to the audience by maintaining eye contact. Let your eyes wander around the group, stopping momentarily on different individuals, bringing people into the picture and giving them a feeling of audience participation.

Do not speak in a monotone. A change in the pitch of your voice could prevent putting the audience to sleep by an incessant drone or singsong, and it can also relax you and your vocal cords.

Avoid annoying mannerisms of action or speech. Listeners may find themselves watching or listening for action or speech mannerisms that are unusual. Avoid these.

William J. McCullough, a recognized authority on public speaking, gives these points:

Avoid mispronunciations or glaring errors in grammar.

Avoid profane or vulgar expressions; the laugh isn't worth it.

Avoid holding the lectern or desk for long periods of time.

Avoid playing with things.

Avoid pacing back and forth.

Avoid memorizing a speech… The bulk of your speech should be extemporaneous.

Avoid reading your speech.

Avoid alcohol. "If you drink, don't attempt to make a speech…"[2]

Give your audience a chance for input. If the situation permits, give your audience a chance for input. People are there because of a special interest or involvement in your topic. Their questions and comments may improve your presentation. Do not let this practice get out of hand, however. Keeping to time restrictions is your responsibility.

Shut Up! The effectiveness of a message can be lost and public relations damaged when a speaker drags on, reducing the audience to fidgeting boredom. One of the most helpful suggestions for making a good speech that will be well received is this: Say what you have to say and SHUT UP!

President Franklin D. Roosevelt said it this way, "Be sincere; be brief; be seated."

Listening

It takes two to speak the truth—one to speak and another to listen.

> Henry David Thoreau (1817–1862),
> American essayist and poet

Common sense tells us that on most jobs a high percentage of time is spent **listening.** Surveys show that most of those at executive levels spend at least one-fourth of their time listening.

---

[2]William J. McCullough, *Hold Your Audience* (Englewood Cliffs, NJ: Prentice-Hall, 1978), pp. 167ff.

Business communication classes traditionally concentrate on writing, because of the acknowledged need for improved writing. However, much communication in business is spoken, as we all recognize. As oral communication is studied thoroughly, it becomes apparent that poor listening is a major culprit in the lack of understanding between speaker and audience—sender and receiver—whether the audience be one or many.

TV Interviewing as a Model for Listening

We may gain some insight into how to improve our listening skills if we take a look at one of our more or less refined forms of listening, the **television interview.**

Bill Moyers, respected for his effectiveness as an interviewer on national TV, recently said that two things make you a good interviewer—in other words, a good listener:

1. Pay attention.
2. Anticipate.

Moyers says he interviews according to a plan expressed by champion ice hockey player, Wayne Gretzky, who said, "I skate to where the puck is going to be, not to where it's been."

Just so in listening on the job: Anticipating does force us to pay attention, and we can try to see if the speaker says what we expect or want to hear. If we have anticipated correctly, we are gratified. If we do not hear what we expected, we have to be alert to hear other ideas, possibly leading to a good question-and-answer session.

Listening for Major Points

A main reason for poor listening is failure to identify major points. (This is why giving audience members a major topics list helps hold an audience and helps them remember.) Listening for major points helps you identify facts that support a point. Our minds can move much faster than anyone can speak, and your mind can wander far away from what you are hearing. Concentrating on major points pulls your mind back to what is being said.

As you listen for major points, you can begin to identify the major plan. When listening to a speech, you usually hear the speaker first make an introduction to what will be presented, then give the body of the presentation, then fill it out with a summary. Anticipating the progress of even a long presentation can help you tune in on what is coming.

Taking Notes

Should you take notes? In one to one interviews or in small or large conferences, diligent note-takers can miss some of the major points of a speaker. Good notes are taken when you listen a lot and write little. Then, the sooner you review your notes in private, the easier it is for you to fill in useful information.

"Hearing" Between-the-Lines Messages

In his writing and speaking, Norman B. Sigband of the University of Southern California emphasizes the advantages if you "listen to what you can't hear." His expression means watching for body language such as facial expressions, listening for voice intonations, and so forth, to get those between-the-lines messages that can be extremely meaningful.

Asking Questions

Don't be afraid to ask questions. In a two-person interview or explanation, or in a large conference, if you feel the need for clarification and have the opportunity, ask questions. Good listeners ask good questions, and any good speaker will be glad to clarify points. Even in a large group, you might say something like, "Could I get something cleared up? I lost the train of thought when you got into ..." You will usually hear a muffled wave of agreement from others in the audience who similarly got lost.

As people realize that everything spoken is not immediately understood, we will probably have more open discussions with people asking to have points clarified. This will lead to better understanding by everyone.

Getting Around Barriers to Good Listening

Recognize that there are many possible **barriers to good listening**. For example, your attention span suffers if you let personal prejudices against a speaker stop you from concentrating on what is being said. Also, good mental discipline forces you to concentrate on your work when you have personal or job problems. When listening, try to ignore personal problems and prejudices, other conversations, airplanes overhead, slamming doors, and so forth. Are you, the listener-receiver, getting the message of the speaker-sender?

Interrupting

The claim is made that we listen at only a 50 percent efficiency rate. Another chief block to understanding is **interrupting.** Some people are more guilty than others of interrupting—a rude habit. If you are a guilty one, do everything in your power *not* to interrupt, no matter what.

Often we don't understand because we bring up another topic right in the middle of what someone else is saying. Or we have the audacity to complete a statement that another person is making, giving the impression that we think we can say it better than the speaker. People who are bothered by constant interruptions often fail to get their messages across, to the detriment of both speaker and potential listener.

Summarizing

As previously suggested, concentrate on what you are hearing by trying to anticipate what is going to be said. Listen for major points and between the line messages. Take brief notes if they will be helpful. Ask questions. Consciously block out anything that interferes with your understanding of what is being said.

Chapter 10   Oral Communications

WRITING IMPROVEMENT EXERCISE

Agreement of Pronoun with the Word It Stands For

Businesspeople find that a common error in grammar is incorrect use of singular or plural pronouns. Also, an objection has developed to the use of a masculine pronoun (he / him / his) when the person the pronoun stands for could be either male or female.

A pronoun should agree in number with the word it stands for—its **antecedent.** If the antecedent is singular, the pronoun should be singular. If the antecedent is plural, the pronoun should be plural. And we should reword our writing so that a masculine pronoun does not stand for both male and female.

1. Pronoun agreement with antecedent: general

    a. Mr. Crawford and Mr. Dowling offered (his/their) assistance in tabulating the votes.

    b. The new man in the department must do (his/their) best to learn the job quickly.

    c. Neither woman wished to boast about (her/their) individual success.

    d. I thought I lost my office key; (it was/they were) hanging on my desk drawer.

    e. We take pride in (ourselves/ourself).

    f. Each woman set (their, her) own pace in the fashion world.

Chapter 10   Oral Communications

WRITING IMPROVEMENT "HANDS ON" ASSIGNMENT

Agreement of Pronoun with the Word It Stands For

Draw a line through the incorrect terms. You might draw an arrow from the antecedent to the pronoun.

1. Everybody on the team earned (their/her) medal.

2. Someone should give (his/their/her/a) seat to the elderly gentleman.

3. Several wanted (his/her, his or her/their) instructions in writing.

4. We promised (ourself/ourselves) that we would do superior work.

5. All of you on this crew can be proud of (yourself/yourselfs/yourselves).

6. Each student has turned in (her/his/the) assignment.

7. Many players made (their selections/a selection/his or her selection) from the instruments on stage.

8. Everyone on the staff should indicate (their/his/her/his or her) preferred vacation dates.

9. Which designer selected this material as (her or his/their) preference?

10. Terry and Koji cannot find (their driver's license/her driver's license/their driver's licenses).

Chapter 10   Oral Communications

ORAL ASSIGNMENTS

1. Make a list of information to be included in a form letter of your own making, and dictate the letter onto a machine.

2. Select a topic from those suggested for reports at the end of Chapter 16 and present to the class a five- or ten-minute explanation of that topic or another approved by the instructor.

3. You are chairman of the next meeting of the class. Prepare an agenda of matters you would like covered in the class.

4. From the local telephone company, get any printed material it has for public distribution that will be helpful in learning to conduct telephone calls properly.

5. Take notes of one class meeting, either in business communication or in another class. Outline the notes as minutes of the class meeting.

6. Watch a news commentator on television for at least a 30-minute program, and give an oral report to the class about his or her most effective and least effective speaking mannerisms.

7. Prepare an agenda for the next meeting of any group of which you are part.

8. If you are preparing a written report for this or any other class, explain to this class what you found most interesting in that report.

9. If you are to make an oral presentation on the job, practice by first giving it to the class, getting suggestions for improvements. (Of course, the job information cannot be confidential.)

10. Get a copy of a public corporation's annual report. (Most libraries will have some.) Give a five-minute speech on the activities of the firm, possibly emphasizing its products and financial standing. Use at least one visual aid for your presentation.

To the instructor: A South African tribe has such a dislike for long speeches that speakers are limited to what they can say while standing on one foot. As long as he can balance himself, a speaker can talk to his heart's content, but the minute his upraised foot touches the ground, his speech is over.

"The Safer Way," quoted in *Religious Digest*

Chapter 10   Oral Communications

REVIEW AND DISCUSSION

1. Why are students who are planning careers urged to take courses in various types of speaking?   <u>Ability to speak well is important in many careers, particularly in</u> <u>upper level positions.</u>

2. The General Telephone Company gives the reason for learning to handle telephone calls in business correctly in the title of its booklet, "Every Time You Talk on the Telephone You <u>Really Are the Company."</u>"

3. The text suggests that on business telephone calls you should usually try to get the name of the person to whom you are talking. Why?   <u>Calls can become disconnected.</u> <u>You may need to call back. You may need to record first and last name of person who</u> <u>called.</u>

4. How can a person learn to improve business dictation?   <u>Practice. Practice. Practice.</u>

5. How is a meeting agenda used?   <u>It is a list of matters to be discussed and work</u> <u>to be accomplished. Keeps meetings on time and on track.</u>

6. If there is no specific purpose for a routine conference, should it be held?   <u>No.</u>

7. Marguerite Grumme, parliamentarian, gives four basic principles of parliamentary law. What are they?

   a.   <u>Courtesy and Justice for All.</u>

   b.   <u>Consider one thing at a time.</u>

   c.   <u>The minority must be heard.</u>

   d.   <u>The majority must prevail.</u>

8. What are the two major responsibilities of conference members?

   a.   <u>Show respect for others attending.</u>

   b.   <u>Bring to meeting any pertinent information—if appropriate.</u>

9. What is a good antidote for the negative effect of office rumors?   <u>Keeping people</u> <u>informed.</u>

10. In any confrontation, what should you keep in mind?   <u>Concentrate on your</u> <u>objective.</u>

11. How can you learn to improve your self confidence in speaking before a group?   <u>__</u> <u>Have something worthwhile to say. Practice. Practice. Practice.</u>

12. Planning a good speech is like planning a good <u>report</u>   .

13. The text furnishes three basics of giving a good speech. What are they?

    a. <u>Stand up!</u>

    b. <u>Speak up!</u>

    c. <u>Shut up!</u>

14. What does "eye contact" mean? <u>Looking individuals directly in the eye.</u>

    _____

15. Why should you avoid annoying mannerisms in your speaking? <u>Audience may</u>
<u>begin to pay more attention to mannerisms than your speech.</u>

16. If the antecedent of a pronoun is singular, the pronoun should be <u>singular</u>   .

    Reword these sentences to eliminate sexism:

17. Here is help if a person is learning English as (~~his/her~~/a/~~their~~) second language.

    _____

18. If anyone wants to volunteer for this hazardous assignment, he can talk to me himself. <u>Those who want to volunteer for this hazardous assignment can talk to me</u>
<u>themselves.</u>

19. If a student wants to discuss his grade, he can see me after class.
<u>If you want to discuss your grade, see me after class.</u>

20. Any real estate broker can discuss ~~her~~ planned contacts for the week.

    _____

11

Computers, the Internet and Other Communication Technologies

The advent of the personal computer, advanced communications and the Internet have had a great impact on business communication. These new, fast paced technologies are changing the means we use to create, edit, communicate, and share information—touching our personal and business lives in dramatic, far-reaching ways.

Computers

Business today runs over a "backbone" network, connecting computers on desktops to share files, printers and communications via the Internet. The new tools used by "wired" business users enable them to produce greater volumes of business documents, with results that can rival the design and quality of professional graphics and design shops.

The nature of office work has changed as a consequence. Most businesspeople compose and edit their own documents (with less need for secretaries doing all the typing from rough drafts or dictation). Documents are easily created, shared, and modified, and expectations have increased correspondingly.

Computers in Written Communications

Word processing software makes letter writing easy. Business reports, memos, flyers, resumes, marketing brochures, press releases, forms, newsletters and innumerable other types of documents are done quite effectively with word processing software.

Early software for word processing had few features beyond the basics. Typical features in current software releases include capabilities for automatic spell checking and correction, grammar checking, a thesaurus, and dozens of additional capabilities. The challenge for most computer users is to be proficient in the basic uses of their word processing system. The "feature creep" in new software releases makes it much more complicated to master, and as a result, they can be a source of frustration and waste of time and money.

Regardless of how easy it is to get started, and how intuitive your first use of word processing seems, there is a considerable benefit in going through the basic tutorials. Hands-on classroom courses provide additional value as do self-training materials. Having a more knowledgeable user available at the ready can also save minutes and hours of frustration and low-quality results.

Page Layout Software

Page layout software, another related class of software application, is best suited for making creatively designed documents. Known for extremely precise control over typeface, graphics and other document elements, page layout applications also allow direct placement and manipulation. This allows layout designers to drop in photos, graphics, text and other design elements on a screen image of the page, move the elements around directly, and preview the results on screen before printing. Page layout software shines best in the creation of brochures, newsletters and a variety of marketing materials.

Best Practices for Computer Word Processing

The effective use of computer word processing can result in high-quality, effective business communications. Selected **best practices** include:

- Compose at the keyboard—type the first version quickly, with little concern for final formatting.
- Edit your writing thoroughly.
- Use the automated tools, but with care—spelling correction software can recommend a word with a totally different meaning.
- Use outlining features effectively.
- Learn the use of the "styles" feature for long documents for which consistent formatting is critical.
- Use standard or custom templates as a starting point for consistent documents.
- For word choices, get accustomed to using the computer thesaurus and/or a hard copy.
- Save multiple versions of your documents.
- Back up your files!
- Take advantage of the computer's ability to let you move text easily.
- Collaborate with other participants for improved results.
- Remember to spell check one last time.
- Did I mention backups?

Many business users stress that the value of an individual working on a stand-alone personal computer is greatly increased by using communications technology to link with other people and devices—"it's the network!"

Local Area Computer Networks

Computers in large business organizations are invariably connected via a **local area network (LAN)** to other computers within the same building or in close proximity. Desktop computers are connected via the LAN to a wide variety of shared devices. File servers over the network allow documents to be easily shared, reviewed, revised and stored for later retrieval. Fast, high-quality laser printers shared over a network enable efficient output of business communications for internal and external use.

Because LAN connections are full time, many other business communication features are available, including internal email, allowing quick and easy messaging. Today's use of email has all but replaced the use of internal paper memos. It's faster and easier for most uses, and less costly. Businesses have also discovered that a well designed company intranet (inside network), running over the company LAN, is a very valuable information source and business communication tool.

Wide Area Networks

With the need to connect local computers to computers in a remote location, various methods can be used, including land lines, satellite communications, microwave transmission and other forms of wireless communications. Such **Wide Area Network (WAN)** connections greatly expand the facilities for communications between individuals and organizations.

The Internet

The Internet uses a vast Wide Area Network of both individual computers and local area networks, all transferring data over a standard communication protocol. With the explosive growth of the World Wide Web, *in 1999 the volume of Internet Email exceeded that of postal mail.*

Unique among the proprietary commercialized communications networks, the Internet is not owned or controlled by any single, central organization or government. Today's Internet has its roots in the 1950s and 1960s (see Figure 11.1). The original network protocol, developed to support defense-related network access in the event of localized attack, enables computers to be easily added with a minimum of administrative delays. Local network outages can be automatically bypassed, and messages lost in midstream sent again without special intervention.

An **intranet** is a variant of the Internet. Its web services and email are set up for use only within an organization. For example, a corporate intranet may have its human resources information system online and employees can use it to evaluate and change their benefits.

Email

"You've got mail," the audible notification one invariably gets when signing on to America Online, is one of the most recognized sound bytes today. Email communications, once used primarily as an alternative to internal memos at a few technical business organizations, has now become the primary tool for written business and personal communications.

Figure 11.1
Brief Timeline of the internet.

internet.com **(Wĕbopēdia)** The #1 online encyclopedia dedicated to computer technology

[ ] [Go!]   [All Categories ▼] [Go!]

MENU
Home
Term of the Day
New Terms
New Links
Quick Reference
Search Utility
Partners
Advertising

Talk To Us...
Internet Jobs
Tech Support
Submit a URL
Request a Term
Report an Error

internet.com
Internet News
Internet Stocks
Internet Technology
Web Developer
Internet Marketing
ISP
Downloads
Internet Resources
International
Search internet.com
Advertising Info
Corporate Info
Internet Trade Shows

internet commerce
Be an Affiliate
Be a Partner
Software Store
Computer Help
Register a Domain
Be Domain Registrar
e-solutions
Internet Jobs
A/V Network
Map Your Website
Rent E-mail Lists
Bookstore
Press Release dist.
Sell Ad Space
Internet Research
Venture Capital
Web Publishing
Build Your Intranet
Expert Advice
Get e-Biz Intell.
Content for Websites

Brief Timeline of the Internet

When we talk about the Internet, we talk about the World Wide Web from the past four or five years. But, its history goes back a lot further; all the way back to the 1950s and 60s.

"Where was I," you ask, "while all this was happening?" Well, it's quite simple really: the Space Program. America was so fascinated with sending men into outerspace, hundreds of miles away, it never saw what was being invented to bring everyone closer together -- eventually.

So, just in case you missed the development of the Internet, I've composed a brief timeline highlighting some of the major occurences over the past 41 years. For more extensive info, you'll find links to other timelines at the bottom of this page.

1958	President Eisenhower requests funds to create ARPA. Approved as a line item in Air Force appropriations bill.
1961	Len Kleinrock, Professor of Computer Science at UCLA, writes first paper on packet switching, "Information Flow in Large Communications Nets." Paper published in *RLE Quarterly Progress Report* .
1962	•J.C.R. Licklider & W. Clark write first paper on Internet Concept, "On-Line Man Computer Communications." • Len Kleinrock writes *Communication Nets* , which describes design for packet switching network; used for ARPAnet
1964	Paul Baran writes, "On Distributed Communications Networks," first paper on using message blocks to send info across a decentralized network topology (Nodes and Links)
Oct. 1965	First Network Experiment: Directed by Larry Roberts at MIT Lincoln Lab, two computers talked to each other using packet-switching technology.
Dec. 1966	ARPA project begins. Larry Roberts is chief scientist.
Dec. 1968	ARPANet contract given to Bolt, Beranek & Newman (BBN) in Cambridge, Mass.
Sept. 1, 1969	First ARPANet node installed at UCLA Network Measurement Center. Kleinrock hooked up the Interface Message Processor to a Sigma 7 Computer.
Oct. 1, 1969	Second node installed at Stanford Research Institute; connected to a SDS 940 computer. The first ARPANet message sent: "lo." Trying to spell log-in, but the system crashed!
Nov. 1, 1969	Third node installed at University of California, Santa Barbara. Connected to an IBM 360/75.
Dec. 1, 1969	Fourth node installed at University of Utah. Connected to a DEC PDP-10.
March 1970	Fifth node installed at BBN, across the country in Cambridge, Mass.
July 1970	Alohanet, first packet radio network, operational at University of Hawaii.
March 1972	First basic e-mail programs written by Ray Tomlinson at BBN for ARPANET: SNDMSG and READMAIL. "@" sign chosen for its "at" meaning.
March 1973	First ARPANET international connections to University College of London (England) and NORSAR (Norway).

Figure 11.1 (Continued)

Timeline of the Internet

1974	• Intel releases the 8080 processor. • Vint Cerf and Bob Kahn publish "A Protocol for Packet Network Interconnection," which details the design of TCP.
1976	• Apple Computer founded by Steve Jobs and Steve Wozniak. • Queen Elizabeth II sends out an e-mail. • Vint Cerf joins ARPA as program manager.
1978	TCP split into TCP and IP.
1979	Bob Metcalfe and others found 3Com (Computer Communication Compatibility).
1980	Tim Berners-Lee writes program called "Enquire Within," predecessor to the World Wide Web.
1981	IBM announces its first Personal Computer. Microsoft creates DOS.
1983	Cisco Systems founded.
Nov. 1983	Domain Name System (DNS) designed by Jon Postel, Paul Mockapetris, and Craig Partridge. .edu, .gov, .com, .mil, .org, .net, and .int created.
1984	William Gibson writes "Neuromancer." Coins the term "cyberspace".
March 15, 1985	Symbolic.com becomes the first registered domain.
1986	5000 hosts on ARPAnet/Internet.
1987	• 10,000 hosts on the Internet. • First Cisco router shipped. • 25 million PCs sold in US.
1989	• 100,000 hosts on Internet. • McAfee Associates founded; anti-virus software available for free. Quantum becomes America Online.
1990	ARPAnet ends. Tim Berners-Lee creates the World Wide Web.
1992	"Surfing the Internet" is coined by Jean Armour Polly.
1993	• Mosaic Web browser developed by Marc Andreesen at University of Illinois, Champaign-Urbana. • InterNIC created. • Web grows by 341,000 percent in a year.
April 1994	• Netscape Communications founded. • Jeff Bezos writes the business plan for Amazon.com. • Java's first public demonstration.
Dec. 1994	Microsoft licenses technology from Spyglass to create Web browser for Windows 95.
May 23, 1995	Sun Microsystems releases Java.
August 24, 1995	Windows 95 released.
1996	Domain name tv.com sold to CNET for $15,000. Browser wars begin. Netscape and Microsoft two biggest players.
1997	business.com sold for $150,000.
1998	US Depart of Commerce outlines proposal to privatize DNS. ICANN created by Jon Postel to oversee privatization. Jon Postel dies.
1999	• AOL buys Netscape; Andreesen steps down as full-time employee. • Browsers wars declared over; Netscape and Microsoft share almost 100% of browser market. • Microsoft declared a monopoly by US District Judge Thomas Penfield Jackson.

http://www.webopedia.com/quick_ref/timeline.html

For a more extensive time-line visit Hobbes' Internet Timeline and Nerds 2.0.1 Internet Timeline. (Reprinted with permission from www.webopedia.com/quick_ref/timeline.html © Copyright 1999 internet.com, Corp. All rights reserved.)

At its most basic, **email** (electronic mail) consists of short text-only messages, entered quickly via computer keyboard with only a couple of mouse clicks to select the "to:" address, and one click to send it immediately. The recipient, who may be in the next cubicle, building, or across the world, can receive the message in a few seconds, and read it on their screen, reply by clicking and typing a short response, and clicking to send it zipping away.

Internet email has become the de-facto standard—for individuals, education and business communications. It's fast, easy, and since email "stamps" are practically free, there are few barriers in its use for all types of communications.

What's Hot

- Using Internet email for direct, one-on-one communications between individuals
- Sending a single message to multiple recipients; easily done by clicking on additional address book entries or typing in new email addresses
- Attaching a computer file to an email message for the recipient
- Creating an *email distribution list,* to use for quickly sending a single message to a large number of list "members"
- Hosting an *email discussion list* so that list members can post a message that all other members receive automatically, and can easily respond to for all to read
- Composing email messages without any special formatting—using plain text—so all recipients can easily read the message without readability problems
- Sending messages and replying promptly, using email features to save time and effort
- Using email as a low impact method to send commercial messages to consumers who've given their permission to receive marketing related email (opt-in email)
- Adding World Wide Web hyperlinks to the email, making it easy for users to double-click and go directly to a specific web page (see Figure 11.2)
- Personalizing the message sent to many email recipients—using "email merge" capabilities that mimic word processing functions

What's Not

- Forgetting to "spell check" and review the message for grammar and composition; what you write *counts!*
- Attaching gigantic computer files to your email—which bogs the Internet down and clogs email server computers—your recipient might not be able to receive your message and any others queued up behind the "attach-clog"
- Formatting the email message with colored text, different fonts and sizes, and using tabs to line up columns—most of which won't look right on the recipient's computer
- Forgetting a salutation at the top of the body of the email—the "to:" may not make this clear, especially with forwarded email messages
- Ditto for the email closing

Figure 11.2
Website hyperlink in email message.

Personalized
Web Hyperlink

> To: ShawnDavis@webstop.com
> From: SavingsClub@DicksSupermarket.com
> Subject: $24.40 INSTANT SAVINGS - Dick's Supermarket Club Saver Shopping List
> Date: Sun, 18 Jun 2000 11:04:55   -0400
>
> Dear Davis Household,
>
> Enjoy INSTANT SAVINGS up to $24.40 with your Club Saver Shopping List! It's available for two weeks, from Monday, 6/19/2000 through Sunday, 7/3/2000.
>
> Click here to access your household's individualized Shopping List:
>
> http://216.168.32.53/c/act.1?-token=3&-resp=1.las
>
> You may print out this Shopping List and take it with you when you shop. No coupons to clip. Simply show the printed copy of your Shopping List to the check out operator at the time of purchase and all special discounts will be automatically deducted on your receipt.

- ☐ Using email for email **"spam"** (see sidebar on page 257)
- ☐ Printing all email messages—wasting paper

Under Consideration

- ☐ Carefully protecting your computer from viruses with a combination of software and safe practices
- ☐ Using email for a legal, carefully done direct email campaign—for legitimate, legal products or services
- ☐ Keeping up-to-date mailing lists for all commercial use, paying particular care to state laws and acceptable commercial practices

Email Style Guide

Well written email messages are effective business communications. It's easy to take shortcuts with electronic mail because they're so easy to create and send. Many people carefully format their business letters but leave all care and consideration out of their email messages. *Remember: All written communications must be completely clear and unambiguous.* Without the immediate feedback of face-to-face communications, or the subtle voice inflections you can hear over the phone, an email message may not result in comments or needed feedback, closing the communication loop.

Email Headers

Internet email messages have certain common elements that are necessary for the message to be valid and deliverable. *The required header elements include a valid*

"To:" Email address, a "From:" Email address, and a "Subject:" line. Nothing else, not even the message body, is required for the message to be valid and able to be sent.

Email Parts

The context of the email is vitally important. The subject line is critical, since it's usually the first thing a message recipient sees. In most email programs, the recipient sees a list of a single line of all incoming messages, including the "from" address and subject. A clear, simple subject is very useful in framing the message that's delivered in the body.

The subject should briefly describe the message contents. Think of the subject as a summary title—it should describe the gist of the communication. Certain email conventions are useful, such as including "URGENT" or "FYI" for your information in the subject to help the reader prioritize.

Also realize that for some forms of business communications, the email subject line may be as important as a front page ad. In targeted email messages, your audience may be interested in your email only if the subject line works in engaging their interest enough to open the message and read the body. The email marketer can't make anything out of a great offer if the message is discarded before being opened. In a recent test of these three subject lines, the last one generated 300 percent more traffic for an e-commerce website:

> **Subject 1:** Genuine Wisconsin Cheese—Order Online Now!
> **Subject 2:** Holiday Gift Boxes, Gourmet Hams, Wisconsin Cheese
> **Subject 3:** One Click Away—Wisconsin Cheese, Gourmet Ham, Brats, Honey

Salutation

Since the message body of an email communication is free-form text, there is no technical requirement for any special entries. *For clarity, it is critical that the message body contain a salutation. Many think that a salutation is unnecessary since they have their email address in the "To:" header. This is not a good practice with email, since email messages are often forwarded again and again. The last person sending the message should always add a salutation and closing to make it clear who the sender and receiver are.*

With formal email messages, "Dear" is an appropriate salutation. More casual messages may use "Hi" or "Hello," followed by the person's first name.

Closing

Make sure you include an appropriate closing in the body of your message. It's too easy with email replies and forwarded copies to lose track of the previous sender.

Signature

Most email software lets you create some standard lines of text as your email "signature." Once you've entered it in the appropriate part of your email program, it will automatically appear at the bottom of each message you send. This is an effective tool for good business communication. Include your key contact information, but keep it fairly brief.

Figure 12.3
Email message parts.

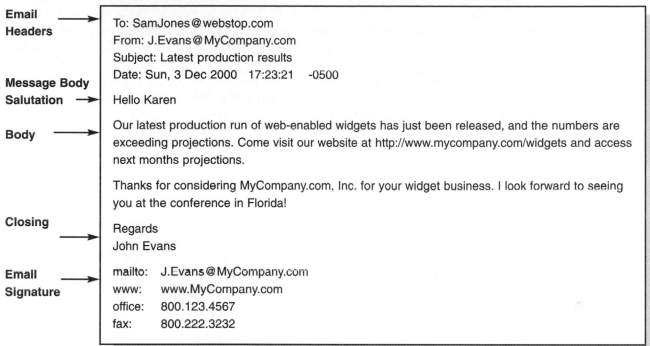

Email
Headers →

Message Body
Salutation →

Body →

Closing →

Email
Signature →

To: SamJones@webstop.com
From: J.Evans@MyCompany.com
Subject: Latest production results
Date: Sun, 3 Dec 2000   17:23:21   -0500

Hello Karen

Our latest production run of web-enabled widgets has just been released, and the numbers are exceeding projections. Come visit our website at http://www.mycompany.com/widgets and access next months projections.

Thanks for considering MyCompany.com, Inc. for your widget business. I look forward to seeing you at the conference in Florida!

Regards
John Evans

mailto: J.Evans@MyCompany.com
www: www.MyCompany.com
office: 800.123.4567
fax: 800.222.3232

Body

This is the message—short or long. Email messages are often received from an unknown source; *it's very helpful if you identify who you are in the opening paragraph.* You want to let the recipient know who you are, whom you represent, how you heard of your correspondent, and what you're interested in. For example:

> Dear Ms. Jones
>
> I am the editor at Acme Publishing Company, and heard your keynote speech at the recent writer's conference in Philadelphia. I'd like to invite you to a luncheon for business authors in our New Jersey offices next month, and include you as a panelist in our discussion forum.

Clear, Careful Writing—Tone and Wording

It's easy to pull a printed letter out of the mailbox after you've sealed it for delivery and decided to make changes. *Email messages, on the other hand, are really gone when you hit the "send" button, so carefully edit them before they're sent.* When you edit email, ask yourself, "Is the tone right? Is the wording clear or does it need revision?"

Spell Check

Most email software includes automatic spell checking. Use it and other aids such as grammar checking.

Replying

Email replies are very easy—one click on the reply icon and the message is formatted with a return address automatically. It's important to make the message response easy for the recipient too, and that takes just a little attention on your part. A good practice is to explicitly "quote" parts of the original message back to the sender. The greater-than sign ">" is the most conventional way to quote the original message, and many email programs do this automatically. Imagine if you will that on Monday morning you received a reply to one of 30 different email messages you sent out on Friday, and the response was:

Ambiguous reply ⟶

> To: J.Evans@MyCompany.com
> From: karensmith@webstop.com
> Subject: Re: a question
> Date: Mon, 4 Dec 2000 09:17:24   -0500
>
> yes

That's obviously not very clear. Here's how it should be done. Let's say this is the original message:

Clear subject ⟶

> To: karensmith@webstop.com
> From: J.Evans@MyCompany.com
> Subject: A Question - attending the meeting?
> Date: Fri, 1 Dec 2000 17:23:21   -0500
>
> Hello Karen
>
> I'd like for you to attend the users conference next week in New York. Can you be there at 2:00 p.m.?
>
> Regards
> John Evans

Karen's response would be much clearer if the relevant context is quoted in the reply, like so:

> To: J.Evans@MyCompany.com
> From: karensmith@webstop.com
> Subject: Re: a question
> Date: Mon, 4 Dec 2000 09:17:24   -0500
>
> Hello John
>
> In your email you said:

Quoted response ⟶

> >I'd like for you to attend the users conference next week
> >in New York. Can you be there at 2:00 p.m.?

Answer ⟶

> Yes, I'll be there.
>
> Regards
> Karen

Plain Text

Use only plain text in your email messages. Avoid using special fonts or type-faces, unusual size fonts, colored text, underlined, boldfaced or italicized text. Don't even use tabs—use the space bar instead. The problem is that, unless you are sure recipients have the same computer platform, the same email software at the same release level, and the same fonts installed on their computer, the message you send may look great on your computer, but terrible on theirs.

Strong Emphasis

It's important to be able to make a strong point of emphasis in an email, but since plain text is recommended, USE UPPER CASE LETTERS! Just remember not to overdo it—some people cap every word, and to the experienced email user it's called "shouting" and should be avoided.

Unregulated Email = "Spam"

Traditional direct mail marketing uses printed materials and postal mail as the primary delivery vehicle for mass mailings of commercial marketing materials. Developing the materials, obtaining mailing addresses, attempting to target the mailings to likely consumers, and the actual distribution is costly. Many consumers go through their mail "over the trash can," quickly discarding all but a few of these direct mail pieces.

The Internet offers a whole new set of opportunities for "push" marketing in the form of email. Internet email users receive many unsolicited email messages from unknown sources. Although some of these "bulk email" communications are from legitimate companies offering quality products or services, many are not. Because the Internet is largely unregulated, some unscrupulous organizations resort to tactics that are often illegal, extremely offensive, and unwanted by many. Such email is called "spam" by most Internet users.

What sets spam apart from other commercial email:

☐ It's often done for get-rich-quick schemes, dubious products, sexually explicit material or illegal services.

☐ The sendings are massive—millions of email messages are sent, indiscriminately.

☐ The target email addresses may be obtained illegally.

☐ The email recipients do not represent a list of users who have agreed to receive these promotions.

☐ It steals resources—using other organizations' email servers without their knowledge or permission.

☐ It uses false identities—probably in an attempt to avoid legal scrutiny or other means of protection; It includes false email "from:" addresses.

☐ There is no facility for users to "opt-out" of future mailings easily and reliably, now a legal requirement in some states and some other countries.

The World Wide Web

The World Wide Web is a universe of information, with a wide collection of data, text, and computer graphics. The web is a system created to provide an easy way to share information globally. Thousands of Internet server computers use standard web protocols to provide millions of "pages" of material for computer users to access via web browser software. Web pages are created with a special computer language called **HTML (Hyper Text Markup Language)**, which enables easy connection to other web pages.

Browsers and Servers

Users access World Wide Web pages with **"browser"** software. **Netscape Communicator** and **Microsoft Internet Explorer** are the most popular browsers for personal computers, and are available for free. Keying in a page **Uniform Resource Locator (URL)** address brings a web page up in seconds. Users save individual URL addresses by **"bookmarking"** their favorite pages for easy retrieval. Hyperlinks on web pages take users to other pages, letting them surf quickly between related information sources.

Web server computers make web pages and other related resources available for users from anywhere in the world. Information in the form of text, graphics, photos, audio and video clips are available from millions of sources.

The Web and Business Communications

The Web, which started as a means of easily sharing information in academia, became commercialized in the early 1990s, and the resulting growth has been phenomenal. Businesses no longer question whether they should have a website—that's a given. However, there are signs of a backlash of sorts—it's no longer fashionable for new firms to include the "dot-com" in the company name.

As a business communications tool, the web is invaluable. Understanding its uses and advantages is as important as knowing the pitfalls and risks associated with creating and growing a web presence.

Website Type	Description
Informational	Current, topical information, easily accessible. Well designed indexes, built-in search capabilities and easy navigation are employed to assist in finding the relevant data
Archival	Historical information containing chronologically organized information
News & Current Events	Up-to-the-minute source or information, updated frequently
Services	Online services, free or for a fee, such as the U.S. government website
Support	Software updates, technical support databases, **frequently asked questions (FAQ)**

Website Type	*Description*
E-commerce	Sales of products or services online, including delivery of services or pickup for physical goods, shipping or online download for software
Marketing, Promotion & Public Relations	Marketing message, promotion, advertising, or a public relations emphasis
Entertainment	Games, stories, and more—focusing on fun for a target audience
Research	General or specialized research tool and content
Sports	News, articles, opinions and current coverage of sports events
Audio	Music formats such as MP3—a whole new area of interest for music servers

Internet Websites

Businesses communicate in a wide variety of ways over the Internet. Well designed websites are a powerful communication vehicle for consumers, investors, business partners and potential employees. Current trends are for business websites to embody more and more capability, and to spawn other related websites when the original one isn't focused on the new target needs. Websites that work bring consumers and others back again and again, and accomplish valuable communications goals 24 hours a day, seven days a week.

Intranet: Internal Communications

Using business communications effectively within large organizations is a complex challenge. Employee benefits, human resources, company policy, marketing, services, and many other areas of information are needed, and should be accessible and current. Intranets have become a very popular means of answering this need, and typically include a website designed for internal communications. To allow access to private information, they usually have user password protection and logon controls. Online forms may be provided to allow easy updating of employee preferences. By keeping company policy and other data online, it's easier to ensure that everyone has access to the latest version, rather than an out-of-date printed copy. Significant cost savings in printing and distribution are benefits that can cover the costs of developing and maintaining a business Intranet.

Intranets are often set up internally on a company local area network (LAN), which allows easy, protected access for employees. Since many business associates travel with laptop computers that have Internet access, a number of Intranets are setup for secure access over the Internet.

Extranet: Business-to-Business Communications

The tremendous volume of paperwork, orders, letters, catalogs and support materials that are processed between business organizations are increasingly being handled by special websites called Extranets. Websites designed specifically for these important communications can streamline information flow, shorten delivery times, and lower costs.

Because of the tremendous potential of e-commerce between businesses, a number of companies are reinventing their whole business process around the use of the web, email, and other technology in a well designed extranet.

PDF: Portable Document Formats

One of the many problems of today's diversity in computer platform is that you can't be sure that a document you create will be readable, and formatted as it was intended, on another person's computer. Computer hardware differences (Mac versus Windows, for example) are part of the cause, but is also due to application program differences. If one computer user creates a document in a program that another user doesn't have, it's a major problem. In addition, computer documents created in WordPerfect may not translate accurately to Microsoft Word, and even more, documents created in Word 2000 may not be readable at all in Word 98, 97 or 95.

There are a number of remedies for a company to consider, including standardizing on a single computer hardware, software and release. This is challenging, costly, and difficult to enforce. There are also translation programs that convert from one format to another; they work well, but don't convert all documents.

Assuming you've found a way to overcome the application program differences between sender and receiver, fonts can be another big issue. If you are using just a handful of standard fonts, your documents may be formatted consistently on other systems. But if you use a font they don't have, another will be substituted, with unpredictable results—all that careful formatting work, gone down the drain.

Enter Adobe's PDF—Portable Document Format—files that overcome these limitations. Adobe PDF files are text and graphic files that can be opened, printed, and read online by any fairly current computer of any platform, and the resulting document is very close to the original. The recipient doesn't need to have the same computer hardware, application software, printer, or fonts—just the free Adobe Acrobat Reader software (available at http://www.adobe.com/). To create such documents, the sender uses a relatively low-cost Acrobat Distiller program to convert their documents to PDF format, so that anyone can read and print them with fidelity. PDF files make an almost ideal means of sharing important attachments via internet email.

Ten Key Website Must-Do's

1. Plan before you design, design before you create, create and test before you launch, and never stop the process.
2. Your business brochures were probably not done by the Information Systems department, so don't let them "do your website." It's a collaborative, team effort that should include outside expertise.

3. Have a clear set of goals and objectives in your plan, identify your audience, and specify the scope of your project.

4. Don't skimp on professional design and layout, but make sure the designers know the web as well as you know your industry.

5. Make sure the navigation works—easily, consistently and intuitively.

6. Personalize the interface appropriately. The consumer will appreciate time savers and customization for a more efficient visit.

7. Use databases and other technology behind the scenes to enable more functionality and less work for the consumer.

8. Integrate email communications with your website, giving consumers simple reminders and easy links to the pages they want.

9. Don't let any of it go stale! Plan for frequent content updates.

10. Be creative, but keep in mind that your target audience probably has slow connections to the internet, a small monitor, and an older release of browser than your website designer.

Fax, Voicemail, Video Conferencing, and Teleconferencing

Fax

Fax (facsimile) machines have accelerated the time in which communications can be shared, and have become a valuable tool in business communications. In many instances, fax transmission has replaced standard postal mail delivery. Business transactions, in the form of text and/or graphics, are faxed and received instantaneously, saving hours, days and dollars.

Fax Machine Do's

☐ Attach a cover page with the recipient's name, department, telephone number and extension.

☐ Indicate the total number of pages being transmitted.

☐ Make sure all page margins are large enough to avoid cutoff.

☐ Use the fax confirmation indicator to verify receipt of important documents.

☐ Make sure the recipient's fax number isn't a home office when setting up autofax with a night-time schedule.

Fax Machine Don'ts

☐ Do not send unsolicited documents. US Code 47.5.II highlights the legal issues involving "junk" faxing.

☐ Don't send email replies by fax.

Voice Mail

Voice mail is a computer-based technology that processes incoming and outgoing telephone calls. In business, it's quickly replacing the receptionist, the written message form and the simple answering machine because of its wide range of additional features. With voice mail, callers are prompted by voice commands to make choices about where to route their calls, and have a range of options for leaving messages and retrieving data, and requesting a fax be sent to their office automatically.

Companies have recently been introducing one-stop solution software for all of their communication needs. These systems enable users to access their email, listen to and answer voice mail messages, and place phone calls simultaneously over one standard phone line, enabling the integration of voice and data communications from remote locations. Some systems offer the ability to retrieve voice mail messages from a Web browser. Additional capabilities are designed to help users screen, prioritize and queue calls, plus route calls automatically to home or cell numbers.

Voice Mail Pro's

☐ Ensures that no phone calls are missed even if you are on the line.

☐ Eliminates the "phone tag" game.

☐ Allows messages to be saved and stored.

☐ Can send a voice message to numerous people simultaneously.

☐ Recorded messages can be left for others when given an access code.

Voice Mail Con's

☐ Can give a "cold," insincere impression.

☐ Punching through menu options can be annoying and time-consuming.

Video Conferencing

These electronic meetings allow participants to see and hear each other via television monitors while communicating from different geographical locations. **Video conferencing** can be useful in viewing a training session or a companywide conference or departmental meeting offered at a remote location, saving hundreds on travel-related expenses.

Video Conferencing Suggestions and Etiquette

☐ Keep in mind that voices will be delayed slightly and images may be somewhat unclear.

☐ All participants may not know you by appearance. It is important to introduce yourself at the beginning of the conference and direct questions to others by name.

☐ Keep in mind that all sounds will be heard. Take caution not to tap fingers and pencils, move chairs or make other noise excessively.

☐ Any visual documentation should be printed boldly and amply sized; also, drawings should be simple.

Teleconferencing

Teleconferencing, or **conference calling** allows three or more people to carry on a conversation over the telephone while at different geographical locations. Users are given a telephone number to call and a lead name and password to join the conversation.

Teleconferencing Suggestions and Etiquette

☐ A lightweight headset allows a person to take notes and move freely during a call.

☐ Identify yourself each time you speak.

☐ Direct questions to individuals by name since the entire group will hear but not see whom the question is meant for.

☐ If a speaker phone is used, keep in mind that all sounds are transmitted into the receiver. Take caution not to tap fingers and pencils, move chairs or make other excessive noise.

Writing Improvement Exercise Misplaced Modifiers

All the original sentences in this exercise were actually found in previously printed material.

A modifier should be placed to show clearly what it describes or modifies. If there is confusion about what is being modified, the meaning is usually made clearer by moving the modifier closer to the word being described. Or for clarity, it may be necessary to rephrase the entire sentence.

A modifier may be a word, a phrase, or clause (subject-word combination). Here are examples of unclear modifying with possible revisions for clearer meaning:

Original	The cowboy roped the calf *on the palomino pony.*
Improved	The cowboy *on the palomino pony* roped the calf.
Original	A university student was convicted of grand theft *just 24 hours after his trial went to the jury.*
Improved	*Just 24 hours after his trial went to the jury,* a university student was convicted of grand theft.
Original	One acre overlooking a waterfall for an unusual buyer, *shaped triangular.*
Improved	For an unusual buyer: *One triangular-shaped* acre overlooking a waterfall.
Original	That is the toughest decision *almost* that we have made.
Improved	That is *almost* the toughest decision that we have made.
Original	He *only* sang for his family.
Improved	He sang *only* for his family.
Original	After hanging on the bulletin board for two weeks, the mail clerk removed the announcement.
Improved	After the announcement had hung on the bulletin board for two weeks, the mail clerk removed it.

Name _____

Date _____ Class Section _____

Chapter 11 Computers, The Internet and Other Communication Technologies

MISPLACED MODIFIERS
WRITING IMPROVEMENT "HANDS ON" ASSIGNMENT

Note: The original form of these sentences came from actual speaking and writing.

Rewrite the following sentences to show clearly what is being modified by the italicized modifiers.

1. During the campaign I *nearly* called a thousand people. → <u>During the campaign I called nearly a thousand people.</u>

2. The crash victims needed medics to take care of them *badly*. → <u>The crash victims badly needed medics to take care of them.</u>

3. He told me what to do *with a smile*. → <u>With a smile, he told me what to do.</u>

4. His book came out after retirement *in a new edition*. → <u>After his retirement, his book came out in a new edition.</u>

5. They announced that they planned to enlarge the warehouse *at the board meeting*. → <u>At the board meeting, they announced that they planned to enlarge the warehouse.</u>

6. The trainer led the lion *cracking a whip*. → <u>Cracking a whip, the trainer led the lion.</u>

7. We have published a booklet about our stocks and bonds, *which we will send upon request*. → <u>Upon your request, we will send you a copy of our booklet on stocks and bonds.</u>

8. What is the company policy on correcting shipping errors *that they want us to follow*? → <u>What is the company policy on correcting shipping errors?</u>

9. The supervisor checked the week's work order and overtime schedule *with a frown*. → <u>With a frown, the supervisor checked the week's work order and overtime schedule.</u>

10. I *only* asked for one copy. → <u>I asked for only one copy.</u>

11. The young lady will lead the elephant *dressed in a sequined bikini*. → <u>The young lady dressed in a sequined bikini will lead the elephant. [Or did the elephant wear a sequined bikini?]</u>

12. *Running down a winding path,* the haunted house was discovered by Benji. → _____
Running down a winding path, Benji discovered the haunted house.

13. This is the domestic crisis center for battered wives *that we helped get started last year.* →
Last year we helped start this domestic crisis center for battered wives.

14. The teacher said that a colleague of hers was hospitalized *at school* for emergency
surgery. →   The teacher said that a colleague of hers at school was hospitalized for
emergency surgery.

15. Mr. Bampkins said he has discussed filling the drainage ditch *with his partners.* →
Mr. Bampkins said he and his partners have discussed filling the drainage ditch.

Chapter 11   Computers, The Internet and Other Communication Technologies

REVIEW AND DISCUSSION

Please compose brief answers. Where you have a choice, draw a line through any incorrect answer.

1. Why has the need for secretaries in offices decreased in the past several years? ____
   Many or most office personnel are composing and writing their own letters, memos,
   etc., on computers.

2. When composing at the keyboard, the text recommends that you (~~try to make your first copy perfect~~/type it quickly with little attention to form).

3. The text recommends while learning to use the Internet you (collaborate with others/~~work independently~~).

4. In a Local Area Network (LAN), computers usually connect to other computers within the organization.

   _____.

5. In 1999 the volume of Internet email was greater than the volume of postal mail. (True/~~False~~)

6. When was the first basic email program written? March, 1972.
   [Instructor: Page 250. At that time "@" was the sign chosen for its email.]

7. What is the well recognized sound byte when signing on to America Online? _____
   "You've got mail!"

8. Because messages can be forwarded again and again, the most recent person forwarding a message must *always* add a __salutation_____ and a signature _____.

9. To make words emphatic in email, seasoned users recommend that you use _____
   capital letters, not italics or boldface. [Receiver's software may not copy.]_____.

10. Browser software gives its users access to __World Wide Web (WWW)._____

11. Why should you not send unsolicited (junk) faxes?_ They fall like heavy rain on __
    _some people's already overloaded desks. [Instructor: They may in fact
    be illegal. Courts currently working on this.]_____.

12. Why is a lightweight telephone headset valuable during telephone conferencing?___
    Makes it possible to wander around while talking.

Rewrite these sentences to show the actual meaning more clearly.

13. They supposedly supplied Hughes, who died while en route to Houston from Acapulco, with codein. Hughes, who died while enroute to Houston from Acapulco, was supposedly supplied with codein.

14. Mr. Simpkins has a wife and three children, all under four. Mr. Simpkins and his wife have three children, all under four.

15. Did the man have a mustache that got out of the car? Did the man who got out of the car have a mustache?

12 Healthy Computing

Preventing Eyestrain, Carpal (Wrist) Tunnel Syndrome, Back Pain

> *As to diseases, make a habit of two things—to help, or at least, to do no harm.*
>
> Hippocrates
> *Early fifth-century* B.C. *Greek physician, called the Father of Medicine. He laid the foundation of scientific medicine and was the first to break away from the theory that disease is a divine punishment.*

Using a Computer: Let's Protect Our Eyes, Wrists and Backs

Question: "Healthy Computing" in a business communication text? Why here?
Answer: If not here, where?

Not long ago, medical professionals began getting alarmed at the increased number of patients coming to their offices with complaints of serious **eyestrain, wrist,** and **back pain**. The back problem was often associated with recurring **shoulder** and **neck pain**.

Confounding them further, people in medical fields recognized that a high percentage of the people reporting these painful conditions spent considerable time at a computer.

Most people working with written communications today spend a substantial amount of time at a computer. People at all levels have learned to respect them for their efficiency, speed and wide-ranging communicating capabilities.

Now several scientific studies show that computer-related injuries can be hazards of working in an office and that the injuries can strike at all levels. It is recognized that long hours at a computer can stress our bodies, specifically contributing to **eyestrain, carpal (wrist) tunnel syndrome,** and **back pain**.

Let's Listen to the Experts

Reliable sources are quoted here for information about what causes and relieves computer-related health problems. More hopefully, these sources also set out ways to prevent them. The following article comes from the *Columbia University Complete Home Medical Guide:*

As a nation, Americans are healthier today than ever before. We have a greater knowledge of the causes of health problems, and new methods for the treatment of illness and injury are continually being developed. ...

Although we may never see headlines proclaiming so, the gains in life expectancy that have occurred in the 20th century were achieved more by prevention and health promotion measures than by treatment and curative medicine. ... few realize that the means of protecting or promoting their health lies within their own hands. Medicine's capacity for the prevention of disease is steadily increasing, but it is up to the individual to act on this knowledge ...

This makes it more important than ever that individuals take great responsibility for their own well-being and that the physician acts as the patient's counselor and educator.[1]

Under the title "Desk Stress" the *New Wellness Encyclopedia of the University of California at Berkeley* states:

Anyone who sits at a desk or computer terminal all day is subject to the physical stress induced by static effort in which muscle groups are contracted for long periods in an unvarying position. ... It generally constrains the way you hold your back, arms, head, and shoulders. ... All of this causes office workers to complain about back, neck and shoulder pains, usually in that order.[2]

Cautioning us about the need for workers to interface with their computers properly, the American Management Association book *Healthy Computing* says:

If medical and surgical treatment attempts only to correct the symptoms, the actual cause of the problem will remain and the injury will be repeated. Much better than resorting to the knife is identifying bad work habits and treating them as well as the painful condition, preferably in good time to prevent chronic problems from occurring. How workers interface with their computers is both the cause of and the solution to most repetitive stress injuries... .

Working at a computer keyboard can be very hazardous to your health. The major occupational injuries and diseases ... will be suffered by those who spend much of their working lives—and perhaps their leisure hours as well—at a keyboard.[3]

Further, a front page *The Wall Street Journal* article titled "Office Pains" says:

Eyestrain tops the list of computer users' complaints. More than 10 million workers visit optometrists each year because of computer-related vision problems, and 40% of them get special glasses for their video display terminals, says

---

[1]*The Complete Home Medical Guide, Columbia University College of Physicians and Surgeons* (New York: Crown Publishers, Inc., 1995), p. 81.

[2]*The New Wellness Encyclopedia, University of California, Berkeley,* (Boston: Houghton Mifflin Company, 1995), p. 440.

[3]Ronald Harwin and Colin Hayes, *Healthy Computing* (New York: American Management Association, 1991), pp. 48ff.

James Sheedy, optometry professor at the University of California, optometrist and president of Corporate Vision Consulting.[4]

To help reduce eyestrain, several medical sources tell us we must take responsibility for ourselves by adapting the computer system and other potentially harmful factors to our individual needs. At the present time, many scientific studies are being conducted into the hazards of working in an office.

Under the title "Eyestrain and Computers," *The New Wellness Encyclopedia* tells of a study of patients who were computer users:

> Clinical studies at the School of Optometry at the University of California at Berkeley suggest that working regularly at a video display terminal may cause a premature loss in the eye's ability to focus. This evidence was preliminary and the conclusions were based on people who had come to the clinic with eye problems—not on a controlled study. Still, of 153 patients who averaged six hours a day at a video display terminal for four or more years, more than half had difficulty changing focus. **Presbyopia,** or loss of ability to focus with advancing age, accounted for half of these problems. The other patients, though, were in their twenties and thirties and should have had good focusing mechanisms.[5]

As we have heard, we should be kind to our eyes. Each of us is granted only one pair.

We experience **eye fatigue** after long sessions at a computer. Now we are told that the tiredness occurs because *eye muscles work harder when focusing on close work than when focusing on distant objects.* Such close work also includes reading a book, doing craft work, working with financial records and so forth.

We Can Prevent and Relieve Eyestrain

Many reference sources say that if the different factors that cause eyestrain are not relieved, they can cause extremely serious sight problems. These sources naturally give recommendations for relieving eyestrain that results from close work, specifically from operating a computer:

- ☐ Blink, blink, blink. Regularly look away from the screen and blink slowly, counting three seconds for each blink. Besides resting your eyes, each blink coats the surface with moisture, relieving dry, stressed eyes.

- ☐ Occasionally look at a distant object. Blink. Shift your gaze back to a near object. Blink. Repeat several times.

- ☐ Take regular breaks away from the computer—probably ten minutes each hour. If at all possible, other activities should frequently be alternated with computer sessions. Some workplaces arrange a buddy system where two people alternate work assignments with each having time away from a computer.

[4]Rochelle Sharpe, "Office Pains," *Wall Street Journal* (Florida Edition), April 9, 1996, p. A1.
[5]*The New Wellness Encyclopedia*, pp. 337–38.

☐ Apply a warm compress four times a day for 10 minutes. Don't rub your eyes.

☐ Should the eye condition get worse, you will get relief even more with over-the-counter eye drops and eye washes that are preservative free. But you should always be aware of possible serious trouble—a strong warning for a rest from close work with your eyes.

Improve the Office Environment

Here are recommendations you can check for making your office a healthier place to work.

☐ Room lighting and sunlight shining in or near your line of vision can be more harmful than you realize. All eye movement is controlled by small muscles that can get just as tight and frozen as any other muscle. According to many authorities, this tightness can also contribute to headaches and body aches, plus back and neck tension.

☐ Light measurements show that the light in most offices is too bright for computer use. *To follow a common test for proper light level, look straight across the room and hold your hand up to block the overhead lights from your eyes, like a sun visor. If you feel your eyes relax, the lights are too bright.*

☐ Within an office or any other working area, many glare problems can be corrected by proper desk placement. Light should come from your back or from your side—far enough back to light your working surfaces but not to shine in your eyes. If you use the computer monitor or screen in natural light, your desk should be positioned so that you are not looking toward light from windows, nor should the light from windows be in your peripheral vision.

☐ Of course, sunlight or other bright light shining on the computer screen can be harmful.

☐ Common eye abusers are indirect bright light coming from various sources such as another worker's desk, sunlight reflecting through windows or doors, or peripheral glare bouncing off white or near white buildings, walls, and other bright objects directly or indirectly in your line of vision. And remember, sunlight changes position during the day, so adjust as you go!

☐ For protection at all times of the day and night, use drapes or blinds, movable partitions, and large portable wall screens around any area.

☐ Also available are glare-resistant screens on the monitor and numerous antiglare computer covers, which can help substantially. Small box screens that fit around a computer might help, but in some positions might not block out other interfering light from farther surrounding areas.

☐ The newer antiglare computer screens are a noticeable improvement over earlier screens.

☐ The computer screen light itself can be a culprit. Adjust your computer. When you are working at a computer you are looking directly at a light at close range. Keep the screen clean so that images are clear and the screen has no reflections coming from it. Experimenting with background screen light will help you find your best adjustment level for avoiding eyestrain and eye damage.

Here are Recommendations for Those Who Wear Glasses

Jay Schlanger, an optometrist practicing at Cedars-Sinai Medical Clinic in Los Angeles, says that **bifocal wearers** who work at computers often have **neck strain** and **back pain** because the computer screen is farther away than most reading material. For a solution he suggests trying separate **prescription glasses for computer use** only.[6]

For computer work, some people who wear glasses find they prefer special **"half-eye" lenses** that can also be used for desk work. When fit properly for computer use, these lenses have a correction area much larger than the traditional reading correction area of full lens bifocals.

Special glasses for computer use eliminate the **"bobbing head" syndrome** of moving in and out of the reading correction area of bifocals. The bobbing tires your eyes, neck, shoulders, and back muscles. (See Figure 12.1.)

For Everybody: Have Regular Eye Exams

Have your eyes checked regularly—every year if you wear glasses. If you don't wear glasses, have them checked every two years. If you experience vision problems like blurred vision and/or poor night vision, make an appointment now.

Many medical authorities say eyestrain and using stronger light to compensate for weaker vision can be harmful to the eyes and may make a person need increasingly stronger glasses, eventually requiring medical attention.

Figure 12.1

[6]Shari Roan, "When It's All a Blur," *Los Angeles Times*, January 19, 1993, pp. E4–5.

Help Prevent Carpal (Wrist) Tunnel Syndrome

Not long ago *carpal (wrist) tunnel syndrome* was a medical mystery—and it might still be a mystery to some. A common theory held that it was an inherited condition because members of the same family were often afflicted by it. However, research reveals that this condition possibly developed because some family members followed similar activities. A symptom of the condition is that fingers begin to draw up into a claw. Without proper attention, it gets worse. (Medical circles alternately call this condition carpal tunnel syndrome **(CTS), repetitive stress injury or repetitive strain injury (RSI).**

An article titled "The Wrist: Preventing Carpal Tunnel Syndrome" from the University of California's *Wellness Encyclopedia* states: "While working with your hands, keep your wrists straight." A *New Wellness Encyclopedia* article supports the theory that people involved in repetitive wrist-intensive work, namely keyboarding, could develop carpal tunnel syndrome and explains:

Deriving its name from the Greek *karpos,* or wrist, the carpal tunnel is the passageway, composed of bone and ligament, through which a major nerve system of the forearm passes into the hand. These nerves control the muscles of this area, as well as the nine tendons that allow your fingers to flex. The wear and tear of repeated movement thickens the lubricating membrane of the tendons, and presses the nerves up against the hard bone. CTS (carpal tunnel syndrome) … usually begins with pain and tingling or numbness. As an occupational injury, it's brought on by repetitive work or movement … anyone who works with her hands for long hours can get CTS.

…If left untreated, the tingling and numbness can progress to a weakened grip and severe pain in the forearm or shoulders. By all means, get medical advice before this happens.[7]

Long hours of working with the hands, such as keyboarding, put constant pressure on the wrist tunnel areas if wrists are bent and moving steadily. Therefore, we benefit from adjusting our keyboard to a low level so our forearms are relaxed and our wrists are positioned straight to avoid injury to them. With wrists straight, fingers should not reach up from the wrist, but should dangle down over the keys.

Figure 12.2 shows the recommended relaxed **keyboarding position** with forearms and wrists horizontal and wrists not flexing constantly. Fingers dangle down to strike the keys.

Here's More on Healthy Office Environment

Figure 12.2 also shows a computer stand and chair arrangement for a healthy office environment. The table or stand should be lower than desk height with other proportions as shown. In this manner, the typing motion is totally in the fingers, with fingers hanging down, striking the keyboard with no motion in the wrists.

Feet are flat on the floor or raised by a footrest that throws weight so that the back of the chair supports the lower back. This way, body weight is shared by but-

---

[7]University of California at Berkeley, *New Wellness Encyclopedia,* pp. 420–21.

Figure 12.2
The right and wrong way to type.

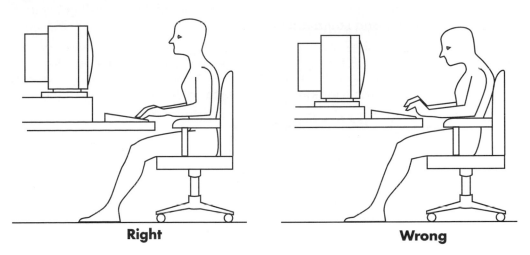

Right   **Wrong**

tocks and lower back, in a relaxed, less tiring position. It is suggested that you can gradually shift around, but three positions are most important:

1. Hand/wrist/arm in straight-line horizontal position
2. Weight distributed between lower back and buttocks
3. Feet comfortably on the floor

When you experiment with this position, you can feel strain relieved from the forearms and wrists when hands, wrists and arms are in the Figure 12.2 straight-line horizontal position. But when tiring occurs, take a break.

A *Time* magazine article discussing the carpal tunnel problem says, "**Repetitive strain injury (RSI)** is caused by too many long hours at the word processor." The article concludes by giving a list of do's and don'ts for avoiding wrist tunnel injury, which are abbreviated here:

Do

take rest breaks before pain begins.

keep hands relaxed.

keep wrists in a neutral position, not twisted or strained.

Don't

work in pain.

overdo home chores or leisure activities such as gardening, cooking, bowling or knitting, that strain your hands.

wear wrist splints while typing—this inaction can cause atrophy in some muscle groups.[8]

[8]Philip Elmer-Dewitt, "Royal Pain in the Wrist," *Time*, October 24, 1994, pp. 60–62.

Suggestions

The American Management Association book *Healthy Computing* supports these opinions and summarizes:

> Computer users are vulnerable to localized swelling of the tissues of [the wrist] area because keyboards, mice, and trackballs encourage us to have bad working habits and to misuse the delicate structures in the arm, wrist, and hand.[9]

Intensive Mouse Work

For **intensive mouse work**, such as designing and editing, become ambidextrous. It's easier than you may think.

As your hand with the mouse, say right hand, tires, first give it a rest. Then, rest your left forearm on the desk. With this changed position, operate the mouse with the left hand. You and the mouse are well acquainted by now, and the change soon becomes easy.

The position, with the arm on the desktop higher than the regular position, allows the relaxed left forearm to slide around with the wrist flat (not bent) and left hand moving the mouse, leaving relaxed fingers free for gently, gently activating the mouse. The flat wrist avoids the carpal tunnel strain while operating the mouse.

Success with Adjustable Chairs and Monitor Stands

As noted, firms are finding success with a combination of easily adjustable chairs and monitor stands. A monitor stand that moves up, down and around would accommodate the ambidextrous position of working with either left or right arm resting on the desktop at the side of the monitor. A change in operating the mouse allows hands, wrists and arms to have alternating rest periods.

Raising the Mouse Pad

Try making an oversized mouse pad from a large box, a book, or something else that has a large smooth surface and is at least two inches thick. With this device, you will be able to move either left or right forearm around the large mouse pad area.

Again, you can use either right or left forearm/hand position. If only the fingers and forearm move and *the wrist is flat*, you're doing it right. In either position, heavy pressure on the mouse builds up stress and pain. Operate it gently, gently.

(You've heard the story about how to catch a large alligator: "Lower the river!" Here, to change your position and rest the mouse-operating wrist, we say, "Raise the mouse pad.")

You Really Can Help Prevent and Relieve Back Pain

Avoid the position that causes your back pain.

That is the first and probably best rule for preventing computer back pain, as stated on a hospital television program titled "Back Pain, the Painful Truth." Partic-

---

[9]Harwin and Haynes, pp. 49–50.

ipating on this symposium were four medical doctors—a family practitioner, an orthopedic surgeon, a neurologist, and the director of the hospital physical medicine and rehabilitation department—plus a practicing physical therapist.

Initially, these five respected authorities gave a revealing reason for the common affliction with the back: Humans are born as quadrupeds. But as we began to stand up and become bipeds, this new stance places unaccustomed pressure on the spinal column. However, the spine was not designed for this upright position. As a result, most increasing back pressure settles down in the base of the spine, eventually causing pain. With this reasoning, the longer the spine endures this pressure, the worse the pain becomes.

One doctor explained, "As we have more birthdays," the pain buildup becomes worse. These practiced experts were quick to acknowledge that back pain affects different people differently. Some experience little if any back discomfort at any age, but others …

Surprisingly, the group agreed that 50 percent of back pain surgery is unnecessary. The orthopedic surgeon, the one of the group who would perform back surgery, inserted, "more than 50 percent." It was emphasized that before surgery a person should get a second opinion, or more than one second opinion.[10]

Preventing Back Pain

We can be sure that back pain must have been under study since cave-dwelling times, and along the way, some theories have been scrapped. However, today most authorities agree on basic principles of prevention.

Compiled from the sources previously given, suggestions for relieving back pain caused by working at a computer or other factors are listed:

- ☐ Regular exercise is your most potent weapon against back problems. Activity can increase **aerobic** (efficient use of oxygen intake) capacity, improve general fitness and help you shed excess pounds that stress your back.

- ☐ Stretching and toning your back and its supporting muscles can reduce wear and tear on your back by warming up muscles, increasing flexibility.

- ☐ Strength training can make your arms, legs and lower body stronger. In turn, your risk of falls and other injuries that could cause back problems decreases.

- ☐ Start slowly if you're out of condition. Your back muscles may be weak and susceptible to injury. Pace yourself: Increase workout time as you become stronger.

- ☐ A doctor or a physical therapist should give you advice before you begin an exercise program, especially if you've hurt your back before or have other health problems.

- ☐ Smart moves like swimming and other water exercises are safest for your back. Because they're nonweight-bearing, these activities place minimal strain on your lower back.

- ☐ Workouts on a stationary bike, treadmill or cross-country ski machine are less jarring to your back and feet than running on hard surfaces. Bicycling is a good option, too.

---

[10]"Back Pain, the Painful Truth," *To Your Health*, Television Symposium (Long Beach, California: St. Mary's Medical Center, May 1992).

☐ High risk moves—movements that cause you to exaggerate the stretch of your muscles—should be avoided. For instance, don't try to touch your toes with your legs straight.

☐ Jogging will probably not put your back at risk if you are in good condition, have a smooth stride, and do not run on a hard surface. Runners with bad backs should swim and/or do exercises to strengthen muscles in the back or abdomen.

☐ Twisting, quick stops and starts and impact on hard surfaces, such as tennis, racquetball, basketball and contact sports pose the greatest risks to your back.

Relieving Back Pain

Your back hurts? Our medical authorities also give these suggestions for relief:

☐ Listen to your body. If your back hurts, stop what you're doing and rest.

☐ Bed rest, medication and physical therapy may provide relief for mild to moderate back pain.

☐ If pain is severe, see your doctor. Bed rest may be advised, although long periods of bed rest are no longer advised because that may cause muscles to lose their strength.

☐ Over-the-counter medications like aspirin or ibuprofen are recommended. Or prescription nonsteroidal anti-inflammatory drugs and muscle relaxants may be advised.

☐ Physical therapy might include warm applications or gentle massage.

Figure 12.3 titled "Your Daily Back Routine," taken from a *Mayo Clinic Health Letter*, shows back exercises that should be followed at least 15 minutes a day.[11]

Sitting at a Desk or Computer for Hours → Muscle Fatigue and Pain

In an article titled "Desk Stress," *The New Wellness Encyclopedia* of the University of California at Berkeley agrees with other medical authorities who state that sitting at a desk or computer terminal all day causes office workers to complain of various physical stresses. The article names back pain complaints as more common than pains in knees, neck and shoulders.

The article further states that blood brings necessary nutrients to all muscle groups. Remaining in an unchanging position for long periods of time can pinch the veins, obstructing blood flow. Not receiving needed food results in fatigue and pain in starved muscles.

Here it is explained that episodes of back pain usually disappear within two weeks with simple measures like rest and over-the-counter pain relievers. Regardless 80–90 percent of back pain disappears within six weeks.[12]

[11]"Your Daily Back Routine," Medical Essay Supplement to *Mayo Clinic Health Letter* (Rochester, MN: Mayo Foundation for Medical Education and Research, 1997), p. 7.

[12]*Wellness Encyclopedia, University of California at Berkeley* (New York: Houghton Mifflin Company), 1995, p. 440.

Figure 12.3
Your daily back routine.

Your daily back routine

Here are basic exercises to stretch and strengthen your back and supporting muscles. Try to work at least 15 minutes of exercise into your daily routine. (If you've hurt your back before or have other health problems, such as osteoporosis, get medical advice before exercising.)

Knee to shoulder stretch — Lie on your back on a firm surface with your knees bent and feet flat. Pull your left knee toward your chest with both hands. Hold for 15 to 30 seconds. Return to starting position. Repeat with opposite leg. Repeat with each leg three or four times.

Chair stretch — Sit in a chair. Slowly bend forward toward the floor until you feel a mild stretch in your back. Hold for 15 to 30 seconds. Repeat three or four times. Don't do this exercise if you have osteoporosis.

"Cat" stretch: Step 1 — Get down on your hands and knees. Slowly let your back and abdomen sag toward the floor.

Step 2 — Slowly arch your back away from the floor. Repeat several times.

Half sit-up — Lie on your back on a firm surface with your knees bent and feet flat. With your arms outstretched, reach toward your knees with your hands until your shoulder blades no longer touch the ground. Don't grasp your knees. Hold for a few seconds and slowly return to the starting position. Repeat several times.

Shoulder-blade squeeze — Sit upright in a chair. Keep your chin tucked in and your shoulders down. Pull your shoulder blades together and straighten your upper back. Hold a few seconds. Return to starting position. Repeat several times.

Leg lifts: Step 1 — Lie face down on a firm surface with a large pillow under your hips and lower abdomen. Keeping your knee bent, raise your leg slightly off the surface and hold for about 5 seconds. Repeat several times.

Leg lifts: Step 2 — Repeat the exercise with your leg straight. Raise one leg slightly off the surface and hold for about 5 seconds. Repeat several times.

Check Your Chair / Computer Stand Combination

Those who study the condition that is sometimes called "desk stress" say that the combination of the desk chair and computer stand is the most important factor to relieve the potential problem of poor circulation. (See Figure 12.2.)

Some offices are finding that the installation of easily adjusted chairs and computer stands a wise investment for prevention of this growing health problem. Claims are made that the ergonomically correct chairs of clerical personnel often protect back and other muscles better than most padded leather chairs of executives. Administrative positions usually require many hours sitting in meetings, conferences, or at a desk and/or a computer.

If you sense a slight backache, quickly check your sitting position. Often a slight shift of back, buttocks or foot position relieves an ache before it gets strong. If a pain gets worse, however—that's a signal for a break.

Maintain Good Health to Prevent Back Pain

The following suggestions for preventing back pain and otherwise improving a person's health are excerpted from an article in the *New Wellness Encyclopedia:*

- □ *Extra weight.* A paunch can strain back muscles, distort posture, and overly compress the lower back.

- □ *Poor posture.* Sitting and standing put considerable pressure on the lower back. Correct posture keeps the head and chest high, neck straight, pelvis forward, and stomach and buttocks tucked in.

- □ *Sleeping.* Don't lie on your stomach, since that makes the stomach muscles sag and increases sway back. Instead, lie on your side with your knees bent to relieve pressure on the spinal disks. If you lie on your back, keep your knees bent by putting a pillow under them. For most people, the ideal mattress has firm inner support. If your mattress is too soft, insert a board under it.

- □ *Exercise.* Regular exercise is vital to the health of your back: calisthenics, stretching, walking, swimming (but not butterfly or back stroke), cycling with upright posture.

- □ *Lifting and carrying.* Bending to pick up an object puts maximum strain on your back and is probably the number one cause of backaches. When you lift, bend at the knees not at the waist, making your leg muscles do most of the work. To pick up something heavy, squat with your legs far apart, tighten your stomach muscles, keep your back straight, holding the object close to your body. Better yet, push a heavy object instead of lifting it. Pulling could injure your back.

- □ *Dress.* Prolonged use of tight pants and girdles may induce weak abdominal muscles and result in back trouble. High heels tend to promote curvature of the spine and increase risk of a fall.[13]

In Sum: Read this Encouraging Information About Back Pain

Beyond the preceding recommendations, the book *Healthwise for Life* reports:

[13]*New Wellness Encyclopedia,* pp. 437–38.

You can strain or sprain ligaments or muscles during a sudden or improper movement, or by overuse.

You can damage your discs the same way so that they tear or stretch. If the tear is large enough, material may leak out of the disc and press against a nerve. A nerve may also become irritated because of swelling or inflammation in other parts of the back.

Any of these injuries can result in 2 or 3 days of acute pain and swelling followed by slow healing and a gradual easing of pain. Pain may be felt in the low back, the buttock, or down the leg. ...

Doctors recommend back surgery much less often now than in the past. Rest, posture changes, and exercise can relieve 98 percent of back problems, even disc problems.[14]

[14]*Healthwise for Life* (Boise, ID: Healthwise, Incorporated, 1992), pp. 33–34.

Chapter 12 Healthy Computing:
Preventing Eyestrain, Carpal (Wrist) Tunnel Syndrome, Back Pain

WRITING IMPROVEMENT EXERCISE
Proofreaders' Marks

Proofreaders' marks are useful in making corrections on paper copy that is to be re-typed or printed. These marks save time and are useful in revising and editing hard copy of written communications. Most have been used for centuries, originating in Latin. You are already familiar with some.

Mark	Meaning
¶	Paragraph
no ¶	No paragraph
∧	Insert
wf	Wrong font—style or size
⊙ ⌃ ⌃	Insert period, semicolon, comma
(delete mark)	Delete. (Draw line through word(s); end with mark.)
∼∼∼ b.f.	Boldface (Make zigzag line underneath word(s); write b.f. in margin.)
ital.	Italics (Draw line underneath word(s); write ital. in margin.)
+ #	Add space
− #	Less space
han⌢d	Close up space
[	Move to left
]	Move to right
⊓	Move up
⊔	Move down
ju(e⌢n)	Transpose (June)
....stet	Let it stand. (Make dots beneath word(s) that were crossed out and write stet—let it stand—in margin.)
l.c. or /	Lower case (Or draw diagonal line through capital letter: Lower Ȼase.)
Caps	Capitals (capitals)
# # #	THE END

Chapter 12 Healthy Computing:
Preventing Eyestrain, Carpal (Wrist) Tunnel Syndrome, Back Pain

WRITING IMPROVEMENT "HANDS ON" ASSIGNMENT
Proofreaders' Marks

In the column at the right, indicate the meaning of the symbol at the left.

1.	$\wedge$	Insert
2.	¶	Paragraph
3.	no ¶	No paragraph
4.	wf	Wrong font, style, or size
5.	⊙ ⌄ ⌄	Insert period, semicolon, comma
6.	℘	Delete
7.	⊏	Move to left
8.	⊐	Move to right
9.	⌐⌐	Move up
10.	∪	Move down
11.	～ b.f.	Type in boldface the words that have zigzag line underneath
12.	-# +#	Less space, more space
13.	....stet	Let it stand. Make dots beneath words that had been crossed out and write *stet* in margin.
14.	_ ital	Type in italic the words that have line underneath.
15.	ju(e n)	Transpose

Chapter 12 Healthy Computing:
Preventing Eyestrain, Carpal (Wrist) Tunnel Syndrome, Back Pain

REVIEW AND DISCUSSION

Please draw a line through the incorrect answer.

1. Today the only people in an office who work with computers are top executives and clerical staff. (~~True~~/False)

2. The capacity of medical science for the prevention of disease is steadily decreasing. (~~True~~/False)

3. Medical authorities encourage people to take responsibility for their own health and well-being. (True/~~False~~)

4. Sitting long hours at a computer terminal or desk can cause eyestrain, wrist, back, neck or shoulder pains. (True/~~False~~)

5. How workers interface with their computers often is both the cause of and solution to many office repetitive stress injuries. (True/~~False~~)

6. Reference sources in your text claim that if a person does not relieve causes of eyestrain it probably will not get worse. (~~True~~/False)

7. Light measurements show that lighting in most offices is too bright. (True/~~False~~)

8. Medical studies show that people involved in constant wrist motion, namely keyboarding, could develop carpal tunnel syndrome. (True/~~False~~)

9. According to a hospital medical TV program which was discussed in the text, the best rule for preventing computer back pain is "Avoid the position that causes your back pain." (True/~~False~~)

10. Room lighting and bright sunlight can be harmful to your eyes. (True/~~False~~)

11. Claims are made that ergonomically correct chairs of clerical personnel probably protect back and other muscles better than the padded leather chairs of many executives. (True/~~False~~)

12. For the health of your back, medical authorities quoted in this chapter recommend exercise such as calisthenics, stretching, walking (but not on hard surfaces), and swimming (but not butterfly stroke). (True/~~False~~)

13 Employment Guides

Finding a Job, Holding a Job, Earning Promotions, Changing Jobs

> *I will pay more for the ability to deal with people than any other ability in the world.*
> *John D. Rockefeller, 1839–1937*
> *U.S. industrialist and philanthropist*

Many of us see our college education as eventually improving our employment prospects. To help you find your place among the working majority, this chapter discusses how to apply for a job, how to be a satisfactory employee, and how to earn promotions. Also, we discuss when and how to change jobs. These steps involve all types of communication—visual, spoken and written.

Big Changes in the Employment Market

Authorities state that in today's employment market most people will change jobs several times. Evidence of this is all around us. Not long ago a person could train for a specific career and expect to stay in the field of that career, often with the same firm, for a lifetime.

This is rarely the case today. Technological advances revolutionize career opportunities in almost all fields. Yet, as job opportunities in one field vanish, entirely new opportunities can develop in others.

Being Flexible in Today's Job Market

So this is the challenge today. You may be able to choose your preferred field with the knowledge that continuing opportunities there should be to your liking. However, in many instances the future might be uncertain. Therefore, you should be flexible, with an eye not only to what is developing in your field, but also to what will be going on there in the future. And you would be wise to learn about unrelated fields that may have better opportunities.

Many aptitudes for one job may be transferable to another you may never have considered. Many people have found that an unwelcome change forced upon them eventually turned out more to their liking and more rewarding than the position they left. Think positive! There is a saying, "Change is good." If you have held a particular job for some time, a move could even help you avoid the trauma of future job burnout from being on the same job doing the same things too long.

Technology Literacy

Now, computer technology has a pervasive impact on nearly all forms of employment. For those directly working with computer systems, maintaining up-to-date knowledge and expertise is critical to your advancement and even to your present value in this fast changing field. In fact, basic technology literacy is a critical success requirement for *all of us*!

Significant improvements in the quality and speed of business communication are available to those who have mastered a level of information technology literacy and strive to keep their skills growing. *In addition, these skills are transferable to nearly any industry, and can often mean the difference between selected job candidates.*

Finding Yourself

First, find yourself. Take time to write down carefully a personal inventory of your own pluses and minuses. Here are 12 points to cover:

1. Long- and short-range goals—responsibilities, money, security, fame.
2. Strengths: What have you enjoyed doing in the past?
3. Weaknesses: What have you *not* enjoyed doing in the past?
4. Finances—needs and desires.
5. Interests.
6. Appearance: Can you improve it for acceptance on the job market?
7. Health: Do you need to improve it?
8. Education and training: List academic and vocational courses that you have particularly enjoyed and in which you have done particularly well. List academic and vocational courses in which you did poorly.
9. Experience: List each job experience and skill you have used, assessing each favorably or unfavorably according to your personal tastes.
10. Hobby interests: Some could eventually be of help on a job.
11. Type of company: small, large, medium-sized? Perhaps you would prefer going into business for yourself.
12. Family situation affecting the employment picture.

By studying your answers to these 12 points, you should get a good picture of the type of work that fits you best and therefore should be the work at which you would best succeed.

Personality

Few people recognize the fact that many personnel choices are made on **personality.** In hiring, promoting and retaining employees, people being considered may have similar backgrounds in education, training, and experience, and the decision is made on "How do they get along with people?"

You must look at yourself as having both positive and negative character traits. You must realize that the greater the positive nature of your personality, the greater the possibility not only for your being hired, but also for upward moves during employment. If you see yourself lacking personality traits that should help make you a satisfactory employee in your preferred career field, work to improve.

Experience

If you hope to get good full-time employment at the completion of your education, seek some part-time employment in the interim, even if you have no financial need. Although the employment may not be related to the hoped-for career, a good recommendation from any former employer is worth having, because it shows your ability in a working situation.

A person looking for work may be confronted with the problem of being unable to list any work experience on a job application form. Applicants often ask, "How can I get experience without experience?" It really is possible to get a job without having worked previously. Even if you have not yet worked for pay, it is valuable to be able to show a potential employer some past record of working successfully with others. If the job market is tight, consider volunteer work, because it, too, can result in favorable employment references. And successful involvement in worthwhile community or campus activities will give the future employer a positive picture of you as an individual. (The Writing Improvement Exercise at the end of Chapter 7 gives the successful experiences of three people, both young and older, who initially believed they had limited backgrounds for applying for work. They successfully turned their negatives into positives.)

Finding a Career

The decision of what career to follow should be each person's own choice. However, this decision should not be made arbitrarily, without considering important influencing factors. You should judge your own desires, capabilities, and limitations. Then, to avoid lifelong frustration, you should try to fit your own background and desires into the current employment scene.

Plato, the ancient Greek philosopher, said, "No two persons are born exactly alike, but each differs from each in natural endowments, one being suited for one occupation and another for another." Following a lifetime career that is personally unrewarding can lead to unhappiness and disappointment. You should try to identify your own preferences in such general matters as the following:

Working conditions. Do you like working with other people? Do you like meeting the public? Do you prefer working alone?

Work location. Do you want the advantages and disadvantages of working in or near a large metropolitan area? Do you prefer the advantages and disadvantages of working in a small town or rural area?

Work hours. Will you accept long hours that might result from being promoted to additional responsibilities? Or would you prefer more free time that might come from refusal to accept promotion? Can you accept the discipline of work-

ing hours prescribed by others, as most work demands? Or do you insist on setting your own schedule?

When you evaluate these general questions relating to working conditions and
personal preferences, you are better able to judge yourself and your own qualifications for a particular type of work.

Opinions of Others

In studying yourself and your career plans, you should seek the opinions of
others, such as employment counselors, teachers, religious leaders, community
members, and interested friends and relatives. These people may or may not have as
much education as you do; they may or may not have the intelligence you do; but
they will have the wisdom of years of experience, both in their own lives and in observing the lives of others.

Selecting a career is a matter of checks and balances, of weighing one factor
against another. You yourself must live with the eventual decision. This decision not
only guides you toward open fields of interest; it also tends to determine your lifetime income and often your position in your community.

The "Family Business"

There is some advantage in choosing to follow the **"family business,"** or any
other type of career with which you have had first-hand contact. Over a period of
time you may have picked up knowledge and skills that give you some proficiency not possessed by those who have not lived in or around that particular atmosphere. You may have what amounts to an internship or apprenticeship in a profession, business, or trade that would make it easy for you to gain true competence
and leadership in that field.

Ultimately, however, weighing all factors objectively, you should choose the
type of work that will be satisfying to you. It may not be the same work as that of
your father or mother, your favorite aunt or uncle, or anyone else with whom you
are acquainted. Spending years at an occupation that conflicts with your true interests or abilities can bring about a physical, mental, or emotional crisis in your later
life. It is hazardous to be locked into work that is too challenging. But it may be even
more hazardous to try to spend your life in a career that is neither sufficiently challenging nor rewarding for you.

A Movie Star's Career Choice

Jack Lemmon, the movie star, tells a story of how his father helped him get
started in acting. At an early point in his career, Lemmon, who had a Harvard education, asked his father for a $300 loan. His father was vice president of a large na-
tional company that made doughnut machines and other bakery equipment.

Lemmon's father said, "OK, you don't want to start in my business. You want
to act."

"I said, 'Yes.'"

"'Do you need to do that?'"

"I answered, 'Yes, I really need to find out if I can get anywhere in acting.'"

"'You love it?'"

"I said, 'Yes, I love it.' I had already done summer stock and some other stuff."

"He handed me the $300 and said, 'The day I don't find romance in a loaf of bread, I'm going to quit.'"

"It was a marvelous, marvelous line. What he was saying was that whatever the _____ you do is not as important as loving it."

Finding a Job

Employment Counseling

Some people can make these career judgments completely on their own. But many benefit from employment counseling experts. You can contact any college nearby (you often need not be a student or former student). Someone there can counsel you or refer you to a job counselor. Also, in some locations, state job services give free aptitude tests. Aptitude tests might reveal you have a good potential for a field you have never considered. Or the tests and counseling might lead you to stay in the field where you have been or want to be.

Counseling services have information on employment possibilities in given fields and also in given geographical areas. Federal government studies are available. The most thorough of these is the U.S. Department of Labor's *Occupational Outlook Handbook,* available in the reference section of your library. This handbook gives *up-to-date* descriptions of hundreds of occupations, with details of type of work performed, training and education needed, salary to be expected, and employment outlook (*excellent, good, may have to hunt some,* or *poor*).

Some college and private employment advising services now have this type of information available on computers to make specific information readily available to you in a paper printout. In many college human resources or personnel offices, announcements are also posted on bulletin boards and in binders that you can study for job openings.

Personnel Recruitment

Some firms specialize in finding employees for other companies, and the people who do the actual looking for employees are called **"headhunters."** Headhunting by computer is becoming common. A computer matchmaker firm sends out their client companies' job openings to college and private job placement centers, where the matches are made. Results are praised for speed and efficiency both by the companies seeking specific types of employees and by career counselors.

A major New York life insurance firm with branches throughout the country recently reported they got their top new agent—rookie of the year—through such a computer service. A firm in Beverly Hills, California, where they train "nannies" for child care, reported excellent results, especially in finding office and clerical help.

Job Sources

Few people looking for jobs realize how many employment sources there are. The following list contains several suggestions for you to explore, and by becoming familiar with a field, you may even add others on your own.

1. *Networking among friends, relatives, neighbors, business contacts of your own.* Such people often know of job opportunities and their personal recommendations can be your best help. Studies show that about 80 percent of new jobs are found through networking.

2. Internet job postings. CareerNet, for example, lists the classified ads from major newspapers on the World Wide Web. The Monster Board is another popular Website for job ads.

3. *College placement bureaus.* Numerous employers contact these agencies looking for students with various types of backgrounds. Many or most of these agencies announce employment opportunities in various fields and types of positions. Lists of job descriptions, salary ranges and sample examinations are available. To avail yourself of these services in public institutions, you need not be a student at the college.

4. *Public and private libraries.* Talk to a librarian about your project. You may be surprised at the wealth of information in your library that relates to possible employers. See Moody's Industrials, Standard & Poor's, Dunn & Bradstreet, and others.

5. *Company web pages.* Most organizations' web pages have a section devoted to employment opportunities.

6. *Business periodicals.* Libraries contain copies of *The Wall Street Journal, National Business Employment Weekly* (published by *The Wall Street Journal*), local business publications and more.

7. *Newspaper ads.* It is reported that only about 5 percent of new jobs are found through these ads.

8. *News items.* Current news can sometimes lead to jobs, such as new business and government job developments.

9. *Public employment agencies.*

10. *Private employment agencies.* Many firms do not like to spend their own time in employee searches; therefore, you may find excellent positions offered through private employment agencies. Some require a fee; some do not. *Do not pay a high fee or sign a contract to pay a high fee unless it is guaranteed in writing that you will be offered a job of your choice.*

11. *Drop-ins on prospective employers.* Appearing in person can be more favorable than telephone and email or postal mail contacts.

12. *Telephone inquiries.* If a position in a distant place especially interests you, you might consider stretching the truth and say something like: "I expect to be in your area next week and would appreciate it if I could talk with you about...."

13. *Trade and industrial organizations such as computer science associations, retail trade marts, and insurance organizations.* Insurance employers and many others regularly hire large numbers of employees in a wide range of work assignments.

14. *Civil service—municipal, state, county, and federal.* Each year a large percentage of college graduates and others are hired by government agencies. Job notices may be found in an agency's headquarters, at job information centers in post offices, and on college placement bureau bulletin boards. Also,

public libraries contain job descriptions, salary ranges and sample examinations. All state and national government agencies are required by law to list their available jobs with state unemployment offices.

15. *Organizations.* Church, YMCA, YWCA, and professional associations often set up career planning centers.

16. *Direct mail.* Applying for a job by mail often puts you in competition with large numbers of people.

17. *Yellow pages of telephone books.*

18. *U.S. Census Bureau.*

19. *Consulting firms looking for people with your specialty.*

The Job Hunt

Sometimes it is an employee's job market—jobs are relatively easy to find. At other times, finding the right job can be a difficult battle. But in good times and bad, personality, education, and experience are put to the test, and the person who rates best will often be given first chance at available positions. Even in the worst of times, some jobs are available.

The **job hunt** can be wearisome, and a person can be conditioned physically and psychologically to only a limited number of turndowns in a given period. But the person who perseveres lands the job—sometimes a better position than the one originally sought.

The job hunt can be one of life's toughest battles, and in this battle being persistent—fighting for a job—can get you the job you want.

James J. ("Gentleman Jim") Corbett, world heavyweight boxing champion at the turn of the century, said:

> Fight one more round. When your feet are so tired that you have to shuffle back to the center of the ring, fight one more round. When your arms are so tired that you can hardly lift your hands to come on guard, fight one more round. When your nose is bleeding and your eyes are black and you are so tired that you wish your opponent would crack you one on the jaw and put you to sleep, fight one more round—remembering that the man who fights one more round is never whipped.

Job prospects for the new millennium are good for communications and computer people, accountants, engineers, nurses, scientists, mathematicians, teachers, and paralegals.

Also, specific industries that have good prospects are recycling and waste disposal firms, the Internet, financial services, long-term care for elderly, high tech machinery, health care, child care, prepared meals, cleaning services. (People are becoming more willing and able to pay for services.)

Study the demand in a particular field and the potential supply of applicants, study yourself, and start looking. Career counseling services and the *Occupational Outlook Handbook* mentioned earlier can help you.

Importance of Money

Selecting career preferences can involve many choices regarding both a field and one's own particular role or roles in that field. Although it must be acknowledged that money buys the necessities and luxuries of life, the amount of **money** you will be able to make over your lifetime in each possible line of employment should not be the overriding reason for making a choice. Much more is at stake here than the money you will earn; for instance, the manner in which you will use your talents, the way you will spend many waking hours, and even many of your dreams at night.

Neither should entry level income be the deciding factor of job choice. Some firms may offer higher-than-average entry level income with scarce opportunity for advancement beyond the entry position. The boss's son or daughter may be training for the only executive position. Another firm may promise you the moon, but the moon never rises. On the other hand, one national electrical supply firm insists that all new employees start in warehouse positions at low pay, to learn the business—even his own son—"from the ground up." Some employees stay at this level only a few weeks or months before progressing into other positions with the firm, in such fields as accounting, data processing, selling, public relations, and administration. Eventually, many reach top executive positions.

Looking, Looking

Surveys of job seekers and job finders show that the more serious study a person puts into the important task of finding a job, the more satisfying is the result. Spend plenty of time in preparation. Study yourself, the type of work you want, and why you want it. Basically, understand that you must try to present yourself more favorably than your competition.

On Being Persistent

Robert O. Snelling, head of a private employment service company with 500 offices across the country, was asked, "What are the mistakes young people most frequently make when they apply for jobs?" He gave this classic advice:

> One common mistake is not being insistent enough—not fighting for an available job. I see this all the time among the sons and daughters of friends and neighbors. The youngsters apply for a job, and I ask them what happened. Often the reply is "Well, they said they'll call me if they want me." When I ask what they're going to do next, they say, "I'll wait to hear about this first opening, but meanwhile I'll apply to other companies."
>
> I tell these youngsters they're taking the wrong tack. They should go back to the first place and tell the employer, "I really want that job." Then they should follow up with a phone call and then with a letter saying, "I want that job. Here's why I'm qualified."
>
> It's amazing to me that young folks won't fight to get a job they really want.[1]

[1]"Are There Jobs Enough for All?" Copyrighted interview in *U.S. News & World Report*, October 30, 1972, p. 72.

Employers want evidence that a person really wants a specific job.

One young woman who planned a career in journalism learned that the university campus correspondent for a daily newspaper was a graduating senior. Figuring that there should be an opening for this position, she mustered her courage, walked into the newspaper office, and approached the news editor. After listening to her, he pulled his half-eye glasses down over his nose, stared her straight in the eye, and said, "You know, of course, that all the other high school journalism seniors in the state are probably applying for that job!"

Returning the stare, she said, "I believe I could do the job as well as any of them." Before she left, she received permission to check in to see if the position had been filled.

And check she did. Every few weeks she dropped in, until the editor would say, "Oh—you again!"

But she got the job.

Further, this led to a full-time position when she graduated.

Frequently, at the completion of education and training, people find it impossible to get employment that they feel adequately suits their background. If this occurs, you should not be too discouraged. One young man, a particularly creative type with a major in theatre arts and a minor in advertising, sought unsuccessfully for the kind of position he wanted. Eventually, in desperation, he accepted a position as meter reader for a power company. After a period of wearing out shoe leather and enduring innumerable assaults from neighborhood dogs, he was advanced to an office position doing routine accounting work. There, through a company bulletin, he learned of an opening in the marketing department—the type of position for which he felt particularly well qualified. Since the firm practiced in-house promotion, he was interviewed for the position, and within $2^1/_2$ years after his initial employment, he began a new career as an assistant account executive in advertising.

In another instance, a woman whose children were grown became tired of volunteer work and sought employment for pay. She had an interest in writing but had found little opportunity to develop it. The best position offered her was as typist and file clerk in the Utah state fish and game department. Gradually she progressed from one position to another, taking some night courses at a nearby university. After a few years, she became editor of the state's fish and game magazine, a popular publication with worldwide circulation. Today she is a published poet, children's nature story writer, and author of three books published by a major New York publisher.

Never Too Late to Look

While God and nature give to the young the plentiful advantages of youth, many employers point out reasons for their preference in hiring the **mature employee.**

These job seekers are recognized as expecting the *work* that goes with the job. They often are more appreciative of being hired, and therefore are more loyal to those who hire them. Thus, they are less likely to job hop. They probably will not miss work to care for small children. Further, tests have shown that people in their 50s learn at the same rate as 16-year-olds. Employers like their stability and reliability.

Older workers seeking employment should follow these suggestions.

☐ *Don't* emphasize your age or possible disabilities.

☐ *Don't* lecture the interviewer about new laws that favor the hiring of older people.

☐ *Do* study this chapter and Chapter 14 for guides in your job search.

☐ *Do* consider volunteer work. Work experience and contacts you make can lead to paid employment.

☐ *Do* try part-time work; it can lead to full time or can connect you with other employers.

☐ Or, *do* try volunteer work as a start.

In all, most employers recognize the advantages of hiring older applicants.

Holding a Job

So now you have your first job and you think that's that. You will soon discover that holding a job takes as much effort as finding one. You must make a continuing effort to perform your duties responsibly. Your success or failure depends upon you. As with most other things, what you get out of a job depends upon what you put into it. You can tell whether or not you can hold your job by asking yourself these questions:

Do I have the qualifications to hold this job?

Do I want to hold this job?

Can I get along with my boss and my fellow employees?

If the answers to all the preceding questions are yes, you will probably hold this job successfully. If the answer to the first question is no and you want the job, you must get additional training or education. If the answer to either of the other questions is no, you should look into yourself for a change in attitude or a change in jobs. Employers have seen too many people who want the *job* but don't want the *work*.

Appearance is also important. A person may not be expected to spend an excessive amount of money for clothes, but a certain standard should be maintained. For both men and women, appearance on the job can be critical. Good introductions to the subject of proper business clothing are the two popular books by John Malloy: *Dress for Success* (for men's wear) and *Dress for Success for Women*.

However, do not overdress on the job. People who overspend on clothing set themselves apart from their fellow employees, which can be difficult for relationships among personnel and even with superiors.

No matter what type of work you do, your success will depend largely upon getting along with people—your boss, your fellow employees, and those who work for you. Actually, in casual conversations and otherwise, people who work for you can be making comments to your superiors about *you* and *your* job performance, even while you are being considered for promotion. If you work with a pleasant, positive, courteous attitude, treating people respectfully, feeling sure that you *can* succeed, you *will* succeed.

Earning Promotions

If you are successful on the job, the next question concerns whether or not you will be considered for promotion. Promotions usually go to the employees who show the following attributes:

Productivity

Productivity is the bottom line for judging most employees—how much quality work does that person do? Mistakes cost money, and a seemingly productive worker who makes more than a tolerable number of errors cannot expect to be kept on the job, much less promoted.

Motivation

Motivation—or drive—comes from a person's attitude toward the job itself. Motivation is a sincere desire to succeed. The salesperson who sells the most, whether the oldest or youngest on the staff, will be a person who is highly motivated.

Initiative

Initiative means doing things without being told—taking the extra step. Initiative also means observing what is going on around you and being interested in the best company-wide performance. It means helping another worker under pressure without being told, if your work load will permit it. It means asking questions and being willing to make decisions when needed. Some people are good at analyzing problems but have no idea how to correct them. Such people are usually kept in the back room, and decision makers use their ideas in instituting changes.

People with initiative often seem to accomplish the impossible when plans seem to have bogged down completely.

Reliability

Time is money, and people who are late often waste not only their own time but also the time of others. A record of tardiness and too many absences has stopped the advancement of many employees.

Reliability also involves promptness with your work. When a job you have been given must be completed by a certain time or a certain day, be sure you have it done by then. This may require pacing yourself carefully and perhaps putting off other work—or play—that does not have such a deadline.

All in all, reliability is one of the most valuable human characteristics, in or out of business. If you can be counted upon, if you are dependable in any normal situation, this quality can outweigh many other minor ones.

Reliability means they can count on you.

Industriousness

Industriousness is the willingness to become totally involved in your work—the willingness to work long, hard hours. Refusal to work overtime shows a lack of interest in the progress of the firm. J. C. Penney once said, "I would like to warn any embryonic executives right now that unless they are willing to drench themselves in their work beyond the capacity of the average man, they are just not cut out for positions at the top."

Use of Good English

As noted earlier in Chapter 4, to thrive in the American career world, a person, native-born American or foreigner, must have good command of the English language. People who use bad grammar are usually kept in low-pay jobs where they do not embarrass the company by meeting with the public.

Work Ethic

In his *Autobiography,* Benjamin Franklin, (1731–1759) U.S. statesman, said:

When men are employed, they are best contented; for on the days they worked they were good-natured and cheerful, and, with the consciousness of having done a good day's work, they spent the evening jollily; but on our idle days they were mutinous and quarrelsome.

Changing Jobs

The Backward Step

Sometimes it is necessary to take a **backward step** when job demands force a person to leave and accept different employment with a lower salary. Like in professional sports, this step can often be an anticipated development for which long-range plans can be made. Or, as stated earlier, sometimes, the backward step is temporary, and the person is able to get into a new field and gradually build up to or beyond previous earnings and position.

Many people, old or young, may at some time have to accept job setbacks because of diminishing physical capacities, corporate mergers, technological advances, or other changes. But it is the person with intelligence, courage and determination who stands the best chance to recover and achieve new heights of success. In the uncommon person, adversity is said to be a source of strength.

Recovering from Losing a Job

If it's you who has just lost a job, it may right now seem impossible to believe that it may have been a "blessing in disguise." But this is frequently the case, and sometimes even in the middle of this dismal picture, there is a sense of relief in not being tied into work you did not like. It may take time to realize that **loss of a job** often occurs because a person really did not want to stay on that job, for whatever reason.

At such a time, take stock of yourself, and *write down* answers to these questions:

- [ ] What are my career options?
- [ ] What type of work would I enjoy doing?
- [ ] What type of work would I *not* enjoy doing?
- [ ] Am I trained for my choice of work? (This could lead to a hunt for interim employment during retraining.)
- [ ] What type of opportunities should I seek?
- [ ] What type of opportunities should I stay away from?

Making the Change

Changing jobs is an act that should never be approached lightly or considered haphazardly. However, as noted, circumstances sometimes force a person to seek new employment. At other times, a person may feel that a voluntary change should be made. According to Drake, Beam, Morin, a leading outplacement firm, people starting a new job will, on average, hold it for five years. This amount of time is shrinking and will continue to shrink.

Before you make a move to change your type or place of employment, you should make a serious study of your current employment and your reasons for wanting to leave. If, after such study, you are convinced you should work elsewhere, you should have your new position firmly lined up before quitting your old job. It is always easier to get a job when you are already employed. If you are still on the job, it is evidence of satisfactory performance.

Sometimes you may cross off a certain type of work because you tried the right job at the wrong time or place. Working at it part time or full time while in school, possibly compounded by family responsibilities, might for a time dim the appeal of the most attractive career. After trying other lines of employment, you may find yourself best suited to your original school-time work, after all. Or perhaps success seemed too easy in some type of employment. Maybe you should try it again, for you could be headed toward higher goals than you originally anticipated.

There can be many reasons for changing jobs. Usually it is done because of a change in personal objectives and goals, sociological changes, or technological advancements. With continuing developments in computer science, nuclear power, laser technology, medical technology and superconductivity, people should look ahead to foresee how these changes can affect the job picture.

A Test before Changing Jobs

An article in Kiplinger's *Changing Times*, "Are You and Your Job Cut Out for Each Other?" covers the topic of changing employment by presenting a self-check test for evaluating yourself and your job. This timeless article for you and yours points out that the choice of a career means "logging 90,000 hours, possibly more, at work. While we do it for money, we also work to fill deep-seated needs for recognition, advancement, learning, and social relationships."

If you are employed and are wondering if you should look for another job, try taking the following test, which, with permission of the publisher, has been slightly abridged from the test in that article.

The Job Itself

1. *Overall, do you find your work at least moderately satisfying? (Yes _____ No _____)*

2. *Are you confident that the skills you've acquired will keep you employable even in bad times? (Yes _____ No _____)*

3. *Are at least some aspects of your work different from what you were doing five years ago? (Yes _____ No _____)*

4. *Are you earning as much as co-workers who have equal training and experience? (Yes _____ No _____)*

5. *Assuming you're interested in a promotion, is the way clear for one? (Yes _____ No _____)*

The Company You Work For

6. *Is your company well established, successful, and in a strong competitive position? (Yes _____ No _____)* There are advantages and disadvantages to working for a small firm new to its field. If it succeeds, you could rise fast. But many small businesses fail or are swallowed up by larger firms. The outlook is generally best in established companies that keep up to date.

7. *Are pay increases and fringe benefits as good as or better than average? (Yes _____ No _____)*

8. *Is the firm's general practice to promote from within on the basis of merit? (Yes _____ No _____)* Seniority should carry you part of the way, but ideally, ability is the clincher in determining who is chosen.

9. *Is your employer respected by you, the community, and other firms in the industry? (Yes _____ No _____)* It's natural to want to be proud of what you do and your employer's products or services. If the product is shoddy, you may mumble when people ask where you work. You'll be happier if you can find an employer whose goals and ideals—possibly even political and social outlook—coincide with your own.

10. *Is the division you're in an essential company operation? (Yes _____ No _____)* When a firm must retrench in bad times, unnecessary functions are the first to get the ax.

The Industry You Work In

11. *Does your industry's chief product or service meet an enduring need? (Yes _____ No _____)* There's money in fads, but not over the long haul. Best job protection is offered by producers of standard items.

12. *Is your industry or occupational group expected to expand in size in the years just ahead? (Yes _____ No _____)*

13. *Has your industry already adjusted to technological change so that few additional job shifts are likely to be caused by it? (Yes _____ No _____)* Hundreds of

clerks have been replaced by computers and other electronic devices. It is difficult to foretell which jobs technology will create or destroy. Be on the lookout for signs of change.

14. *Is your industry large enough to absorb you elsewhere in the event your company fails or you get the itch to switch?* (Yes _____ No _____)

15. *Are there related industries that could also use your services with little or no re-training?* (Yes _____ No _____)

Scoring. Count three points for each "no" answer in the "your job" section, two points for each "no" in the "your company" section, and one for each "no" in the "your industry" section. Add the total.

A total score of around ten points indicates that you should be on the lookout for a more suitable position, most likely outside your present company.

Fifteen or more points means that you should be on the pavement actively searching. With so many things going against you, another job at the same pay is likely to be better than the one you have. But don't quit until you have a solid offer and until you've subjected the new job to the same kind of scrutiny.

If your score is under ten, congratulations. No job is perfect, of course. If you're relatively happy most of the time where you are, stay put. If not, happy hunting.[2]

Watch Yourself When (If) You Leave

Unfortunately, sometimes a primary reason for wanting to leave a position is the desire to tell off someone in authority about all the negative aspects of the position, the firm, and the people working there. But in the long run, this can only hurt you, since at some time in the future, you may need references attesting to your performance on the job and your ability to get along with people. If inability to get along with people is a major reason for leaving a position ("It was *only* a matter of personality conflict"), be careful. The next employment interviewer may seriously question your claim that the responsibility rested entirely with others—even if it did. People shy away from hiring someone who might bring such potential personality problems.

The wise employee who decides for any reason to seek employment elsewhere controls personal feelings, calmly assesses the situation, finds other employment (listing the current employer as a reference), turns in a pleasant resignation, and is off to a new assignment.

Welcoming the New Employee

Do you remember your first day on a new job? Or perhaps you have not yet had this experience. Everything is strange. Not just your job, but the building you work in, the area where you work, and the people around you. Obviously, any friendly gesture is welcome.

One phase of employee communication that should be practiced by all is that of **welcoming the new employee.** The success of newcomers will help your company and, in the long run, should help you.

[2]"Are You and Your Job Cut Out for Each Other?" *Changing Times*, August 1972, pp. 41ff.

Let's say that you are now an established employee. A new woman is starting her first day of work at a desk in the same office as yours. There are many ways in which you can give that new employee the boost that may assist her in becoming an effective working member of the team.

"Hello"

Greet the newcomer and introduce yourself, or repeat your name if you met previously. Welcome her aboard, and get her acquainted with a few people who work nearby. Repeat the newcomer's name to them and identify them in some manner, such as saying what type of work they do or making some pleasant personal comment that will help her remember them. This will prevent the new employee from feeling engulfed in a sea of strangers.

The Grand Tour

Don't just explain where things are, but take time to point out to the newcomer the location of such things as the cafeteria, the stockroom, the restroom area, and the employee parking lot. Show her the location of manuals or other instructions that will aid in her daily work.

Lunch Hour, Coffee Break

During her first days on the job, frequently invite the new employee to join you and your friends at lunch or for other break periods. Then draw her into the conversation occasionally, so that she does not feel like an outsider. Don't worry that you will always have to include her with your group whether you want to or not. As she gradually moves among other people, she will find a group of her own.

Friendly Help

For the first few days on a job, an employee is hesitant to ask help of anyone, especially of an immediate superior. Without intruding, try to offer any suggestions that you believe will be of assistance. Also, encourage the new employee to refer to higher officials at the proper time. At the end of the day, take time to seek her out for a friendly "good night."

Loneliness is said to be the world's most prevalent disease. The new employee needs your help, patience, and friendship.

Writing Assignments

Writing assignments for Chapters 13 and 14 are at the end of Chapter 14.

> **To the instructor:** After weeks searching for a job that suited his background, a San Diego man finally accepted a position cleaning apartments for a maintenance company. One evening he answered the door of a vacant unit and found a woman standing there in coveralls wearing a utility belt filled with tools. "Hi," she said, "I'm the telephone man here to disconnect the phone." "Come on in," he replied, "I'm the cleaning lady."

Chapter 13   Employment Guides: Finding a Job, Holding a Job, Earning Promotions, Changing Jobs

WRITING IMPROVEMENT EXERCISE
PASSIVE SENTENCES → ACTIVE SENTENCES

Active Sentences Are Usually Preferred

Why are some writers good and some just so-so? If we analyze their writing, we can pinpoint some patterns of the better writers.

Most good writers help make their writing clearer by using the **active** sentence form more than the **passive** sentence form in sentences that show movement in action or thought. In the **active** sentence, the **subject performs the action.** In the **passive** sentence, the **subject receives the action.** Somehow, our minds follow the active sentence more quickly: Subject–Verb–Direct Object.

Active: Subject performs action.

Mr. James <u>dictated</u> the letter.

Passive: Subject receives action.

The letter <u>was dictated</u> by Mr. James.

Passive sentences lend variety to our writing and can be used in good writing. However, if a piece of your writing somehow does not seem to be as clear as it should be, you will probably find that direct statements are not being used enough—that the passive sentence form is used too frequently. Then, if you follow the type of editing that has been done with the following sentences, your writing will be more alive and clear.

Subject   Verb

Passive   Many <u>orders</u> <u>have been taken</u> by Mr. Thompson.

Subject   Verb

Active   <u>Mr. Thompson</u> <u>took</u> many orders.

S   V   V

Passive   The computer <u>memory</u> was <u>destroyed</u> by a faulty surge protector.

S   V

Active   A faulty surge <u>protector</u> <u>destroyed</u> the computer memory.

Chapter 13 Employment Guides: Finding a Job, Holding a Job, Earning Promotions, Changing Jobs

WRITING IMPROVEMENT EXERCISE: PASSIVE SENTENCES → ACTIVE SENTENCES

Writing Improvement Worksheet

Change the following sentences from the passive to the active form. Answers may vary in some details. In some sentences, you may have to supply your own subject.

1. The sentences were revised by the students. → _Students revised the sentences._

   _____

2. The cabin was built by Mr. Swallow. → _Mr. Swallow built the cabin._

   _____

3. The records were brought to the office by Mr. Stone. → _Mr. Stone brought the_
   records to the office.

4. Last month's meeting was attended by only fourteen members. → _Only fourteen_
   members attended last month's meeting.

   _____

5. Copies of the report were sent to all board members from the chairman of the board.

   → _The chairman of the board sent copies of the report to all board members._

   _____

6. Between 10:00 last night and 6:00 this morning, our store was burglarized. → _____
   Between 10:00 last night and 6:00 this morning, someone burglarized our store.

7. This letter was received by our office today. → _Our office received this letter today._

   _____

8. The invoice was placed on my desk by the mail clerk. → _The mail clerk placed_
   the invoice on my desk.

9. A request for his or her desired vacation period should be turned in by each
   employee. → _Each employee should turn in a request for his or her desired_
   vacation period.

10. The word processing staff often received praise from the office manager → _____
    The office manager often praised the word processing staff.

Chapter 13 Employment Guides: Finding a Job, Holding a Job, Earning Promotions, Changing Jobs

REVIEW AND DISCUSSION

Make answers brief. Where there is a choice, draw a line through any incorrect answer.

1. What ability did John D. Rockefeller say was most important to him in employees? The ability to deal with people. _____

   _____

2. On today's employment market you (a. ~~should choose your preferred career and stay with it~~; b. be open to the possibility of a career change).

   _____

3. What four matters should a person study when choosing a career?

   a. Working conditions. _____

   b. Work location. _____

   c. Long hours. _____

   d. Supervision of/from others. _____

4. On the average, the college-trained person still earns _2 to 3_ times as much as the noncollege-trained.

5. Name two advantages of part-time work.

   a. (Accept any two of these responses.) $$$. Job reference. Satisfaction from

   b. helping others. Testing for yourself a type of employment. Others?

6. How can a record of volunteer work aid a person seeking employment? _____ Shows ability to work, get along with others, accept responsibility.

7. What are the advantages of following the "family business" or any other business with which you have a long-time familiarity? You probably have picked up a familiarity with a career that might take others years to learn.

8. What course should you follow if you feel you are not the type of person that someone would employ? Improve yourself. Go into business for yourself.

9. Why is it important that you try to follow a career that is right for you? Influences you in many ways: style of living, money, self-respect, position in community, even your dreams at night.

10. Name at least five fields that should have good job opportunities in the new millennium.

    a. (Accept any five of these responses.) Communications, technology, teaching,

    b. health fields, paralegal, engineering, accounting.

c. _____

d. _____

e. _____

11. Should entry-level income be the major consideration in selecting a position? Explain.
    May never increase. You may be promised the moon, but the moon never rises. Work
    may not be satisfying, or even may not be honest.

12. Name ten sources of job information.

    a. [See pages 293–295.]

    b. _____

    c. _____

    d. _____

    e. _____

    f. _____

    g. _____

    h. _____

    i. _____

    j. _____

13. Is it advisable to use the influence of friends or relatives, if available, in seeking
    employment? By all means. Successful networking is common.

14. Robert O. Snelling, employment counselor, says young people make a common mistake in applying for jobs. What is that mistake? Not being persistent. They should
    keep on trying for the job they want.

15. What three questions can you ask to determine your capability for holding a job?

    a. Do I have qualifications?

    b. Do I want this job?

    c. Can I get along with my boss and fellow employees?

16. Why is a person's appearance on the job important? Communicates about you
    nonverbally. Different positions require different dress.

17. Is it possible for a job to have some undesirable features and still rate as being satisfactory employment? You bet.

18. Why should you "Watch yourself when you leave"? Your parting interview may
    be the most lasting impression your employer has for future reference.

19. Why is a record of "personality conflict" a difficult trait to be reported on an employment record? It may raise the suspicion that you can't get along with others.

20. Why should you try to make a new employee feel welcome? New employee
    probably needs help, patience and friendship. Helping that person be productive
    benefits the firm and you.

14 Employment Resumés and Application Letters

Miscellaneous Employment Communications

> The harder you work, the luckier you get.
> Gary Player,
> Professional golfer

The Employment Resumé

Almost everyone who works for someone else will at some time have to prepare an employment **resumé** (REZ-oom-ay). You may be asked to furnish one at the time of an employment interview. Or, if you are applying for a position by mail, you may follow the standard procedure of enclosing a resumé with your letter of application. A resumé is sometimes called by another name, such as *vita*, or *bio* (biography).

This form is a summary presentation of your background and employment qualifications. It should be prepared before the letter of application is written. Properly prepared, it sets out in a logical, organized manner major facts concerning an applicant that should be of interest to a potential employer. Therefore, it furnishes a good pattern for choosing the parts of this information that should be highlighted by being included in the letter of application.

Because your employment resumé can determine whether or not you will get a job, a professional writing consultant might charge you a high fee for preparing one. However, studying a few examples and seeing how they are written should make you able to write a professional resumé for yourself.

Any communication so important in applying for a job should not be written hurriedly. Take care to compose one or more rough drafts of each section, and select the best of each for inclusion in the final draft.

As you study how to make up a resumé, look at the examples shown in Figures 14.1 and 14.2.

Resumés for Entry Level or Early Level Positions—and Later

Resumés are generally prepared either for entry level and early level employment or for advanced level positions after a person can show evidence of work experience.

In this text we will give most of our attention to setting out basics for the first group, entry and early level positions. Then, when preparing your later employment applications, you can build on the background of the basics here, adjusting and emphasizing sections that are to your individual advantage.

FIGURE 14.1
Employment application resumé or data sheet.

MARIA HELEN GOMEZ

POSITION SOUGHT: ADMINISTRATIVE ASSISTANT AT ACME FOODS

45 Olympia Avenue
West Grove, Penn. 19390
(215) 555-1239

Education	20XX–20XX: Cerritos College, Norwalk, California. AA degree; Office Administration major.
	Courses taken that would be useful in an Office Administration Position:

Advanced Office Procedures	Machine Calculation
Advanced Word Processing	Office Services
Business English (grammar)	Basic Accounting
Business Communication (writing)	Human Relations in
Machine Transcription	Business

	20XX–20XX: Downey High School, Downey, California. Pre-college major.
Experience	20XX–present: Student assistant in office of Business Division, Cerritos College. General office duties: take shorthand; answer telephone; act as receptionist; file.
	20XX–20XX: Volunteer worker in office of Principal, Warren High School, Downey, California.
Special Qualifications	Bilingual: Competency in writing and speaking both English and Spanish.

Personal	Health excellent	Hobbies: Tennis; styling own clothes.
	Age 20	Memberships: Alpha Gamma Sigma;
	Height 5′ 7″	college honor society; Phi Beta Lambda,
	Single	college business fraternity; Future Business Leaders of America, high school business club.

References	Mrs. Margaret W. Baird, instructor, Business Division, Cerritos College, 11110 East Alondra Blvd., Norwalk, California 90650. Telephone: (213) 860-2451
	Mrs. Merle Davidson, Office Manager, Warren High School, 8131 East DePalma Street, Downey, California 90241. Telephone: (213) 923-6711.

FIGURE 14.2
Employment application resumé or data sheet.

RESUMÉ: ROBERT D. ARMSTEAD   1522 South Jellison Avenue
                                   Rowland Heights, California 91748
                                   (213) 964-0000

CAREER ACCOMPLISHMENTS

In each of my three years as department manager of J.C. Penney, Culver City, California, my departments had significant sales gains while total store showed losses. Prior to my arrival, my department had also shown losses.

EDUCATION

20XX–present   CALIFORNIA STATE POLYTECHNIC UNIVERSITY, POMONA, Pomona, California. Will receive B.S. degree in Business Administration in June 20XX. Current grade point average 3.9 on 4-point scale.

2/20XX–6/20XX   RIO HONDO COLLEGE, Whittier, California. GPA 3.9. Completed lower division requirements.

EXPERIENCE: J.C. PENNEY COMPANY

Left retail management position in January 19XX, to complete my B.S. degree.

2/XX–present   <u>Selling Specialist</u>, Sporting Goods Department, Puenta Hills Mall, City of Industry, California.

6/XX–2/XX   <u>Management Trainee</u>: Earned early promotion to Department Manager, Stonewood Shopping Center, Downey, California. <u>Duties</u>: Responsible for purchasing, merchandise assortment planning, hiring, training, and managing up to 25 employees.

HONORS AND ACTIVITIES

Dean's Honor List since beginning Cal Poly. Member of Information Technology Association, university club.

Enjoy family activities, snow skiing, singing and playing acoustic guitar. Won two prizes for original oil paintings. Elected president of Key Club, high school honor club.

PERSONAL

Health: excellent   Hobbies: Jogging; spectator sports;
Age 28   photography.
Height 6′   Job preference: Like it here; willing
Weight 180   to relocate

REFERENCES

References will be furnished on request.

Resumés on Computer Software

Computer software packages for preparing resumés can be purchased from college bookstores, other bookstores, and computer stores.

Any resumé package will have a choice of programs with blanks for you to fill in, and you will have to decide whether or not you want to use one. Quality varies, but before purchasing a computer package, put yourself in a position to make a good choice by studying the resumés in the following pages. After reviewing these basics, you are in a better position to select a good quality resumé package or to decide whether you prefer to make your own completely personalized application.

Problem Areas in Resumés

In a survey of 500 largest corporations listed in the *Fortune* magazine directory, top Human Resources officers of those corporations listed these problem areas as showing up too often in resumés:

Applicant does not clearly show specific job objectives.

Appearance of resumé is unsatisfactory compared to others.

Applicants oversell themselves and are vague instead of specific about how their qualifications fit job requirements.

Their abilities in spelling, grammar, and writing are poor.

Appearance of Resumé

The **appearance** of your resumé may be crucial. It is foolish to make up one that is less than perfect looking. You should be aware that an employer may be so deluged with resumés that any excuse, reasonable or unreasonable, may narrow the number of prospective job candidates. A resumé that is too long, is on cheap paper, or has even a single typo will often be rejected without being read. Right or wrong, employers look at your resumé to judge how you present yourself. Too often, they are harsher here than they are in person.

Be brief. One interviewer says, "We get hundreds of job applications from college students. If the resumé is longer than one page, I don't take time to read it." The vice president of another company says, "If a resumé is too long, I probably won't read it. Even the best job applicant can get the message across in two pages."

Later after you have had experience, you should certainly make your resumé longer than one page if you have significant details to present. Try to picture what competing applicants are listing and show your possible superiority. Be honest but don't be modest. Tell of career accomplishments, evidence of leadership, how many subordinates you had, and especially your contributions to company success. If something is worth saying, say it. Do not make the potential interviewer try to read between the lines for any additional information. Other applicants may be clearer and more specific.

In any resumé, eliminate minor details and mention only matters that will be of help in getting a position.

Nevertheless, in being brief, do not list a last name of a reference without giving the first name or initials. Also, do not use confusing abbreviations or titles for business, campus, or other organizations.

Not This	*This*
Dr. Reeves, veterinarian	Dr. D. J. Reeves, veterinarian
Ms. Frances	Ms. Lorraine Frances
B of A	Bank of America
Alpha Gamma Sigma	Alpha Gamma Sigma, community college honor society
VA	Veterans Administration
GPA	grade point average

Paper and Printing

For attractive appearance, use a laser printer. (If you do not have access to one of these, you will find it worthwhile to pay the small charge of a secretarial service for making a final draft.)

Be sure that you use first quality paper, preferably rag content bond, for your resumé. Do not use duplicator or mimeograph-quality paper, even if it is of a special color of your choice. Use white paper. Or, to make your application stand out from others, you might select first-quality paper of a soft shade of gray, cream or beige. Sharp, deeper colors might turn the reader off, unless you are applying for a creative position such as in advertising.

If you have several copies of your resumé printed, be sure that copies are similarly on letter-quality bond paper. Good copies can be made for a minimal cost. Purchase extra paper and matching envelopes for cover application letter and mailing.

Value of White Space

Make good use of **white space.** That is, leave top, bottom and side margins at least 1¼ inches wide ("white"). Also, leave blank lines between sections. This spacing shows off individual parts, and among papers with more crowded printing, it also makes your paper more inviting because it is easier on the reader's eyes and therefore easier to read.

Good Will Tone

Write at a conversational level and make the resumé "you-oriented." That is, set material out according to the reader's interests—what will help make someone hire you because you fit that person's needs.

Don't be modest. You are selling yourself. State your case clearly and forcefully. On the other hand, don't brag. One person in charge of company personnel said, "Don't make it sound as if you can jump over mountains or, if you can't jump over them, you can move them."

Clear, Complete and Concise Message

There is no single good format for setting up your resumé. You might center your headings or place them at the margin. Material might be set out in sentence format or in columns. Look at business communications book illustrations, or make up a distinctive, attractive plan of your own. Remember to leave white space in margins and between paragraphs, making the resumé appealing and easy to read.

Format

Be consistent in sentence or phrase format in all sections of the resumé. In the explanation of duties performed, the following lists of verbs might be handy. Use them as verbal phrases, avoiding the overuse of "I" with complete sentences: *"Compiled information for department report. Planned daily work routine for five employees. Maintained... ."*

The following verbs describe skills that are transferable from one job or career field to another. Use them in your resumé to describe your experience.

achieved	designed	interviewed	provided
adapted	determined	invented	purchased
administered	developed	investigated	recommended
advised	directed	led	recorded
analyzed	distributed	maintained	reported
assembled	documented	managed	researched
assorted	edited	monitored	reviewed
classified	established	motivated	revised
communicated	estimated	negotiated	scheduled
compared	examined	obtained	selected
compiled	gathered	operated	served
conducted	guided	ordered	sorted
constructed	handled	organized	stocked
consulted	hired	performed	supervised
contracted	implemented	planned	trained
coordinated	improved	prepared	translated
counseled	increased	produced	utilized
created	inspected	programmed	wrote
delegated	installed	promoted	

The message or content of the resumé can be set up in sections: *heading, special qualifications* (if any), *education, experience, career accomplishments* (if any), *personal details,* and *references.*

To make up your resumé, refer to information in your employment profile as set out for the first section of Chapter 13, "Employment Guides."

Heading

For the heading, set out your name, postal and email addresses, and telephone number including area code clearly at the top so it identifies you and shows you are available for contact.

Authorities disagree about the advantages of setting out your employment objective. Most say it is advantageous because it shows you have a goal. Others say that stating a specific objective may exclude you from other fields that may lead to a better future. If you have a specific position in mind, name it.

One applicant who was successful in obtaining a highly contested position in city management did not list an employment objective on his resumé. When asked this question in the interview, he replied, "Well, if you and I are happy with my work here, I may stay until I am an old man. Then again, I may eventually leave for a position in another field. Or, I may just use this position as a stepping stone to another position in city management."

He was later told that only a few applicants were called in for a second interview. A member of the interviewing committee said one reason he got the job was that the committee felt he was the only one of the group who gave an honest answer to this question.

After the heading, the sections under *special qualifications* or *career accomplishments, education,* and *experience,* should be set up in order of their importance, with details of the section that will best impress a potential employer being listed first.

Special Qualifications or Career Accomplishments

One of these two headings should be set out next, if you have background material that suits such a classification. Figure 14.2 shows the section *Career Accomplishments* first, because it was judged worthy of this emphasis.

Following are examples of qualifications that can be considered of high value on the employment market and could be listed under one of the headings above:

- ☐ Outstanding employment in a specific field
- ☐ Competent bilingual or multilingual ability
- ☐ Writing ability and experience (with examples)
- ☐ Artistic ability (with portfolio)
- ☐ Research in a specific field
- ☐ Work with someone outstanding in a field

Competence in a foreign language could be a valuable special qualification. The job markets of today and the future show a need for people with foreign language skills. With recent waves of immigration from Asia, Latin America, Eastern Europe, and the Middle East, business persons increasingly find themselves in a "global village," managing El Salvadoran employees working for a Vietnamese boss or working side by side with Asian co-workers.

One expert on international travel emphasizes that the tourist industry, especially on the Internet, is thriving, with great promise for new employees in the future, but few Americans bother to learn foreign languages, making great employment opportunities for people who speak English well and another language or other languages.

U.S. businesses and industries continue to expand into many foreign markets, and the number of foreign-owned companies is growing in the United States. Learning a foreign language or polishing up on one could be extremely worthwhile. If a language other than English is spoken in your home, study that language in a classroom.

Education and Training

For most college students with no special qualifications or applicable work experience, education would be listed first.

Set out information concerning your education in reverse chronological order, with your current or most recent education first. This is of most interest to an employer. If some time has elapsed since high school and there is a record of college work, leave out high school information. With little or no college work, having a high school diploma shows you persevered through this work. Identify fully any college degree and/or special training certificates you have received and the town and state of educational institutions you attended.

List specific courses you have completed that would directly help in performing duties of the position you are seeking, along with other major courses that would be of general help in your employment goal. Completion of courses in business writing, public speaking, and computer technology should be listed. All these courses could be applicable to present employment, and they should all speak well for your possibility for future advancement.

Do not list courses by number, such as "Marketing 101." Instead, list each course by its full title, such as "Survey of Marketing," because course numbers probably mean nothing to others. If you have attained a certain level of competency in office skills or in operating common business software programs, list your ability according to tests you have passed or certificates you have received.

No diplomas or degrees? List special courses you may have taken. Completion of any training shows perseverance. List special talents you have shown such as selling the most tickets to a fund raiser, assembling or repairing a motorcycle or other complicated machinery.

Experience

Work experience is of high value in employment applications. As with data referring to education, list the most recent or current employment first, then go in reverse chronological order, ending with the earliest. If part-time work is not related to the position sought, do not list it if there is a sufficient record of full-time work. All full-time employment should be reported, as well as terms of military service. Be ready to explain blank periods.

Military experience could lead off your resumé if your work experience is limited. Emphasize courses completed, skills learned, promotions earned and leadership shown.

Report *volunteer work* if paid work experience is nonexistent or limited. Include the following with each employment position, giving information briefly and eliminating unnecessary details:

- [ ] Job title
- [ ] Date of employment
- [ ] Firm name (no abbreviations) with city or town
- [ ] Duties performed

As a matter of fact, volunteer workers are sometimes absorbed into the full-time work force. Or, this could be your first step into a network where someone on the staff could recommend you to another employer looking for a person with your capabilities. Recommendation from someone who already knows you personally is a good asset.

Personal Details

Unless there is a bona fide need for a given position, employment interviewers are forbidden by law to ask for the following personal information before, during, or after employment: height, weight, race, creed, color, national origin, sex, marital status, children and who takes care of them, or physical challenge.

On the other hand, employers like to see you as a whole person. Thinking of your future success on the job, *potential employers are interested in answers to many of the preceding questions, even if they cannot ask for them.*

Therefore, in the "Personal" section, it is legal for you to voluntarily furnish standard information plus answers to any of the preceding questions *or other questions that you believe might be helpful in getting you the job* or, at least, will not be harmful.

A given organization may have need for a person with diverse talents, so consider listing hobbies and other pastime interests. Include such items as artistic capabilities, campus or community organizations in which you are or have been active and the type of work done, publications worked on and type of work you did (writing, editing, selling ads, etc.) Some of your best assets could be revealed here.

One young woman, recently graduated with a degree in health science, wanted to work in pharmaceutical sales. For lack of experience, she was quickly turned down by two companies. At the third interview she emphasized her extracurricular activities and was chosen from 600 applicants because she was so active on campus.

To repeat: Employers want to know the whole person. Listing extracurricular activities could reward you with a job.

When given, personal details should be listed briefly and modestly. (None of the "People tell me I am good looking" sort of thing on a business application.) You might give hobbies, sports, and organizations in which you are active. Such information should be clear, and sports should be listed as *active* or *spectator* if both types are shown. This would preclude the puzzling notation made by one college freshman: "Favorite sports: tennis, baseball, bullfighting."

When listing organizations to which you belong, identify clearly the name and type of each organization. Not everyone who reads the resumé will be able to determine what an organization is if it is identified only by name, initials, or Greek letters.

References

Many employment resumés do not give names of references. Instead, a statement like this is made: "References will be furnished if requested."

If you do give references, try to give three and list them last. There they serve as natural lead-ins for the employer to telephone or write the people listed.

Give the name of a supervisor or administrator who can vouch for your job proficiency in preference to the name of a fellow worker or a higher official who might not remember you personally. If you have no previous employment or other suggested references, you might list names of instructors, religious leaders, youth activities leaders, business people with whom you or your family have traded, friends, or neighbors. Do not give names of relatives as references except in rare cases.

If you do not want your current employer advised that you are seeking employment elsewhere, make a statement like, "Please do not contact my present employer," and be ready to explain your request to an interviewer.

For each reference, give the appropriate title, such as Dr., Mr., Ms., Miss, or Mrs., together with the first name or initials; address complete with ZIP code; telephone number, including area code; and your association with that person. Omission of any of the details of a reference might make the person reading it feel that it would be easier to inquire about another potential hiree.

You should request a person's permission before using his or her name as a reference. Most people will willingly do you this favor. An example of a request for letter of reference is given later in this chapter. Also shown is the type of information you might ask to have included in such a letter.

The Employment Application Letter

Address your letter of employment application to a person by name. Several Human Resources officials who were asked about this matter agreed that a letter that is not addressed to the specific official by name is often disregarded. One said, "If you really want a job, take the time to look up the name of the proper official who would receive the letter." This information can be obtained from the company by telephone or letter. For a large organization, you will find personnel officers listed in business directories in the library. Visit the library or phone the reference librarian.

After setting out the information for a good employment resumé, you have the information before you for writing a good letter of employment application. This letter is truly a selling letter. As stated before, the product you are selling is yourself.

Appearance of Application Letter

All the basic qualities of a good letter apply here. Appearance is important, because from this letter a judgment will be made of you personally.

Good Will Tone

Naturally, the letter must be written in a good will tone. You should show an interest in the firm and have some knowledge about it. In addition, you might show a special interest in the type of position you are seeking.

The tone of the letter should be as natural as possible, as if you were talking directly to the person who is to read it. However, avoid being too casual or informal. Avoid using contractions.

Clear, Complete and Concise Message

The clear, complete and concise message that must be given is that you are applying for a position for which you feel qualified, and you would like to be granted an interview to discuss this matter. As part of the message, you should present an abbreviated version of some major points in your resumé that would aid you in getting the job.

The employment application letter that encloses a resumé should be short, almost always just one page. Fuller details are set out in the resumé enclosure, and you should always mention it. As much as possible, this letter should have the *you attitude* instead of the *me attitude*. This way, you *stress how your qualifications can benefit the employer instead of how you would expect to benefit from the employment.*

This letter is about you, and use of the words *I, me, my,* and *mine* is necessary. However, avoid overusing these words, and in particular, limit the number of sentences that begin with *I.*

Figures 14.3 and 14.4 are examples of good employment application letters.

The standard formula for writing a selling letter can be followed: attention-getter, buildup of interest and desire, and action closing.

Attention-Getter

State clearly that you are applying for a position. If possible, name some factor that especially qualifies you for the position or that makes you want to work for the firm to which you are applying. Show some specific interest in or knowledge of the firm.

FIGURE 14.3
An example of an employment application letter.

1314 Gladys Avenue
Long Beach, California 90803
May 15, 20XX
(000) 000-0000

Dr. Armand C. Teague
Professor of Marketing
California State University
   at Long Beach
6101 East Seventh Street
Long Beach, California 90801

Dear Dr. Teague:

As a current business student at CSULB I saw in your bulletin posted at the placement bureau that you are looking for a student to work part time as an assistant in charge of marketing research. I believe that my educational background and my experience working with people could be put to good advantage for you in your research work.

On June 15 I received an AA degree with a marketing specialty from Rio Hondo College, Whittier. As my resumé shows, I have been holding two part-time jobs: one as assistant to a professor of marketing at Rio Hondo College, one as night supervisor at a local pet clinic. My work at the clinic is mostly summers and holidays. While I enjoy my work at both of these jobs, I would prefer to do more in marketing, as I hope for a career in that field.

I feel that I work well with people, and in my position at the college, supervise the work of a crew of three students.

The resumé you requested is enclosed. You may reach me or leave a message at my home telephone: (562) 000-0000. May I see you soon?

Sincerely,

Enc.

FIGURE 14.4
Employment application letter.

Roger E. Morrison
3103 Lexington Avenue
Baltimore, Maryland 87577
(000) 000-0000

Mr. James T. Jones
Director of Human Resources
Jones Manufacturing Company
200 North Park Avenue
Baltimore, Maryland 87577

Dear Mr. Jones:

Your advertisement for a Payroll Manager in the *Baltimore Sun* on Sunday, January 25, 20XX interests me considerably. I feel my background is well suited to the position you describe.

My experience has been very diversified in the following areas:

Payroll systems and payroll taxation
Accounting and taxation problem solving
Supervision of 10 staff people

I have a Bachelor of Science degree in Business Administration with heavy accent on financial courses. My experience has been in payroll for more than five years with computerized systems. I would he happy to negotiate salary with you.

A resumé is enclosed which summarizes my background and experience. May I have the opportunity to further discuss my qualifications in a personal interview?

Sincerely,

Roger E. Morrison

Enclosure

Interest and Desire Buildup

To build up in the reader an interest in you and a desire to employ you, choose from your resumé the most pertinent facts that qualify you to hold the position sought. Make your request plain, and make it with the "you attitude," as already noted. That is, make it from the viewpoint of the potential advantages to the firm, not to you. If you refer to yourself, be sure not to brag. For example, instead of saying, "I believe I have a pleasant personality," say something like, "I enjoy working with people and feel that I get along well with others."

Action Closing

The purpose of the combination letter of application and job resumé is to get an appointment for an employment interview. The closing section of the letter should make this request clear. Also, give information that makes it easy for the potential employer to contact you, either by giving your telephone number and address here or by mentioning that this information is on your enclosed resumé.

Will Travel for Interview

If the position is some distance out of town, you might end with something like, "I plan to be in (name another town) near you sometime in the next two weeks, and I really would like to drop in to talk about this position. Could you tell me a time that would be convenient to you?"

Employment interviewers are reluctant to ask an applicant to travel very far for an interview, even an applicant who sounds very good, because they don't want to feel obligated. They might believe you are pushing the truth with your statement, but they will get a good impression of your attitude because you are willing and eager to make the trip.

Signature

The letter must be signed in either blue or black ink. If a woman wishes, she can type a title (Ms., Miss, Mrs.) before her name, below her signature. A man would not have a title typed before his name unless he has a first name that might be used for a man or woman, such as *Shawn, Leslie, Terry, Lynn, Pat, Lee, or Cory.*

A person with a professional degree could give this information by having his or her name typed below the signature space with the standard abbreviation for the degree shown (Ph.D., M.D., CPA, J.D., etc.). Here is an example:

Christopher T. Rynersen
Christopher T. Rynersen, J.D.

Editing the Resumé and Application Letter

It is an excellent idea to make a rough draft of your planned resumé and application letter. For editing, show them to a teacher, counselor, businessperson (perhaps one of your references) or another whose opinion you value. An experienced person can often help you avoid mistakes by seeing them from another point of view. After they are thoroughly studied by yourself and others, you are ready to make the final copies.

The Employment Interview

At an advisory committee meeting of business executives and college business faculty members, the business people were asked, "How can we help our graduates compete on the job market?" Replying for the group, one man advised:

Teach them how to present themselves properly at a **job interview**.

So much has to be decided in the brief time of employment interviews that it may not seem fair. But the individual's appearance and also that person's ability to participate in an interview both at the time of employment and later during personnel progress reports on the job can be more important than educational background. We will hire a two-year college graduate in preference to the four-year individual if the two-year person has a good appearance, speaks up and *looks you in the eye*, and in general makes a positive impression. The person who dresses carelessly, mumbles answers, slouches in a chair, and evades looking you in the eye will be passed by regardless of otherwise good qualifications.

In regard to people being interviewed for a job, a national survey of employment interviewers listed the following qualities in order of their relative importance: (1) appearance, (2) manner of dress, (3) personality, (4) speech and voice, (5) manners, and (6) skills.

Planning Ahead

Before the interview, you can take steps to aid in presenting yourself favorably and give you self-confidence during the interview.

Study the Company

A man who had been interviewing college students for a major national corporation said that if any applicant had shown some knowledge of his firm, he would have hired that person on the spot. He objected to the fact that everyone interviewed seemed interested only in personal job goals and was not applying because of any interest in the organization.

Your college placement bureau will have information on companies interviewing students. Libraries carry books and periodicals with information about specific companies. Again, ask your librarian. The World Wide Web has excellent informa-

How NOT to get the job.

tion on most companies. The company itself may, on request, furnish employment brochures and annual reports that are very informative.

Prepare Yourself

It would seem unnecessary to mention the importance of a person's appearance at a job interview. But another personnel officer who interviews graduating applicants said, "You wouldn't believe the appearance of some of our job applicants—even graduates of universities and junior colleges."

You should dress for the job you want, not for the job you have. A day or two in advance, check to see that your clothes are clean and neatly pressed, and that your shoes are shined and new looking. If necessary, it may be advisable to go into debt to get one suitable outfit for making that good first impression. The choice of clothing for this purpose should be conservative. A suit for men is not always necessary; attractive go-togethers of jacket, slacks, shirt, and tie will usually do nicely. The style and cut of hair for both men and women should also be conservative. If a man does not choose to be clean shaven, his beard and/or mustache should be neat and trimmed. Women should consider a little shaping of their hair, and should use only a minimum of makeup.

If possible, bring a portfolio of your work and any written job references you may have. Also, you might bring a copy of a resumé in case it is requested, or a copy of other materials you may wish to leave with the interviewer. On a card or a small piece of paper you might bring a short list of questions you may wish to ask, or you should have in mind some appropriate questions. You will be given an opportunity to ask them. Do have a pen or a pencil with you, as you may be asked to fill out an application blank or an interview form. Asking to borrow this equipment gives a negative impression.

Time the Interview

Selecting the day and time of an interview can be important. Also, there are additional matters that should be planned in advance.

Try to Choose Your Day. Because the job interview is important to you, try to make it on a Tuesday, Wednesday, or Thursday. Try to avoid Mondays—we all know about "blue Mondays," when both you and your interviewer might not be at your best. Also try to avoid Fridays, when the interviewer's mind may be full of plans for the weekend, and "If this applicant weren't here today, I could have left already." However, if you must make your appointment on a Monday or Friday, you could be very successful. Much satisfactory business is done on these days.

Be on Time. The interviewer's time is valuable, and in evaluating an applicant, tardiness for an appointment may be overemphasized. Give yourself ample time for the vagaries of traffic and parking. (Asking where you can park is a valid question.) Arrive in time to catch your breath, check on your appearance, and relax a few minutes. In the waiting room, there may be reading materials available that can give you current information on the organization that you can discuss with the interviewer. Be sure to phone the day before to confirm your appointment.

Being Interviewed

At a Business Communication conference in Las Vegas, the introductory keynote speaker, the manager of a large hotel casino there, related the following:

All our employees do not work on the gaming floors. Ours is a large business and we employ many people behind the scenes in management, sales, advertising, offices, to name a few. We find that in employment interviews we often get a choice of people. This is where you want to shine.

All applicants for a given position will usually come with somewhat similar education and training as well as somewhat similar work experience. Now, we have come to realize that our final choice is frequently made solely on *personality*. We have our own appropriate training courses for various positions. But in hiring we are looking for people who have the proper attitude toward our patrons and get along well with other employees.

Most personnel officers will agree that this is a common picture in employee hiring.

Let the Interviewer Lead the Interview

Resist the temptation to take over the lead in the interview unless encouraged to do so, and do not ask too many questions relating to job benefits. The interviewer gets an extremely negative picture of an applicant whose questions relate mostly to such matters as vacations, insurance, sick benefits, and stock options. You should show more interest in the company and your possible position in it. Toward the end of the interview, it is usually proper to discuss potential salary, if this matter has not been discussed previously. However, a few extremely conservative companies have a sharply negative attitude toward such a question.

Figure 14.5 is a list of questions frequently asked during employment interviews.

Keep Calm

Some nervousness during an employment interview is expected and accepted. If some embarrassment arises, try to recover gracefully. For example, as one applicant for a position with a Florida airline entered the door of the Human Resources director, he tripped on a rug and fell flat on the floor. His aplomb at recovering from such an experience probably helped him get the job.

Answering Questions Briefly and Honestly, State Your Case as Clearly as Possible

Answer questions briefly and honestly; do not boast; do not be too humble. Show that you are making a straightforward appeal for the position and that you feel qualified to fill it.

A nationwide authority on hiring practices says that the thing to keep uppermost in mind is that typical employers are looking for reasons to hire you. They may be desperate for good workers, and may not want to interview more applicants, so they are begging you to tell about yourself.

Don't Try for Pity

If you feel that a bid for pity is one of the chief appeals you can make, don't make it! If the interviewing official represents a large corporation, the firm is probably suffering through enough people problems already, and they certainly do not want you to add to them. And if you are applying for a position with a smaller firm where contacts may be closer, the person who will make the hiring decisions is

FIGURE 14.5
Questions frequently asked during employment interviews.

Questions Most Asked During Interviews[1]

1. What are your future vocational plans?
2. In what type of position are you most interested?
3. Why do you think you might like to work for our company?
4. What jobs have you held? How were they obtained? Why did you leave?
5. Why did you choose your particular field of work?
6. What percentage of your college expenses did you earn? How?
7. What do you know about our company?
8. What qualifications do you have that make you feel you will be successful in your field?
9. What salary do you expect?
10. What are your avocations?
11. Do you prefer any specific geographic location? Why?
12. How did you rank in your graduation class in high school? Where did you rank in college?
13. What do you think determines an individual's progress in a good company?
14. What personal characteristics are necessary for success in your chosen field?
15. Why do you think you would like this particular job?
16. Are you looking for a permanent or temporary job?
17. Do you prefer working with others or by yourself?
18. What is the most important aspect of the work you do?
19. Can you take instructions without feeling upset?
20. Did you enjoy your last job? Why?
21. What have you learned from some of the jobs you have held?
22. Can you get recommendations from previous employers?
23. What interests you about our product or service?
24. What do you know about opportunities in the field in which you are trained?
25. Do you like routine work?
26. Do you like regular hours?
27. What is your major weakness?
28. Define cooperation.
29. Do you demand attention?
30. Do you have an analytical mind?
31. Are you eager to please?

[1]"Questions Most Asked During Interviews," *You and Your First Job,* Personnel and Industrial Relations Association, Inc., Los Angeles, CA, undated, p. 12.

FIGURE 14.5
(Continued)

32. What do you do to keep in good physical condition?

33. Have you any serious illness or injury?

34. Are you willing to go where the company sends you?

35. Is it an effort for you to be tolerant of persons with a background and interests different from your own?

36. What books have you read recently?

37. What type of people seem to rub you the wrong way?

38. Do you enjoy sports as a participant? As an observer?

39. What jobs have you enjoyed the most? The least? Why?

40. What are your own special abilities?

41. What job in our company do you want to work toward?

42. Would you prefer a large or small company? Why?

43. What is your idea of how industry operates today?

44. Do you like to travel?

45. How about overtime work?

46. What kind of work interests you?

47. Are you interested in research?

48. To what extent do you use liquor?

49. What have you done that shows initiative and willingness to work?

probably even less inclined to want someone who may seriously handicap business operations because of financial or family difficulties.

If You Take a Test ...

If you take a **test** during the interviewing process, follow these guidelines:

1. Bring your own pencil.
2. Listen to instructions and read printed instructions thoroughly.
3. Read each question through.
4. Write legibly.
5. Don't dwell too long on one question.

Figure 14.5 gives 49 questions that are frequently asked during employment interviews.

Do Not Overstay Your Allotted Time

Be alert for signals that the interview is near a conclusion, but try not to leave until you are satisfied that you have furnished an effective presentation of all information and material that could help you get the job. Tedious repetitions will do little to assist your cause, unless the interviewer is clearly interested in hearing them.

Reason for Leaving Previous Employment

You need not volunteer a **reason for leaving a previous position.** However, if you are queried on this matter, make your answer as brief and positive as possible and do not "bad mouth" your previous employer. Your interviewer might think that this may be the way you would describe leaving this new position. Remember, many people have been fired a time or two—your listener may have had this very experience. It is known that this can be a lesson well learned.

Saying "It was only a personality conflict" can be perilous.

On Leaving, Sincerely Thank the Interviewer for His or Her Time

Besides sincerely **thanking the interviewer** for his or her time, it is also proper to thank the receptionist who conducted you to the interview, if it is convenient to do so.

Suggestions for writing a thank you letter are given later under the "Miscellaneous Employment Communications" section.

Why They Don't Hire

In a study of reasons for *not* hiring applicants, 166 employers were contacted. Figure 14.6 lists negative factors, in order of frequency, mentioned as reasons for not hiring. Notice that **negative personality factors** and **lack of communication skills** were the two most common reasons that applicants failed to get the job.

FIGURE 14.6
In a survey of 166 employers, these reasons were given for not hiring applicants. Reasons are shown in order of frequency given.

Why They Weren't Hired

Reasons	Frequency of Mention
Negative personality or poor impression: lack of motivation, ambition, maturity, aggressiveness, or enthusiasm	110
Poor communication skills	62
Lack of competence—inadequate preparation	56
Low grades—poor grades in major field	38
Unidentified goals	32
Unrealistic expectations	28
Lack of interest in type of work	25
Unwillingness to travel or to relocate	23
Poor preparation for the interview	14

Source: Frank S. Endicott, *The Endicott Report: Trends in the Employment of College and University Graduates in Business and Industry* (Evanston, IL: Northwestern University), p. 8.

Miscellaneous Employment Communications

Interview Follow-Ups

Immediately after the job interview, be sure to write a **letter of thanks** to the person who talked to you. This letter should be brief and will serve two purposes: (1) to thank the interviewer, and (2) to remind that person that you still want the job. This letter also helps keep your file active and shows that you are aggressively interested, something the employer would like to know. Further, even if someone else is hired, your letter helps keep you a step ahead of others if another opening occurs. This letter should have an upbeat, positive tone.

If a panel of people conducted the interview and the interview is important to you, be sure to write each one a personalized letter of thanks. Otherwise, if they compare letters that are all alike, they might be offended that you sent them a "form letter."

One employment interviewer tells the story of interviewing 15 college students on a Friday morning. When he returned to his office Monday, on his desk were letters from three of these applicants thanking him for the interview. These were the first three applicants he considered. Two were hired for the two positions.

Figures 14.7 and 14.8 are letters that thank the employment interviewer.

There is another type of follow-up employment letter. If you have applied for a position and have not heard that it has been filled, after a short period of time you should telephone to ask if it is still open. If it is, your next step is to try for another interview, expressing your continued interest in the position and your confidence in your ability to fill it. If it is not open, you should ask to be kept in mind if something else in your field opens. Further, you should continue to look for employment with the firm as long as you are interested and you feel there is any possibility of your being hired.

One woman applying for an executive position with Los Angeles County did not fit all the background requirements, yet in many ways she did qualify. Eventually, after more than 18 months of courteous, patient persistence, she was hired for the position. For many years she served the county in an executive capacity and was the pride of those who had hired her.

Refusal of a Job Offer

Usually, a refusal of a job offer is made orally in person or by telephone. This personal interview should be a natural, open explanation of the reasons for not accepting the position. It is always easier to explain a matter if you are candid about the reasons, whether they involve making a personal change of plans or taking a position that seems better to you.

Sometimes a job refusal brings forth a better offer than the original. Here again, it is risky to try this as a ploy. A better offer may or may not be made, and you will have refused the original offer.

Occasionally it is necessary to write a letter refusing a position that has been offered to you. When writing this letter, keep in mind the possibility that someday in the near or far future, you may have business contacts with the person or firm to whom you are writing. You may even, at some later date, desire to reapply for a position with this same firm. By the good will of a well prepared job refusal, you can try to keep the door open for any future developments.

FIGURE 14.7
Employment interview thank you letter.

Your address with

ZIP code

Your telephone

with area code

Date

Mr. John E. Onthespot
Kimball Electronics
141 West Eighth Avenue
Oshkosh, Wisconsin 00000

Dear Mr. Onthespot

    I do thank you for taking time today to talk with me about joining the Management Training Program there at Kimball Electronics.

    My experience in electronics combined with my earlier two years in personnel work as shown on my resumé should give me a strong background for this program.

    Mr. Onthespot, I surely hope we will be working together in the future and that I will hear from you soon.

Cordially,

(Signature)

Your name

Following is an example of a job offer refusal:

Dear Mr. Kirby:

Neutral, leading to → negative

    Little did I think when I was talking to you last Wednesday that if you offered me a position with Kirby and Kirby I would even consider not accepting that position.

Explanation → of negative
Negative →

    However, just this morning I was offered a similar position with a manufacturing firm in Abilene, Texas, my wife's home town. I believe you can understand why I am accepting it.

Pleasant → closing

    While my wife and I will both be glad to return to our native state, I would otherwise have been very happy to be working with you. I do thank you for your time in considering me for employment with your company.

                             Very sincerely yours,

FIGURE 14.8
Employment interview thank you letter.

```
                                                    Your address
        with ZIP code
                                                    Your telephone
        with area code
                                                    Date


        Miss Ann T. Locks
        Personnel Director
        Acme Electronics
        3400 Palo Verde Avenue
        Tucson, Arizona 85726

        Dear Ann T. Locks

            Thank you so much for our interview today. I enjoyed
        meeting you and learning more about Acme Electronics.

            Now I am even more interested in being part of your
        sales force. Acme's plan to increase the market area
        interests me, and the expansion sounds exciting. As I told
        you, I am single and available for travel.

            Again, I do appreciate having the interview with you. I
        hope to hear from you soon.

        Respectfully,

        (Signature)

        Your name
```

Turndown of Job Applicant

The **turndown letter** of a job applicant is a negative message that should be handled most delicately. If at all possible, it should contain a compliment and/or some word of encouragement. Naturally, this is a "bad news" message, but the applicant undoubtedly felt qualified for the position and should get some hope so that the turndown message does not create a deep hole for that person to crawl into. This letter is best when it ends on some kind of alternative suggestion or other uplift.

Examples of employment turndowns are hard to find, but here are some that have been used satisfactorily. Notice that all these messages are short, not dragging out the negative. Some are results of intense work of committees or other groups.

Turndown 1

Thank you for taking the time to send your resumé for our consideration. However, at this particular time, there are no openings for your area of expertise.

We will keep your information on file, and should there be any positions available that would be suitable, we will contact you.

Again, thank you for your interest in our company.

Turndown 2

We appreciate your taking time to apply for the position of Knowledge Engineering Consultant.

We received many highly qualified applications such as yours. However, your background does not fit our rather specific requirements.

May we otherwise wish you success in your career.

Turndown 3

We received your resumé and wish to thank you for your expression of interest in our firm.

Your experience and background are quite impressive. However, there does not appear to be a match between your skills and our present needs.

Should our needs change so that we could take advantage of your qualifications, we will contact you.

Again, thank you for your interest in ZOO, Inc. We wish you success in finding a new and challenging position.

Turndown 4

Thank you for applying for a position in _____. We were very pleased to receive many high quality applications for our department position.

Our MHR members reviewed the applications and we are inviting several candidates for interviews. Your application was not among those chosen at this stage.

We appreciate your interest in our firm and wish you much success in your career.

The last of these letters is an obvious "kiss off," but it would be perfectly proper to follow up by telephone, letter or a call in person any of the other replies until you are satisfied that the position for which you applied is filled and that there are no other positions for which you qualify.

Many people eventually get the job after an initial turndown. Robert O. Snelling, the nationally known job counselor, said one common mistake job applicants make "is not being insistent enough—not fighting for an available job."

Asking for a Raise

Many people—especially women—do not know how to bargain for a raise.

But there can come a time when you feel undervalued on the job. First, you should do some homework. Get good information about what people in comparable jobs are making in your company and at other companies. Such information is hard to get, and you may have to resort to social occasions when conversations are more relaxed.

Then, approach your boss and ask if the firm is satisfied with your work and if you have a future there. If the answer is yes, simply say, "I am underpaid. What can we do about it?"

You may get a satisfactory answer, or you may get a promise for a raise in the future. If the latter, you can probably have some patience, but maybe you should be looking elsewhere.

Don't whine. Don't plead the high cost of living—this doesn't influence facts about your value to the organization. Don't plead the high amount of your indebtedness—this could lead you right out the door.

Do have a specific amount of raise that you believe would be fair, and be ready to negotiate.

Requests for Employment References

Sometimes it is necessary to write letters **requesting employment references.** At times, you will be requesting that the letter of reference be written to a particular potential employer. At other times, you may ask for a letter addressed to you or "to whom it may concern." You can carry these letters as part of your portfolio, or you can forward copies to interested persons. If the letter is not addressed to a specific individual or firm, you may leave copies with interviewers.

Your request for a reference letter should be brief, polite, and direct. You should immediately state the purpose of the letter, closing on a friendly tone of gratitude. It should follow these guidelines:

☐ State that you would like a letter of reference and give the particular reason for your request.

☐ Explain how you want the letter addressed. If you want it sent to a particular person, give that person's first name or initials so that a letter can be addressed to him or her properly. Be sure to give the complete address, including city, state, and ZIP code, even if it is to be addressed to the city in which you are living.

☐ List specifically the type of information you would like included in your letter, such as the dates of employment and the nature of your duties. To facilitate checking the records, furnish approximate dates of employment. It is also helpful if you mention specific responsibilities you had that you wish mentioned in the letter, to jog the memory of the person answering.

☐ Include any appropriate personal comments to help close the letter on an "up" note.

☐ In some manner, close with an expression of appreciation for this favor.

A letter requesting a reference might read:

Dear Mr. Cooper:

I would appreciate it very much if you could write a letter of reference to help me obtain a position with Hostetter Manufacturing Company.

The position I am seeking is in the accounting department, and I would be handling all accounts receivable. The letter should be addressed

Mr. T. Hee, Director of Human Resources
Hostetter Manufacturing Company
Suite 1301, Majors Towers
Philadelphia, Pennsylvania 00000

My employment with you, as you may recall, was during the summers of 20XX and 20XX. During this time I posted all accounts receivable and accounts payable and also performed general office duties and both computer and hard copy filing.

I enjoyed working for you, Mr. Cooper, and this is part of the reason I am seeking full-time work in an accounting position. Also, the money surely helped me in completing my education.

If you would write a letter verifying my employment with you, I would be very grateful.

Sincerely,

Letters of Reference

Standard Information

Letters of reference need planning so that they will be brief, honest, specific, and sincere. It is rarely necessary to write a negative letter in this situation. A person will usually not list you as a reference unless you can be expected to give a good recommendation. Today especially, people must be acutely aware of the possibility of legal action that might be taken to elicit proof of any negative statements that are made.

This letter should cover the points requested by the job applicant, and should also include other comments you would like to make. The major consideration is that it should sound sincere.

This information is usually desired in an employment reference letter: dates of employment, nature of duties, manner in which the employee performed the work, special abilities of the employee that would be of interest to an employer, and personality traits of a positive nature, such as neatness, drive, imagination, punctuality, resourcefulness, dependability, and attitude.

The following letters are examples of favorable employment references. Any such letters can be fleshed out to include more favorable comments.

To Whom It May Concern:

I gladly recommend _____ as a potential employee. _____ has been in my classes for two semesters and has proven himself to be a dependable, hard-working student. He is in the upper quarter of the class. Also, he is pleasant to know and would be an agreeable person to have as an employee.

Sincerely,

Dear Ms. Sussman:

I am writing to recommend that you favorably consider Debbie Jacobsen for employment in your firm. She has been a completely satisfactory part-time employee here at Ross hardware for nearly two years.

Debbie is an efficient, competent worker who gets along well with fellow employees and customers. Her reliability and punctuality are excellent.

Her duties here consist of greeting customers in person and on the telephone, typing, and other clerical activities. Debbie willingly accepts assignments under time pressure and produces excellent work on time. We will certainly miss her fine work and also her pleasant personality.

Cordially,

Sometimes it is necessary to dismiss an employee for reasons not related to the employee or the job performance, such as when there is a cutback in work. At such times, it can be helpful to furnish any affected employee with a letter of reference explaining the reason for the termination. Such a letter might read as follows:

To Whom It May Concern:

Recently, due to a major cutback in government spending in our region, many people have moved out and we have been forced to reduce our sales staff.

One of the people affected was Mr. Eric G. Cain, who was one of our newest employees. During his year in our employment, Mr. Cain was a very effective salesman who not only handled old accounts well but succeeded in bringing in more than his share of new customers.

Mr. Cain is an honest, reliable employee who gained the respect and friendship of all those who worked with him. We are sorry that we are unable to retain him. We would be happy to recommend him for another position.

We will be glad to furnish additional recommendations for him by telephone or postal or email letter.

Sincerely,

Legal Guidelines in Letters of Reference

If you do have reservations about making a full recommendation, you might consider that everyone deserves another chance and that anyone can improve. Emphasize positive attributes.

However, when asked to recommend a truly poor worker, you should be selective and not write a letter for that person. In this way you help prevent such workers from being able to jump from job to job. You also may avoid potential legal action.

Do not write potentially negative reference letters. Currently, lawsuits are being filed for reporting some matters that were formerly considered acceptable to report and helpful to the person inquiring. Something like this could cause trouble: "His letter of reference kept me from getting a position for which I am well qualified."

Employment references today are extremely sensitive communications.

Requesting Permission to Use Name as Reference

A letter requesting to use a person's name as a reference should be short, with as little or as much detail as is needed. Following is a letter sent to a former instructor:

Dear Mrs. Hunter:

I am applying for a sales position that is now open at Myers Corporation.

Since I was a student in your Marketing Research program in 20XX and received excellent practical instruction on selling principles, I would like to use your name as a reference.

I have enclosed a self-addressed envelope for your reply.

Cordially,

Resignations

A heavy record of frequent job-hopping does not look good to a potential employer. Yet occasionally you may find it necessary or desirable to make a change in employment. If you can make your **resignation** in person, this method is preferred, with the natural discussion and feedback that are possible. For your own good, you should approach this important interview with an extremely positive mental attitude. Do not give vent to any grievances you have unless you feel that they can be interpreted as constructive criticism. When the employer is later contacted for a job reference for you, that person's most vivid recollection may relate to this resignation interview.

An employment resignation may bring forth a counterproposal so attractive that you may decide to remain in your current employment. Do not let this be the primary reason for submitting your resignation, however, because your plan might backfire and you might find yourself out on the street sooner than expected.

Sometimes it is necessary to resign by letter. This communication should be patterned as the negative message that it is. You can assume that it will be necessary to replace you and that your employer will regret losing you and the training you have received in the organization. The resignation should have three parts:

1. *Opening:* neutral, pleasant statement probably relating to experience with the firm

2. *Middle:* clear statement or resignation, with reasons given in positive terms.

3. *Closing:* "up" tone, making positive statements about work, firm, and employees. Offer to train replacement; if it is not presumptuous, suggest a replacement; express appreciation for employment with firm.

Two letters of resignation follow:

Dear Mr. Brando:

Neutral, pleasant →
Lead into

For the past four years I have enjoyed my work with Brando Brothers and have also enjoyed the association with the many fine employees here.

negative →
Negative (resigna-

Recently, however, I was offered the position of Junior Management Consultant with Farrell-Lynch, Inc., and I feel that this larger firm can offer me considerable chance for advancement.

tion) →
Pleasant

I would like to resign the end of this month. I believe that this will give you time to find my replacement.

closing →

I do thank you personally, Mr. Brando, for a pleasant association with your firm.

Sincerely,

Dear Mr. Plunkett:

Neutral,
pleasant →
Lead into
negative →
Negative
(resigna-
tion) →

When we came to Burlington on a skiing vacation, we did not expect that we would try to make it our permanent home. However, we like Vermont so well that my husband interviewed for a position. As a result, he will be a reporter and assistant editor on the local newspaper staff, and I will be a part-time legal secretary while I learn the work of a woman who will retire in a few months.

As this letter should reach you two weeks before the end of my vacation, I hope that this will give you time to find my replacement.

Pleasant
looking to
future →

I am truly sorry to leave Fargo Wells, because I have enjoyed my work there and certainly like all the people with whom I worked. Please give my best wishes to the other members of the firm, and also to Mrs. Plunkett.

I surely appreciate the training I received in the Legal Department, Mr. Plunkett, and I wish you continued success with Fargo Wells.

Cordially,

Employment Resumé Checklist

1. Identify your reader(s) and write at that level.
2. Appearance:
   a. Is it short?
   b. Is it neat, clean, and attractive?
   c. Is it uncrowded, with margins of at least $1^1/_4$ inches?
   d. Is there at least one blank line between sections?
3. Good will tone:
   a. Is material set out courteously according to interests of employer?
   b. Minimize use of *I, me, my,* and *mine.*
4. Clear and complete message:
   a. Have you set out information concisely under appropriate headings?
   b. Are education and employment listed with most recent or current experience first?
   c. If resumé is overlong, reread it to eliminate information least helpful in securing the position.
5. Writing improvement points: Recheck for all writing improvement points, especially correct grammar and spelling.

Employment Application Letter Checklist

1. Identify your reader(s) and write at that level.
2. Appearance?
3. Good will:
   a. Have you shown interest in and/or knowledge of the firm?
   b. Have you tried to point your background toward needs of the potential employer?
   c. Minimize use of *I, me, my,* and *mine.*

4. Clear and complete message: Follow the AIDA plan.
   a. Attention: Focus on the firm or your special background.
   b. Interest and desire buildup: What especially qualifies you for the position that will make them *interested* in you and should make them *desire* to hire you?
   c. Action: Is the closing designed to move the reader to the action you want?

5. Writing improvement points: Check for all writing improvement points, especially grammar and spelling.

To the instructor: For classroom variety and for students' experience in a "first" job interview, you might count them out in pairs to interview each other. Give them copies of these six questions, or others of your choice:

1. Why do you think you might like to work for our company?
2. What kind of work interests you?
3. What qualifications do you have that make you believe you will be successful in your field?
4. What jobs (or classes) have you enjoyed the most? The least?
5. What do you do to keep in good physical condition?
6. What are your future vocational plans?

Chapter 14   Employment Resumés and Application Letters: Miscellaneous Employment Communications

WRITING IMPROVEMENT EXERCISE

Using a Thesaurus to Improve Your Vocabulary

Winston Churchill, a master in the use of the English language, said, "Short words are best, and the old words when short are best of all." Our study of the Fog Index in Chapter 16 supports this idea by encouraging the use of a long word only when a short word will not do. Many studies support this attitude.

At the same time, our study here on how to use a thesaurus will demonstrate three distinct advantages of finding and using longer words when they are needed. First, synonyms from a thesaurus will improve your vocabulary by showing a choice of words of specific meaning to help make your speaking and writing clear and precise. As you will see from the following examples and from your own homework for this exercise, so-called synonyms do not have exactly the same specific meaning. It is up to you to choose the best word for your own purpose, referring to a dictionary if necessary. Also, most word processing software has a built-in thesaurus.

Be sure that the synonym you choose has the proper shade of meaning. For instance, wanting to express his extreme pleasure at having been invited to dinner with a dean and his wife, one student searched a thesaurus for a strong synonym for the word *desire*. At first his sentence read, "I really *lust* to meet Mrs. _____." Fortunately, his business communication professor helped him find a more acceptable synonym.

Second, learning to find and use synonyms from a thesaurus or dictionary will help you avoid awkward overuse of the same common words or terms.

Third and last, enlarging your vocabulary with a command of specific words when needed improves your speaking and writing, marking you as a better-educated person.

A thesaurus also contains a limited number of antonyms for most words. At times this information, of course, can be helpful.

There are a few different thesauruses (or thesauri) on the market today. The old standby—*Roget's International Thesaurus,* published by Thomas Y. Crowell Company—is widely used and respected. Also, Simon & Schuster Inc.'s book, *Websters New World Thesaurus* has gained wide approval. Although not providing as many choices as the larger hard-cover books, pocket-size paperback editions provide a good help.

Following are selections from Charlton Laird's reference book, *Webster's New World Thesaurus* (New York: Simon & Schuster, 1997):

believe, v. 1. [To accept as true]—Syn. accept, hold, think, conclude, have faith, be convinced, be certain of, deem, understand, regard, take at one's word, consider, affirm, be of the opinion, postulate, opine, conceive, give credence to, have no doubt, rest assured, swear by, take one's word for, cherish a belief, keep the faith, be credulous, entertain or nurture a belief.—Ant. doubt, deny, suspect.

2. [To assume]—Syn. suppose, guess, gather; see **assume** 1.

sweet, modifier. 1. [Sweet in taste]—Syn. toothsome, sugary, luscious, candied, sweet as honey, sweet as sugar, like honey, like sugar, honeyed, saccharine, cloying, like nectar, delicious; see also **rich** 4.—Ant. sour, bitter, sharp.

2. [Sweet in disposition]—Syn. agreeable, pleasing, engaging, winning, delightful, patient, reasonable, gentle, kind, generous, unselfish, sweet-tempered, even-tempered, good-humored, considerate, thoughtful, companionable; see also **friendly** 1.—Ant. selfish, repulsive, inconsiderate.

3. [Not salt]—Syn. fresh, unsalted, uncured, unseasoned, freshened.—Ant. salty, pickled, briny.

4. [Dear]—Syn. sympathetic, loving, winsome; see **beloved.**

hungry, modifier.—Syn. starved, famished, craving, ravenous, desirous, hankering, unsatisfied, unfilled, starving, edacious, insatiate, voracious, of keen appetite, famishing, half-starved, hungered, ravening, omnivorous, carnivorous, supperless, greedy as a hog, dinnerless, piggish, hoggish, peckish, half-famished; on an empty stomach; hungry as a wolf, empty; see also **greedy** 2.—Ant. satisfied, full fed.[2]

[2]See dictionary for usage.

**Chapter 14 Employment Resumés and Application Letters:
Miscellaneous Employment Communications**

USING A THESAURUS TO IMPROVE YOUR VOCABULARY
WRITING IMPROVEMENT "HANDS ON" ASSIGNMENT

Using a thesaurus for reference, find at least five synonyms for each of the following words:

1. awful horrible, terrible, dreadful, lofty, exalted, majestic, appalling, disgusting, repulsive, gigantic, colossal, stupendous, frightful, grand, offensive

2. friend schoolmate, playmate, roommate, bedfellow, companion, intimate, confidant, comrade, chum, buddy, sidekick

3. happy joyous, glad, cheery, sparkling, satisfied, delighted, pleasant, overjoyed, radiant, vivacious, sunny, smiling, content, animated, lively, good-humored, thrilled

4. like (verb) to take pleasure in, to find agreeable or congenial or appealing, regard with favor, take a fancy to, dote on, take an interest in, go for in a big way, cotton to

5. long (modifier) lengthy, extended, elongated, interminable, boundless, prolonged, long-winded, for ages, eternal, lanky, gangling, farseeing

6. stupid foolish, shallow, irrational, ridiculous, nonsensical, unintelligent, misguided, injudicious, narrow-minded, moronic, senile, giddy, dippy, half-baked, unsophisticated

7. thing * article, object, item, commodity, device, gadget, entity, body, something, anything, everything, element, substance, piece, stuff, good (*or be specific*)

8. neat tidy, trim, dapper, shipshape, methodical, regular, orderly, immaculate, spick-and-span, proper, in good order, spotless, systematic

9. weird uncanny, ominous, eerie, ghastly, mysterious, unearthly, unnatural, gruesome, pallid, strange, abstruse

10. wonderful amazing, astonishing, incredible, unusual, fine, enjoyable, pleasing, pleasant, excellent, admirable, remarkable, marvelous, extraordinary, magnificent

*[Usually a weak word; try to use a word that is more specific.]

Chapter 14   Employment Resumés and Application Letters:
Miscellaneous Employment Communications

WRITING ASSIGNMENTS

1. Make up an employment resumé and application letter that you might use either (a) at the completion of your college work this year, or (b) at the completion of your college work some time in the future. If you wish, you may use your imagination for details. Try to make the assignment something that will eventually be useful for you. This assignment may open your eyes to additional education and training you should pursue.

2. Write a letter requesting an employment reference for the job for which you are applying in assignment 1. If you are currently employed, write a letter that you might actually use. If you are not employed, use an imaginary situation.

3. Write a letter supposedly to an instructor, asking to use his or her name as a reference on an employment application.

4. You have a small accounting firm and have employed a student as part-time receptionist and typist. She has also done some basic bookkeeping for you. Since she worked for you, she has received a B.S. degree in accounting and has applied for full-time work as a junior accountant. Write her a letter of reference for this position.

5. It is early Friday evening. This morning you were interviewed for a position with Rockefeller Corporation, 1111 Vine Street, Your Town, Your State (with ZIP code). Your interviewer was John Jacob Astor, Director of Human Resources Personnel. You want to have a letter on his desk Monday morning. Write Mr. Astor thanking him for the interview. Make up an explanation about why you are now more than ever interested in becoming a member of the staff of Rockefeller.

6. A week ago you applied for a position that you would really like to obtain, and you have had no response. Write a follow-up letter to the person who interviewed you and thank her for her time in granting you the interview. You should consider phoning or calling in person.

7. Write a letter of reference for yourself that you would like to have prepared for you some time in the future when you have completed the education and training for the position you eventually wish to hold. (Believe it or not, this situation frequently happens when an employee is doing completely satisfactory work but is seeking a higher position.) Of course for this assignment, you will have to fictionalize some details of matters in your background that have not yet been completed.

Chapter 14   Employment Resumés and Application Letters: Miscellaneous Employment Communications

REVIEW AND DISCUSSION

Give brief answers. If given a choice, draw a line through any incorrect answer.

1. Today's typical employment application letter consists of two parts. What are they?

   a. __Resumé__

   b. __Application letter__

2. What does "white space" mean in relation to written or printed communications?

   __Empty space between printed or written material; wide margins.__

3. What are the main sections of an employment resume?

   __Heading. Special qualifications. Career accomplishments, if any.__

   __Education and training. Experience. Personal details. References.__

4. What should be included in the heading of the resume?

   __Name, Address(es), Phone and Fax number. Possibly: Position sought.__

5. If you took a course titled, "Speech 118: Public Address," how would you list it on a resumé?

   __Public Address *or* Speech__

6. On an employment application blank, education and employment should be listed (most recent first/~~most recent last~~).

7. Name three specific types of information you should list about any employment.

   a. __(Accept any three of these responses.) Firm name with address,__

   b. __dates of employment, duties performed, full name of person to be contacted,__

   c. __outstanding employment experience__

8. Name five qualities that could be considered for inclusion under "Special Qualifications."

   a. __Outstanding employment experience.__

   b. __Bilingual or multilingual ability.__

   c. __Writing experience with examples.__

   d. __Speaking ability and experience.__

   e. __Artistic ability with portfolio. Special research. Other?__

9. Why might it be to your advantage to give some details under a "Personal" heading?
   <u>Laws prohibit potential employers from asking many personal questions. However, they are</u>
   <u>interested in learning about you. Take advantage by telling them any personal details you wish.</u>

10. On a resumé it is (not acceptable/acceptable/<u>acceptable and often recommended</u>) that you give information that by law cannot be asked by a potential employer. <u>Underline the best answer.</u>

11. Why are references usually listed last? <u>Here they are natural lead-ins for being</u>
    <u>contacted.</u>

12. Whose names can you list as references if you have had no previous employment?
    <u>Old family friends, business contacts of family, religious leaders, instructors.</u>

13. What pattern should the application letter follow?
    <u>Sales letter pattern: You are selling yourself; put your best foot forward.</u>

14. What can be the source of information for your letter of application?
    <u>The resumé. [That is why you write resumé first.]</u>

15. What is the best tone for a letter of application? (~~formal~~/conversational/~~casual~~)

16. How should a letter of application be signed?
    <u>In blue or black ink. Do not put title before name.</u>

17. In planning ahead for a job interview, there are two areas in which you should prepare. Name them. <u>Know something about the company. Prepare yourself: clothes,</u>
    <u>style and cut of hair, written materials that could be helpful.</u>

18. The text lists eight steps to help carry you well into and through your interview. List them.
    a. <u>Try to choose your day.</u>
    b. <u>Be on time.</u>
    c. <u>Let interviewer lead the interview.</u>
    d. <u>Keep calm.</u>
    e. <u>Briefly and honestly, state your case clearly.</u>
    f. <u>Don't try for pity.</u>
    g. <u>Do not overstay your allotted time.</u>
    h. <u>On leaving, thank interviewer for his or her time.</u>

15

Planning a Business Report or a Term Paper

> *Once begun, half done.*
> *Old proverb*

Advantages to the Student, Job Applicant, and Employee

The advantages to the student in learning how to write effective reports or term papers are in three chief areas: (1) as a student, (2) as a job applicant, and (3) as an employee.

For the Student

Colleges are placing more emphasis on writing courses because employers emphasize business's need for writers and because people in technical, scientific, and professional fields recognize the same need. Students who learn to organize and write good, clear reports can noticeably raise their grades in classes that require any kind of writing, particularly the writing of reports.

For the Job Applicant

With many firms conducting their own courses in language skills, such as English grammar and writing, the job applicant who already has an ability to organize information and write good reports will frequently be hired and/or promoted ahead of those who cannot. Although writing ability is helpful in preparing daily correspondence, there is also a great demand for the person who can prepare longer letters, sometimes called **report-letters**, and the essential reports of business and industry.

For the Employee

Business reports must be written for three reasons:

☐ For management to know what is taking place, for its own efficient operation and for meeting competition
☐ For legal obligations to investors, government, customers, employees, and suppliers
☐ For customer relations and various public information uses

349

On the job, employees must frequently turn in many different types of reports. Upper management studies these reports not only for the information contained in them but also for leads in locating people who can write clearly and concisely. The employee may feel that routine reports are filed away where no one sees them. But to high-level officials, these reports are often their only concrete evidence of a person's progress on the job. The person who carefully prepares routine reports will often be singled out for consideration when promotions arise.

Unnecessary Reports

Business leaders caution that today, too many reports are being produced and circulated. Too many reports are being furnished to people who don't need them and won't read them. The result is that essential reading is sometimes overlooked in the morass of reports. This comes from two causes: (1) Unnecessary, overlapping, irrelevant reports are being prepared; and (2) copies of necessary reports are being circulated not only to those who have need for them, but also to those who neither need nor want them.

One airline reduced its report budget by 43 percent when it inaugurated a system of monitoring distribution of reports according to circulation and use. Through its findings, the company eliminated the preparation of some reports and curtailed distribution of many copies of others. Figure 15.1 is a copy of an "Evaluation of Report" form that can be attached to a report to determine if each person who receives it needs or uses it.

Also, we must be cautious of being wooed too often by the siren call of electronic data processing. Electronics enables us to record and classify data much more quickly and efficiently than was possible earlier. But a result has been that, by pushing a few buttons, voluminous reports are frequently prepared and distributed when they are in no way helpful to the enterprise.

Research

In general, two types of research are conducted, primary and secondary. Primary research—obtaining original data—is done from observational studies, in-plant surveys, opinion polls, and experimental research with actual testing of solutions. Secondary research—written from studies made and reported by others—is usually done from public and private library sources.

Chapters 15 and 16 of this text will deal chiefly with the second method, library research, with references to gathering data by the other methods. In reporting much primary research, many procedures here can be followed. Primary or original research often also includes some secondary research, reference to printed materials.

Steps in Seeking Solutions to Problems or Completing Other Research

To solve your problem or complete your research for your report topic, take the following steps:

1. Identify the problem or the research topic.
2. Identify the people who will read and use the report.
3. Identify the parts of the problem.

FIGURE 15.1
A report evaluation form that can be attached to a
report to determine the need for it.

EVALUATION OF REPORT		
Ref. SPLIT 1-02-011		
TO:	FROM:	
TITLE OF REPORT:		

PLEASE ANSWER THE FOLLOWING QUESTIONS AND RETURN THIS FORM TO THE SENDER.
IF YOUR ANSWER TO THE FIRST QUESTION IS "NO," NO FURTHER ANSWERS ARE REQUIRED.

DO YOU REQUIRE THIS REPORT? YES ☐ NO ☐	IF YES, AT WHAT FREQUENCY? WK ☐ MO ☐ YR ☐ OTHER (EXPLAIN)

IS PRESENT FORMAT ACCEPTABLE? YES ☐   NO ☐   (IF "NO," SPECIFY CHANGES DESIRED)

ARE OTHER REPORTS, FORMS, ETC. PREPARED FROM THIS REPORT?   YES ☐ NO ☐

(IF "YES," ENUMERATE)

IF YOU KNOW OF ANY OTHER REPORT THAT DUPLICATES INFORMATION IN THIS ONE, INDICATE.
TITLE:

PREPARED BY:

BRIEFLY JUSTIFY YOUR REQUIREMENT FOR THIS REPORT

4. Ask questions about each part.
5. Write down what you know—and what you must find out.
6. Allow for limitations on time, money, and availability of data.
7. Get authorization to prepare the report.

Identify the Problem or the Research Topic

The most helpful step in writing any report is to clearly identify the problem or the research topic. Everything in the report must hinge upon this central idea. Making a brief statement of this problem or research subject is very helpful. Even though this statement may never be used in the actual report, it will give you a framework into which all the research and writing must fit. It should be kept uppermost in the mind of anyone working on the report. In this manner you are able to zero in on wanted material and eliminate extraneous information.

A common error in students' choices for term papers is that the selection of topic is too broad for the planned presentation. Undergraduate students often try to choose a term paper project that would be more suitable for a graduate dissertation—or more. For example, one college sophomore wrote on his 3 by 5 term paper proposal card, "Data Processing"; another wrote "Explorations in Outer Space."

To help choose a topic you can cover properly, write down the name of the field of study you want to research, such as "The Internet." Then list subtopics under your chosen title that would interest you for doing research. On broad topics, you and your instructor might agree on a subtopic or even a sub-subtopic for your paper.

Identify Those Who Will Read and Use the Report

Identification of the people who will read and use the report will affect the information to be included and will help determine the detail into which the report must go. Further, it will affect the physical aspects of the report, such as method of printing, types of illustrations, quality of paper, types of covers, and tone of writing. An in-house report might economize on printing, illustrations, paper, and cover, and it might have a relaxed, informal tone. Reports for clients, customers, board of directors, and government agencies would probably receive more formal treatment in these areas.

Identify Parts of the Problem

Any problem or research topic can be studied and reported more easily when it is broken down into small segments, making it simpler to find solutions. This is particularly true when the large unanswered problem seems almost beyond comprehension. Step-by-step solution of these parts can be combined into the solution of the whole.

Ask Questions about Each Part

As each part is identified, list questions that can be helpful in finding the solution. Questioning may eliminate some parts and add others not previously listed.

Write Down What You Know and What You Must Find Out

Make notes on what you know and what you need to find out about each part of the problem or topic. At this stage, business often uses the advantages of brainstorming—freewheeling, open-end group discussions with few limits on ideas and suggestions. Brainstorming usually helps clear the air, giving significant help in the search for solutions.

Allow for Limitations on Time, Money, and Availability of Data

Reports must be structured within certain limits of time, money, and availability of data. This applies to all reports, from the college term paper to the annual report of a major corporation.

Businesses must especially recognize limitations of time and money in respect to the value of the research and report writing being done. Any type of report must be of sufficient interest and value to justify the expenditure of time and talent required.

Get Authorization to Prepare the Report

If proper authorization to prepare the report has not been received before this time, specific authority should be obtained before more work is completed. For the classroom, of course, an instructor should agree that the planned topic will be acceptable and of proper length and depth for class requirements. Properly authorized personnel must give approval for a go-ahead for the on-the-job project.

Sources of Information

Now you are ready to begin research for the project.

Business reports must above all else be accurate and up to date. As a rule of thumb, use no reference that is more than five years old unless it is an exceptional case or the data are needed for historical comparison. The business scene changes rapidly, and in some fields of study, information even one year old is outdated. Further, factual information must be documented by footnotes with reference to its source if there can be any question about its accuracy, or if further study of that information might be made by readers.

In the Beginning—

In the beginning, encyclopedias will usually give you general information on your research topic, so they can guide you in selecting which part of a large general subject you wish to study. Also, they might help you find a good order of presentation. There are general encyclopedias, and encyclopedias for specific fields. Ask your reference librarian.

Reference Librarian

Probably your best help in doing library research is the reference librarian. One librarian says, "If you don't know, ask." Another says, "Don't leave without asking." Reference librarians are trained to help researchers locate information. They will guide you to locating sources you ask for, and probably will guide you to good sources you had not considered. As a matter of fact, your first step in doing library research might be to explain your topic to the reference librarian and ask for help. "You'll be glad you did." Further, you will find you can do your next research paper far more easily because you will have become familiar with some of the sources of information in the library.

Computerized Sources

Libraries are moving from space-consuming card indexes and bound book indexes to computerized systems which are updated regularly. Here you might at first need the help of the reference librarian.

Computerized sources gather materials into a **database** that contains related information on a given subject. Sometimes the information is similar to that in card and catalogue indexes: subject, author, title.

Other times the entire text of the article is available. ABI/Inform is a good example of a database that contains both citations for some periodicals and the full text of others.

A number of private information services compile databases available to the public, usually charging a fee according to usage. Also, prominent business resources, such as *Harvard Business Review, Dow Jones & Company, New York Times,* and *Los Angeles Times,* make their files available to others via the internet.

Many college, university and public libraries are beginning to offer database services to the public free or for a fee charged according to computer time used.

With all the material available through computer research, a major problem might be narrowing down the pertinent selections you wish to use.

CHECK YOUR INTERNET RESEARCH SOURCES: A STUDENT RESEARCH PROJECT

The internet is usually the first place students turn to when doing research. The problem with this is the quality of internet information varies wildly—from reliable and scholarly to misleading or even false.

Your college may offer access to databases through its web pages that are usually good sources. Further, company, government, trade association and other web pages can be good sources. If you are in doubt about the validity of information on the web, don't hesitate to ask the opinion of a reference librarian or your instructor.

A good example of web based research for a student business report occurred in a class of one of the authors of this text (DWMcC). Students were required to form small teams and create an imaginary company. Next, they were assigned to make a computerized slide show presentation to a group of supposed "investors" (the rest of the class). The students were to decide whether or not to put their "money" into this new business. A well-researched report accompanied the presentation.

One team planned to start a Mexican restaurant. They found excellent reliable information on the web from an association of restaurant owners, the city's Chamber of Commerce, "Creating Business Plans" on the Small Business Administration pages and other dependable sources.

One non-productive member had to be dropped from the team. However, at last report, other team members were continuing research into actually starting a restaurant at the location that their on-site, primary research had selected.

Periodicals

All libraries, including public, corporate, and other private libraries, have three basic classifications of materials: periodicals, references, and books in stacks.

For business reports, much information might come from authoritative periodicals—magazines, newspapers, and journals—because they are, by their nature, of more recent publication than most other sources.

Periodical Indexes

One type of periodical index is the *Magazine Index.* Prepared on a computer and updated monthly, this index is viewed on a microfilm screen. You can easily call up five, ten or more years' indexing of subject matter in magazines, and it is efficiently cross-indexed like other periodical indexes. Older materials can be found in bound book indexes.

Other helpful indexes for researching business or industrial subjects in a library are listed here. Probably the most helpful will be the *Business Periodical Index* and *Reader's Guide to Periodical Literature.*

Name of Index	*Periodicals Indexed*
Applied Science and Technology Index	Engineering, trade, business
Business Periodicals Index	Business, industrial, trade
Humanities Index	History, economics, international relations, political science
New York Times Index	*New York Times,* including business section of *Times;* oriented to eastern U.S. and international business
Reader's Guide to Periodical Literature	General periodicals on all subject matters; covers major business periodicals

Business Periodicals. These are the major authoritative business periodicals:

Business Ethics	Monthly magazine covering socially responsible business
Business Week	Weekly business news magazine
Changing Times	Kiplinger's monthly business magazine for general readership
Dun's Business Monthly	Periodical for business executives; regional coverage
Forbes	Magazine for business executives published every two weeks
Fortune	Magazine containing articles on business firms and business problems published every two weeks
Harvard Business Review	Magazine on business activities published every two months
Money	Monthly business and investment magazine for general readership
Nation's Business	Published by U.S. Chamber of Commerce; articles on business for general readership
The Wall Street Journal	Daily Monday—Friday business and financial newspaper, which also contains general news; regional issues

Besides these major business periodicals, the library may contain copies of other magazines and journals pertaining to business in general, as well as those devoted solely to a particular field of business. Library indexes should be studied for names of such periodicals. Each library makes its own selection of materials found on its shelves; these decisions are usually made according to demand.

The library can be checked for periodicals in many different categories, such as these:

Accounting	Human resources	Personnel
Communication	Labor and labor relations	Retailing
Computers	Law	Secretarial science
Economics	Office management	Transportation

E-commerce   Marketing
Environment   Mines and
Finance   minerals
Food   Waste management

In-House Libraries

Many large companies and other major organizations have their own exten-sive libraries staffed with librarians and reference works of their own company as well as other general and specific topics related to their operation. Some of their information can be top secret relating to business and industrial matters, and therefore appropriate precautions are taken for protection from unauthorized in-dividuals.

Directories and Encyclopedias

Business directories and business encyclopedias in the library's reference sec-tion can be of great help in writing business reports. The corporation directories are good general references.

Corporation directories list information on specific corporations and business-es by name, as well as listing government units that offer opportunities for invest-ment. These directories will give such information as the address of a business main office and divisions, its current status, its history, types of products or services, and detailed financial statistics. Your reference librarian can help you locate current major corporation directories. Much of this information is, of course, also available on the World Wide Web and can be found using a search engine.

Other corporate directory references can be found in these areas:

Automotive and aviation   Import and export
Chemical and engineering   Metals and machinery
Coal and mining   Mining
Drugs   Petroleum
Electronics and data processing Textiles and apparel
Food and food processing

Books in Stacks

Fiction Books
Fiction books are shelved alphabetically by author.

Nonfiction Books
Computerized sources, library card catalogues, or bound catalogues list each nonfiction book under three different classifications: author, title and subject.

To aid us in locating them, nonfiction books are placed in library stacks accord-ing to subject matter. The two major classification systems used are the Library of Congress and the Dewey Decimal systems.

The Library of Congress system. College, state, and federal libraries are in-creasingly adopting the Library of Congress system of classification. This system facilitates inter-library lending opportunities offered by the automated system of the Library of Congress so that through your own library you can borrow books from other libraries. This system uses letters of the alphabet combined with numbers to place materials in specific categories. Following are the Library of Congress classifications.

A	General, Work, Polygraphy
B	Philosophy, Religion
C	History—Auxiliary Sciences
D	Universal and Old World History
E—F	America
G	Geography, Anthropology, Folklore, Customs, Sports and Games
H	Business, Political Science
K	Law
L	Education
M	Music
N	Fine Arts
P	Language and Literature
Q	Science
R	Medicine
S	Agriculture
T	Technology
U	Military Science
V	Naval Science
Z	Bibliography and Library Science

The Dewey Decimal system. The Dewey Decimal system, the most widely used library classification system in the United States, is based on a progressive use of arabic numbers 0 to 9.

Most information of interest to business and industrial research is listed under the classifications "300: The Social Sciences," and "600: Technology (Applied Sciences)." The following list contains the major classifications of the Dewey Decimal system and also includes subheadings of the 300 and 600 classifications:

000	GENERALITIES	
100	PHILOSOPHY AND RELATED DISCIPLINES	
200	RELIGION	
300	THE SOCIAL SCIENCES	
	310	Statistical method and statistics
	320	Political science
	330	Economics
	340	Law
	350	Public administration
	360	Welfare and association
	370	Education
	380	Commerce
	390	Customs and folklore

400 LANGUAGE

500 PURE SCIENCES

600 TECHNOLOGY (APPLIED SCIENCES)

    610 Medical sciences

    620 Engineering and allied operations

    630 Agriculture and agricultural industries

    640 Domestic arts and sciences (home economics)

    650 Communications, business

    660 Chemical technology, etc.

    670 Manufactures

    680 Mechanical trades

    690 Building

700 THE ARTS

800 LITERATURE AND RHETORIC

900 GENERAL GEOGRAPHY AND HISTORY, etc.

Doing Library Research

With a Computer

Know your Source!

Most business reports and term papers today are prepared with the use of computers for research and writing.

The chief problem in using computer references is choosing reliable sources. As you know, no screening process—public or private—evaluates the authenticity of information that shows up on your monitor. To get around this, you should refer to standard reliable publishers, dependable trade and government sources, and in-house publications and information. Again, your reference librarian can guide you further.

Watch this. As emphasized earlier, once you report inaccurate information as valid, anything you say or write from then on will be suspect.

You Can Keep Notes on a Computer

You may want to use the library's computer and keep your notes on a disk that you bring yourself. Or you may be able to use your own portable computer. Titles of report sections can be saved in the computer memory and then easily accessed for placing information under each title. For long reports, an individual disk might be used for notes on each report section title.

Essentially, you will be able to follow the procedure for making out note cards.

With Note Cards and Xerox Copies

As you collect information, printed or otherwise, record your research notes on a computer, on 3 by 5 or 4 by 6 cards, or on standard 8 1/2 by 11-inch paper. Xerox copies of printed research are valuable and certainly are exact copies of wanted materials. Xerox pages, clippings and other pages can be held together separately with headings in order, corresponding to the order of headings on the cards. You will find the cards handy for carrying and for stacking in order of presentation.

When you are writing the report, you will find the cards handy for carrying and stacking in order of presentation of material. Cards are also useful for fitting other materials into the proper place in the report. You will not only use these notes as references when writing the report, you will find them useful if you wish further details from this source or wish to recheck the information on it with other information that may conflict.

Figure 15.2 is an example of a typical library research card. The card can be set out in sections:

1. At the top of the card in the left corner, list a key word or phrase identifying the part of the report this card covers. Placing this information here makes it easy for you to rearrange the cards and pages. This also give you the order in which to "cut" parts of your computer word processing file and "paste "them correctly.
2. In the upper right corner, put the library call number for possible future reference. From the database you are using or the title page of the book or periodical, copy the full name of the author, full title, name of publisher, place and date of publication, and the page number(s). This accurate information may be used for reference, footnotes and bibliography. If several notes are made from the same source, abbreviate this information on different cards or pages by listing just the name of the author or key words in the title of the article. If you use more than one reference for the same author, identify each one clearly. Always note exact page numbers.
3. Leaving a blank line below this source material, write pertinent research information, using the back of the note card if necessary.

FIGURE 15.2
Example of library research card for report writing.

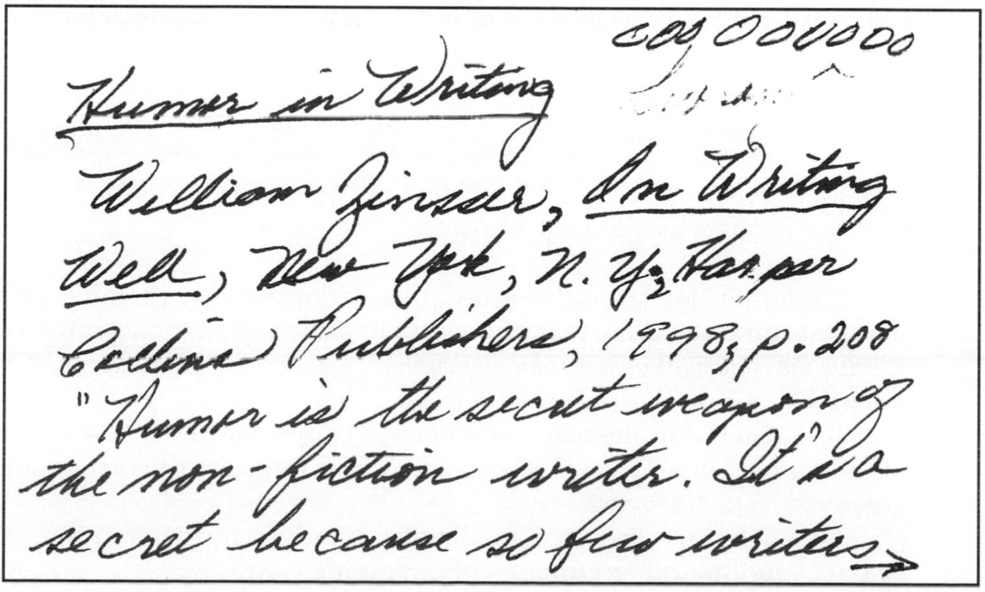
Humor in Writing

William Zinsser, On Writing Well, New York, N.Y.; Harper Collins Publishers, 1998, p. 208
"Humor is the secret weapon of the non-fiction writer. It's a secret because so few writers

For a Longer Report

For a longer report, it might be more helpful to keep your bibliography notes separate from your research notes. If you are using a computer, you could keep bibliographic information at the end of your word processing file and your research notes in the beginning. If you are using cards you may want to keep two sets of research cards: One set of 3 by 5 inch bibliography cards would contain full information as shown in Figure 15.2—name of author, full title of source, place of publication, publisher, and date of publication. However, your research notes would not be put on these bibliography cards.

The second set of larger, 4 by 6-inch cards would be used for all research notes. Both front and back of these cards might be used. You could identify the source of this information at the *bottom* of these cards in abbreviated form, such as *Felber and Koch, p. 67*. Each large card should also have at the top the title of the major report section to which the card refers.

Organizing Notes

Make a good table of contents for the report. The note cards can then be compiled under the major headings. By placing the note cards in a logical order of development of the report, you are organized and ready to write the table of contents, which will be the pattern you can follow for the entire report. Subheadings can be made up from the organization under the major headings.

With notes in order and outline written, you are ready to write your report. Chapter 16 contains detailed information about writing a report.

Copyright Laws

Copyright laws are passed to protect writers and other creators from those who would appropriate their work without paying for it. Because technological changes have made copying and sending electronic, printed and recorded materials much easier than in times past, newer laws have been passed. Supporting and updating old copyright laws, Section 107 of Public Law 94-553, reads in part:

> … the fair use of a copyrighted work, including such use by reproducing copies … for purposes such as … teaching (including multiple copies for classroom use), scholarship, or research, is not an infringement of copyright. [Factors to be considered shall include] whether such use is of a commercial nature or is for nonprofit educational purposes….

Under its "fair use" provisions, this law apparently permits copying of printed materials for use during research, providing such use is noncommercial and *does not deprive the copyright owner from money that would otherwise be derived from the sale of the material.*

If registered in the name of a person, copyright protection is issued for the life of the author plus 50 years. If registered by a business or corporation, protection is given for 75 to 100 years.

"Plagiarism," discussed in Chapter 16, gives further caution and explanation against "quoting other writers without giving credit."

Writing assignments for Chapters 15 and 16 are at the end of Chapter 16.

Chapter 15   Planning a Business Report or a Term Paper

REVIEW AND DISCUSSION

1. Tell how report writing ability can help you as a student.

   It helps you write better, especially for class reports and essay questions.

   _____

2. Business people say that ability to write reports is important because reports have to be written for three reasons. What are the reasons?

   a. For efficient operation of the business—to review and preview.

   b. For legal obligations.

   c. For customer relations and other public information.

3. Tell how report writing ability can help you as a job applicant.

   Many businesses and other employers are looking for people who can write.

   _____

4. Tell how report writing ability can help you as an employee.

   Many reports are written on the job. Upper levels are often on lookout for writers to

   place them in higher positions.

5. What do business leaders say are two causes of excessive report writing and report circulation?

   a. Unnecessary reports are being prepared.

   b. Too many copies of reports are often circulated to people who won't read them.

6. When airline officials studied the distribution and use of their reports, they reduced their report budget by __43__ percent.

7. Name two types of research that are conducted for reports.

   a. (Accept any two of these responses.) Library research. In-company surveys. Opinion polls.

   b. Observational research (surveys). Experimental research with actual testing. Other?

8. What is the most helpful first step in solving any problem?

   Identify or define the problem.

9. Give the seven steps to follow in seeking solutions to problems.

   a. [See pages 350–351.]

   b. _____

   c. _____

   d. _____

   e. _____

   f. _____

   g. _____

10. Why should you always keep in mind the people who will use the report?

 Helps determine information to include and detail needed. Helps determine

 physical aspects: type of reproduction, paper, cover, limitation of cost and so forth.

11. When a problem is so large it seems almost unsolvable, what is a good method to follow for its solution?

 Break it down into small parts.

12. What is a common error that students make in choosing a topic for reports they are preparing?

 They want to choose a topic that is much too large for the assignment.

13. What are the criteria for determining the amount of time and money that can be spent on preparing a report?

 Interest in study and value of study.

14. As a rule of thumb, references used in writing a business report generally should not be more than __5__ years old.

15. Name three sources of information for researching a business report.

 a. Periodicals

 b. Reference works

 c. Books in stacks

16. Under what three categories are nonfiction books in the library stacks catalogued?

 Author, title, subject

17. Colleges and government agencies are increasingly beginning to classify materials under the Library of Congress system. Why? Makes it possible to borrow

 from other member libraries.

18. Identify the information that should be included on a card or other note that will be used as reference in writing a report.

 Key word or phrase that identifies subject matter of card. Full name or identity

 of source. Full name of author. Library call number. Date of publication, publisher,

 place of publication, page number. Pertinent information from this source.

19. Under the *fair use* provisions of current copyright laws, we are permitted to copy printed materials for use during research and for educational purposes, providing this use is noncommercial and does not deprive copyright owner of money.

16

Writing a Business Report or a Term Paper

Writing a Business Contract Proposal

At a pub in Dublin known as a haunt of the late Irish poet, Brendan Behan, men around the bar were discussing the talent of writing. One "wee lad of 60," Jocko, concluded: "Ah, now. You know it's not the writin' down. It's the assembly."

What do you do when all you have is a jumble of ideas, plus a handful of notes that must be enlarged into a complete, understandable report?

When Writing Comes Hard

If you are like most people, writing your first business report or term paper comes hard. Just keep in mind that the purpose of writing the report or paper is to set out ideas clearly so that readers can easily understand what you have written. Also, recognize that good organization simplifies the entire process.

So how do you organize? Following ideas set out in the preceding chapter, take these steps:

First: Define the Problem or Make a Statement of the Purpose

Certainly, the first step in solving any problem is to define the problem. Odd as it may seem, both in our personal lives and in our careers, we waste much time and effort trying to solve a problem when we have not actually faced up to what the problem is. So it bears repeating: *The first step in solving any problem is to define the problem.*

Many reports are written not to solve a problem, but to set out facts or ideas. If your report is of this nature, *make a statement of the purpose of the report.*

Summarize that problem or statement in as few words as possible, so that it is clear and you can readily recall it to mind. Everything that appears in the report should be pertinent to this announced problem or purpose. As you do your research, you may constantly need to ask yourself, "Does this relate to my basic problem (purpose)?"

Second: Gather Research Materials

As you gather research materials, make sure you have cards, notes, papers, clippings or other backup on everything you have learned on the subject. Written with each have all bibliographical data you may need. While you were doing research, these notes should have been put on your computer or on cards or pieces of paper. Don't be concerned yet about good grammar, complete sentences, neatness and so forth. You may or may not use everything you have gathered. (File it away for another project?)

Keep a folder or file box where you can collect all the notes or other relevant material over a period of time. If you are working with a computer, be sure to regularly back up your files and make a hard copy to file in the box.

Third: Start with a Random List of Items or Ideas to be Included in the Report

As was said by the self-proclaimed critic in the quotation that introduces this chapter, ". . . it's not the writin' down. It's the assembly."

From your list of report items, assemble the first random list of notes for your Table of Contents. Then, arrange the random list items in logical order. Subheads and sub-subheads can be listed under these main heads. Remember: Your list is not cast in concrete. As your work continues, you might adjust and change it, adding, deleting, and altering its order. Writing down this first phase Table of Contents with major divisions and subdivisions gives you a skeleton that you can flesh out as you complete your research. Also, your report may change as you get information on the ideas you first had in mind. These major report divisions with their subheadings will eventually be the heading and subheadings of the Table of Contents at the beginning of the report. The headings let readers quickly scan the contents of the report and find specific parts.

Fourth: As You Work, Tag Research Material to Match Contents Headings

If you haven't done it already, you are now ready to put the random list of Items into a List in Order. This becomes the TOC, the pattern for the report.

List of Items In Random Order —>	List of Items In Order —>	Table of Contents
1 _____	1 _____	1
4 _____	2 _____	2
2 _____	3 _____	3
3 _____	4 _____	4
5 _____	5 _____	5
7 _____	6 _____	6
8 _____	7 _____	7
6 _____	8 _____	8

Order of Presentation

Choose a logical order of presentation of material. Because the purpose of preparing the report is to have material that will be read and understood by other people, one step should lead to the next and then on to the next. Select a method of presentation that will set out your major points and conclusions best, such as one of the following:

The Inductive Problem Solving Technique

This method is sometimes called the scientific "parts to whole" method. All positions relating to the problem—pro and con positions or arguments—are clearly identified. Then all these "parts" or positions are evaluated, even those that initially seem least appealing.

At this point of making important decisions, a **free-wheeling unrestrained discussion** by people involved (sometimes called "brainstorming," "bull session," or "toro ballistics") should bring forth the best solution. During these sessions, members are free to toss in any ideas, even seemingly lunatic ones. All options are considered in making a decision about the "whole," the problem.

In using any method, some members may learn that a position they have previously held must be scrapped because evidence proved the earlier position invalid. (Exception: When the dissenter signs everyone's paycheck.)[1]

The Deductive Problem Solving Technique

This technique can be called the "whole to parts" method. An answer (the whole) is agreed upon and then all positions that support that conclusion are considered and stated. Potential arguments against the agreed-upon decision are ignored. This might be called the nonscientific method of decision making. Unfortunately, costly business, industry, government and personal life problems are sometimes "solved" by this deductive problem solving technique.

Cause → Effect

Many reports are written in the cause → effect style: As a result of this, this, and this, the following happened (or may happen).

Chronological Order

This type of report is common and is easiest to organize but is of course not appropriate to all studies. Matters are related in the order of occurrence.

Geographical Order

Geographical order reports state matters by areas or regions, such as showing activities of various branches of a firm. As much as possible, all matters reported from each area should be given in similar order making them easier to find and compare.

---

[1]Before Henry Ford's time, all cars were basically custom built. Ford was the first to effectively use the assembly line for manufacturing cars. All Ford cars were similar and sold at a low price, making them available to the average person. After much success, executives asked for a meeting to discuss making cars of different colors to satisfy their customers. Ford's reply, which held because he owned the company: "People can have any color they want, as long as it's black."

Fifth: Identify Your Readers and Write to That Level

Decide how much detail you must include to serve your readers properly.

Sixth: As You Work, Check and Change the Order of Your List as You Wish

Now, take a good look at your list. Have you kept your reader or readers in mind so that the report will be understood from the viewpoint of your audience? Is it set out in a sensible order that will lead a reader logically from one idea to another throughout the entire report?

You can use numbers and/or letters to label parts of the report contents. These symbols show the relation of parts of a report to each other and show when you have covered one section or subsection and are going into another.

Preparing the "Random List —> List in Order —> Table of Contents"gives you a useful pattern to follow, which simplifies your writing. Also you now have a necessary item, the Table of Contents, ready for its place in the front matter of your report.

Seventh: As You Work, Label Your Research Papers

Label your research cards and notes with tag lines that match major headings. Then stack your cards and notes according to their corresponding position in your report. At this point, you will probably add or delete some headings or subheadings to follow your research discoveries.

On a computer, access research note section and make changes.

Make a Rough Draft of the Report

Now, referring to your list of main heads and your research papers, start to write your report.

Never submit the first draft as a final copy. Always prepare a **rough draft** of the entire report. Don't feel that you are exhibiting amateurism because you make a first "practice" copy. Far from it. Harry Shaw was an internationally known editor and author of respected books on writing. He also taught writing classes at both New York and Columbia universities. Shaw said, "There is no such thing as good writing. There is only good rewriting."

Shaw says further that those who are unwilling to revise and rewrite are skipping a major step in becoming better writers. He recites the experiences of other professional writers:

William Faulkner on his novel, *The Sound and the Fury*: "I wrote it five times."

Thornton Wilder, dramatist and novelist: "There are passages in every novel whose first writing is the last. But it's the joint and cement between those passages that take a great deal of rewriting."

Frank O'Connor, short story writer, when asked about rewriting, said that he did so "endlessly, endlessly, endlessly."

James Thurber, asked if the act of writing was easy for him: "It's mostly a question of rewriting. It's part of a constant attempt to make the finished version smooth, to make it seem effortless." He told of having rewritten one story 15 times.[2]

Before writing your first draft, however, read through the rest of this section.

Open-Minded Attitude

If there is a controversial aspect in your report, keep an open-minded attitude, and recognize that there may be some biases or pet theories relating to certain studies. To conduct valid research, report theories that are supported by facts. If opinions or biases are given, they should be shown as such and should not be given the weight of being factual. Otherwise, an entire study loses credibility—the parts that are valid as well as those that are not. Such research reporting is considered unprofessional and should not be done.

If you hide facts or problems in trying to prove your point, most readers will become suspicious of your one-sidedness. Instead, deal gracefully and intelligently with opposing viewpoints. You will strike your readers as being fair-minded, ethical and balanced, giving credibility to your report.

When people are not open-minded about problem solutions, they sometimes solve a problem somewhat related to the matter at hand, while ignoring the true problem. This can happen in studies related to our personal lives, as well as studies related to our careers or college work.

Reporting Opinions

Opinions from authoritative sources are valuable in research. As for including your own opinion, anyone seriously interested in writing should study Strunk and White's *The Elements of Style*. In this classic authority still revered by today's writers, we are told:

> Unless there is good reason for its being there, do not inject [your own] opinion into a piece of writing. We all have opinions about almost everything, and the temptation to toss them in is great. To air one's views gratuitously, however, is to imply that the demand for them is brisk ...[3]

Relevance vs. Irrelevance

You may find a great deal of material that seems interesting but is not relevant to the study. To determine whether or not this material should be reported, go back to the original statement of purpose, and decide whether or not this information is relevant to that purpose. Even if the material is extremely interesting, leave it out if it is not pertinent. You might, of course, take notes for use at another time or place or make a copy of it for your file. If material is quasi-relevant to the topic at hand and

---

[2]Harry Shaw, *20 Steps to Better Writing* (Totowa, NJ: Littlefield, Adams & Co., 1978), pp. 124ff.

[3]William Strunk, Jr., and E. B. White, *The Elements of Style*, 3rd ed. (New York: Macmillan, 1979), p. 80.

if it warrants such treatment, you might consider making a footnote reference to it. (See footnote reference to Henry Ford on page 365.)

Plagiarism

In Chapter 15, you were reminded that it is legal and ethical for you to copy written material while doing research if you are not copying so much that you are preventing the sale of a copy of the original work. When you report information found in other sources, copy it verbatim or paraphrase the writing of others. That is, state the information in your own words and show where you got it.

Do not appropriate the writing of another person and try to pass it off as your own. To quote another person without giving credit is to plagiarize. There are laws against plagiarism—that is, quoting other writers without giving credit. For term papers and most business reports, you may quote others without getting their permission, but you should give them credit in some way, either in the context of the report or in a footnote. If material is to be circulated widely, such as in a periodical or book, permission to quote lengthy material must be sought and granted.

Copying the work of another and pretending it is your own is not only unlawful; it is unethical and damages the reputation of the writer. Further, readers of your material may be quite knowledgeable and may actually recognize the writing as coming from another source. Writing styles do vary. It may be jarring to the reader to go from a student's writing style to the style of a different person—a person who may be a recognized authority in a given field. Your own writing may be quite authoritative, but keep it in your own words. Short quotes should be within quotation marks; lengthy ones should be indented as extracts.

Tone

Writing Up and Writing Down

Avoid writing up or writing down to your reader. Keeping your audience in mind, make your report understandable and logical. If technical terms must be used, explain them without belittling those who are trying to understand them. How much you must explain is determined by the level of understanding of your readers.

Improve your vocabulary in order to have grasp of the appropriate terms in your field. However, choose a long word only if a short word will not do. After all, the best writing in any field is made up of short, easily understood words, using longer terms only when necessary.

Charles T. Brusaw, a recognized authority on business writing, says:

> In business writing, tone can be especially important; just as it can help you gain your reader's sympathy, so it can rub him or her the wrong way. When you write you must always consider your objective; in addition, you must then maintain an appropriate tone....
>
> The tone used in reports should normally be objective and impersonal.... The important thing is to make sure that your tone is the one best suited to your objective. To make sure that it is, always keep your reader in mind.[4]

---

[4]Charles T. Brusaw and others, *The Business Writer's Handbook,* 2nd ed. (New York: St. Martin's Press, 1982), pp. 559–60.

Definitions

Define all terms that may not be understandable to readers of the report. A new term should be defined the first time it is used. If you use a number of new terms, you might have an alphabetized glossary at the end of the report where definitions are repeated.

Formal vs. Informal Tone

Business today is often adopting an informal tone in reports by the use of first- and second-person form, saying, "We found that ...," or "You will note ..." With business's growing interest in better direct communications, you can see why the less formal conversational tone is the trend in business report writing.

However, formal business reports are written in the impersonal, third-person form. In other words, formal reports do not use *I, me, my, we, our, you, your, yours.* Instead of saying, "We found that ...," the report would read, "Our study found that ..." Looking at a few formal business reports will show how effective and easy this writing style is.

The "Breezy" Writing Tone

In business communications, do not use the breezy writing style that you frequently find in bulletins and newsletters distributed among people who are well acquainted. The tone of such writing may be appreciated and accepted within some small groups, but this style can be deadly in business writing.

This is the type of stream-of-consciousness writing that you should avoid altogether in business writing:

> Well, buddies, isn't it about time you heard from your reckless, feckless reporter? That's me—good ol' Dan. And here are some fresh grapes right off the vine (grapevine, get it???).
>
> If you didn't get to our annual Fall roundup, let me tell you, you really missed a bash! 'Frisco never looked better—the Cannery, Pier 39, Golden Gate. To name a few!
>
> Grant M. showed off his latest—car, that is. And Roxie L. kept button-holing everybody (including yours truly) to give endless details about her latest tour....

Sexism in Writing

Prentice Hall, Inc., gives its authors the following advice on avoiding sexism in writing:

In your writing, be certain to treat men and women impersonally in regard to occupation, marital status, physical abilities, attitudes, interests, and so on. Depending on the requirements of your subject, avoid attributing particular characteristics to either sex; instead, let your writing convey that one's abilities and achievements are not limited by gender. Your text should support the fact that both sexes play equally important roles in all facets of life and that activities on all levels are open to both women and men alike.

The preceding guidelines on sexism should also be followed by writers of business reports and term papers.

Tense

Do not slip from present to past tense in writing the report. Some writers favor using past tense, such as, "This survey *revealed* that ..." But use of the present tense throughout the report might make the information seem more alive and current: "This study *reveals* that ..." Whichever form is selected, be consistent. Repeatedly changing from past to present and back to past is not only poor writing form, it can be disconcerting to the reader and could detract from the clarity of the report.

Sentence Length

In their manual for training consultants how to write reports clearly, a national business consulting firm strongly recommends short sentences. They suggest that "getting stuck" in the middle of a sentence probably means you have too many ideas in it. The solution: Break it down into two, three, or four sentences; however, don't make the sentences so consistently short that they sound childish or choppy. Their recommended average sentence length: 15 to 20 words.

Readability of Written Material: The Fog Index

Many studies have been made on readability of written material, and there are various yardsticks for judging this quality. One of the most reliable and simplest to use is the Fog Index, originated by Robert Gunning. (*Fog* in this use refers simply to lack of clarity.) Gunning has earned high fees from business and government to edit material before publication to make it more readable. Among his clients are *The Wall Street Journal*, General Motors, du Pont, and Standard Oil of New Jersey.

The Fog Index is based on the premise that short words and short sentences result in clear writing. This index number is determined from sentence length and count of long words, and it includes a factor enabling this number to represent the number of years of schooling needed to readily understand the written material. Thus, the higher the Fog Index number, the more difficult the material is to understand.

Even for exceptionally well educated people, "foggy" writing is slow reading. Many reports and letters sit unread on desks of business, technology, and professional people. Their potential readers know that in their own fields the readability index of written material is generally too high. The writers are trying to impress their peers with long words and long sentences. But their peers know those stacked unread papers would probably be slow reading and therefore are not inviting to those well educated, busy people.

Readability studies show that written material with a Fog Index level above 10 or 11 is difficult to understand and is extremely slow reading even for those with college and advanced degrees. Writing authorities recommend that all writers, including business writers, seek to write at a level no higher than 10.

The Fog Index level of writing is determined by first finding the length of the average sentence in a selected piece of writing and the percentage of difficult words in that segment. From these two figures, the index is determined in this manner:

1. Select a representative sample of the writing. Count 100 words, ending with the complete sentence that is nearest the 100 count.
   Example: Selected sample contains: 103 words
   Find the average number of words in a sentence by dividing the number of words in the sample by the number of sentences.

Count each independent clause as a sentence. *"We came. We saw. We conquered"* would be counted as three sentences whether these clauses were separated by periods, semi-colons, or commas.

Example: There are 5 sentences in the sample:

$103 \div 5 =$ Average length of sentence   20.6

2. Find the number of difficult words in the sample this way: *Of the first 100 words in the sample,* count the words that have three or more syllables. Do not count:
   - Capitalized words.
   - Words that make their third syllable by combining two words, such as *typewriter* or *underlying.*
   - Verbs that form the third syllable by adding *es* or *ed.*

   Example: Number of difficult words: 5

3. Take the figure that represents the average sentence length: 20.6
   Take the figure that represents the number of difficult words: + 5

   Add these two figures: 25.6

4. Multiply that sum by .4 (In the answer, disregard figures after the decimal).

   $\times \ .4$

   10.24

5. FOG INDEX   10

In order to understand easily the sample of writing studied in this example, the reader would have to have completed at least 10 years of schooling. Reviewing the works of the best writers in the English language will prove that our best writing is around or below the level of ten. Ernest Hemingway said he went to the King James version of the Bible for his instructions in clarity of writing. Here are Fog Index studies from this edition of the Bible, from Hemingway, and from other outstanding writers:

King James Bible	
23rd Psalm	5
Ten Commandments	9
Ernest Hemingway	
Farewell to Arms, first page	10
Old Man and the Sea, selection	3
Lincoln's Gettysburg Address	10
Winston Churchill speeches	
"Blood, sweat, and tears …"	11
"Give us the tools and we will finish the job …"	5
John Feinstein	
A Good Walk Spoiled: Days and Nights on the PGA Tour,	9
Average of random selections	7.75

Graphics and Visuals

> *I hear and I forget.*
> *I see and I remember.*
>   *Confucious*

On the theory that a picture is worth a thousand words, graphics, or illustrations of every kind are used in business reports. Although information dealing with figures

FIGURE 16.1
Examples of line graph, pie chart and bar graph.

Index of
Business Activity (1977 = 100)

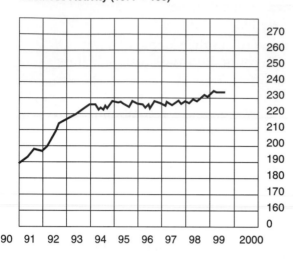

Line Chart

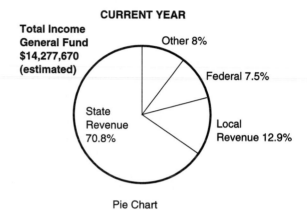

Pie Chart

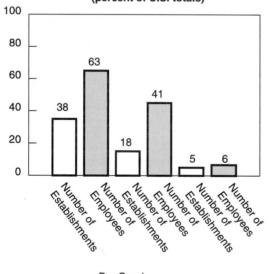

Bar Graph

could be simply set out in paragraph form, for instance, these figures are usually clearer if set out in a table, a chart, or in a bar or line graph. Maps, photographs, and drawings are also used when applicable.

Graphics should not be set out alone in the report. Before each illustration is given, it should be introduced with a summary of its contents. Figure 16.1 shows a line graph, a pie chart (generally used for percentage figures), and a bar graph.

Today with electronics unbelievably eye-catching graphics can be prepared.

Documentation: Footnotes

To give credit to those whose ideas are being used and to document authority for statements made, footnotes and bibliographies are included as part of a report. Documentation—supplying supporting evidence for what you are saying—is also useful to those who may wish to read further on the subject and would appreciate seeing additional sources.

Footnotes can be placed within a report or at the end of sections; a bibliography is placed at the end of the finished report.

For classroom reports and many business reports, footnotes are usually placed at the bottom of the page on which the reference is made. Technical papers sometimes include footnote documentation within the written material of the report, in brackets at the end of the sentence containing the reference. Longer texts sometimes list all the footnote data in a separate section at the end of the book or report.

A reference number is shown as a superior number at the end of the material that pertains to the footnote. Then the same superior number introduces the footnote.

Footnote references can be shown in different manners, but the ones shown here are clear, complete, and acceptable for most purposes.

In a footnote references to a book show the items in this order; (1) name of author(s) or editor(s) as shown on the title page, with the first name first (if there are more than two authors, list "and others"); (2) title of book, underlined or printed in italics; (3) edition, if other than the first; (4) city of publication; (5) name of publisher as it appears on the title page; (6) date of publication; (7) and page number(s)—"p." for one or for more than one page. Punctuation should be as shown.

Following is an example of a footnote copied from page 368.

[4]Charles T. Brusaw and others, *The Business Writer's Handbook*, 2nd ed. (New York: St. Martin's Press, 1982), pp. 559–60.

In a footnote reference to a magazine, newspaper, newsletter, or any other periodical, items can be shown in this manner: (1) author, if shown; (2) title of article, within quotation marks; (3) title of periodical, underlined or printed in italics; (4) date of publication; (5) page number(s). Following is an example of a footnote for a magazine article:

[1]Carrie Gottlieb, "Technology to Watch," *Fortune*, March 20, 1995, p. 34–36.

Later parts of this chapter show how to make up a bibliography.

Revising Your Rough Draft

After the first draft of your report is completed, set it aside for a while, if possible, to let it cool off so you can come back to it totally fresh. Now is the time to check meticulously for grammar, spelling, and punctuation. Then reread it, checking closely that it follows the table of contents. If the report does not follow along in a logical order, change the report or change the table of contents. This helps make sure that the report tells what you want it to tell and that your ideas proceed logically from one to another. You will also find it helpful at this point to have someone whose opinion you respect read it for form and content.

Compiling the Complete Report

After carefully proofreading and correcting the body of your report, you are ready to set up the complete report with title page, table of contents, and so forth.

From the proper authorities, specific instructions can be obtained for setting up the typing, printing, and binding of a business report. A term paper should be typed double spaced with paragraphs indented. If paragraphs are not indented, make a triple space (two blank lines) between paragraphs.

Major Parts of the Report

The major parts of a business report are the cover, the title page, table of contents, introduction and summary, body of the report, bibliography, and report cover. Figure 16.2 is an example of a title page of a report; Figure 16.3 is a sample table of contents; Figure 16.4 is a sample first page. Following are details of the preparation of each part of the report.

Report Cover

The cover can be an extremely important part of the report and, for business, should be prepared according to the value of the material inside. For some classroom assignments, no special report cover is required; for others, a special cover is requested. In business, much care and expense are spent in preparation of report covers to identify the report both for future use and for the detailed piece of work that it is. Report covers may be printed and/or embossed, with two- or four-color illustrations. They should be designed to withstand wear.

Title Page

The title page should be an attractive introduction. Items should be well spaced and well balanced for good visual effect. Information on the title page should include the title, person(s) or firm that authorized it, name of the person or persons who prepared it, and date of submission. Other information might be included according to the specific nature of the report. For a classroom assignment, the name of the class for which the report was prepared should be shown.

Table of Contents

As stated previously, the final table of contents should be prepared after the entire report has been written, because some adjustments may have been made as writing progressed. You may add some sections, combine sections, delete sections, or change their order. But the major purpose of the report must be kept uppermost in mind in making any changes, and only those that improve the original form should be made.

FIGURE 16.2
Title page of a report.

COMMUNICATIONS:
BARRIERS AND BRIDGES

Presented to

Ralph E. Bristol

Associate Professor

Rio Hondo College

Submitted by

Gregory H. Walker

May 4, 20XX

Business Communications
MWF 9:00

Introduction and Summary

The person who receives your report wants to know immediately its main message and the specific parts that are of most interest to that person. The **introduction-summary,** which is the first part of the report, must give this information. It should explain what the report is about and summarize it, giving the purpose and major findings. From this, some readers may see that they need to read the entire report; others may find that they will need to read only specific sections.

Sometimes, business firms ask for a **synopsis** of a report, and the introduction-summary can be used as the report synopsis. In other instances, a detailed **letter of transmittal** may be the first part of the report, and this letter may contain the essen-

FIGURE 16.3
A sample of table of contents page for a report.

TABLE OF CONTENTS

tials of the introduction-summary. If a synopsis or a detailed letter of transmittal containing major information introduces the report, it is not necessary to set out this basic information again in summarized form at the beginning of the report. You can then proceed directly to the next major section, the body of the report.

Most business reports are set out as presented in the foregoing paragraphs—that is, with some type of introduction-summary first, followed by details or the body of the report. Two other popular formats are these:

1. Introduction; body of report (details); summary
2. Introduction-summary; series of findings and recommendations

FIGURE 16.4
An example of the first page of a report.

INTRODUCTION

<u>What is communication</u>?
Communication, it has been said, is not a chapter in the book of
management; it is the whole book. The ability to communicate effectively
is regarded as an essential skill for integrating the company.

Communication is the transmission and interchange of facts, ideas,
feelings, and courses of action. Mental or emotional concepts are
conveyed by means of symbols from one person to another, each being
compelled to think in terms of who says what, to whom, how, and with
what effect. Good communication is the result of clear thinking.

A system of communication developed and maintained in a company
should keep employees informed. Management can build attitudes.

Findings and Recommendations Report

Figure 16.5 is an example of another type of report made by a management consultant. This report shows findings and recommendations.

The Body of the Report

The rough draft of your report, which was covered in an earlier section of this chapter, is, of course, the body of your report. After preparing the front matter of the report, set out this, the body, always beginning on a new page. Figure 16.4 shows a typical first page for a report. The copy should begin at least two inches from the top of the page; frequently it starts in the middle of the page, as the example shows. (This leaves room for late brief revisions of the early part of the report.)

FIGURE 16.5
Sample page of findings and recommendations report format.

FINDINGS

It is essential to security of your computer that backup disks be
maintained in a separate location. In reviewing your procedures, Mr.
Steele reported that backup disks are being stored in the main vault and
that backup documentation is also on file. This procedure is to be
recommended; however, the surest approach is to allow no one
employee access to both off-site and on-site files.

RECOMMENDATIONS

It is recommended that the duplicates being maintained by you be
retained in the vault of the State Street Branch, rather than remaining on
the premises. This would make certain that a serious catastrophe would
not destroy both current copies and backup copies. It would also remove
the possibility that one employee could destroy all copies.

FINDINGS

At the present time you have no formal contract arrangement with an
outside firm to supply hardware (computer) backup in case of a serious
breakdown.

RECOMMENDATIONS

Under the circumstances, it is recommended that the manager of your
computer facility continue to make inquiries to insure that backup
computer hardware would be available to you in the event of an
extended breakdown.

Documentation: Bibliography

The bibliography is a list of all materials used for reference in the report. It contains essentially the same information for each entry as is contained in the footnote, except that the last name of the author is listed before the first name or initials (for alphabetical listing), and page numbers are not listed. Bibliography entries are listed alphabetically by the name of the author. When there is more than one author for an entry, the authors after the first one are listed with first name or initials preceding last name. If no author's name is shown, the entry is listed alphabetically by the title. (See the second entry following.)

For longer bibliographies, entries can be separated under headings like *Books, Periodicals, Government Documents*, and *Unpublished Works*. For a shorter bibliography, all entries can be included alphabetically in one listing.

Interviews, Print Bibliography. Following is an example of a print bibliography that includes books, periodicals, a government pamphlet. The hanging indent paragraph form used here is recommended for bibliographies, because the alphabetical headings can be located most easily.

Burchfield, R.W., Editor. *New Fowler's Modern English Usage* 3rd Edition. Oxford: Oxford University Press, 1996.

Designing Letter Mail, Publication 25, August 1995. United States Postal Service.

Gates, Bill. "Everyone, anytime, anywhere. The next step is universal access." *ASAP Forbes,* October 4, 1999.

Jones, Scott L. "A Guide to Using Color Effectively in Business Communications," *Business Communication Quarterly,* New York, NY, June, 1997.

Peters, Tom. "Please...I just need some quiet time." *ASAP Forbes,* October 4, 1999.

Webster's New World College Dictionary, 3rd Edition. New York: Simon & Schuster Macmillan Company, New York, NY, 1997.

Zinsser, William Knowlton. *On Writing Well,* 6th Edition. Harper Collins Publishers, New York, NY, 1998.

Interview Bibliography. A citation for a personal interview should show the name of the person interviewed, last name first; the type of interview (personal or telephone) and date:

Barrett, John C. Personal interview. August 14, 1999.

Personal interviews can be listed alphabetically with other sources. Or, if there are several interviews, all interviews can be set out together alphabetically under the heading "Interviews."

Minor Parts of the Report

Minor parts not always included in a report are a list of illustrations, a letter of transmittal, miscellaneous items that might be placed in an appendix at the end, a glossary of terms, and an index.

List of Illustrations, Charts, or Graphs

A separate list of illustrations, charts, or graphs is included if several of these items are in the report. This list would immediately follow the table of contents.

Letter of Transmittal

A short letter of transmittal might be part of any report, even one prepared for credit as a classroom assignment, and would usually follow the table of contents or the list of illustrations, if there is one. The message of this letter is basically, "Here is the report I prepared." It might read:

Dear Dr. Albanese:

Here is the report I prepared as partial fulfillment of requirements for Introduction to Business, Spring 20XX.

I found the work very interesting, particularly charting the progress of my selected stocks.

Respectfully submitted,

Appendix

Most short reports do not have appendixes, but this section can hold detailed information considered useful but not essential to the basic study. Here you would include a copy of a questionnaire used for a survey, or the full text of some materials that have been only highlighted in the report. In the body of the report, reference must be made to the fact that this information can be found in the appendix.

For example, for study and reference, this book contains the following materials as appendix items:

Appendix A: Spelling Rules and Spelling Lists
Appendix B: Punctuation

Glossary of Terms

A glossary, if there is one, comes at the end of the study right before the index. If only a few technical terms are used in the report, instead of having a glossary, the terms can be defined within the text of the report itself or with occasional footnotes. If there are many terms that will not be easily understood by readers, they can all be defined in an alphabetized glossary.

Index

In an extremely long, detailed report, an alphabetical index might be prepared to assist readers in locating specific information. If there is an index, it is at the end of the report.

Order of Major and Minor Report Parts

For a long report, major and minor parts would be included in the following order:

1. Title page
2. Table of contents
3. Table of illustrations, charts, graphs
4. Letter of transmittal
5. Introduction-summary
6. Body of report
7. Bibliography
8. Appendix
9. Glossary of terms
10. Index

Desktop Publishing

Desktop publishing is in every phase of business communication. This type of publishing is called "desktop" because the computer equipment used can fit on the average desk. Printed material produced will appear the same as if it had been sent out to a print shop.

With the proper combination of software package, computer and printer, professional printing can be produced within any office. Besides other work, your computer can produce forms, letterheads, and one-page brochures as well as major reports and proposals. Printing costs are reduced enormously. For example, a report that formerly cost $3,000 would cost about $300 produced in-house with desktop equipment.

Also, saving time can be important. A project that might previously have taken two weeks when farmed out to a printer can be completed within three or four days.

With your own desktop publishing you can

- choose varying layouts of pages with columns of different widths.
- combine different font sizes and styles for text, headlines, etc.
- choose even or uneven right margins, or have certain sections even and other sections uneven.
- make layouts for master pages so that an overall style can be set automatically for all pages throughout a publication.
- edit the text during preparation.
- have on one page any combination of text, photos, diagrams or other graphics with explanatory text set in any type style. This information can be placed in any position on or near illustrations.
- use all combinations of two colors or the four basic colors (black, red, blue, yellow), to produce any tint for text or illustrations. They can be printed on any type of paper from inexpensive newsprint to more expensive glossy paper like that in many of the better magazines.
- save any page format for future use on other papers.

Competition for the widening desktop publishing market is heavy, and considerable study must be made in your selection of software. Decisions must be made about capabilities, adaptability, cost and ease of mastering software of any new machines purchased.

As in any other field, desktop publishing (DTP) brings us new terms and new usages of old terms. Printers have used some of these terms for centuries. With print shop work coming into offices, office workers will benefit from learning and using the time saving helpful old and new.

WRITING A BUSINESS CONTRACT PROPOSAL

Because of the complexity and high cost of many work projects today, detailed written bid proposals are required for selling many products and services. Businesses, industries, government, and individual buyers are demanding that these proposals be written specifically according to their requirements.

There are two types of bid proposals, *unsolicited* and *solicited.*

Unsolicited Proposals

Unsolicited proposals can be handled like *sales letters* (Chapter 7) because you are trying to sell your product or service. According to the nature of what you are proposing, your presentation can be in the form of a detailed letter or a letter with various enclosures that give fuller information.

Enclosures can be photographs, charts, graphs, and so forth. Bold or soft color can be very effective when appropriate. If your proposal involves something that could be helped by including a sample (like selling an artificial grass installation), include the sample. "Hands on" experience can be effective in promoting sales.

The chief aims of your unsolicited proposals are (1) to get their *attention* (2) build up their *interest* in your proposed work and their *desire* to discuss it with you and (3) move them to *action,* that is, to get them to contact you.

If you do not receive a response, phoning or visiting the office could give you an opportunity to discuss the matter personally.

Solicited Proposals

Large organizations (and often smaller ones) will usually initiate **solicited proposals** by issuing a **request for proposal** (RFP). An RFP asks for bids from contractors for each project or each phase of a large project. Commercial, industrial, government and other big customers usually do not do their own research. Instead, they rely on bidders to be knowledgeable about fulfilling their needs for specific types of products and services.

Contracts—Highly Competitive

Contracts obtained by successfully responding to such requests for proposals are almost always highly competitive with eyes on the bottom line, the cost. Therefore, *the proposal you prepare must show how you can satisfy their needs better than any competitor.*

The most important concern in writing a proposal is to follow all guidelines and regulations set out in the Request For Proposal (RFP) information kit available to bidders. Worthwhile proposals may be turned down if instructions are not followed to the letter.

Proposal Format

A proposal usually has five parts: heading, introduction, customer's needs, proposed plan, your qualifications. In making your proposal, copy the format of the RFP prepared by the specific organization, using the headings given there, and cover items in that order. Remember, this may be in a different order from a proposal you submitted for similar work for another organization. Check all numbers carefully.

Heading

Because a party might have several requests for proposals circulating, at the top of the first page clearly identify the proposal request you are answering, such as:

A PROPOSAL IN RESPONSE TO RFP #GB-4-1234
TO PLAN AND INSTALL SECURITY PROCEDURES
FOR SKYLINE COMPUTER SYSTEMS

Introduction

While the introduction is the first major part of your proposal, you will probably benefit from writing it after you have completed the other sections. In the introduction you get the customer's attention by promising to satisfy their specified needs; also, you set out additional effective work you can do to benefit them. You should include a summary background of key personnel who will be doing the work, emphasizing their strengths and experience. Further, promise that you or your representative will be available for any follow-up work on the project.

Proposal Content

Customer's Needs

Set out specifically from your own experience and observation what you see as the **customer's needs,** constantly referring to the RFP. Show that you have studied the situation thoroughly and understand how you can solve their problems. Tell of possible future problems related to the matter at hand and how to avoid or correct them. Avoid any discouraging attitude, but approach the work positively, displaying confidence. Showing that you have studied beyond specifications in the proposal will help give the customer the assurance that is wanted. It will also probably put you ahead of some competitors who do not include this factor.

Proposed Plan

The **proposed plan** is the heart of your proposal and this is the place to spend most of your time and talent. In your first drafts, set out the plan that you believe from the beginning to be most logical. Then, set out alternate plans that might be considered by you or your competitors. After studying all possible options, you are ready to choose solutions to make the plan you will offer.

Following the format of the RFP, set out by number exactly how you propose to complete the project. Numbering items helps make discussions with you, your workers and the customers clear.

Set up a reasonable time frame with a schedule for completing each phase of the operation. In stating the time expected for completion of the project, make clear whether it will be calendar days or working days. If your expected time varies from the time projected in the RFP, give clear reasons for the difference. It is best to schedule the number of working days needed for completion of each phase. Uncontrollable factors may cause work interruptions, such as weather or natural disasters that might delay shipments of needed goods or might otherwise delay completion of work. Also, the customer might postpone inspection time, and you will be protected by saying how many *working days* will be needed for completion of each phase.

Your Qualifications

Here you show **your qualifications** that make your firm a better choice than your competitors.

Describe the *type of work your firm performs and your facilities*. If you will need to add to your present capacity, tell how it can be done efficiently and effectively. Show that you have thought through all possible developments. Name past and current projects of your firm so the customer can actually check your work, giving names, addresses and phone numbers of references.

Also, it is important that you *identify and give background experience of key personnel* who will be in charge of the project. Give as much detail as might be helpful. *Make this an individual presentation for this customer, not a standard list that can be added to any proposal.*

Copies of letters of appreciation from satisfied customers who have given permission to be references can be strong persuaders.

Summary

Make the entire proposal as attractive as possible. Use the best in-house printing facilities or contract with outside printers to give it a professional appearance. Give special attention to the cover, possibly setting out in vivid color an important diagram or illustration taken from the report. You must catch the attention of the reviewers.

The actual presentation of your proposal should be done in the best possible manner. Hand carry it to the top executive if possible and try to get an interview at that time. If you must mail it, be sure to follow up with a telephone call and see that it has reached the correct destination. Many proposals have been lost because papers were misfiled or delivered to the wrong person.

If you have not received a response within a reasonable time, make one or more follow-up personal or telephone calls. Don't delay these calls too long or a competitor may get ahead of you. As you know, many contracts are group decisions made by people with several different demanding interests. Showing your active interest in getting the contract can jog the memory of a customer. Besides being a reminder that you are ready and eager to do the job, sometimes you are reminding them that a particular job has to be done.

Chapters 15 and 16   Writing a Business Report or a Term Paper: Writing a Business Contract Proposal

WRITING/ORAL ASSIGNMENTS

1. Write a library research report of approximately ten pages counting the title page, table of contents, etc. Complete the following steps:
   a. Select a topic of interest to you.
   b. Get topic approved.
   c. Conduct research in the library, on the internet, and through other reliable sources; also, possibly, interviews.
   d. Make a list of items in correct order for a table of contents order of presentation.
   e. Prepare a rough draft.
   f. Make a final copy of the report.
   The report should contain:
   a. Title page
   b. Table of contents
   c. Report proper
   d. Footnotes—at least three
   e. Graphics (optional)
   f. Bibliography (at least three entries)
   Suggested report topics:
   - A study of a career of interest to you.
   - A study of an organization for which you might like to work.
   - A study of some topic that has come up in class on which you think you would like to read further.
   - A study of some phase of the life of a successful person.

2. Prepare a shortened report format.* This report writing assignment will give experience in the mechanical aspects of report preparation with very limited report research and writing. To complete this assignment, select a topic that would be of interest to you if you were writing a report. (For suggestions, see assignment 1.) Then follow these steps:
   a. Prepare a title page of the report.
   b. Prepare a table of contents. This should mainly be fabricated and not necessarily what the table of contents would be if you actually wrote the report. Make it sound logical.
   c. Prepare the first page of the report. (It can be a half page.)
   d. From a magazine, take a copy of a selection of at least ten lines that might have been part of your report if you had written it in full. Paraphrase this selection— that is, write it in your own words. Turn in both copies as part of your minireport.
   e. Make a footnote reference for this material; also, make a footnote of a book reference and a government source.
   f. Make an alphabetized list of the footnotes in item *e* and prepare a bibliography of them. Use the hanging-indent style.

3. Give a five or ten minute oral summary of your report.

> *Thanks to Joan Teufel.

Chapter 16   Writing a Business Report or a Term Paper: Writing a Business Contract Proposal

REVIEW AND DISCUSSION

1. What is the first step in solving a problem?

   Identify what the problem is.

2. How can the report list be used for the completed report?

   It can be converted to a table of contents.

3. Name six different methods of setting out the major points of a report.

   a.   cause to effect

   b.   chronological order

   c.   inductive order

   d.   deductive order

   e.   geographical order

   f.   order of importance

4. Which order of presentation is considered scientific reporting?

   Inductive order, parts to whole, considers all possibilities before drawing conclusion.

5. Name the two most common forms of outlining materials.

   a.   Headings

   b.   Subheadings, sub-subheadings, etc.

6. Should you make a rough draft of any report? Explain. YES. It gives you an almost finished plan to follow—to add, subtract, alter.

7. Is it acceptable to give the writer's personal theories and prejudices in a report? Explain.
   Usually not unless it has been requested.
   Usually not unless writer is recognized authority in field.

8. How can you determine whether or not information you discover is relevant to your study and should be reported in it? Go back to statement of purpose and determine whether it is relevant to purpose. Identify the problem.

9. What is plagiarism? Appropriating the original work of another person and trying to pass it off as your own.

10. Business reports today are becoming (~~more~~/less) formal.

11. Is it proper to give definitions of terms in a business report? Explain.
    By all means, if needed to make them understandable to readers. If there are many,
    consider putting a glossary of terms at the end of the report.

12. Why should you be consistent in the use of verb tenses in writing a report?
    Inconsistent verb tense leads to bumpy writing and could detract from clarity of
    report.

13. Why are graphics used in reports?   _"A picture is worth a thousand words." Makes_
    report understandable, interesting.

14. Name two types of documentation that are often used in reports.
    a.   _Footnotes_
    b.   _Bibliography_

15. Give three uses for documentation.
    a.   _To give credit where credit is due._
    b.   _To show validity of statements._
    c.   _To aid readers who may want further study._

16. What information is included in a footnote citing a book reference?
    Name(s) of author(s) or editor(s), book title, place of publication, publisher, date of
    publication, page number.

17. What are the advantages of placing a summary at the beginning of a business report?
    To give today's busy reader a quick overview to decide which parts may be of
    interest to her or him or if all parts are of interest.

18. Why is the cover of a report important?   _First impression reader gets can indicate_
    value of report.

19. In writing a business contract proposal, what is an RFP and how is it used? _____
    Request for proposal is an announcement asking for bids from contractors._

20. Name two categories of information that should be included under "your qualifications" in a business contract proposal.   _Customer's needs. Proposed plan. Your_
    qualifications, including chief personnel who will work on project.

Appendix A
Spelling Rules and Spelling Lists

> *For instance, if you cause the reader to say, "Why he can't even spell," the even implies "So, of course, he can't be depended on to know anything else either."*
> J. H. Menning and C. W. Wilkinson
> Writing Business Letters
> *(Homewood, Ill.: Richard D. Irwin, Inc., 1971)*

Learning to Spell

Practice, practice, practice.

This is the best advice to follow if you wish to improve your spelling. As any text on business communication will tell you, in personal and career life you are often judged on how well you can spell. If you are not a good speller, you will certainly benefit from spending the time and effort needed to improve your spelling.

To improve your spelling, say and spell a problem word correctly; write it or type it ten times; look at the correctly spelled word and try to remember how it looks—commit it to visual memory. Above all, keep a dictionary handy for quick reference when you are not sure of the spelling of a word. Good software programs that check spelling are available for computer systems. (One woman executive tells that she is aware of her difficulty with spelling. However, she attributes part of her career success to carrying a small speller's dictionary in her purse or pocket.) Also, using spell checking computer software is a tremendous boost.

Most improved spelling is achieved by rote, memory—repetition, as just described. However, mastering a few basic spelling rules will help you with a high percentage of questionable spellings.

You may find the rules more helpful if you memorize the pattern of *one word* from each rule. Then apply the principle of spelling that word to the spelling of other words that fit the same pattern.

Phonetic Spelling

Most words are spelled phonetically. Say them slowly by syllable and spell them by sound.

Spelling Rules[1]

Rule 1: Adding a Prefix to a Basic Whole Word

Some long words can be broken into parts, leaving a basic whole word with a prefix. To spell such words correctly, simply add the prefix to the basic word.

book/keeping	re/affirm
co/axial	re/commend
dis/advantage	un/crowded
dis/satisfaction	retro/active
extra/ordinary	un/announced
fore/closure	un/known
fore/going	un/necessary
il/legal	un/noticed
inter/state	with/draw
mis/spell	with/held
mis/conduct	

Rule 2: Words with ie or ei: Remember the old ditty:

I before e, *except after* c,
Or when sounded like a,
As in neighbor and weigh.

This old rhyme will help you with many words that have the *ie* or *ei* combination. Remember, as the rhyme says, most words with one of these combinations are spelled *ie*, such as these few examples:

achieve	grievance
alien	hosiery
belief	lien
believable	mischief
chief	niece
client	piece
clientele	proprietor
convenience	relief
friend	vacancies

[1]From Phyllis Davis Hemphill, *Career English: Skill Development for Better Communication* (Englewood Cliffs, NJ: Prentice-Hall, Inc., 1980), p. 219ff.

Choose the far less common combination *ei*, generally "after *c*, or when sounded like *a*."

ceiling	chow mein
conceit	eight
conceive	freight
deceit	neighbor
deceive	sleigh
perceive	vein
receipt	weigh
receive	weight
beige	

Exceptions. Memorize these common words that are the chief exceptions to this rule:

either	neither
foreign	seize
height	their
leisure	weird

Some words have the *cie* combination as in *science*:

ancient	efficient
conscience	proficient
conscientious	science
deficient	scientific

Rule 3: Adding Suffix to a Word Ending with y Preceded by a Vowel

To add a suffix to a word ending with *y* preceded by a vowel (*a, e, i,o, u*), simply add the suffix to the base word without changing the *y*:

annoy	annoyed, annoying, annoys
attorney	attorneys
convey	conveyed, conveying, conveys
employ	employed, employee, employer, employing, employs
holiday	holidays
journey	journeyed, journeying, journeys
portray	portrayed, portraying, portrays
survey	surveyed, surveying, surveys
valley	valleys

Rule 4: Adding Suffix to a Word Ending with y Preceded by a Consonant

To add a suffix to a word ending with *y* preceded by a consonant, generally change the *y* to *i* before adding any suffix except *ing*. The only two common words in the English language with two consecutive *i's* are

Hawaii
skiing

accompany	accompanied, accompanies, accompanying
annuity	annuities
apply	applied, applies, application, applying
beneficiary	beneficiaries
busy	busily, business, busier, busiest
casualty	casualties
copy	copied, copier, copies, copying
dictionary	dictionaries
discrepancy	discrepancies
necessary	necessarily
opportunity	opportunities
quantity	quantities
satisfy	satisfied, satisfies, satisfying
satisfactory	satisfactorily
vacancy	vacancies

Rule 5: Adding Suffix Beginning with a Vowel (-ing, -ed, -en, -ance, -ally)

To add a suffix beginning with a vowel to a word that ends with a single consonant preceded by a single vowel: If the word is of one syllable, double the final consonant.

One Syllable

bag	baggage
drop	dropped
fit	fitted, fitting
get	getting
hop	hopped, hopping
plan	planned, planning, planner
stop	stopped, stopping
wrap	wrapped, wrapping

If the word is of more than one syllable and *the accent is on the last syllable* follow the same rule by doubling the final consonant.

Multisyllable

admit	ad•mit'tance, ad•mit'ted, ad•mit'ting
allot	al•lot'ted, al•lot'ting
begin	be•gin'ning
confer	con•ferred', con•fer'ring (con'fer•ence)
control	con•trolled', con•trol'ling
equip	e•quipped', e•quip'ping
infer	in•ferred', in•fer'ring (in'fer•ence)
occur	oc•curred', oc•cur'rence, oc•cur'ring
omit	o•mit'ted, o•mit'ting
recur	re•curred', re•cur'rence, re•cur'ring
refer	re•ferred', re•fer'ring (ref'er•ence)
remit	re•mit'tance, re•mit'ted, re•mit'ting
transfer	trans•ferred', trans•fer'ring

To add a suffix beginning with a vowel to a word ending with a single consonant preceded by a single vowel, do *not* double the final consonant *when the accent is not on the last syllable.*

confer	con'fer•ence
exhibit	ex•hib'it•ed, ex•hib'it•ing
infer	in'fer•ence
limit	lim'it•ed, lim'it•ing
profit	prof'it•able, prof'it•ed, prof'it•ing
refer	ref'er•ence

Exceptions[2]

cancel	cancelled or canceled, cancelling or canceling
equal	equalled or equaled, equalling or equaling
travel	travelled or traveled, travelling or traveling

Rule 6: Adding Suffix to a Word That Ends with a Silent *e*

To add a suffix to a word that ends with a silent *e*, keep the *e* if the suffix begins with a consonant.

achieve/ment	hope/ful
approximate/ly	immediate/ly

[2] Word study shows that these words were misspelled so often that dictionaries eventually accepted both spellings.

comparative/ly	love/ly
definite/ly	manage/ment
disburse/ment	nine/teen
ease/ment	nine/ty
encourage/ment	require/ment
endorse/ment	sincere/ly
grate/ful	use/ful

To add a suffix to a word that ends with a silent *e*, drop the *e* if the suffix begins with a vowel.

argue	arguing, arguable
arrive	arrival, arriving
believe	believable, believing
collate	collating, collator
come	coming
compare	comparable, comparing, comparative, comparability
desire	desirable, desiring, desirous
duplicate	duplicating, duplicator
execute	executing, executive, executor
fascinate	fascinating
receive	receiving
write	writing

Exception: If a word ends with *ce* or *ge,* retain the *e* to soften the *c* or *g*.

changeable
chargeable
manageable
noticeable
serviceable

Spelling Lists

The following lists are chiefly compiled from a collection of words commonly misspelled on student papers and professional papers submitted for editing. They also come from miscellaneous sources of common spelling errors seen in business and other career writing, plus some new technology terms.

Study 1	Study 2	Study 3	Study 4
1. abandoned	1. accustomed	1. allocate	1. affluent
2. accessible	2. acquaintance	2. allotted	2. agenda
3. accumulate	3. approximately	3. already	3. alien
4. assistance	4. beneficiary	4. apparatus	4. allies
5. beginning	5. casualty	5. beneficial	5. belligerent
6. believes	6. deficiency	6. binary	6. committee
7. calendar	7. economical	7. concealment	7. cyberspace
8. component	8. equitable	8. conceive	8. dilapidated
9. concede	9. follow-up	9. definitely	9. empathy
10. desirable	10. grammar	10. effect	10. February
11. enthusiastic	11. inevitable	11. excellent	11. flammable
12. envelope	12. infinite	12. fascinating	12. forcible
13. environment	13. initial	13. grievance	13. immediately
14. familiar	14. microcomputer	14. height	14. liberation
15. fiery	15. necessary	15. incidentally	15. license
16. foreword	16. obvious	16. leisure	16. memorandums
17. handwritten	17. peripheral	17. meticulous	17. microprocessor
18. imminent	18. privilege	18. millionaire	18. miscellaneous
19. installation	19. requisition	19. nineteenth	19. occasionally
20. integrate	20. restaurant	20. ninety	20. quandary
21. knowledge	21. suitable	21. personnel	21. ramification
22. maintenance	22. trivial	22. pollution	22. satellite
23. personally	23. unforgettable	23. sabotage	23. television
24. ratification	24. whether	24. scarcity	24. undoubtedly
25. vacancies	25. vacuum	25. width	25. willful

Study 5	Study 6	Study 7	Study 8
1. abbreviation	1. accede	1. acceptable	1. accommodation
2. absenteeism	2. accidentally	2. altogether	2. adjustment
3. allowance	3. already	3. ambiguity	3. amateur
4. anonymous	4. aluminum	4. arbitration	4. amendment
5. basically	5. conscientious	5. automation	5. architect
6. cellular	6. conspicuous	6. believable	6. booster
7. collateral	7. depreciation	7. clientele	7. comparatively
8. disappear	8. embarrass	8. constitution	8. competitive
9. ecology	9. foreign	9. disappointed	9. discrepancy
10. eliminate	10. heretofore	10. executor	10. eminent
11. foreclosure	11. interface	11. flexible	11. electronic
12. foregoing	12. intrastate	12. independence	12. formally
13. grateful	13. librarian	13. innovation	13. interdependence
14. helpful	14. manager	14. nonessential	14. journeys
15. illegible	15. omitted	15. parallel	15. manifestation
16. incredible	16. paradoxical	16. precarious	16. morale
17. lien	17. polyester	17. precede	17. opposite
18. manageable	18. reaffirm	18. predominant	18. prerequisite
19. misspell	19. receive	19. recommend	19. proceed
20. occurred	20. seize	20. recommendation	20. rebellious
21. paid	21. seminar	21. separate	21. remunerate
22. pamphlet	22. temperament	22. serviceable	22. requirement
23. reference	23. unique	23. signature	23. similar
24. referred	24. vandalism	24. theory	24. studying
25. satisfactory	25. warranty	25. variable	25. weather

Study 9	Study 10	Study 11	Study 12
1. assembled	1. accompanied	1. appropriate	1. apparel
2. attorneys	2. announcement	2. arguing	2. applicable
3. bookkeeping	3. annuity	3. artificial	3. astronaut
4. conquer	4. antagonistic	4. brochure	4. attached
5. controlling	5. bankruptcy	5. coaxial	5. business
6. convenience	6. chaplain	6. collator	6. contingent
7. database	7. chargeable	7. dependent	7. continuous
8. dissatisfaction	8. endorsement	8. dictionary	8. defendant
9. exercise	9. energy	9. easement	9. disbursement
10. extraordinary	10. famous	10. fundamental	10. elementary
11. fuselage	11. internet	11. guarantee	11. ethical
12. itinerary	12. litigation	12. interference	12. exaggerate
13. mortgage	13. mathematics	13. invalidate	13. facsimile
14. optimism	14. parentheses	14. loose	14. gratuitous
15. partial	15. phenomenon	15. municipal	15. interrupt
16. prestige	16. processing	16. past due	16. manuscript
17. pursue	17. procrastinate	17. proprietor	17. opportunity
18. recurrence	18. replica	18. psychology	18. participant
19. recycle	19. souvenir	19. questionnaire	19. penalize
20. retroactive	20. statistics	20. reimburse	20. pressurized
21. reveal	21. supersede	21. reimbursement	21. reinforcement
22. succeed	22. surgeon	22. stationery	22. subpoena
23. sympathize	23. unpretentious	23. stewardesses	23. symbolic
24. synonymous	24. vehicle	24. transit	24. symmetrical
25. versus	25. withheld	25. verbatim	25. voluntary

Appendix B
Punctuation

> *The primary purpose of punctuation is to ensure the clarity and readability of your writing. Although punctuation is, to some extent, a matter of personal preference, there are many required uses, and while certain practices are optional, consistency is mandatory. Be sure to use the same punctuation in parallel situations.*
>
> Joseph Gibaldi and Walter S. Achtert
> MLA Handbook for Writers *(New York: The Modern Language Association of America, 1988)*

Over Time, American English Grammar Changes

Over a long period of time, the English language has slowly changed. Gradually it has gone from the Old English of the early Anglo-Saxons, through the Middle English of Chaucer during the 1400s, and on through the Early Modern English of Shakespeare's time in the 1600s. Continuing to accept gradual differences slowly over the years, today's Late Modern American English has shifted in many ways from the Early Modern English of Shakespeare's time and the current British English. The appearance of dictionaries in the mid-1700s helped make the English language uniform and continues to do so.

Over the centuries, language authorities have said that any grammar form that is understood and is used long enough by enough people eventually becomes standard. That is how changes have taken place over the centuries. You can see such acceptable changes in current respected magazines and newspapers. In our own usage, therefore, we should neither try stubbornly to stay with outdated forms nor lightheartedly adopt all modern innovations.

Currently, there is a trend toward omitting some **punctuation** marks. Today's disappearing punctuation marks are unnecessary commas, hyphens, apostrophes, quotation marks and capitalization. However, before we decide to follow any new, simplified punctuation style, we must first clearly understand why we use punctuation marks—to make writing clear. Early written English did not have punctuation at all, as shown in Chapter 4.

Use common sense in applying rules of punctuation. Also realize that the simpler usage—less punctuation—is the newer usage. The simpler usage of grammar is almost always preferred over an older style.

Here are a few punctuation rules that will answer many common questions on this subject. For additional information, consult *current* editions of the following: a grammar text or an unabridged or desk-size dictionary that contains punctuation rules.

The Period

1. Use a period at the end of a sentence that is not a question or an exclamation.

2. Use a period after a polite request phrased as a question.
    Would you please send us the complete title of the book you requested.

3. Standard dictionaries do not agree on the use of periods with abbreviations. In general, periods are disappearing. The newer and simpler forms without periods are appearing more frequently.

a.m.	MD, M.D.
Dr, Dr.	MP, M.P.
f.o.b., F.O.B.	Mr, Mr.
ft.	Mrs, Mrs.
gr.	Ms, Ms.
kilo	oz.

    Here are commonly used abbreviations for government agencies, military services, and other well-known organizations.

AFL-CIO	NAACP
CIA	UPI
FBI	USA or U.S.A.
IBM	USN
IRS	USSR, U.S.S.R.
NBC	

4. In a typed manuscript, abbreviations and initials of names do not have space between periods.

    U.S.A.
    p.m.
    A.R. Russon

5. In a typed manuscript, two spaces follow a period at the end of a sentence.

The Comma

1. Use a comma before the conjunctions *and, or, nor, but, yet, for* when they join the independent clauses of a compound sentence. Between most short clauses and between many long ones when the meaning is clear, omit the comma.
    We read the report he had made, and everyone approved what he said.
    They were waiting to hear the speech, but we were preparing for the next meeting.
    They arrived and we left immediately.

2. Omit a comma after a short introductory clause or phrase. Use a comma in this position for emphasis, or use a comma here if you would tend to pause at that point in speaking. Also, use the comma if it is needed to make the meaning clear.
    When they arrived we left.

> If you will cooperate with us, we can meet the deadline.
> Last night we received our final instructions.
> Eventually everything worked out all right.
> Certainly, our office will cooperate.
> As a matter of fact, several notices have been mailed.
> If you hit, the umpire will be ready.

3. Use a comma to set off an introductory *yes* or *no*, mild exclamations, and words of direct address. Use a comma after a transitional adverb conjunction such as *however, anyway, nevertheless, therefore, later*, etc. If it is an interrupting element and if in speaking there would normally be a pause at that point, use a comma.

> Yes, they own the laundry.
> Oh, I did not know they were in business.
> Here, Jerry, is a current list of our customers. [Direct address]
> Nevertheless, this is the Internal Revenue Service report.
> The judge began to address the jury; therefore, the room was quiet.
> The attorneys remained calm; actually, they appeared unconcerned.

4. Use a comma to separate parts of dates and addresses.

> The first manuscript was mailed on August 10, 1974, from my home.
> He lived in a hotel at 19400 Collins Avenue, Miami Beach, Florida for three years.

5. Set off titles and appositives with commas.

> I am writing to Dr. Olga Swenson, Dean of Admissions.
> This is our chief comptroller, James P. Post.

6. Use a comma to separate words, phrases, and clauses in a series. Do not use a comma before the conjunction at the end of the series unless it is needed for clarity.

> We had a choice of hamburgers, hot dogs or pizzas.
> The memorandum was carried out this door, down the hall and into the mailroom.
> If you plan your letter, draft a copy and then write the final form, you should have a good letter.

Use a comma before conjunctions when needed for clarity: pancakes, waffles, and bacon and eggs.

7. Use a comma to separate coordinate adjectives (adjectives of equal form) modifying the same noun. If you can substitute *and, or* or *nor* for the comma, the adjectives are coordinate.

> Her window box holds lush, green, healthy plants.
> Margaret has brown, bright, mischievous eyes.
> Did you order beige, blue or yellow notepads?

Do not use a comma between noncoordinate adjectives.

> Two ancient red clay pots were discovered in the ruins.
> We studied the fine old English manuscript.

8. Use a comma or commas to set off nonrestrictive (nonessential) words, phrases or clauses from the rest of the sentence.

> The tower, actually, was directly in front of us.
> The letter, when it did arrive, was unimportant.

9. Use a comma to set off direct quotations from such expressions as *she said, he replied,* etc.

    She said, "We will meet the printing deadline on schedule."

    "We will be ready," he answered, "when we receive it."

    Do not use a comma to introduce part of a quotation within a sentence.

    Churchill is quoted as saying that "old words when short are best of all."

10. In a typed manuscript, a comma is followed by one space.

The Semicolon

Proper use of the semicolon is said to be a mark of an educated person.

1. Use a semicolon between two independent clauses not joined by a coordinating conjunction (*and, or, nor, but, yet, for*)

    Mr. Clark's company is prospering today; he foresaw the current business problems.

    Most supervisors attended the convention; a few remained at home.

    Note: At the choice of the writer, a period could be used in place of this semicolon, capitalizing the next word for a new sentence. A semicolon is used to show a close relationship between the two thoughts expressed.

2. Use a semicolon to separate independent clauses joined only by conjunctive adverbs (*however, therefore, furthermore, nevertheless, consequently, also, then, moreover,* etc.). In such instances, at the writer's choice, the second clause could be written as a new sentence.

3. Use a semicolon to separate elements of a series when the elements themselves contain one or more commas.

    We went to Englewood Cliffs, New Jersey; Philadelphia, Pennsylvania; Wilmington, Delaware; and Baltimore, Maryland.

4. In a typed manuscript a semicolon is followed by one space.

Index

Chapter Tests

NOTE: *Asterisks indicating correct answers must be removed from a separate set of masters before making student copies.*

Chapter 1: You and Business Communication: The Communication Theory

Select the letter of the best answer. Read all answers before making your choice.

1. The text states that in a study of 2000 business executives, most of those responding rated _____ as the most important factor leading to promotion.

    a. education   **c.** good appearance   **e.** ambition

    b. experience   **d.*** ability to communicate

2. Studies show that managers and other executives spend at least _____ percent of their time writing and speaking. (**a.*** 25; **b.** 50; **c.** 80).

3. Which of the following items cannot be considered an advantage of written communications?

    a. Work at a time convenient to sender and receiver.

    b.* Have an opportunity for immediate feedback.

    c. Have a written record.

    d. All are advantages of written communications.

4. The cost of sending email is far less than the cost of sending postal mail. (**a.*** True; **b.** False)

5. The text proclaims that learning to master today's communication technology is well worth the effort. (**a.*** True; **b.** False)

6. In discussing today's computer use, the text states that computer literacy is not enough, but that

    a. Effective communications also require skills and experience in technology.

    b. Effective communications also require skills and experience in composing business communications.

    c.* Both a. and b. are true.

7. Noting that business communication classes have become prestige courses, the text states that organized writing means organized

    a. earnings.

    b.* thinking.

    c. writing.

    d. operations.

8. Today, managers and other executives often create and write communications at their own computers. (**a.*** True; **b.** False)

9. Raising your hand in class is an example of a(n) _____ form of communication.

    a. unwelcome

    b. feedback

    c.* nonverbal

    d. brain drain

10. Nonverbal forms of communication can carry a stronger message than written or spoken communication. (**a.*** True; **b.** False)

11. The first and highest level of communication is
    a.   the telephone.
    b.   the computer.
    c.   the office grapevine.
    d.* face to face.
    e.   written.

12. Business communications perform which of the following functions?
    a.   They inform management about internal operations to help the business continue to function.
    b.   They inform workers of job requirements—those that change and those that remain the same.
    c.   They can improve morale by keeping employees informed of overall business operations and personnel matters.
    d.* a., b., c.
    e.   a., b.

13. What are the major uses of communications outside an organization?
    a.   To receive and sell goods and services.
    b.   To make necessary reports to owners, stockholders and government.
    c.   To create and maintain good will for the business.
    d.   b., c.
    e.* a., b., c.

14. How you express yourself
    a.   Affects your readers' confidence in you.
    b.   Affects your ability to influence your readers.
    c.* Both a. and b.
    d.   Neither a. nor b.

15. A major problem of the communicating process is that the receiver often misunderstands the original message. (**a.*** True; **b.** False)

Chapter 2: Qualities of an Effective Business Communication: Attractive Appearance

Select the letter of the best answer. Read all answers before making your choice.

1. Our readers pay little attention to the appearance of our communications.
   (**a.** True; **b.*** False)

2. Full responsibility for the appearance of communications should be with the secretarial or word processing staff. (**a.** True; **b.*** False)

3. Standard size stationery is (**a.*** 8¹/₂ by 11 inches; **b.** 6 by 9 inches; **c.** 8¹/₂ by 14 inches).

4. High-quality stationery might be chosen because it
   a. looks and feels attractive.
   b. wears well.
   c. resists yellowing.
   d. costs less.
   e.* a., b., c.

5. Many firms choose tinted stationery for
   a. reduction of glare.
   b. color coding.
   c. psychological effect.
   d.* a., b., c.

6. The second and following pages of a letter should be of the same quality as the first page. (**a.*** True; **b.** False)

7. The two most popular letter styles are
   a. AMS and block.
   b. block and picture frame.
   c. modified block and AMS.
   d.* block and modified block.

8. If you do not have your name, address (with ZIP code) and phone number (with area code) on your personal business letterhead, you should have it typed at the head or foot of the first page of the letter, because envelopes with return addresses are often separated from letters. (**a.*** True; **b.** False)

9. The biggest innovation today in preparing business communications is
   a. satellite communication.
   b. electric typewriters.
   c.* automation, computerization.
   d. the 35-hour work week.

10. A famous newspaper writer quoted in the textbook said, "Typewriters do work infinitely better than computers." (**a.** True; **b.*** False)

11. A letterhead identifies the name, address and other information about the receiver. (**a.** True; **b.*** False)

12. All lines of the address should be checked carefully, especially (**a.** numbers; **b.** spellings and markings of names; **c.** words in a foreign language; **d.*** a., b., c.

13. The inside address on the letter and the outside address on the envelope should be the same. (**a.*** True; **b.** False)

14. Conforming with current simplified punctuation trends, the colon or comma after the letter salutation and the comma after the complimentary closing are disappearing. (**a.*** True; **b.** False)

15. On the envelope, special mailing instructions like *Registered Mail* and *Certified Mail* should be placed below the stamp position. (**a.*** True; **b.** False)

16, 17, 18, 19, 20: *Select the preferred form of each of these sentence groups.*

16. **a.**   Enclosed please find the brochure you requested.

    b.* Enclosed is the brochure you requested.

17. **a.**   This is to inform you that our next meeting will be held April 2.

    b.* Our next meeting will be on April 2.

18. **a.*** This will take a long time.

    b.   Well, you know, this will take a long time.

19. **a.**   The thing is, all stockholders will be present.

    b.* All stockholders will be present.

20. **a.*** We must cover all these points.

    b.   You know, we must cover all of these points.

    c.   You know, we must cover all these points.

Chapter 3: Qualities of an Effective Business Communication: Good Will Tone

Select the letter of the best answer. Read all answers before making your choice.

1. The tone of a message does not affect the meaning of a letter or memorandum. (**a.** True; **b.*** False)

2. The tone of a message is part of the unwritten message "between the lines." (**a.*** True; **b.** False)

3. The best level for most business communications is
   a. writing in a sophisticated tone to impress your audience.
   b. writing down to your audience.
   c.* writing as if you are eyeball to eyeball, facing each other.

4. Empathy means
   a. a snide remark.
   b.* trying to put yourself in the other person's position.
   c. the Golden Rule.
   d. various unspoken meanings.
   e. ethics.

5. Effective business letters communicate an acceptable tone by all but one of the following. Which one?
   a. writing at the reader's level.
   b. writing naturally and courteously
   c. emphasizing the positive.
   d.* showing your superiority.

6. Use of good grammar makes a favorable impression, helping create good will and also helping people have confidence in you. (**a.*** True; **b.** False)

7. Following unethical practices in business will help keep you from having trouble with the law. (**a.** True; **b.*** False)

8. If possible, negative and positive messages should be handled with
   a. either a negative or positive tone.
   b. a negative tone.
   c.* a positive tone.
   d. none of these.

9. Advertisers generally write from the (**a.** we; **b.*** you) viewpoint.

10. Euphemisms
    a. replace blunt expressions with more acceptable words or terms.
    b. are often chosen to avoid using words with unpleasant connotations.
    c. should not be used if they lead to obscure writing.
    d. are used by good writers.
    e.* all of the above.

11. A touch of humor can be a welcome relief in business communications. (**a.*** True; **b.** False)

12. The text shows that many of our best, most effective communications are written during temper tantrums. (**a.** True; **b.*** False)

13. If you cannot stifle an urge to write a letter exhibiting your powerful temper, write it and *immediately* destroy it. (**a.*** True; **b.** False)

14. Answering letters promptly does all but one of the following. Which one?

    a. Shows courtesy to those receiving your letters.

    b.* Shows you have nothing else to do.

    c. Helps keep matters current in your own business.

    d. Helps keep matters current in your customer/client businesses.

    e. Helps retain customers.

15. Violating company policy could cost you your job. (**a.*** True; **b.** False)

16. In business communications, resale is

    a. practiced when company promotional or sale materials are enclosed in correspondence.

    b. anything that reinforces customer or client's decision to do business with you.

    c. selling old letters and memos to a recycling plant.

    d.* a., b.

    e. a., b., c.

17, 18, 19, 20: *Select the preferred form of each of these sentence groups.*

17. **a.** You were wrong when you presumed your video cassette recorder has a lifetime guarantee.

    b.* Your video cassette recorder comes with a 90-day warranty.

18. **a.** You should have read the instructions before complaining over the phone.

    b.* We are enclosing another copy of the instruction booklet.

19. **a.*** Accidents should be reported immediately.

    b. You were negligent in not reporting the accident immediately.

20. **a.** You'll have to wait while I answer the person on the other line.

    b.* Excuse me a moment. I'll be right back.

Chapter 4: Qualities of an Effective Business Communication: Clear and Complete Message

Select the letter of the best answer. Read all answers before making your choice.

1. Why is English spoken around the world?
   a. Passengers and crews of early British sailing ships spread their language to many countries around the globe.
   b. Sailing ships helped Great Britain acquire foreign colonies until it was said, "The sun never sets on the British Empire."
   c. English became the major language spoken by people in many countries.
   d. Today English is the chief language spoken in worldwide radio and television broadcasts.
   e.* All of the above.

2. In corresponding with people in other countries, we should try to impress them by using their foreign language even if our command of it is poor. (**a.** True; **b.*** False)

3. Mastering another language is strongly recommended for which reasons?
   a. There is growing international traffic in business.
   b. Foreign language mastery leads to attractive employment offers.
   c. There are benefits both on and off the job
   d.* a, b., c.

4. In writing in English to foreigners, try to impress them by using long words and sentences. (**a.** True; **b.*** False)

5. In email, casual expressions might be accepted better than in more formal printed messages. (**a.*** True; **b.** False)

6. Do consultants say that most offices produce many unnecessary memos, letters and reports? (**a.*** Yes; **b.** No)

7. To express your thoughts clearly and completely in your writing and speaking, you should make a list and then organize list items in a logical order. (**a.*** True; **b.** False)

8. Electronic machines with their "cut" and "paste" capabilities (**a.*** do; **b.** don't) simplify the arrangement of items on your list.

9. If you let inaccurate information slip into your memos, letters, reports, etc., people will usually forgive you. (**a.** True; **b.*** False)

10. We should make our messages brief and clear because
    a. The clearest, most effective writing is concise.
    b. You owe your receivers the courtesy of eliminating unnecessary verbiage.
    c. You can be proud of your improved writing.
    d.* All of the above.

11. Foreigners will understand your jargonistic, long-winded gobbledygook. (**a.** True; **b.*** False)

12. Educated people seldom refer to dictionaries. (**a.** True; **b.*** False)

13. A thesaurus
   a. Contains synonyms.
   b. Contains antonyms.
   c. Is the same as a dictionary.
   d. Is a good reference for writers and speakers.
   e.* All but c.

14. The more words you put in a sentence, the better it will be understood. (**a.** True; **b.*** False)

15. Right or wrong, poor spelling often makes your readers classify you as
   a. stupid.
   b. lazy.
   c. uneducated.
   d.* any or all of the above.

16. To make sure your letter, memo, or report is clear and complete
   a. compare it with the early list you made when planning your writing.
   b. check it for legality: defamation of character, etc. (See pages 72–73.)
   c. proofread carefully. (Read the sentence from the Prentice Hall *Author's Guide* that is quoted on page 73, paragraph 4.)
   d.* All of the above.

17, 18, 19, 20. **Pronouns in Subject or Object Form.** *Select the preferred form.*

17. She and (**a.*** I; **b.** me) attended the concert.

18. I went to the concert with Joe and (**a.** she; **b.*** her).

19. The chairman sent (**a.*** her and me; **b.** she and I) to the conference.

20. Between (**a.** you and I; **b.*** you and me), I didn't think we had a chance.

Chapter 5: The Routine Information, "Yes" or Good News Communication: News Releases

Select the letter of the best answer. Read all answers before making your choice.

1. The letter pattern that is used most is the _____ pattern.
   a.* routine information, "yes" or good news
   b. negative communication
   c. sales or persuasive request

2. In the routine information pattern, the main message should be
   a.* in the beginning.
   b. in the middle.
   c. at the end.

3. Email has become popular partly because
   a. It is fast and is more flexible than fax.
   b. It can be sent any time, day or night.
   c. Computer word processing has special features, such as copy and paste.
   d. Feedback is fast.
   e.* All of the above.

4. Form letters should be prepared carefully and reviewed frequently because they will be used many times. (**a.*** True; **b.** False)

5. Postcards should not be used for routine messages. (**a.** True; **b.*** False)

6. We are cautioned that we should frequently send out many letters because most people like junk mail. (**a.** True; **b.*** False)

7. Mail merge letters
   a. Place messages closer together on a page.
   b. Encourage cooperation among workers.
   c.* Make it possible to combine the same main message with different specific messages.
   d. None of the above.

8. Even though routine, an order blank or an order letter must be clear and specific
   a. for the interests of the customer/client.
   b. for the interests of the seller.
   c. because it is the first step in a legal contract to buy.
   d.* a., b., c.
   e. a., b.

9. An order acknowledgment is generally considered a
   a. sales letter.
   b.* routine communication.
   c. negative communication.

10. In a routine claim letter, you are not expecting the receiver to comply with your request automatically. (**a.** True; **b.*** False)

11. A routine request is a negative letter and you should not expect the receiver to comply immediately. (**a.** True; **b.*** False).

12. Because news releases are important, new employees are never assigned the duty of writing them. (**a.** True; **b.*** False).

13. Small news outlets, like community newspapers, TV and radio stations, should not be considered for your news releases. (**a.** True; **b.*** False)

14. An unusual twist at the beginning of a news release will usually help your story get the editor's attention. (**a.*** True; **b.** False)

15. When submitting a news release to print or broadcast media, use single spaced typing and crowd as much print on the page, as you can, leaving little white space for top, bottom and side margins. Who cares about damaging the editor's eyesight? (**a.** True; **b.*** False)

16,17,18,19,20. **Variety in Sentence Form.** *Select the choice that gives the sentence variety by not beginning with the subject.*

16. **a.*** Yesterday the news from all branch offices was good.

 b. The news from all branch offices was good yesterday.

17. **a.** We distributed the news release after we received the reports.

 b.* After we received the reports, we distributed the news release.

18. **a.** We alternate assignments among our staff members frequently.

 b.* Frequently, we alternate assignments among our staff members.

19. **a.*** In the appendix at the end of the report is the completed survey.

 b. The completed survey is in the appendix at the end of the report.

20. **a.** I can leave after I send all these emails.

 b.* After I send all these emails, I can leave.

Chapter 6: The Negative Communication: The "No" Message

Select the letter of the best answer. Read all answers before making your choice.

1. Champion Canadian skier Jean Paul Killey, quoted at the beginning of this chapter, says that concentrating on negative possibilities during his races helps him win. (**a.** True; **b.*** False)

2. In writing negative communications, what usually presents the greatest challenge?

   a. appearance

   b.* good will

   c. clear and complete message

3. The negative message is usually most effective if the negative is carried in which section?

   a. first

   b.* middle

   c. closing

4. The buffer of the negative is planned to

   a. Leave a pleasant impression at the closing of the message.

   b. Include the main negative.

   c.* Cushion a blow—the coming negative.

   d. Quote company policy.

   e. None of the above.

5. Negative communications should almost always be written with which kind of tone?

   a. negative

   b.* positive

6. All but one of the following are true about "flaming emails." Which one?

   a. Are angry email replies.

   b. Should be avoided, not sent.

   c.* Are replies that should make you proud.

   d. Usually create a shock value that gains notice, but are not good form and should be avoided.

7. Candor is

   a. subtle humor.

   b. putting on airs.

   c. being dishonest.

   d.* openly admitting an unpleasant fact.

8. Using "company policy" as the reason for a refusal is generally not satisfactory to a customer or client. (**a.*** True; **b.** False)

9. Since insurance companies began to eliminate unnecessary legal terminology from their policies, they have received (**a.** more; **b.*** fewer) complaints and inquiries from clients about the meaning of terms in their policies.

10. *Caveat venditor* means

    a. Do unto others as you would have others do unto you.

    b. Do unto others before they do unto you.

    c. Let the buyer beware.

    d.* Let the seller beware [**Instructor:** From Latin *venedere*, to sell.]

11. A good refusal letter should do all but one of the following. Which one?

    a. Suggest an alternative.

    b. Advise that a substitute is being sent.

    c. Suggest future business under other circumstances.

    d.* Say "I hope we can be of service to you again."

12. You should not send a message with a "bee sting" because

    a. People may give the message the attention it deserves and ignore it.

    b. People may retaliate spitefully.

    c. It may hurt your relationships with people who receive the sting.

    d. a., b.

    e.* a., b., c.

13. Although most businesspeople don't like to write refusals to their customers, they find that for economic reasons they sometimes have to do this. (a.* True; b. False)

14. In writing a partial adjustment, you should minimize what you can do and emphasize what you cannot do. (a. True; b.* False)

15. When a customer makes a ridiculous request, a cutting or pointed comment will probably

    a. Satisfy the customer.

    b.* Lose the person as a customer.

16. For the complaint letter you write yourself, you should follow all but one of the following. Which one?

    a. Don't put yourself in someone else's "crackpot" file.

    b.* Try to go immediately to the top official.

    c. Avoid criticism of the reader.

    d. Start with a neutral statement with which the reader can agree.

17, 18, 19, 20. **Negative ——> Positive.** *Select the form of each of these pairs that sounds positive instead of negative.*

17. a.* May I please sit at your desk?

    b. Will it bother you if I sit at your desk?

18. a. You cannot park in the VIP parking lot.

    b.* You may park in the visitors' parking lot.

19. a. Scott Scuffs won't bind your feet and make them feel cramped.

    b.* You'll be walking on clouds in your new Scott Scuffs.

20. a. Construction will not begin before June 1.

    b.* Construction will begin soon after June 1.

Chapter 7: Sales Letters and Persuasive Claims and Requests

Select the letter of the best answer. Read all answers before making your choice.

1. Winston Churchill's quote at the beginning of Chapter 7 ends by portraying business enterprise as
   a.   a target to be shot.
   b.   a cow to be milked.
   c.* a sturdy horse pulling the wagon.
   d.   none of the above.

2. The employment application letter is a type of selling letter. (**a.*** True; **b.**   False)

3. Sales letters are written only to sell goods and services. (**a.**   True; **b.*** False)

4. Compared with other types of advertising, selling by mail usually costs (**a.**   more; **b.*** less).

5. Advertising helps
   a.   Keep businesses competitive.
   b.   Make people aware of new products and services.
   c.   Make people aware of improvements in some older products and obsolescence of others.
   d.   Sell goods, services and ideas.
   e.* a., b., c., d.

6. To sell successfully, you need not try to be personally familiar with the product or service you are promoting. (**a.**   True; **b.*** False)

7. Lists of prospective customers are usually
   a.   purchased.
   b.   made up from your own list of present and former customers/clients.
   c.   made up free from government and other public records.
   d.   taken from the phone book.
   e.* a., b., c.

8. Most ads are in the (**a.**   innovation; **b.**   imitation; **c.*** competition; **d.**   saturation) stage of advertising.

9. You should conscientiously avoid using an advertising style that is in which stage set out in question 8? (**a.; b.; c.; d.***)

10. The first part of the sales letter should be considered the (**a.**   action hook; **b.**   interest and desire buildup; **c.*** attention-getter).

11. The ending of the sales letter should be the action hook. (**a.*** True; **b.**   False)

12. Some attention-getters are placed on envelopes of sales letters. (**a.*** True; **b.**   False)

13. Which typical Website attention-getters are losing their effectiveness?
    a.   animated graphics
    b.   audio sound bytes
    c.   "screaming" ads
    d.* all of the above

14. Unsolicited emails are often which of the following?
    a.   a pain in the neck
    b.   junk mail
    c.   signs of a "spam scam"
    d.* all of the above

15. Addressing sales letters to "Occupant" or "Resident" is a way of getting the reader's attention. (**a.** True; **b.*** False)

16. Most readers react the same way to any given sales appeal. (**a.** True; **b.*** False)

17. All sales letters should be only one page long. (**a.** True; **b.*** False)

18, 19, 20: **"We Attitude"** ——> **"You Attitude."** *In each of these couplets, select the choice that has the best sales pitch.*

18. **a.**   Our research and development section has applied our best technique for this new product.
    b.* You and yours can benefit from the years of research devoted to this new product.

19. **a.*** You may enjoy the safety features built into your new "Swing Along" improved titanium scooter.
    b.   We have put three years into developing safety features in our newest model "Swing Along" titanium scooter.

20. **a.**   We have spent 27 years making Jurgen the finest backhoe on the market.
    b.* Behind your backhoe are 27 years of research and development.

Chapter 8: Credit and Collections

Select the letter of the best answer. Read all answers before making your choice.

1. The four C's of credit are capital, capacity, conditions and (**a.** cash; **b.*** character; **c.** criminal record).

2. (**a.*** More than half; **b.** Less than half) of business is conducted on a credit basis.

3. Which of these figures is closest to the total of business credit losses each year? (**a.*** 0.5 percent; **b.** 5 percent; **c.** 10 percent; **d.** 25 percent)

4. In reporting the credit status of an individual, you should
   a. Give any information you think the inquirer would like to hear.
   b. Give only what information a *prudent* individual would report, being aware of possible legal entanglements.
   c. Give information only to persons legally authorized to receive it.
   d. Give personal evaluations and opinions.
   e.* b., c.

5. Usually the first and best source of credit information on a person is
   a. friends and neighbors.
   b. the employer.
   c. the local credit bureau.
   d.* the credit applicant herself/himself.
   e. other businesses.

6. Information on the trade credit status of other businesses, like milk, sours fast. (**a.*** True; **b.** False)

7. Today most credit applications are made (**a.*** by filling in a form; **b.** by writing a letter asking for credit; **c.** by giving information over the phone).

8. The letter granting credit is a (**a.*** "yes"; **b.** negative; **c.** selling) letter.

9. The letter granting credit to new customers should have a tone of (**a.** routine information; **b.** ho-hum; **c.*** welcome; **d.** neutrality).

10. Because all retail credit agreements are basically the same, you need not explain terms of credit in a letter granting credit. (**a.** True; **b.*** False)

11. Certain laws govern statements that must be made in a letter granting credit. (**a.*** True; **b.** False)

12. The letter refusing credit should have the refusal in the (**a.** beginning; **b.*** middle; **c.** end) of the message.

13. Are computer form letters effective in collections? (**a.*** Yes; **b.** No)

14. People with overdue accounts (**a.** are surprised to hear from you; **b.*** know they owe and expect to hear).

15. Speaking over the phone or in person is often more effective than sending written collection notices. (**a.*** True; **b.** False)

16. The most productive collection procedures may be totally different from any that have been tried before. (**a.*** True; **b.** False)

17. Collection letters to government agencies and large businesses should be directed to (**a.*** high-level; **b.** low-level) officials.

18. Early stage collection letters should carry good will. (**a.*** True; **b.** False)

19. As letters progress through the collection letter series, their tones (**a.** become more cautious; **b.*** become firmer; **c.** do not change).

20. The last stage of the collection letter series is the (**a.** pressure; **b.** inquiry/appeal; **c.** saturation; **d.*** ultimatum; **e.** none of these).

21. When you have written to or otherwise contacted a person with an overdue account and have been ignored repeatedly, one of your major concerns is still maintaining good will. (**a.** True; **b.*** False)

22, 23, 24, 25: *Choose the preferred business form from each of these sets.*

22. **a.** The complexity of his complex problems overwhelmed him.
    b.* The complexity of his problems overwhelmed him.

23. **a.** When I heard the threat of their unethical plan, I felt threatened.
    b.* When I heard the threat of their unethical plan, I was frightened.

24. **a.*** Researchers say they can determine which study is most important.
    b. Researchers say they can determine which research is most important.

25. **a.** We designed the design for this floor plan.
    b.* We designed this floor plan.

Chapter 9: Courtesy Messages You Don't Have to Send, but Should

Select the letter of the best answer. Read all answers before making your choice.

1. The dollar and cents value of a firm's good will can never be listed. (**a.** True; **b.*** False)

2. Because of the expense of writing letters, we should not write a business letter unless we can see a potential for making money. (**a.** True; **b.*** False)

3. The most common communications a customer receives from a business are (**a.** bills and statements; **b.** bills and good will letters; **c.*** bills and advertisements).

4. It is never appropriate to write a letter of congratulations to a high-level executive of your organization whom you may never have met. (**a.** True; **b.*** False)

5. Businesses recognize that getting new customers is commonplace, so they do not write letters to welcome these people. (**a.** True; **b.*** False)

6. At times of bereavement, people usually appreciate (**a.** cards; **b.** telephone calls; **c.** personal letters; **d.*** a., b., c.).

7. Writing a letter of condolence gives you an appropriate chance to promote your own religious beliefs. (**a.** True; **b.*** False)

8. Even though time is money, in business there are occasions when a handwritten letter is appropriate. (**a.*** True; **b.** False)

9. A U.S. representative quoted in the text stated that for him and his colleagues, _____ are one of the best gauges of public opinion. (**a.** telegrams; **b.** phone calls; **c.** person-to-person interviews; **d.** TV and radio commentaries; **e.*** personal letters)

10. Our public officials are very busy at their duties and generally pay little attention to letters from their constituents. (**a.** True; **b.*** False)

11. Western Union has special low rates for sending Public Opinion Messages to elected state or federal officials. (**a.*** True; **b.** False)

12. If you want to write to a public official about two separate matters, you should write (**a.** one; **b.*** two; **c.** three) letter(s).

13. In general, public officials have a strong aversion to (**a.** cards; **b.** typed letters; **c.** handwritten letters; **d.*** form letters).

14. Today faxes are taking the place of much of the regular mail we formerly used. (**a.*** True; **b.** False)

15. You need not be concerned about appearance, good will tone, and clear and complete message in your communications to public officials, because they are not customers of your firm. (**a.** True; **b.*** False)

16, 17, 18, 19, 20: Misplaced Modifiers. *Choose the form of each of these sentences that is clearer and therefore gives the intended meaning.*

16. **a.** He was presumed drowned by the Coast Guard.
    b.* The Coast Guard presumed that he was drowned.

17. **a.*** The President feels strongly that mothers of young children should not be compelled to enter the job market.
    b. The President feels strongly that mothers should not be compelled to leave young children to enter the job market.

18. a. Driving near the Miami airport, office workers can sometimes be seen sunning themselves in a penthouse atop the Eastern Airlines building.
b.* Driving near the Miami airport, you can sometimes see office workers sunning themselves in a penthouse atop the Eastern Airlines building.

19. a. It is going to mostly consist of a write-in campaign.
b.* It is going to consist mostly of a write-in campaign.

20. a. They supposedly had supplied Hughes, who died while enroute to Houston from Acapulco, with codeine.
b.* When Hughes died while enroute to Houston from Acapulco, they supposedly had supplied him with codeine.

Chapter 10: Oral Communications

Select the letter of the best answer. Read all answers before making your choice.

1. A telephone company brochure emphasizes, "Every time you talk on the telephone you really are (**a.** important; **b.** responsible for what you say; **c.*** the company)."

2. Because no one meets the switchboard operator in person, his or her tone and attitude are unimportant. (**a.** True; **b.*** False)

3. The textbook says that in telephoning, "The name of the game is (**a.** honesty; **b.** speed; **c.*** names; **d.** costs)."

4. The best way to improve dictation is (**a.** practice; **b.** practice; **c.** practice; **d.*** a., b., c.).

5. Who is ultimately responsible for all details of a meeting or conference?
   a.* the conference leader
   b. the conference leader's administrative assistant
   c. the program chairman
   d. the low person on the totem pole

6. Of the basic parliamentary principles Marguerite Grumme listed as a framework for successful meetings, which is listed first as most important?
   a. Consider one thing at a time.
   b. The minority must be heard.
   c. Majority must prevail.
   d.* Courtesy and justice to all.
   e. Get on your knees and bow toward the leader.

7. To win a confrontation, you are advised to do all but one of the following. Which one?
   a. Avoid arguments.
   b. Maintain eye contact to show you honestly believe in what you are saying.
   c.* Hold your temper, but yell if you *must* win.
   d. Concentrate on your objective.
   e. If the opponent holds a weak position, ask him or her to repeat it, maybe making that person realize how weak the position is. You have a moment to think of a rebuttal.

8. Business students are encouraged to take speech courses because your speech can influence your career. (**a.*** True; **b.** False)

9. A good, well-received speech usually (**a.*** follows; **b.** does not follow) a plan or list.

10. An agenda is
    a. a substitution of an acceptable term for a word or term that might be objectionable.
    b. use of body motions to send messages.
    c.* a list of matters to be covered at a meeting.
    d. various associations and unspoken meanings that a particular word might bring to another person's mind.

11. When you have finished your speech, you should
    a. Try to think of another long example to give.
    b. Tell a long, involved joke or story.
    c.* Shut up and sit down.

12. Executives have much to say and spend little time listening. (**a.** True; **b.*** False)

13. You should try to avoid taking an excessive amount of notes during a speech. (**a.*** True; **b.** False)

14. Some barriers to good listening are:
    a. personal prejudices against a speaker.
    b. concentrating on matters other than what is being discussed.
    c. nearby or distant noises.
    d. interrupting.
    e.* all of the above.

15. People sometimes miss the best parts of a speech because they are not listening well. (**a.*** True; **b.** False)

16, 17, 18, 19, 20: *Choose the preferred form of the word or sentence.*

16. We did it (**a.** ourself; **b.*** ourselves).

17. Everybody offered (**a.** his; **b.** their; **c.*** some) assistance.

18. You can be proud of (**a.*** yourselves; **b.** yourselfs).

19. **a.** Each tourist will handle his own luggage.
    b.* All tourists will handle their own luggage.

20. **a.*** All supervisors were assigned their new offices.
    b. Every supervisor was assigned his new office.

Chapter 11: Computers, the Internet and Other Communication Technologies

Select the letter of the best answer. Read all answers before making your choice.

1. In the past several years, the need for stenographers and secretaries in most offices has increased. (**a.** True; **b.*** False)

2. When composing at a computer or typewriter, we are advised to try to make the first copy perfect. (**a.** True; **b.*** False)

3. The text recommends that while learning to use the Internet, you work completely independently. (**a.** True; **b.*** False)

4. In a Local Area Network (LAN), you usually connect with other computers around the world. (**a.** True; **b.*** False)

5. In 1999, the volume of email was greater than the volume of postal mail. (**a.*** True; **b.** False)

6. In its early development, before it was common, Queen Elizabeth II sent an email message. (**a.*** True; **b.** False)

7. Sending a single message to multiple recipients can be done easily by clicking on additional address book entries or typing in new email addresses. (**a.*** True; **b.** False)

8. Because many people receive long strings of emails, the subject line must briefly tell what the message is about. (**a.*** True; **b.** False)

9. We are told to use only plain text in emails, not boldface, italics, etc., because the word processing program of the receiver may not accept our fonts. (**a.*** True; **b.** False)

10. Unsolicited emails and faxes may equal "spam." (**a.*** True; **b.** False)

11, 12, 13, 14, 15: **Misplaced Modifiers.** *Select the form of these sentences that shows the actual meaning more clearly.*

11. **a.**   The cowboy roped the calf on the palomino pony.

    b.* The cowboy on the palomino pony roped the calf.

12. **a.**   A university student was convicted of grand theft just 24 hours after his trial went to the jury.

    b.* Just 24 hours after his trial went to the jury, a university student was convicted of grand theft.

13. **a.**   One acre overlooking a waterfall for an unusual buyer, shaped triangular.

    b.* For an unusual buyer: One triangular shaped acre overlooking a waterfall.

14. **a.*** This is almost the toughest decision we have made.

    b.   This is the toughest decision almost that we have made.

15. **a.**   We have published a booklet about our stocks and bonds which we will send you on request.

    b.* Our stocks and bonds booklet will be sent to you on request.

Chapter 12: Healthy Computing: Preventing Eyestrain, Carpal (Wrist) Tunnel Syndrome, Back Pain

Select the letter of the best answer. Read all answers before making your choice.

1. According to an article in the *Columbia University Complete Home Medical Guide,* the gains in life expectancy that occurred in the 20th century were achieved by
   a. medical treatment.
   b. curative medicine.
   c. prevention and health promotion measures.
   d. a., b., c.
   e.* a., b.

2. Under the title, "Desk Stress," *The New Wellness Encyclopedia of the University of California at Berkeley* states, "Anyone who sits at a desk or computer terminal all day is subject to the physical stress in which muscle groups are contracted for long periods in an unvarying position. ... All of this causes office workers to complain about back, neck and shoulder pains, usually in that order." (a.* True; b. False)

3. The American Management Association book, *Healthy Computing,* states that, much better than resorting to surgery,
   a. Identify and treat bad work habits.
   b. Treat the painful condition in time to prevent chronic problems.
   c.* a, b.

4. At the top of the list of computer physical stress complaints is
   a. back problems.
   b. wrist problems.
   c.* eyestrain.

5. The *New Wellness Encyclopedia* also recommends:
   a. Blink, blink, blink.
   b. Blinking coats the surface of the eye with needed moisture.
   c. Take breaks away from the computer.
   d. Quit your job.
   e.* a., b., c.

6. Some office environmental hazards to your eyes are
   a. room lighting or sunlight shining in or near your line of vision.
   b. poor desk placement.
   c. possibility of glare from white or near-white objects nearby, such as walls and buildings.
   d.* a., b., c.

7. Wearing bifocals at the computer might cause neck and back pain from the "bobbing head" syndrome. (a.* True; b. False)

8. Light in many offices today is too bright. (a.* True; b. False)

9. Medical authorities say that a weakened grip and severe pain in the forearms are warnings that should be checked to prevent serious wrist trouble. (a.* True; b. False)

10. To prevent carpal (wrist) tunnel syndrome, doctors recommend keeping your wrists straight. (**a.*** True; **b.** False)

11. Concerning back pain, authorities recommend all but one of the following. Which one?

    a. Listen to your body. If your back hurts, stop and rest.

    b. Bed rest, medication and physical therapy may provide relief.

    c. Over-the-counter medications are recommended; nonprescription drugs like aspirin or ibuprofen and muscle relaxants are often advised.

    d.* If your back hurts severely, ignore it.

12. For care of the back, the text does not recommend one of the following. Which one?

    a.* Bending to pick up objects, putting maximum strain on the back, probably the number one cause of backache.

    b. Bending at the knees to lift instead of bending at the waist, so that leg muscles do most of the work.

    c. Pushing a heavy object instead of lifting or pulling.

    d. All are recommended.

Chapter 13: Employment Guides: Finding a Job, Holding a Job, Earning Promotions, Changing Jobs

Select the letter of the best answer. Read all answers before making your choice.

1. John D. Rockefeller, wealthy industrialist quoted at the beginning of the chapter, said he would pay more for _____ than any other ability in the world. Which would he pay more for?

   a. a good education

   b. satisfactory appearance

   c. a record of satisfactory employment

   d.* the ability to get along with people

   e. the ability to write well

2. In preparing for almost any position in today's job market, a person should have some competence in computer technology. (**a.*** True; **b.** False)

3. In planning for a career, you should first

   a. Study the job market.

   b. Study the salary level you want.

   c. Study promising careers.

   d.* Study yourself.

   e. Don't study anything.

4. You should not take advantage of personal connections when you are seeking employment. (**a.** True; **b.*** False)

5. Most colleges have job placement services to help students obtain temporary and permanent employment. (**a.*** True; **b.** False)

6. Articles in the news can sometimes can give you leads about possible job openings. (**a.*** True; **b.** False)

7. Municipal, state and federal government agencies employ large numbers of people in various types of jobs. (**a.*** True; **b.** False)

8. Robert O. Snelling, head of a major national private employment firm, says that in job hunting, the biggest mistake most young people make is (**a.** not dressing properly; **b.** not showing interest in the job; **c.*** not being persistent in seeking a specific job; **d.** not being on time).

9. At graduation time, most college students are able to obtain the jobs of their choice. (**a.** True; **b.*** False)

10. After a person has worked with a firm for a time, it is not necessary to be concerned about personal appearance. (**a.** True; **b.*** False)

11. By making casual comments to your superiors, people who work for you can influence your possibilities for promotion. (**a.*** True; **b.** False)

12. J.C. Penney said that to be an executive, a person must be willing to work longer hours than the average employee. (**a.*** True; **b.** False)

13. Even if your job is negative in some respects, it may be the right job for you. (**a.*** True; **b.** False)

14. Choose the statement that is not good advice: If you want to leave a position under unpleasant circumstances, remember that:

   a. You may need a reference for your next position.

   b. The best memory your previous employer has of you will probably be of the last time he or she saw you.

   c.* You don't plan to come back, so take advantage of the opportunity to blow off steam.

   d. You may want to come back in the future.

   e. You should wait, calmly assess the situation, and find another job, listing the current employment as a reference—it is easier if you are employed.

15. Why should you welcome a new employee?

   a. You want to practice the Golden Rule.

   b. You try to do unto others as you would have done to you.

   c. You want to be liked.

   d. You want to help make the new employee an effective working member of the team.

   e.* All of the above.

16, 17, 18, 19, 20: *Select the preferred form of these sentences.*

16. a.* Dr. McCormick called the class to order.
    b. The class was called to order by Dr. McCormick.

17. a.* Her copying talent is so outstanding that she even tricks experts.
    b. Her copying talent is so outstanding that even experts have been tricked.

18. a. The report will be mailed on Friday.
    b.* We will mail the report on Friday.

19. a. Most player contracts were signed immediately.
    b.* Most players signed their contracts immediately.

20 a.* Was the letter sent to the right office? [**Instructor:** Avoid a negative accusation.]
    b. Did you send the letter to the wrong office?

Chapter 14: Employment Resumés and Application Letters: Miscellaneous Employment Communications

Select the letter of the best answer. Read all answers before making your choice.

1. An employment resumé might be called all but one of the following terms. Which one? (**a.** bio; **b.** data sheet; **c.*** feedback; **d.** vita)

2. In giving education or work experience, you should list (**a.** earliest employment first; **b.*** earliest employment last).

3. To give readers a favorable impression, get all possible information on each page of the resumé, leaving little space for margins and no blank lines between sections. (**a.** True; **b.*** False)

4. For employment today, bilingual or multilingual ability is a definite asset in a high percentage of cases. (**a.*** True; **b.** False)

5. You (**a.** should; **b.*** should not) use abbreviations in your resumé to identify such items as places of employment, organizations to which you belong, and so forth.

6. While law prohibits employment interviewers from asking certain personal questions, the law does not prohibit you from furnishing any personal information that you feel may further your cause. (**a.*** True; **b.** False)

7. Because English is becoming the universal language, the text suggests that Americans should not study foreign languages. (**a.** True; **b.*** False)

8. The employment application letter should usually be written as a _____ letter.
   a. routine information
   b. negative
   c.* selling

9. At an employment interview, most potential employers are favorably impressed if you show interest in and knowledge of (**a.** potential salary; **b.** fringe benefits; **c.** working hours; **d.*** the company you are hoping will employ you).

10. The text suggests that you try to make an appointment for an employment interview on a (**a.** Monday; **b.** Friday; **c.*** Tuesday, Wednesday or Thursday; **d.** weekend).

11. It is usually wise to use pity as a means of trying to help you get a job. (**a.** True; **b.*** False)

12. A record of frequent job changing usually indicates to the potential employer that you are a wide-awake go-getter. (**a.** True; **b.*** False)

13. Whether you are resigning in person or by letter, it is usually best if you start with a pleasant buffer statement. (**a.*** True; **b.** False)

14. Resigning from a job gives you a good chance to tell people in authority everything that is wrong with the firm and the people in it, and you should take advantage of this opportunity to express yourself. (**a.** True; **b.*** False)

15. Sending a letter to an employment inteviewer to express thanks for the appointment can
   a. Show that you know how to express appreciation.
   b. Show that you are courteous.
   c. Show that you are seriously interested in the position.
   d.* a., b., c.
   e. a., b.

16. In the Northwestern University study of "Why They Weren't Hired," the negative factor listed most frequently was
    a. poor education.
    b. lack of interest in type of work.
    c.* negative personality or poor impression.
    d. unwillingness to travel or relocate.

17. Under no circumstances should you ever ask for a raise. (**a.** True; **b.*** False)

18. Use of a thesaurus shows that you are trying to improve your vocabulary. (**a.*** True; **b.** False)

19. Educated people never use dictionaries, because they already know everything. (**a.** True; **b.*** False)

20. Enlarging your vocabulary by word study in a dictionary and/or thesaurus
    a. Helps make your writing and speaking clear and specific.
    b. Enables you to avoid using the same words constantly.
    c. Enables you to better understand what you read and hear in and out of classrooms.
    d. Helps you understand new words used in classrooms and classroom texts.
    e.* All of the above.

Chapter 15: Planning a Business Report or a Term Paper

Select the letter of the best answer. Read all answers before making your choice.

1. Due to demands of business, technical and professional fields, colleges today are placing added emphasis on writing courses. (**a.*** True; **b.** False)

2. Costs of preparing business reports are often high; therefore, we must realize that we should not prepare unnecessary reports. (**a.*** True; **b.** False)

3. Primary research is conducted by checking printed reference materials in college, company or public libraries. (**a.** True; **b.*** False)

4. Businesspeople today say their reports are written
   a. to aid management in making decisions.
   b. for legal obligations.
   c. for public information, potential investors, and public relations.
   d. to keep the public relations department busy.
   e.* a., b., c.

5. Electronic data processing records and classifies information so quickly and efficiently that much unneeded printed material is produced and kept in computer memory and/or hard copy (paper) files. (**a.*** True; **b.** False)

6. In solving any problem, the first and most important step is to
   a. Select the person or persons to solve the problem.
   b.* Identify the problem.
   c. Find money for research.
   d. Decide how many copies are needed.
   e. Determine the method of seeking the solution to the problem.

7. You should not bother reference librarians by asking them to use their years of training to help you find reference sources. (**a.** True; **b.*** False)

8. The only type of research done for business or education purposes is library reference research. (**a.** True; **b.*** False)

9. Why must you know how much money can be spent on a report?
   a. Somebody has to pay the bills.
   b. To determine the amount of time that should be spent on it.
   c. To determine who will work on it.
   d. To determine the type of printing, paper, illustrations, cover, etc.
   e.* All of the above.

10. The three classifications of printed library materials are books in stacks, periodicals and (**a.** newspapers; **b.** magazines; **c.** librarians; **d.*** reference works).

11. For business reports, the text says that authoritative periodicals are valuable because they can be _____ than other printed sources.
    a. cheaper
    b. more readily available
    c.* more up to date
    d. all of the above

12. For information such as the specific name and address of a business, its history, names of its officers, types of products and services, and so forth, check (**a.** periodicals; **b.** books in stacks; **c.*** business directories in the library reference section).

13. Most colleges use the _____ system of classifying materials because it permits book loans between libraries. (**a.*** Library of Congress; **b.** Dewey decimal; **c.** college's own; **d.** colleges do not classify materials—they just stack things up).

14. Your library research cards or pages should include library reference numbers for

    a. checking accuracy of questionable information.

    b. easily finding materials again.

    c.* a., b.

15. The Internet can contain inaccurate information—nobody screens everything.

    (**a.*** True; **b.** False)

Chapter 16: Writing a Business Report or a Term Paper; Writing a Business Contract Proposal

Select the letter of the best answer. Read all answers before making your choice.

1. The text says that the first step in writing a report or term paper should be to
   a. Decide upon the length of the report.
   b. Identify who should receive copies.
   c. Find a typist.
   d.* Define the problem or identify the purpose of the report or paper.

2. Everything in a research report or paper should relate to its stated purpose. (a.* True; b. False)

3. Make a good list and stay with it, never changing the order of items as you work. (a. True; b.* False)

4. Just as an architect follows a blueprint, a report writer should follow (a. the leader; b. instructions from others; c.* a report list).

5. Cause to effect, chronological order, deductive order, inductive order, and geographical order are all
   a. Dewey decimal systems.
   b.* methods of organizing research materials.
   c. methods of doing observational research.
   d. names of new music groups.

6. The inductive problem technique
   a. is called the "scientific" method.
   b. considers all pro, con, and off-the-wall solutions.
   c. takes the position, "My mind's made up; don't confuse me with the facts."
   d. can lead to drastic changes in the original list.
   e.* a., b., d.

7. In any kind of writing, rewriting
   a. shows that a person is an amateur writer.
   b. usually helps improve the finished product.
   c. is done regularly by good professional writers.
   d. a., b.
   e.* b., c.

8. The writer's opinion on a report topic should always be included as part of the report. (a. True; b.* False)

9. In trying to decide whether to include specific information in a report, you should decide whether
   a. the information is interesting.
   b. the information is funny.
   c.* the information relates to the statement of purpose of the report.

10. Paraphrasing means (a. documentation; b.* restating written or spoken material in your own words; c. making a rough draft).

11. Plagiarism (a. is copying the work of another person without giving that person credit; b. is illegal; c. is unethical; d. can damage the reputation of the person committing plagiarism; e.* a., b., c., d.).

12. Formal reports avoid use of the first person pronouns "I," "me," "my," "we" and so forth. (**a.*** True; **b.** False)

13. For information such as the specific name and address of a business, its history, names of its officers, types of products and services, and so forth, check (**a.** periodicals; **b.** books in stacks; **c.*** business directories in the library reference section).

14. Most colleges use the _____ system of classifying materials because it permits book loans between libraries. (**a.*** Library of Congress; **b.** Dewey decimal; **c.** college's own; **d.** colleges do not classify materials—they just stack things up.)

15. Your library research cards or pages should include library reference numbers for
    a. checking accuracy of questionable information.
    b. easily finding materials again.
    c.* a., b.